PLANT CLOSINGS

PLANT CLOSINGS: PUBLIC OR PRIVATE CHOICES?

Revised Edition

Richard B. McKenzie
Editor

Indiana
Purdue
Library
Fort Wayne

This book was made possible by a grant
from the Scaife Family Charitable Trusts.

CATO
INSTITUTE

Copyright © 1984 by the Cato Institute.

Library of Congress Cataloging in Publication Data
Main entry under title:

Plant closings.

   Includes bibliographical references and index.
   1. Business relocation—United States—Addresses, essays, lectures.
2. Plant shutdowns—United States—Addresses, essays, lectures.
3. United States—Industries—Location—Addresses, essays, lectures.
4. Industry and state—United States—Addresses, essays, lectures.
I. McKenzie, Richard B.
HC110.D5P55   1984   338.6′042   84–14957
ISBN   0–932790–42–9

Printed in the United States of America.

CATO INSTITUTE
224 Second Street SE
Washington, D.C. 20003

5 - 21 - 91

CONTENTS

THE CONCEPTUAL ISSUES

THE LEGAL ISSUES

CONCLUSION

APPENDIX

PREFACE

In writing for the Conference on Alternative State and Local Policies, William Schweke declares, "The problems of capital mobility and major job losses are real and growing. The major victims are the laid-off workers and their families. The massive job cuts often flood the labor market, overwhelming local employment opportunities. States and municipalities also face several fiscal difficulties, as their tax base erodes and public spending rises to pay for the social costs of economic dislocation, which include rapid increases in juvenile delinquency, crime, divorce, mental illness, and despair."[1] The proposed remedy: restrict the ability of businesses to close their doors, to move, and to reinvest their earnings by requiring firms (1) to give long-term notice of their intention to close, (2) to pay substantial severance benefits to unemployed workers, and (3) to make restitution payments to the affected community.

Simply stated, the central purpose of this revised edition remains that of the original: to bring together studies that critically evaluate the claims of those proposing restrictions on plant closings. First, the question of whether there exists a need for restrictive legislation is examined with reference to the facts on business closings and relocations. Second, the question of whether restrictions on plant closings will actually improve people's welfare is considered through an examination of the logical consistency of arguments put forward in favor of such intervention in the market system. Generally speaking, the studies presented here argue against the proposed restrictions and for continued reliance on the free play of market forces. This case against restrictive legislation is not a case against workers or their unions. Quite the contrary, it is a prolabor argument. The writers in this volume tend to see restrictive legislation as counterproductive and detrimental to the welfare of workers in general. With the debate over restrictions joined in Congress and in at least 24 state legislatures, the studies in this volume add important, but

---

[1]*Plant Closings: Issues, Politics and Legislation,* ed. William Schweke (Washington, D.C.: Conference on Alternative State and Local Policies, 1980).

not generally well understood, arguments on a policy topic that is likely to be widely discussed during the 1980s.

However, in two important respects this revised edition expands the coverage of topics. First, plant-closing restrictions have been offered as an important component of proposed "national industrial policy," namely a set of government actions designed to override market forces and to reallocate by collective means human and physical capital across industries and regions of the country. Many proponents of a national industrial policy want not only to prevent plants from closing but also to "target" industries for government aid and, thereby, "pick winners." Because such policies will also necessarily "pick losers," the plant-closing potential of national industrial policies cannot, and has not, escaped the attention of national industrial policy enthusiasts. For this reason, three new chapters (8, 9, and 12) on the myths and folly of national industrial policy have been added. Second, courts have progressively over the past two decades been drawn into the plant-closing controversy, resulting in a number of decisions that have prescribed in somewhat loose terms the legal rights managers have to close their plants. To a significant extent, the two chapters added on the legal consequences of plant closings (13 and 14) reveal that legislative efforts to prevent and restrict plant closings are being preempted by decisions of the courts and the National Labor Relations Board.

RICHARD B. MCKENZIE

Clemson, S.C.
February 1984

viii

INTRODUCTION

I. The Right to Close Up Shop

Richard B. McKenzie

There is a movement afoot that seeks to destroy one of the last remaining vestiges of the free-enterprise system in the United States: the right of the firm to close up shop. Make no mistake about it— this movement is well financed, dug in, broadening its political support at the federal and state levels, and (especially when there is a rash of large-plant closings) attracting more and more media attention.

The leaders of the movement at the federal level include Congressman William Ford (D-Mich.) and Senator Donald Riegle (D-Mich.). They have a growing number of followers on the political left: Nader's Raiders, the now-defunct Progressive Alliance (an assortment of 130 union, civil-rights, environmentalist, and feminist organizations), and, when restrictive legislation was last introduced in Congress in 1983, more than thirty congressmen. More recently, proponents of a national industrial policy have included plant-closing restrictions as a centerpiece of their comprehensive programs to reindustrialize America.[1]

At one time, not too many years ago, proponents of restrictions were primarily concerned with containing the regional movement of plants, mainly from the North to the South, by requiring firms to give as much as two years' notice of any intention to move and imposing tax penalties on firms that moved without "adequate justification." Now the movement has directed its attention toward restricting closing (for whatever reason) of virtually all large and

---

[1]For a review of the national industrial policy issues, see Richard B. McKenzie, "National Industrial Policy: An Overview of the Debate," *Backgrounder* (Washington: Heritage Foundation, July 1983). For the specifics of the programs of national industrial policy advocates, which include plant-closing planks, see Robert Reich, *The Next American Frontier* (New York: Times Books, 1983); Barry Bluestone and Bennett Harrison, *The Deindustrialization of America* (New York: Basic Books, 1982); and Samuel Bowles et al., *Beyond the Wasteland: A Democratic Alternative to Economic Decline* (Garden City, N.Y.: Anchor Press, 1983).

even modest-sized plants by proposing that workers be granted handsome severance pay for up to a year and by effectively institutionalizing federal government "bailouts" of ailing firms.

The lobbying efforts of this movement were once concentrated almost exclusively on the passage of a federal law. Now, with a Congress apparently less receptive to new interventionist measures, the proponents of restrictive legislation have shifted to the state level. In fact, over the past several years bills similar to the proposed federal law have been repeatedly introduced in 24 states.[2] In addition, two cities—Philadelphia and Pittsburgh—have passed ordinances to restrict plant closings within their jurisdiction.[3] The backers of these bills apparently fail to see that the passage of restrictive legislation in their states will place their states and cities at a serious competitive disadvantage in their attempts to attract industry. They fail to realize that restrictions ultimately translate into a "tax" on businesses, their workers, and the consumers of their products and that any restriction on plant closings is also a restriction on openings (points stressed in chapters 2, 7, 10, and 11).

By expressing concern over the reinvestment of profits outside the communities in which the profits are earned by incorporating plant-closing restrictions within much broader national reindustrialization programs, this movement shows every sign of shifting its interest in the future toward control of the free flow of investment funds.[4] The argument so often made in defense of such an intrusion by the federal government into the traditional domain of business decision making is twofold. First, businesses have a "duty" or "moral obligation" to reinvest profits in the company and, indeed, in the community in which they are earned; those who help to make the profits should be the beneficiaries of the reinvestment plans of the companies, or so the proponents argue.

Second, the reinvestment of a company's profits in its community will have a "multiplier effect"; that is, the employment growth will be several times the number of jobs directly associated with the investment projects. The workers in the expanded plants will spend

---

[2]For a comparativie analysis of the federal and various state bills, see Littman and Lee (chapter 7), and Richard B. McKenzie, *Fugitive Industry: The Economics and Politics of Deindustrialization* (San Francisco: Pacific Institute, 1984).

[3]The Pittsburgh ordinance was declared unconstitutional in state courts.

[4]See Reich, *The Next American Frontier;* Bluestone and Harrison, *Deindustrialization of America;* and Bowles et al. *Beyond the Wasteland.*

their incomes in local businesses that will need additional workers. Such an argument is not dissimilar to the contentions made by the mercantilists 200 years ago: The purchase of domestically produced goods will increase the health and wealth of the domestic economy by not drawing down the country's hoard of gold. Modern-day supporters of control of investment decisions apparently do not see that their distorted mercantilist philosophy, the subject of James C. Miller's essay (chapter 12), could equally be applied to workers: Workers, it could be said, have a duty to spend their incomes on local goods and services because such expenditures would have a multiplier effect. Such a rule, however, would destroy the rights workers now have to find the best deals they can from suppliers inside and outside their own community.

Proponents of restrictions apparently do not see that any law requiring firms to reinvest their profits in their community would, itself, be a law that restricts companies in other areas from investing in their community. In addition, such a restriction would discourage people from assuming the risks of operating a business and would, in the aggregate, deter saving and investment. Pittsburgh might be able to force its firms to reinvest their earnings in the city; however, such a law would not, on balance, necessarily lead to a multiplier effect in Pittsburgh. Firms outside Pittsburgh would also be required to reinvest their earnings in their communities; hence, Pittsburgh could not then be the beneficiary of the flow of investment funds from elsewhere. The net effect of such restrictions would not be economic and positive, contrary to the contentions of the advocates, but would be political and negative: a denial of individual freedom.

The case for restrictive legislation that has been offered to the public raises a number of interesting and profound questions for the future of the American economy. The first is empirical. Has the interregional movement of business been as dramatic as advocates of restrictions claim? In short, is there a "need" that must be addressed by public policymakers? From a number of studies, several of which are included in this volume, the answer to these questions now seems reasonably clear: No. By careful examination of the best data available, which are from the files of Dun & Bradstreet, James P. Miller (in chapter 3), John Hekman and John Strong (in chapter 4), and Carol Jusenius and Larry Ledebur (in chapter 5) reveal that interregional business movements account for a relatively small share of all employment losses in economically distressed regions, such as the northern industrial corridor. The North definitely has serious economic problems, but the outmigration of firms is not one of them. Most of the North's employment losses are due to the "deaths" and "contractions" of firms. Hekman and Strong write,

> Many people consider plant closings and layoffs in the Northeast and North Central regions important contributors to higher unemployment rates in some parts of these regions. Accordingly, plant-closing laws have been proposed in many states to prevent "capital flight" from the Frostbelt to the Sunbelt. . . . The evidence suggests that the number of relocations to the Sunbelt which have been positively identified is quite small relative to the total number of closings in the Frostbelt and relative to total employment change. The rate of plant closings does not differ much between regions. [p. 77]

Jusenius and Ledebur draw a strikingly similar conclusion:

> In contrast to widespread publicity, this paper has found that the recent employment problems of New England are not the result of significant outmigration of firms. Previous evidence to support the outmigration thesis has been, at best, anecdotal. Generalizations have been made—based on the identification of relatively few migrating firms—which are not supported in fact.
>
> Indeed, the migration of firms in either direction [in or out of New England] has not been significant. To the extent that migration has occurred, New England was a net beneficiary between 1969 and 1974. [p. 116]

By employing a markedly different data source and focusing on the problem of labor turnover, Robert Premus and Rudy Fichtenbaum (in chapter 6) confirm the results of these studies and conclude that "economic stagnation in the Frostbelt region is due to the inability of the region to stimulate business starts and expand existing businesses at a rate sufficient to absorb the growing labor force" (p. 125). The evidence shows, Miller (chapter 3) has found, that most businesses, when they move, most often relocate in their own regions (indeed, in their own states) and tend to move from states with relatively high growth rates in taxes to states with relatively low growth rates in taxes. Many proponents of plant-closing restrictions hold that workers who lose their jobs because of plant closings represent a major component of the unemployed. Daniel Littman and Myung-Hoon Lee (chapter 7) conclude that simply is not the case and argue further that plant-closing restrictions will have other distorting effects on labor markets.

In their article, Hekman and Strong also compare the economy of Sweden, which already has extensive plant-closing legislation on the books along with a variety of other means of controlling firm opening, closing, and reinvestment decisions, with the economy of New England, where several plant-closing laws have been recently introduced in state legislatures. Hekman and Strong conclude that plant-closing legislation alone would have a meager impact on the employment opportunities in either New England or Sweden. Further, they write,

> Sweden's labor transition or "redundancy" problems would seem to offer a comprehensive approach to this problem [of unemployment]. However, Sweden's experience indicates that these programs have diverted an increasing share of the labor force into subsidized work and public employment rather than assisting workers in making the desired transition to profitable industries. Notification of layoffs in Sweden does not seem to help workers find new jobs more efficiently as much as they lock workers into subsidized programs. [p. 77]

In chapter 2, I explain why one must be careful in accepting claims that the health of the North, for example, is impaired because of a decline in manufacturing employment. I argue that although manufacturing employment was at about the same level in 1980 as in 1969, it was on the upswing in the northern region during the last half of the 1970s; furthermore, employment gains in nonmanufacturing sectors of the northern economy had, during the 1970s and generally speaking, more than compensated for the net employment losses in manufacturing in the North. Restrictions on plant closings and moves could, therefore, work to the detriment of the North by choking off the rise in northern employment opportunities and the resurgence in manufacturing jobs that was underway before the 1980–1982 recession. Of course, one can point to isolated areas and regional subdivisions that have, from time to time, experienced employment declines because, in part, of business outmigration. That sort of evidence, however, argues against a national policy on plant closings. Charles L. Schultze and William H. Branson (chapters 8 and 9) restate, in their own terms, several of these findings and reveal the extent to which the national industrial policy movement is largely founded on a modern industrial mythology.

The second important question raised by the claims of the advo-

7

cates of restrictions is whether restrictions on business closings and mobility will serve the interests of those workers the legislation is presumably designed to protect. Bernard Weinstein and John Rees (in chapter 10), while examining the growing political competition among states and regions for federal dollars, stress that the relative prosperity in the South is not necessarily detrimental to the North, or any other region of the country. Indeed, southern prosperity very likely has contributed to the growth in income and employment opportunities in the North. They also point out that marginal shifts in the flow of federal funds will do little to dampen the relatively stronger growth of southern and western states.

In chapter 11, I survey a number of theoretical points raised by proponents and find them all wanting. I argue that businesses locate their plants to minimize their production costs. Economic conditions in any dynamic economy are constantly changing, and businesses must be allowed the flexibility to fit their location to those conditions. Restrictions on business closings will, in the long run especially, lead to greater costs of production, higher prices on consumer goods, and lower real incomes—and not only in the region in which they are imposed: They are, in the long run, necessarily detrimental to all regions. Nevertheless, plant-closing restrictions are gradually becoming part of the law of the land by way of court and National Labor Relations Board decisions, the central point of the work of John Irving and of Edward O'Keefe and Seamus Tuohey (chapters 13 and 14).

The studies in this monograph reveal that restrictions on the investment decisions of firms are a bad idea from both a conceptual and an empirical perspective. However, restrictions on business have strong emotional and political appeal, and unless the proponents of the restrictive legislation are watched closely, businesses may, in the future, be hamstrung. We would all suffer as a consequence.

THE EMPIRICAL ISSUES

II. Business Mobility: Economic Myths and Realities

Richard B. McKenzie

Business mobility—the mirror image of the free play of economic forces—is a normal, indeed inevitable, feature of any dynamic and growing economy. Nonetheless, particular moves (plant closings, relocations, and the like) can and do evoke protests by the communities and workers left behind. These people see themselves as somehow wronged, and among the political remedies they seek are restraints by government fiat on business mobility.

Cities are worried about losing employers and tax revenues to the suburbs, the Frostbelt is worried about losing both of those and skilled workers as well to the Sunbelt, and politicians everywhere seem attracted to the notion that economic stability in their areas can be ensured by checking management's freedom to pull up stakes. In 1978, when American Airlines announced its decision to move its headquarters from New York to Dallas, for example, New York Mayor Edward Koch termed it a betrayal, and a taxi union vowed to stop serving the airline's New York terminals. Fortunately for the airline and its passengers, as well as the cabbies, the threat was never made good. And American's headquarters was moved.

In recent years, bills that would seriously restrict business mobility have been introduced in the U.S. Congress and at least 24 state legislatures.[1] The scheme is also the centerpiece of Ralph Nader's campaign to "democratize" corporate America, to make major corporations more responsive to the "general interest." His vehicle is the Corporate Democracy Act of 1980, H.R. 7010. If such a measure became federal law, it would substantially increase government

---

This chapter is drawn from two previous works by Richard B. McKenzie: "Frustrating Business Mobility," *Regulation*, May/June 1980, pp. 32–38; and "Myths of Sunbelt and Frostbelt," *Policy Review*, Spring 1982, pp. 103-114.

[1]For a comparative analysis of these bills and laws, see Littman and Lee (chapter 7).

intervention in business decision making, alter our national economic system in fundamental ways, and be, on balance, detrimental to the regional and local economies of the country in the bargain.

The "Runaway Plant Phenomenon"

The purpose of the restrictive legislation, which already has been enacted in Maine and Wisconsin, is to remedy what has been called the "runaway plant phenomenon." Typically, the bills provide for a government agency to investigate business moves and rule on their appropriateness. For example, the National Employment Priorities Act, a 1977 proposal that was reintroduced in the House in May 1983 by Rep. William Ford (D-Mich.) and 31 cosponsors, would set up a National Employment Priorities Administration within the U.S. Department of Labor to investigate plant closings; to report its findings on the economic rationale for the decisions to close or cut back, and on employment losses and other impacts on the affected community; and to recommend ways of preventing or mitigating these harmful effects. (In the 1977 version, the investigation would determine whether "such closing or transfer" was "without [and presumably also "with"] adequate justification.")[2] A bill introduced in the New Jersey General Assembly would vest similar responsibilities in a state agency called the Division of Business Relocation.

A second typical feature of bills designed to curb business mobility is the levying of penalties on firms that move. The Ohio bill, for instance, would require such firms to dole out to the employees left behind severance pay equal to one week's wage for each year of service and to pay the community an amount equal to 10 percent of the gross annual wages of the affected employees.

Under the Ford bill (H.R. 2847), a business that moved or closed would have to pay the workers left jobless 85 percent of their last two years' average wage for a period of 52 weeks, less any outside income and government assistance. Besides, the firm would have to make a year's normal payments to any employee benefit plan and cover relocation expenses for employees who decided to move to any other company facility within the next three years. Workers over age 54 at the time of a move or closing would be entitled to full retirement benefits at age 62 instead of the normal retirement,

[2]See Appendix, page 315, for statements Congressman Ford made in support of his legislative efforts in 1974, 1979, and 1983.

if it is above 62. Failure to comply with the act would carry severe penalties—a combination of fines and the denial of the tax benefits associated with a move. Finally, the local government would be owed an amount equal to 85 percent of the firm's average tax payments for the last three years. If the firm moved abroad and an "economically viable alternative" existed in the United States, the firm would have to pay "damages" equal to 300 percent of any tax revenue lost to the U.S. Treasury. Any payment required under the act, not met by the firm, and paid by the federal government would become a debt owed by the firm to the federal government.

Third, the kind of legislation under consideration here generally provides for government assistance to the people and entities adversely affected. Under the Ford bill, for instance, the U.S. secretary of labor, with the advice of a relocation advisory council, would be empowered to provide financial and technical assistance to employees who lost their jobs, to the communities affected by plant relocations, and even to businesses themselves—those that might decide *not* to relocate if government assistance were available. Assistance to employees would take the form of training programs, job placement services, job search and relocation expenses, in addition to such existing welfare benefits as food stamps, unemployment compensation, and housing allowances. Federal grants for additional social services and public-works projects would go directly to the community. Assistance to businesses would be given as technical advice, loans and loan guarantees, interest subsidies, and the assumption of outstanding debt, but only if the secretary of labor were to determine that the aid would "substantially contribute to the economic viability of the establishment." The New Jersey and Ohio proposals provide for similar community and employee aid.

Fourth, under the various bills, firms are required to give advance notice of their plans to move or close—up to two years' notice in the Ohio bill and in the proposed Corporate Democracy Act of 1980. The prenotification requirement in the Ford bill varies with the size of the anticipated loss in jobs: one year for firms expecting the loss to be greater than 100 and six months for less than 100. The legislation proposed in New Jersey requires only a one-year notice. Exceptions could be made, of course, but generally only if the firms can show that meeting the requirement would be unreasonable.

Fifth, the various bills usually require that businesses offer their employees, to the extent possible, comparable employment and pay at the new location. And finally, each of the bills contains some minimum-size cutoff point. The proposed National Employment Priorities Act, for example, would apply only to firms with more than 50 employees. The bills' reach, typically, is both wide and deep.

Drawing the Battle Lines

In describing the changing regional structure of the U.S. economy, *Business Week* magazine observed: "The second war between the states will take the form of political and economic maneuver. But the conflict can nonetheless be bitter and divisive because it will be a struggle for income, jobs, people and capital" (May 17, 1976). When he introduced the original National Employment Priorities Act in 1974, Congressman Ford gave us a preview of the economic rationale of the political battle lines and some flavor of the ensuing debate:

> The legislation is based on the premise that such closings and transfers may cause irreparable harm—both economic and social—to workers, communities, and the Nation. . . . My own congressional district suffered the effects of the runaway plant in 1972 when the Garwood plant in Wayne moved and left 600 unemployed workers behind. . . . [T]he reason these firms are moving away is not economic necessity but economic greed. For instance, the Federal Mogul Co. in Detroit signed a contract in 1971 with the United Auto Workers and 6 months later announced it would be moving to Alabama. A spokesman for the company was quoted as saying they were moving "not because we are not making money in Detroit, but because we can make more money in Alabama."[3]

Five years later, in introducing his significantly revised 1979 bill, Congressman Ford stressed that business movements from the Northeast during the last decade had resulted in a million lost jobs in manufacturing and pointed to studies showing the suicide rate among workers displaced from their jobs by plant closings at thirty times the national average. He also noted,

> It is well established that the affected workers suffer a far higher incidence of heart disease and hypertension, diabetes, peptic ulcers, gout, and joint swelling, than the general population. They also

[3]See Appendix.

14

incur serious psychological problems, including extreme depression, insecurity, anxiety, and loss of self-esteem.[4]

So it should come as no surprise that the campaign for government restrictions on business mobility adopts the rhetoric of war. Phrases like "second war between the states," "counterattacks," and "fierce and ruinous state warfare" fill popular accounts of regional shifts. The economic conflict at the heart of attempts to control business relocations is viewed as "us" against "them"— North versus South, the Frostbelt versus the Sunbelt.

Although the rhetoric is stirring, there is, frankly, little in the positions articulated by *Business Week* and Ford that is correct. From such journalistic prose, however, monumental myths have been erected. And the casual reader is likely to surmise that the whole of the South and West is prospering, while the whole of the North is rapidly sinking into an economic abyss. Steeped in tales of the northern woes, made dramatic by silent pictures of idle plants and interviews with workers distressed by recent news of their own plant's shutdown, the inattentive viewer of nightly television news is likely to agree that "dramatic" government action must be taken to save the northern industrial tier states, that a new "industrial policy" is needed to augment the free play of market forces—in other words, that the times justify denying firms their traditional rights to retrench in production, to lay off workers, and to shut down. Consider the following thirteen myths, several of which are evaluated in detail in following chapters.

Myth 1: The North is losing population.

The reality of the 1980 census is that the population in the Northeast-Midwest industrial corridor that runs from Minnesota to Maine has remained more or less stable or has grown (except for New York), although very slightly. The nub of the concern is that population has generally grown less rapidly in the Northeast and Midwest than elsewhere, reducing the Northeast-Midwest's representation in Congress from 213 to 196 House members.[5]

Granted, during the 1970s nearly two million people left the Mid-Atlantic states, and two-thirds of those migrants left one state, New

---

[4]Ibid.

[5]Jacqueline Mazza and Bill Hogan, *The State of the Region: 1981* (Washington: Northeast-Midwest Institute and Congressional Coalition, 1981), p. 10.

York. One and a half million people migrated out of the East North Central region. News accounts of these migration flows give the impression that all of these people were whistling Dixie as they left, all too eager to get their hands on their first bowl of grits.

The fact is that the outmigration flow from the Mid-Atlantic states was relatively meager on an annual basis, amounting to about one-half of one percent of that region's 1970 population. Further, many of the people who left the Mid-Atlantic states settled in New England or the East North Central region, and many of the people who left East North Central states headed west to other midwestern states or east to Mid-Atlantic states. Many went south and others went west. Still others returned home from an earlier move north. Many who left the Frostbelt were adults, but many were children. In short, they were free people doing free things, going where they pleased.

Myth 2: The North is losing jobs.

Employment in every northern and midwestern state has grown over the last 10 or 15 years—maybe not as rapidly as in the South, but the growth is evident. Even employment in *relatively* depressed cities like Gary, Indiana, grew during the 1970s, quite slowly and irregularly at about 1 to 2 percent per year.[6] Total employment in Illinois grew at a compound rate of 1.2 percent, meaning that total employment grew by about 20 percent during the 1965–1980 period.[7]

In the 1970s, New York, the state with the worst overall employment record, experienced some slight growth in employment (0.25 percent per year compounded) in spite of a loss of about 3 to 4 percent of its population. And because of the growth in the so-called subterranean economy, which may now exceed $700 billion annually and exists almost exclusively to avoid the narcotics squads and the IRS tax auditors, the recorded growth in relatively high tax northern states is understated.[8]

[6]Based on calculations made from *Employment and Earnings,* various issues.

[7]Between 1965 and 1980, total employment in the Northeast grew at a compound rate of 1.06 percent; North Central, 2.00 percent; South, 3.69 percent; and West, 3.97 percent. All rates of growth and decline in this article are compound rates calculated from trend values for 1965 and 1980.

[8]The IRS estimated that in 1976 income unreported to the IRS was a minimum of $135 billion and may actually run up to four times that amount, or $540 billion—more than a fourth of the Gross National Product that year. See Mortimer Caplin, "Uncovering the Underground Economy," *Wall Street Journal,* March 31, 1980, p. 20.

Without question, manufacturing employment has declined in the Northeast-Midwest, but at less than one percent per year—hardly "swift." The "destruction" of northern manufacturing jobs has been more than offset by expansions in job opportunities in other sectors of the northern economy. Further, although much has been made of the fact that between 1969 and 1976 the North lost about a million manufacturing jobs, little has been said about the rebound in northern manufacturing employment—about 650,000 jobs between 1976 and 1980.

The economic rebound in New England has been so dramatic that observers have referred to the area as the "Sunbelt of the North." In the last few years New Hampshire's growth in manu-facturing employment has been on par with the growth of manu-facturing employment in the Greenville-Spartanburg area of South Carolina, touted as a major industrial seedbed. And the growth in overall employment in New Hampshire during the 1965–1980 period was 50 percent higher than in South Carolina. It's not the "low-paid southern serfs" who are "stealing" jobs from New Yorkers; it's those gophers from New Hampshire.

Myth 3: Fifteen million jobs have been lost during the last decade to plant closures, and a disproportionate share of these job losses were in the North.

The picture painted by such statistics, developed by economists for the now-defunct Progressive Alliance (a conglomerate of 130 union, environmental, consumer, and feminist organizations), is bleak.[9] The statistic makes the private sector out to be an economic black hole; and left dangling by itself in news stories, the statistic is a gross distortion of what has actually happened in national employment opportunities. During the 1970s, total employment in the United States rose by 20 million, suggesting that (if there were 15 million jobs lost) 35 million jobs were created. Job losses can, and generally do, mean job gains. Many people lose their jobs

[9]Barry Bluestone and Bennett Harrison, *Capital and Communities: The Causes and Consequences of Private Disinvestment* (Washington, D.C.: The Progressive Alliance, 1980), p. 59. Although the number of "jobs created" is included in their tabular presentations, emphasis in the text is almost exclusively on the "jobs destroyed" in the economy. For an updated version of the argument, see Barry Bluestone, untitled paper in *Basic Industries in Trouble: Why . . . And Are There Solutions?*, ed. Julian Scheen (Dallas: LTV Corp., 1983), pp. 15–34.

because their companies are being run out of business by more successful, expanding firms.

Myth 4: The southward and westward trek of northern industry is the source of much of the North's unemployment problem.

According to the best studies available, undertaken primarily at Harvard and MIT, less than 2 percent of all employment losses in the North are attributable to plant relocations, meaning that 98 percent of all northern job losses can be credited to the "deaths and contractions" of northern firms.[10] Less than 2 percent of the South's job gains are attributable to the in-migration of business. The average annual rate of job losses due to plant relocations during most of the 1970s in northern industrial tier states was a mere three-tenths of 1 percent. Can such losses be characterized as "plummeting"?

Myth 5: Most northern firms that relocate move to the South or West.

Wrong again. According to U.S. Department of Agriculture economist James P. Miller (chapter 3), about 97 percent of the Mid-Atlantic firms and about 94 percent of the East North Central firms that moved during the 1970s stayed within their respective regions. And more than 75 percent stayed within the same state. Most firms move relatively short distances because many of their employees and managers are bound economically and culturally to their regions and because moves are costly: the longer the move, the greater the cost.

Myth 6: The migration of industry is only in one direction, from the North to anywhere else.

Would you believe that would really be the case in a diverse economy? According to a study conducted by Peter Allaman and David Birch in the early 1970s, 118 firms migrated from the Mid-Atlantic to the South Atlantic at the same time that 23 firms migrated in the opposite direction (each flow representing about an equal percentage loss of their industrial base).[11] I am sure that all of these

---

[10]Peter M. Allaman and David L. Birch, "Components of Employment Change for States by Industry Groups, 1970–1972," (Cambridge, Mass.: Joint Center for Urban Studies of MIT and Harvard University, September 1975).

[11]Ibid.

firms would cite different reasons for moving. In general, they moved because of the economic advantages the new locations provided. The North has many economic advantages over the South, and that is why so many people live and work there. A major southern textile manufacturer recently moved back to Rhode Island because he felt the wage advantage he once found in the South had largely been eroded by competitive forces; he moved, principally, to employ more highly skilled workers than he could find in the South.

One of the greatest myths that has come out of the Sunbelt/ Frostbelt controversy is that *regions,* bounded artificially and arbitrarily by dark lines drawn on a map, somehow have a meaning of their own, independent of the motivations of people. Perhaps, to those who wish to inspire sectional economic warfare and to form political coalitions to play the only game Washington knows— beggar-thy-neighbor—geography matters. But to most of us out here in the hinterlands who wish to make the best living we can, geography, per se, matters little. What matters is people and what they want. When contemplating a move, most of us think little of the imaginary Mason-Dixon Line; we think mainly about the costs and benefits of our decision, regardless of whether they leave us in Texas or New York. New York is relatively depressed not because it happens to be in the Frostbelt (remember New Hampshire is even further north), but because for many prospective firms, costs of production and taxes have gotten out of line and now exceed the benefits of locating and expanding in New York. New York has operated as though there were no alternatives—as if it were the only place to be, regardless of the costs.

Myth 7: The North has been economically buried by a rash of plant closings unequaled in other parts of the country.

John Hekman and John Strong (chapter 4) report a different reality: The Sunbelt has had a slightly higher rate of plant closings than the Frostbelt (33 percent versus 30 percent). Further, many Sunbelt cities like Houston, acclaimed for their prosperity, have experienced a higher rate of plant closings than Frostbelt cities like Boston.[12] Certainly, the North has experienced many more plant

[12]David M. Smick, "What Reaganomics is All About," *Wall Street Journal,* July 8, 1981, p. 26.

closings than the South, but that is in part because the North has far more plants than the South.

Plants close for a variety of reasons. Firestone closed its Dayton tire facility because many people no longer want the bias-ply tires it produced. Consumers have demonstrated by their purchases that they want more reliable, fuel-efficient radial tires. Butte Knit Industries recently closed a factory, employing 1,200 workers, outside Spartanburg, South Carolina, because consumers no longer care for double-knit clothes at the prices Butte would have to charge. Other firms close simply because they cannot keep up with the competition in terms of meeting prevailing wage rates or product prices. Of course, competition is "destructive," as the opponents of capitalism ardently maintain, but it is "creative destruction," a process whereby consumers get more of what they want at more favorable prices. Plant closings may just as well signal a growing, dynamic economy as a dying one. After all, we hear little of plant closings in the Soviet Union or the People's Republic of China. We hear only of bread lines, shoddy products, and empty shelves.

The North's major economical problems appear to center not so much on plant closures but on the absence of new plants and plant expansions. Recognizing that fact, we are led to wonder what it is about policies internal to the North that are stifling business "creativity," choking off the flow of new capital and the emergence of new firms. People in the North, not Washington, will ultimately have to answer that question. Regional prosperity in the long run will depend on the "rollover" of capital, not on restrictions on closures.

Myth 8: The relative growth in employment in the South is critically dependent upon the in-migration of large manufacturing plants from the North.

When large manufacturing plants move into North and South Carolina, their arrival is typically accompanied by considerable media fanfare, including news conferences hosted, on occasion, by the respective governors of the two states. The news coverage of these events probably leads people to believe that the growth in jobs of the Carolinas would rapidly wane if it were not for the influx of "big businesses" from the Frostbelt. Appearances, however, are deceiving. A study of the movement of new industrial plants into the Carolinas undertaken at Clemson University paints a picture grossly at odds with common perceptions: The jobs created by the in-migration of large industrial plants from the whole of the Frost-belt (including the New England, Mid-Atlantic, East North Central, and West North Central regions) during the entire decade of the 1970s represented a scant 0.7 percent of South Carolina's 1980 total employment.[13] The majority (80 percent or more) of jobs created in the South, as well as elsewhere, are dependent upon small firms.

Myth 9: The North has experienced a higher rate of worker layoffs.

That isn't true either, at least over the long haul. According to Robert Premus and Rudy Fichtenbaum at Wright State University in Ohio (chapter 6), the layoff rate over the last two decades has been significantly lower in the North (1.45 per hundred) than in the rest of the country (1.60 per hundred).

Myth 10: Income in the North is plummeting, leading to reduced tax bases for northern states and communities.

Restricted growth in worker productivity and income is a serious problem nationwide. However, in spite of higher taxes and an onslaught of government regulations, real personal income per capita has continued to climb in the North, although at one-half or less the growth rate experienced in the South and West. Because of lower growth in personal income, northerners have experienced a decline in their *relative income.* In other words, they no longer have twice the income of southerners, but only, maybe, 15 or 25 percent greater incomes. Furthermore, taxes have continued to climb through legislated increases in tax rates and through inflation-induced "bracket creep." Nationwide, the after-tax purchasing power of the median-income family fell by $467 between 1971 and 1981. What people are probably concerned about is that the tax base of government *has* expanded, leaving them with more work and less to show for it.

Myth 11: Through out-migration, the North is being stripped of its highly skilled workers and is being left engorged with low-income, welfare cases.

The South has historically had a higher incidence of poverty than the Northeast, and the poverty rate in the South is still about one-

[13]Nancy T. Mathews and Richard B. McKenzie, "New Plants and Employment Gains in South Carolina During the 1970s," *Business and Economic Review* (October 1982), pp. 31–37.

third higher than in the North. In addition, a disproportionate share of those migrating into the South over the last decade has been low-income, unemployed workers and their families.[14] This is especially true if the legal and illegal Mexican, Cuban, and Haitian immigrants are counted. One would expect the low-income and unemployed workers to move where opportunities are more abundant—just as the skilled workers do.

The North has an unemployment problem partly because many of its workers are paid relatively high wages to compensate for unstable employment in cyclical industries. Moreover, unemployment is no longer the burden it once was. Unemployment compensation has, over the last two decades, grown in real terms but has remained steady relative to worker wages (in the range of 35 to 37 percent). However, given our inflationary history and the forces of "bracket creep," the spending power of the unemployed has risen faster, relative to the spending power of the working population, than the growth in dollar payments indicates.[15]

According to Rex Cottle, an economist who has studied exten-

[14]See McKenzie, "Frustrating Business Mobility," *Regulation* (May/June 1980), p. 35:

"Now, the new wave of outmigration from the North of course includes many highly educated and skilled people; but the proponents of restrictive legislation [on plant closings] greatly exaggerate the quite undramatic facts. For instance in the 1975–1977 period substantially more unemployed male workers moved from the Northeast to the South (23,000) than from the South to the Northeast (14,000), and virtually the same pattern held for unemployed female workers. The Northeast also exported more unemployed workers to the West than it imported from the West.

"Other considerations are equally revealing. Far more people below the poverty line migrated from the Northeast to the South (133,000) than vice versa (39,000) in the 1975–1977 period. (Much the same point can be made about the migration of low-income people between the Northeast and West.) In addition, while more people with one or two years of college migrated from the Northeast to the South (151,000) than from the South to the Northeast (102,000), those with *some* college education were a significantly greater proportion of the southern migrants to the North (56.3 percent) than the other way around (40.3 percent). (The same cannot be said about the migration of college-educated people between the Northeast and the West.) In short, it simply is not clear that the South or the West is receiving from the North a disproportionate number of highly trained, high-income people. Some—but no tidal wave."

[15]People on unemployment compensation do not pay taxes on their benefits. Hence, when inflation pushes working people up into higher and higher current income brackets, their tax rates are increased (there is "bracket creep") and the *relative* spending power of unemployed workers on unemployment compensation rises.

22

sively the effects of unemployment compensation and welfare benefits, unemployed workers react like workers in most other labor markets.[16] If worker wages are raised in an industry, more people will take up that occupation. Similarly, if the benefits—or "wages"—for being unemployed are raised, you will find more people willing to take up the occupation of being unemployed. One of the reasons the unemployment rate is higher in the North relative to the South is that states in the North tend to pay a higher "wage" for being unemployed. Illinois's average weekly unemployment compensation is 42 percent higher than in South Carolina. Pennsylvania pays 35 percent more in average weekly benefits than South Carolina. Again, the problems of the North are at least partially of the North's own making.

Myth 12: Defense expenditures are concentrated disproportionately in the South and Southwest, creating a gross disparity in the growth rates between those regions and the North.

Texas Congressman Charles Wilson was probably correct when he recently lamented that the "whole world believes we get 90 percent of the defense contracts in the country."[17] While the West gets a large portion of the defense dollars, it is pure nonsense that the South has made off with a disproportionate share. John Rees of the Center for Policy Research at the University of Texas–Dallas has found that during much of the 1970s the "manufacturing belt" of the North, while encompassing one-quarter of the nation's population, got more than one-third of defense dollars allocated for "prime contracts."[18]

The South and Southwest, on the other hand, had one-third of the population and received a little over 20 percent of prime contract

[16]See Rex L. Cottle, "Unemployment: A Labor Market Perspective," *Journal of Labor Research* (Fall 1980), pp. 231–44. Cottle estimates that for the country as a whole, a $1 increase in the national average weekly unemployment check will add approximately 390,000 people to the unemployment roles for at least one week. Those already on unemployment compensation will stay on the unemployment roles longer.

[17]Christopher Bonner, "Sun Belt Congressmen Form 'Defense' Lobby," *Greenville* (S.C.) *News*, June 26, 1981.

[18]John Rees, "Manufacturing Change, Internal Control and Governmental Spending in a Growth Region of the USA," in *Industrial Change*, ed. F. E. I. Hamilton (London: Longman, Ltd., 1979), pp. 155–74.

dollars. Of the five largest recipients of prime defense contracts, three prominent northern states stand out—New York, Connecticut, and Massachusetts—and all three lost manufacturing jobs during the 1970s. Furthermore, not all prime contract dollars are spent in the state or region in which they are received. Many of the dollars allocated to Texas end up in New York and vice versa. On balance, for most of the 1970s, the northern manufacturing belt received nearly 50 percent of the subcontracted dollars whereas the South and Southwest wound up with 12 to 15 percent.[19]

Myth 13: Since many federal grants are allocated on the basis of formulas that include a population factor, the shift in the population from the North to the South and West, reflected in the 1980 census, will mean dramatic regional shifts in federal grant money.

John Goodman of the Urban Institute believes that there will be some shifts in the regional allocation of federal funds, but for several reasons the shifts are not likely to be as dramatic as one might suppose.[20] First, many of the grant formulas devised during the 1970s were based not on the 1970 census, but on population estimates for the year the formula was devised. Second, grants are often allocated on the basis of offsetting variables, like population and income levels; the South, which has experienced a relatively high population growth rate, has also experienced relative increases in income. Third, only a small portion, say 20 percent, of many programs subject to grants are allocated on the basis of formulas; there is, in other words, a great deal of room for bureaucratic discretion that is not easily predicted. And, fourth, many grant programs have minimums and maximums, which will restrict the reallocation of funds.

Concluding Comments

In summary, the Frostbelt has some serious economic problems. For that matter, the whole country has serious problems. We have recently suffered severe recessions, and it is not clear that the recovery will be permanent. However, to a considerable extent the Sunbelt/Frostbelt confrontation is built on modern regional mythol-

[19]Ibid.

[20]John L. Goodman, Jr., "Federal Funding Formulas and the 1980 Census," *Public Policy* (Spring 1981), pp. 179–96.

ogy, reflecting what has been called Newton's "third law of journalism": For every adverse economic action, there is an opposite overreaction by the media. Nonetheless, the myths that have been recounted have caused many observers to conclude that we need a new policy to control and redirect the migration patterns of people across this nation; that we need a new industrial policy (euphemistically termed a "reindustrialization policy") to restrict disinvestment, to control reinvestment, and to direct new investment across regions; and that we need an array of new federal social initiatives to compensate regions and states for "migratory redistribution."[21]

We must be skeptical of the arguments put forth for one principal reason. The arguments do not make reasonable sense from both empirical and conceptual perspectives. Even if northern manufacturing firms were to be restricted by legislation from moving South, the movement of manufacturing jobs to the South, though impeded, would not be stopped. Firms move because costs of production in the new location are lower—and anticipated profits higher. Restrictions on business mobility would cause new firms to spring up in southern locations and existing southern firms to expand by more than they otherwise would. Because of cost disadvantages, firms in the old northern locations would be induced by natural market forces—*which relocation rules attempt to override*—to contract their operations or to go out of business.

And this of course is the key, this ill-conceived attempt to improve on "nature" by those who urge regulation to restrict business mobility. Even at the risk of accentuating the obvious, it is helpful to return to a first principle or two. People in different parts of the country trade with one another because differences in their costs of production make it to their mutual advantage to do so. Specialization in trade leads to maximum output from the resources available to the community as a whole. And, because the conditions of production—the availability of resources, technology, consumer preferences for work and for goods—continually change, so do the comparative costs from region to region. What once was relatively advantageous to produce in the North may, for various reasons, become less costly to produce in some other region. This constantly

[21]For a good example of the type of justification given for new forms of control over people and capital migration, see Peter A. Morrison, "America's Changing Population: Demographic Trends," *USA Today* (September 1981), pp. 20–24.

25

shifting calculus of costs can be altered by changes in the relative scarcity of resources, worker education levels, or regional preferences for services. Whatever the reason, the cost of producing any particular good in one region can go up, and, as a consequence, the production of that good moves elsewhere—all, to repeat, very naturally.

Pinning down the precise reasons for changes in regional economic structures is difficult. In recent decades, however, the comparative advantages of the North have indeed changed, and for two principal reasons. First, the demand for services in the North has increased rapidly, more so than in other parts of the country; and this in turn has increased the cost of resources, including labor, for all other sectors of the northern economy. Also, environmental legislation has placed more severe restrictions on industrial production in the congested North than in many other parts of the country and has increased the relative costs of manufacturing there. The unavailability of "pollution rights" in the North has caused many firms to look to locations with less pollution and less stringent pollution-control standards—to the South and West, for example.

Undeniably, these changes in regional production costs, and the economic adjustments that result from them, can and do cause hardship for some. But restricting business mobility is a cure worse than the disease. Such restrictions would force employers to lock labor and other resources into comparatively inefficient uses—resources that could and should be moving into expanding sectors of various regional economies. Thus governmental rules that impede the movement of manufacturing industry out of the North would not only retard the development of industry in the South (or elsewhere) but would also retard the development of the service sector in the North. The overall result would be increased nationwide production costs and reduced national production and income.

States and communities that are mulling over restrictions may believe they would be protecting their economies by protecting their industrial bases, but in fact they would be hurting them—and themselves. What company would want to move into an area that had substantial economic penalties for moving out? What entrepreneur would want to start a business in a community or state that had penalties for changing locations? Companies interested in profits will always try to settle in those areas that leave them free to make the basic decisions on when to shift among products, when to close, and when to move. States or communities that do not

26

impose restrictions will obviously have a competitive advantage over those that do, which makes it equally obvious why Congressman Ford and others, who want restrictions in their own areas, are seeking through federal legislation to have *all* areas of the country abide by the same rules. And this simply tightens the squeeze on U.S. industry in world markets and provides yet another marginal inducement for U.S. firms to locate their production facilities in foreign countries where such restrictions are not in place.

Indeed, viewed from whatever perspective, restrictions on business mobility constitute an idea whose time one hopes will never come. Predictably, restrictions would tend to reduce the efficiency of resource allocation; reduce national and regional income levels; and reduce the ability of the economy to respond to changes in people's tastes and to changes in technology, in the availability of resources, and in the mix of demand for particular goods and particular services. In short, they represent a bad bargain all around—for the communities and workers affected (in spite of the appearance of near-term relief), for Congressman Ford's constituents as much as everyone else, for the U.S. economy generally, for entrepreneur and taxpayer alike.

III. Manufacturing Relocations in the United States, 1969–1975

James P. Miller

Introduction

Much of federal, state, and local development effort, historically, has been aimed at encouraging the establishment of new industry. In recent years, however, as the manufacturing sector entered a "postindustrial" period of decline, the stock of potential candidates opening new manufacturing operations has been sharply reduced, forcing state and local development authorities to compete more actively either to attract or retain plants currently in operation. Plant closings and outmigration have become a major concern. The fear of losing manufacturing jobs and income through plant abandonment has been so great in certain distressed areas that national legislation was proposed in 1979 to discourage the abandonment and relocation of plants to other areas. Two bills, H.R. 5040 and S. 1608 (cited together as the National Employment Priorities Act of 1979), were introduced in the House and Senate. Both bills sought to develop a comprehensive national policy for easing the adverse economic impact of plant closings and relocations by (a) requiring firms to give notice of their plans to move, (b) imposing penalties such as requiring severance pay for employees, (c) requiring payments to the community, and (d) denying tax benefits to the relocating firm.[1]

State legislators have also been active in proposing new restrictions on plant abandonment. Bills requiring that plant closings be announced at least a certain length of time in advance were introduced in twenty state legislatures between 1979 and 1981: Alabama, California, Hawaii, Illinois, Indiana, Maine, Massachusetts,

The author is an economist in the Economic Development Division, Economic Research Service, of the U.S. Department of Agriculture.

[1]See Richard B. McKenzie, *Restrictions on Business Mobility: A Study in Political Rhetoric and Economic Reality* (Washington, D.C.: American Enterprise Institute, 1979).

Michigan, Minnesota, Missouri, Montana, New Jersey, New York, Ohio, Oregon, Pennsylvania, Rhode Island, Washington, West Virginia, and Wisconsin.[2]

With the current high level of public concern over state and local job losses due to plant closing and relocation, it is surprising that so little is known or has been documented about industrial relocation in the United States. Recent studies provide some insight into the importance of relocation and the factors that appear to influence the volume, distance, and direction of plant movement, but narrowly focus on selected urban areas,[3] states,[4] and regions.[5] Other studies provide some information on relocation in a national context but are concerned primarily either with the trend in Great Britain or the decisions of the large, multiplant "Fortune 500" firms in this country.[6] No study, to my knowledge, has been undertaken on the

---

[2]McKenzie, "The Right to Close Down: The Political Battle Shifts to the States," Working Paper (Clemson, S.C.: Department of Economics, Clemson University, 1981).

Each bill either failed to pass or is still in committee, however. Public concern over plant abandonment due to relocation was also evident in earlier area development legislation, which routinely included "antipiracy" clauses prohibiting financial assistance "if the result is to transfer from one area to another any employment or business activity" (Public Law 92-419, the Rural Development Act of 1972) or "to assist establishments relocating from one area to another if it increases unemployment in the original location" (Public Law 89-136, the Public Works and Economic Development Act of 1965).

[3]See Rodney A. Erickson and Michael Wasylenko, "Firm Relocation and Site Selection in Suburban Municipalities," *Journal of Urban Economics*, vol. 8, no. 1 (July 1980): 69–85; Leon Moses and H. F. Williamson, "The Location of Economic Activity in Cities," *American Economic Review*, vol. 57, no. 2 (May 1967): 211–41; and Roger W. Schmenner, *The Manufacturing Location Decision: Evidence from Cincinnati and New England* (Cambridge, Mass.: Joint Center for Urban Studies of MIT and Harvard University, March 1978).

[4]See David L. Barkley, "Plant Ownership Characteristics and the Locational Stability of Iowa Manufacturers," *Land Economics*, vol. 54, no. 1 (February 1978): 92–99.

[5]See John A. Kuehn and Curtis Braschler, *New Manufacturing Plants in the Nonmetro Ozarks Region* (AER no. 384) (Washington, D.C.: U.S. Department of Agriculture and the University of Missouri Agricultural Experiment Station, September 1979); and James P. Miller, *Nonmetro Job Growth and Locational Change in Manufacturing Firms* (RDRR no. 24) (Washington, D.C.: U.S. Department of Agriculture, Economic Research Service, August 1980).

[6]See R. A. Henderson, "Industrial Overspill from Glasgow," *Urban Studies*, vol. 11, no. 1 (February 1974): 61–79; Morgan Sant, *Industrial Movement and Regional Development: The British Case* (Elmsford, N.Y.: Pergamon Press, 1975); Schmenner,

overall trend and geographic pattern of industrial movement in this country.

This paper seeks to expand the base of facts on industrial relocation in the United States by examining the volume, origin-destination flows, and characteristics of the manufacturing plants that changed county locations between December 31, 1969, and December 31, 1975. The first section demonstrates how plant relocations have contributed to the growth and decline of manufacturing employment in each of the nine U.S. census divisions. A second section investigates the origin-destination flows of establishments relocating during the period. The final section examines the distance of movement and attempts to identify whether or not certain factors, such as size of firm, ownership status, or the difference in relative state-tax burden at the origin and destination of relocation, influence the distance of movement.

Identifying Relocation with Dun & Bradstreet Data

Manufacturing "relocation," for the purpose of this paper, refers to the intercounty movement of establishments—branch plants, corporate headquarters, and noncorporate single-unit operations—in all industries classified as manufacturing by the U.S. Office of Management and Budget in its standard industrial classifications, for example, SIC 20 (food products), SIC 21 (tobacco products), . . . SIC 39 (miscellaneous products). Relocations were identified by comparing the records of over 300,000 individual manufacturing establishments in two annual data files, 1969 and 1975, provided by Dun & Bradstreet Corporation.[7] For a move to qualify as a relocation, an existing plant operation must have closed in one

---

The Location Decisions of Large, Multiplant Companies (Cambridge, Mass.: Joint Center for Urban Studies of MIT and Harvard University, September 1980); and P. M. Townroe, Industrial Movement—Experience in the U.S. and U.K. (Westmead, England: Saxon House, 1979).

[7]Dun's Market Identifiers (DMI) files containing records on most manufacturing establishments in the United States are compiled and marketed by the Dun & Bradstreet Corporation. The establishment's address on each record allows researchers to identify changes in plant location over time. Readers desiring further information on Dun & Bradstreet data and the procedure for identifying relocations should refer to the earlier studies by David L. Birch [The Job Generation Process (Cambridge, Mass.: MIT Program on Neighborhood and Regional Change, 1979)] and James P. Miller [Nonmetro Job Growth; and "Research with Dun and Bradstreet Data," EDD Working Paper no. 4903 (Washington, D.C.: U.S. Department of Agriculture, ERS, March 1979)].

county and reopened under the same company name in another county between December 31, 1969, and December 31, 1975. The plants that did not reopen under the same company name are classified as "closings."[8] Plants that began operation under new company names are identified as "starts." Plants that kept the same company name and remained at the same county locations during the period are labeled "stationary."

Manufacturing Relocation as a Factor in Regional Growth and Decline

In the early 1970s automation, foreign competition, and a recession (1974–75) continued to diminish the role of the manufacturing sector as a major employer. Employment over the 1969–75 period declined 8.0 percent, while the number of plants in operation decreased 5.1 percent. Most of the decline occurred in the Northeast. Manufacturing employment continued to expand in four census divisions.

The disparity in the rate of employment change between regions has led to much speculation about the importance of manufacturing relocation. Plant outmigration is often perceived as the major cause of regional decline.

The evidence, however, refutes this perception. Plant relocations do not appear to be a major factor in either national or regional manufacturing growth and decline. Nationwide, only 6,639 manufacturing plants out of 326,123 in operation in 1969 (2.0 percent) changed county locations between 1969 and 1975, and the number of jobs involved (309,581) represented only 1.6 percent of all manufacturing jobs in 1969 (table 3.1). This was also true for regions. The number of outmigrating plants by census division rarely exceeded 3.0 percent of the total in manufacturing in 1969—the one exception was the Middle Atlantic division. The number of jobs lost because of plant outmigration was consistently under 3.0 percent of total manufacturing employment in each region. Employment gains due

[8]Some relocations may have been falsely recorded as closings during the period. A comparison of establishment records in the 1969 and 1975 DMI files does not guarantee completely accurate identification of all relocations. For example, plants that were acquired and then consolidated under a new company name at a new location would be identified as, first, closings and, then, a plant start elsewhere and not as relocations. However, a recent study has found that only 5 percent of the relocations identified with Dun & Bradstreet data are either falsely recorded or missed moves (Schmenner, *The Location Decisions of Large, Multiplant Companies*).

Table 3.1

COMPONENTS OF CHANGE IN THE MANUFACTURING SECTOR, 1969–1975

	1969 Total	Net change in stationary firms	Components of change, 1969–75 Natural change			Relocation			Total change 1969–75
			Starts[a]	Closings	Net change	Gains	Losses	Net change	
	Establishments		Percent of 1969 Total						
United States	326,123[b]	—	33.8	38.9	−5.1	2.0	2.0	0	−5.1
New England	24,894	—	29.7	35.8	−6.1	2.5	2.1	0.4	−5.7
Middle Atlantic	85,014	—	22.5	38.6	−16.1	2.8	3.1	−0.3	−16.4
East North Central	72,500	—	27.5	35.1	−7.6	1.7	1.8	−0.1	−7.7
West North Central	23,900	—	29.8	38.2	−8.4	1.4	1.5	−0.1	−8.5
South Atlantic	36,595	—	37.9	40.4	−2.5	2.6	2.2	0.4	−2.1
East South Central	14,641	—	32.1	38.3	−6.2	1.2	0.9	0.3	−5.9
West South Central	25,519	—	41.9	42.8	−0.9	1.2	1.1	0.1	−0.8
Mountain	9,035	—	57.3	42.9	14.4	1.5	1.2	0.3	14.7
Pacific	34,025	—	65.2	45.7	19.5	1.4	1.4	0	19.5
	Employment		Percent of 1969 Total						
United States	19,348,791	5.7	8.5	22.6	−14.1	2.0	1.6	0.4	−8.0
New England	1,566,268	−1.3	7.6	26.4	−18.8	3.6	1.3	2.3	−17.8
Middle Atlantic	4,308,698	−1.7	7.1	25.2	−18.1	2.3	2.8	−0.5	−20.3
East North Central	5,140,825	11.3	5.5	19.6	−14.1	1.3	1.2	0.1	−2.7
West North Central	1,126,675	14.7	11.4	24.7	−13.3	1.4	1.8	−0.4	1.0
South Atlantic	2,458,512	2.1	9.3	24.4	−15.1	3.2	2.0	1.2	−11.8
East South Central	1,051,635	17.4	8.4	22.0	−13.6	1.1	0.6	0.5	4.3
West South Central	1,084,899	13.4	15.8	27.5	−11.7	2.1	2.0	0.1	1.8
Mountain	302,046	9.9	16.1	28.6	−12.5	4.2	0.9	3.3	0.7
Pacific	2,309,233	1.5	11.6	16.6	−5.0	0.9	0.5	0.4	−3.1

SOURCE: Dun's Market Identifiers, Dun & Bradstreet Corporation, 1969, 1975.

[a] Because Dun & Bradstreet does not provide the starting dates on branch plants, the percentages are unavoidably biased downwards. The net effect is to bias total percentage change downward by the actual number of new branch starts during the period.

[b] This number includes 24,872 firms that did not report employment to Dun & Bradstreet.

to plant inmigration were similarly low, ranging from 0.9 percent of 1969 employment in the Pacific division to only 4.2 percent of manufacturing employment in the Mountain division.

Plant closings, starts, and stationary operations clearly had more influence than relocation on regional manufacturing employment during the period. Regions lost employment primarily because of plant closings. The losses ranged from 16.6 percent in the Pacific division to 28.6 percent in the Mountain division. Regions gained employment, on the other hand, primarily through new plant starts and expansions by stationary plants. Relocations did not constitute a substantial proportion of the number of jobs (or plants) gained and lost by each division.

The low volume of plant relocations in the United States is not surprising. Manufacturing firms rarely make decisions to relocate plant operations when other options are available, such as retooling and expanding the operation at the original site, maintaining the old operation while starting a new branch plant elsewhere to handle the overflow, selling out to another firm, or even going bankrupt.[9] The consensus of previous studies is that most relocations are "decisions of last resort" that involve a large element of risk and uncertainty.[10] Plants are closed and opened elsewhere only when considerable inertia at the original site is overcome.[11] The net gain from sales and reduced operating costs at the new location must outweigh the loss of largely depreciated facilities, equipment, and trained employees at the old location. The costs of interrupting production, employee relocation, and pension funds for displaced employees must also be considered. Thus relocations do not commonly occur, because they are often the least attractive option.

While it is important to emphasize the fact that relocations contribute very little to the growth and decline of regional manufacturing employment, one should be aware that other, less obvious forms of industrial mobility can also shift the locus of employment. Companies can open new branch operations while either maintain-

[9]M. T. Daly and M. J. Webber, "The Growth of the Firm within the City," *Urban Studies*, vol. 10, no. 3 (October 1973): 303–17.

[10]See Schmenner, *The Manufacturing Location Decision;* and David F. Walker, "A Behavioral Approach to Industrial Location," in *Location Dynamics of Manufacturing Activity*, ed. L. Collins and D. F. Walker (London: John Wiley, 1975), pp. 135–58.

[11]Dennis K. Smith, "Industrial Plant Location Decisions: Implications for Community Activity," staff paper, Virginia Agriculture Economic Cooperative Extension Service, Virginia State University, Blacksburg, March 1975.

ing stable employment or phasing out operation at the old site. In addition, corporate acquisitions, divestitures, and mergers can shift organizational emphasis on expansion from one region to another; that is, plant operations may be shifted to other regions under new company names. One recent study has shown that "organizational control" shifts of this type contributed much more to the disparity of growth between regions than the actual relocation of plant operations during the 1960s and early 1970s.[12] A study of industrial movement in a wider context, therefore, should consider the "corporate organizational" aspect.[13]

Origin and Destination Flows

Previous research has revealed very little about the pattern of industrial movement in the United States "except by implication through studies of relative rates of growth and decline in different regions [and] states."[14] This section provides some background information on the pattern of movement between census divisions, states, and counties as a first step toward investigating factors that appear to influence the distance of movement.

Regional Flows

Manufacturing firms, typically, do not make high-risk decisions to move plant operations to distant locations in other regions. The low incidence of interregional movement is clearly evident from the census division origin-destination flow data presented in table 3.2. Only 751 out of 6,639 relocations (11.3 percent) were to other census divisions. The proportion of jobs displaced by moves to other divisions was also low: 28.2 percent of the total number involved in all plant relocations.

Because so few plants were involved, no clear, discernible pattern of movement emerged during the period. Some net migration did occur from the Middle Atlantic (264 plants), East North Central (73 plants), and West North Central (6 plants) census divisions to the other six divisions. The South Atlantic census division gained the most plants through net migration (132 plants). Census division losses and gains of jobs through net plant migration followed a similar pattern.

[12]See Schmenner, *The Location Decisions of Large, Multiplant Companies.*

[13]Townroe, *Industrial Movement*, p. 211.

[14]Ibid., p. 210.

Table 3.2

REGIONAL (U.S. CENSUS DIVISION[a]) FLOWS OF MANUFACTURING ESTABLISHMENTS AND JOBS INVOLVED IN RELOCATIONS, 1969–1975

A. Establishment Flows
Region of 1975 Location

Region of 1969 Location	NE	MA	ENC	WNC	SA	ESC	WSC	Mt.	Pac.	Total
NE	486	25	6	0	7	4	1	0	3	532
MA	127	2,278	33	3	118	13	14	10	29	2,625
ENC	10	23	1,173	19	39	23	14	11	14	1,326
WNC	1	2	12	313	4	3	9	4	4	352
SA	0	23	11	1	768	10	4	1	5	823
ESC	0	1	9	1	9	105	5	1	1	132
WSC	0	2	3	1	4	6	252	5	2	275
Mt.	1	1	4	3	2	1	3	91	3	109
Pac.	0	6	2	5	4	4	6	16	422	465
Total	625	2,361	1,253	346	955	169	308	139	483	6,639

Table 3.2 cont.

B. Job Flows (Percent)[b]

Region of 1969 Location	Region of 1975 Location									
	NE	MA	ENC	WNC	SA	ESC	WSC	Mt.	Pac.	Total
NE	5.2	—[c]	0.3	—	0.2	—	—	—	—	5.9
MA	9.4	25.4	1.7	1	3.1	0.5	0.5	—	0.5	41.4
ENC	0.2	0.3	14.3	0.2	4.6	0.8	0.3	0.4	0.6	21.7
WNC	—	—	0.5	3.6	—	0.1	0.2	—	0.2	4.6
SA	—	0.3	0.1	—	12.3	0.1	—	—	—	12.9
ESC	—	—	—	—	0.1	1.2	0.1	—	—	1.6
WSC	—	—	—	—	—	0.1	4.6	—	—	4.9
Mt.	—	—	—	—	0.1	—	—	2.3	—	2.6
Pac.	—	0.1	—	0.1	—	—	0.1	0.3	3.7	4.2
Total	14.8	26.2	17.1	4.1	20.6	3.0	5.9	3.1	5.2	100.0[d]

SOURCE: Dun's Market Identifiers, 1969, 1975.

[a]NE = New England   ENC = East North Central   SA = South Atlantic   WSC = West South Central   Pac. = Pacific
MA = Middle Atlantic   WNC = West North Central   ESC = East South Central   Mt. = Mountain

[b]Percent of 1969 employment involved in relocation (309,581 jobs).

[c]—indicates values less than 0.1 percent of all relocation employment in 1969.

[d]Percentages may not add up exactly to 100.0 percent because of rounding off.

The largest movement of plant operations occurred out of the Middle Atlantic (118 plants) and East North Central census divisions (39 plants) to the South Atlantic census division. The Middle Atlantic division also experienced the highest proportional loss of employment from the net migration of plant operations (15.2 percent).[15]

Most evident from table 3.2, however, is that interregional relocations are not very important. This is clearly brought out by comparison with the total number of manufacturing plants and jobs in existence in 1969. Out of 326,123 establishments, 6,639 (2.0 percent) relocated, but only 751 plants (0.02 percent) relocated to other census divisions. Out of 19,348,791 jobs, 309,581 (1.6 percent) were displaced by relocations, but only 87,302 jobs (0.04 percent) were displaced to other census divisions.

State Flows

About one-fourth of all relocations occurred across state borders—1,603 plants (21.1 percent). Most of the interstate relocation activity involved movement over relatively short distances to adjacent states in the Middle Atlantic and New England census divisions. The major flows of relocations to adjacent states—New York to New Jersey, New York to Connecticut, Massachusetts to New Hampshire, Illinois to Wisconsin, and Missouri to Kansas—occurred within the metropolitan areas (SMSAs) of New York City, Boston, Chicago, and Kansas City. There were few major flows to nonadjacent states. The largest flow of relocations to a distant state occurred out of New York to Florida (37 plants).

County Flows

Most manufacturing movement occurred between counties within the same state. Approximately three-fourths of all relocations (5,036) involved intrastate, intercounty moves.

The flow of movement was primarily to less urbanized counties. This is clearly illustrated in table 3.3, which shows the flows of plants and jobs between county groups classified according to level of urbanization. The dominant flow, involving 46.7 percent of all relocations and 53.4 percent of all jobs, was to less urbanized counties. The most common type of relocation was from urban core to

[15]See table 3.2; the net migration loss of employment in the Middle Atlantic division is obtained by subtracting the column total (26.2 percent) from the row total (41.4 percent).

Table 3.3

MANUFACTURING PLANT RELOCATIONS AND JOBS BY LEVEL OF
COUNTY URBANIZATION,[a] 1969–1975

	Percent of Total Relocations (6,639)	Percent of Total Relocation Employment (309,581)[b]
Flows to less urbanized counties		
Metro core to metro fringe	26.5	24.1
Metro core to other metro	8.5	17.4
Metro core to nonmetro	3.9	5.7
Other metro to nonmetro	3.3	2.8
Metro fringe to other metro	2.5	1.5
Metro fringe to nonmetro	2.0	1.9
Total	46.7	53.4
Flows to more urbanized counties		
Metro fringe to metro core	11.6	11.8
Other metro to metro core	2.6	6.0
Nonmetro to other metro	2.3	1.0
Other metro to metro fringe	1.7	1.2
Nonmetro to metro core	1.0	.9
Nonmetro to metro fringe	.8	.6
Total	20.0	21.5
Lateral flows		
Metro core to metro core	15.8	12.0
Other metro to other metro	6.9	5.9
Metro fringe to metro fringe	6.2	4.2
Nonmetro to nonmetro	4.4	3.0
Total	33.3	25.1

SOURCE: Dun's Market Identifiers, 1969, 1975.

[a]*Metro core*—Core counties in SMSAs (Standard Metropolitan Statistical Areas) with at least one million residents in April 1973, e.g., Cook County, Ill., Fulton County, Ga.;

Metro fringe—Fringe counties outside core counties in SMSAs with at least one million residents;

Other metro—Metropolitan counties with fewer than one million residents but at least 50,000 residents in one urban center;

Nonmetro—Nonmetropolitan counties are those with fewer than 50,000 residents in the largest urban center and not socially or economically integrated with an SMSA.

[b]This is employment at the county of 1969 location.

urban fringe counties within the largest metropolitan areas of the United States, e.g., Chicago, Atlanta, New York City. A smaller number of manufacturing plants (33.3 percent) and jobs (25.1 percent) were involved in lateral moves to counties classified at the same level of urbanization. The smallest flow of plants (20.0 percent) and jobs (21.5 percent) was to more urbanized counties.

It appears that the level of county urbanization is a factor in relocation decisions. The fact that most plants relocate over short distances, primarily to less urbanized counties within the same state, suggests two things. First, many plant operations have been forced to move out of major urban areas because of unfavorable local economic conditions such as restrictions on facility space, congestion, high labor costs, taxes, and other factors associated with densely populated areas. Second, the forces of "locational inertia" appear to be sufficiently strong to limit most movement to sites that are not too distant from the original location. The large incidence of short-distance relocations to less urbanized counties is not unexpected. Previous research on plant relocation decisions in both Great Britain and the United States reveals that most relocations involve short-distance moves by small, noncorporate plants that are interested in retaining former workers, suppliers, services, and customers.[16]

Distance of Movement

Manufacturing plant moves over longer distances to other states and regions appear to be motivated by circumstances different from those confronting short-distance, intrastate movers. Intrastate relocations typically involve small, noncorporate, single-unit, rapidly growing companies moving out of urban core areas to fringe locations.[17] These relocations are primarily motivated by the need for space and the desire to retain workers and contacts with former suppliers and customers. Plant moves to other states and regions, on the other hand, typically involve more cost-conscious and larger corporate operations that are attempting to consolidate operations

[16]See Moses and Williamson, "The Location of Economic Activity in Cities"; Schmenner, *The Location Decisions of Large, Multiplant Companies;* idem, *The Manufacturing Location Decision;* and Townroe, *Industrial Movement.*

[17]Schmenner, *The Manufacturing Location Decision;* and Townroe, *Industrial Movement.*

because of profitability problems at the old site.[18] Better access to markets, transportation, and even state and local financial inducements including tax incentives can be important motivative factors.

Some suggestive evidence is offered in table 3.4 that compares selected plant characteristics for three categories of movers: intrastate, intraregional (U.S. census divisions), and interregional. Statistical examination of the incidence of relocations in each distance category generally indicates significant differences in age, employment size, ownership, and industry.[19] The degree of significance, however, indicates that there is most likely a strong relationship between distance and only two variables: ownership and employment size. The relationship is much weaker for age and industry.

Age, as an indicator of a plant's future profit potential, does not appear to be a strong motivative factor in intrastate relocations. Relatively new plant operations (under six years old) were proportionately more active in longer-distance moves—14.8 percent of the interregional relocations and 11.5 percent of the intraregional relocations, compared to only 7.2 percent of the intrastate moves. Plants over thirty years old, however, also appear to be more active in longer-distance moves—19.2 percent of the interregional relocations compared to 13.8 percent of the intraregional relocations and 14.6 percent of the intrastate moves. The evidence, thus, does not consistently suggest that older plants are more likely to make interregional moves to the most cost-efficient locations in order to overcome low growth and profitability problems.

Employment size differences were more evident. Small plants (under fifty employees) were proportionately more active in shorter-distance moves (intrastate and intraregional) than in longer, interregional moves. Plants in the three size categories with over fifty employees, conversely, were more active in longer-distance interregional moves.

[18]Schmenner, "Industrial Location and Government Policy," paper prepared for the National Commission on Employment Policy, Washington, D.C., 1981.

A recent study of rural manufacturers in Iowa reveals that corporate firms have a higher propensity to consolidate (i.e., to abandon and relocate) branch plants during periods of slumping demand, particularly if the plants are low-wage, labor-intensive operations. See Barkley, "Plant Ownership Characteristics."

[19]Chi-square tests were performed on each cross-tabulation in table 3.4. Significant chi-square values were computed in each case indicating likely differences in the age, employment size, ownership status, and durable-nondurable industry structure of intrastate, intraregional, and interregional relocations.

Table 3.4

AGE, SIZE, OWNERSHIP, AND INDUSTRY DIFFERENCES OF
INTRASTATE, INTERSTATE, AND INTERREGIONAL MOVERS

	Intrastate Movers	Intra-regional Movers	Inter-regional Movers	Total
Number of Establishments	5,036	852	751	6,639
Age				
Under 6 years	7.2%	11.5%	14.8%	8.5%
6–10 years	31.5	28.3	24.9	30.4
11–20 years	29.6	29.8	27.0	29.4
21–30 years	17.1	16.5	14.1	16.7
Over 30 years	14.6	13.9	19.2	15.0
Total	100.0	100.0	100.0	100.0
Employment				
Under 20 employees	59.0	54.8	48.3	57.3
20–50	24.1	23.1	21.4	23.7
51–100	8.9	10.7	11.9	9.5
101–500	7.0	10.6	15.6	8.5
Over 500	1.0	0.8	2.8	1.0
Total	100.0	100.0	100.0	100.0
Ownership				
Single operation	74.8	65.5	49.4	70.7
Headquarters	20.5	32.5	47.7	25.1
Branch operation	4.7	2.0	2.9	4.2
Total	100.0	100.0	100.0	100.0
Industry				
Durables	62.5	48.7	52.7	59.6
Nondurables	37.5	51.3	47.3	40.4
Total	100.0	100.0	100.0	100.0

SOURCE: Dun's Market Identifiers, 1969, 1975.

Ownership status appears to be another important factor in the distance of relocation. Corporate headquarters and branch plants were less active in relocating within the state (25.2 percent) than outside the state: 34.5 percent of the intraregional moves and 50.6 percent of the interregional moves. Noncorporate, single-unit plants, on the other hand, were proportionately less active in relocating outside the state compared to inside the state.

Product susceptibility to changes in national markets also could be a factor in the distance of movement. Durable-goods producers were proportionately more active in intrastate relocation (62.5 percent) than nondurable-goods industries. Producers of durable goods may have opted for less risky intrastate moves because of slumping markets in the early 1970s. Durable-goods industries, traditionally, are more susceptible to cyclical downturns over time than nondurable-goods industries.

State and Local Taxes

State and local taxes, generally, are not an important consideration in industrial location decisions. The consensus from previous studies of manufacturing location decisions is that taxes are not a critical element in the cost structure of the firm and, thus, will rarely influence the choice of site.[20] The cost savings from favorable state personal income taxes, local property taxes, and various tax exemptions and moratoriums on industrial income and property are seldom large enough to overcome the other cost disadvantages (e.g., labor and transportation) facing the firm at any given site.

In some relocation decisions, however, tax savings can be an important "swing-factor," particularly in moves over short distances to neighboring city jurisdictions, counties, and states.[21] Taxes are likely to be a motivative factor in these decisions because labor, transportation, and raw material cost differentials are usually small between neighboring locations and can be easily offset by lower tax bills. Areas adjacent to areas with higher tax burdens are thus expected to attract more plant operations than they lose through migration.

The evidence on interstate manufacturing relocation in the early 1970s suggests that state and local taxes may have, indeed, been a factor directing the flow of movement. A comparison of the major interstate flows of relocations in table 3.5 reveals that the direction of movement was primarily to states that had lower relative growth in state and local tax burden (1967–74) compared to the states where relocations originated. States with lower relative changes in tax burden gained 520 plants through net migration (table 3.6). States

[20]See Erickson and Wasylenko, "Firm Relocation"; Robert Kleine, "State-Local Tax Incentives and Industrial Location," *Revenue Administration*, NATA Proceedings, 45th Annual Meeting: pp. 178–89, 1977; Schmenner, "Industrial Location and Government Policy"; and idem, *The Manufacturing Location Decision*.

[21]Advisory Commission on Intergovernmental Relations, *Regional Growth, Interstate Tax Competition* (A-76) (Washington, D.C.: ACIR, March 1981).

43

Table 3.5

MAJOR FLOWS[a] OF INTERSTATE MANUFACTURING RELOCATIONS, UNITED STATES, 1969–1975

State of Net Loss	State of Net Gain	Flows From Net Loser to Net Gainer	Flows From Net Gainer to Net Loser	Positive Net Flow (State)	Net Flow was to Adjacent State	Net Flow was to State with Lower Relative Change in State-Local Tax Burden[b]
N.Y.	N.J.	283	45	238 (N.J.)	yes	yes
N.Y.	Conn.	87	0	87 (Conn.)	yes	yes
N.Y.	Fla.	37	1	36 (Fla.)	no	yes
Mo.	Kans.	46	14	32 (Kans.)	yes	yes
Mass.	N.H.	28	2	26 (N.H.)	yes	yes
D.C.	Md.	26	2	24 (Md.)	yes	yes
N.Y.	Cal.	19	1	18 (Cal.)	no	yes
N.Y.	Va.	13	0	13 (Va.)	no	yes
Penn.	N.J.	37	25	12 (N.J.)	yes	yes
Ill.	Fla.	14	2	12 (Fla.)	no	yes
Ill.	Wisc.	21	10	11 (Wisc.)	yes	no
N.Y.	Penn.	26	17	9 (Penn.)	yes	no
Cal.	Nev.	9	0	9 (Nev.)	yes	yes
N.Y.	Ohio	8	1	7 (Ohio)	no	yes
Ill.	Mo.	9	2	7 (Mo.)	yes	yes
N.Y.	Ga.	6	1	5 (Ga.)	no	yes
Ill.	Ohio	6	1	5 (Ohio)	no	no

Table 3.5 cont.

State of Net Loss	State of Net Gain	Flows From Net Loser to Net Gainer	Flows From Net Gainer to Net Loser	Positive Net Flow (State)	Net Flow was to Adjacent State	Net Flow was to State with Lower Relative Change in State-Local Tax Burden[b]
Ind.	Ill.	9	4	5 (Ill.)	yes	no
N.Y.	Ill.	11	6	5 (Ill.)	no	yes
N.J.	Conn.	5	0	5 (Conn.)	no	yes
N.Y.	Mass.	11	7	4 (Mass.)	yes	yes
Ohio	Ky.	8	4	4 (Ky.)	yes	yes
Ill.	Mich.	6	2	4 (Mich.)	no	yes
Tenn.	Miss.	5	1	4 (Miss.)	yes	yes
N.Y.	N.C.	6	3	3 (N.C.)	no	yes
Ill.	Tex.	5	2	3 (Tex.)	no	yes
Okla.	Tex.	5	2	3 (Tex.)	yes	no
Ill.	Cal.	5	2	3 (Cal.)	no	yes
Mass.	Conn.	5	3	2 (Conn.)	yes	yes
N.Y.	Cal.	5	4	1 (Cal.)	no	yes

SOURCE: Dun's Market Identifiers, 1969, 1975.

[a]5 or more relocations.

[b]State rankings on relative tax burden change are taken from an earlier study by ACIR (*1*, p. 56).

Table 3.6
SUMMARY OF POSITIVE NET FLOWS OF RELOCATIONS

| | Total | | — Net flow to states with — | | | |
| | | | Lower Tax Burden Change | | Higher Tax Burden Change | |
	No.	Pct.	No.	Pct.	No.	Pct.
Net flows to adjacent states	477	78.9	411	68.8	66	11.1
Net flows to nonadjacent states	120	20.1	109	18.3	11	1.8
All flows	597	100.0	520	87.1	77	12.9

SOURCE: Table 3.5.

experiencing higher relative changes in tax burden gained only 77 plants. The largest net flow of plants occurred between adjacent states, from states with high growth in tax burden to states with lower growth in tax burden (477 plants). Net migration was lowest to nonadjacent states with higher relative changes in state and local tax burden. These states gained only 11 plants (1.8 percent) through net migration.

Summary and Conclusions

This paper has presented a descriptive analysis of manufacturing relocation in the United States, 1969 to 1975. The primary aim of the paper was to provide background information, previously unavailable, on (a) the role of relocations in reallocating manufacturing employment among regions, (b) the geographical flow of relocations, and (c) selected characteristics of plants involved in relocations over short and long distances.

The major findings are: (1) that relocations play a very minor role in reallocating manufacturing employment among regions compared to the net effect of starts, closings, and stationary plants; (2) that when relocations do occur, the majority involve short-distance, intrastate moves by small, non-corporate-affiliated employers; and (3) that the direction of plant movement is primarily to less urbanized counties and to states with lower relative growth in tax burden.

The implications for current and proposed industrial development policy are fairly obvious. First, the recent proposals to restrict plant movement in the United States tend to exaggerate the importance of plant abandonment and outmigration. Very few manufacturing plants actually migrate, and when they do move, it is usually to other sites within the same metropolitan area, state, and almost certainly the same region. The adverse economic impact of plant outmigration on a state or region is minimal. Second, there is little to be gained by either encouraging or discouraging manufacturing plant relocations. An alternative strategy for state and local industrial development is to foster the survival and expansion of plants already in operation and to encourage new plant starts. Far more manufacturing jobs were involved in starts, closings, expansions, and contractions than in plant relocations during the early 1970s. Third, a favorable tax climate may be a factor in plant outmigration to neighboring states. In the early 1970s, the major flow of interstate relocations was to neighboring states experiencing lower growth in state and local tax burdens.

IV. Is There a Case for Plant-Closing Laws?

John S. Hekman and John S. Strong

The older industrial states of the Northeast and the Midwest have been experiencing a marked decline in manufacturing employment over the last fifteen years. Public attention has been drawn repeatedly to the closing of large industrial plants, causing pockets of high unemployment to develop even during periods of national economic expansion. To a large extent the cause of the problem has been ascribed to the Frostbelt-Sunbelt migration of industry. In its most basic form, the idea is that firms are said to be fleeing high labor costs and unionization in the North by moving to the low-wage, nonunionized South; the terms coined for this process are "capital flight" and "runaway plants." Some North-South migration of workers took place starting in the 1970s, but not enough to prevent unemployment rates in some Middle Atlantic and North Central states from remaining well above those of the Sunbelt. Especially in smaller cities, plant closings have resulted in workers experiencing underemployment, lower paying jobs, or early retirement.

Various attempts have been made to deal with this problem, for example via more aggressive industry location incentives in northern states. However, the campaign with the most far-reaching potential is probably the current spate of so-called plant-closing laws which seek to change the terms under which large business establishments may close down or lay off large numbers of workers.

"Is There a Case for Plant-Closing Laws?" by John S. Hekman and John S. Strong is reprinted with the permission of the authors from the *New England Economic Review*, July/August 1980, pp. 34–51.

John S. Hekman is an associate professor of business administration at the University of North Carolina–Chapel Hill; John S. Strong is a doctoral student at Harvard Business School. At the time this article was written, both men worked at the Federal Reserve Bank of Boston, Mr. Hekman as economist and Mr. Strong as research assistant.

The purpose of this article is to describe and analyze both sides of the debate over plant-closing laws and to clarify the myriad issues involved. As one way of illustrating the possible policies toward plant closings or industrial transition, a description of Sweden's extensive labor policies relating to these issues is included. Parallels are drawn between the size and industrial nature of New England and Sweden.

Legislation to regulate plant closings and layoffs has been proposed in several states of the Northeast and the North Central regions, including Massachusetts, Connecticut, Rhode Island, Pennsylvania, New York, Ohio, and Illinois. Three types of provisions are contained in most of the bills: These come under the headings of worker notification, severance pay, and community assistance. For example, several of the bills introduced in the Massachusetts legislature would require that one year's notification of an impending closing be given to employees, that one week's severance pay for each year of service be paid, and that 15 percent of the annual wage bill be given to the local community as adjustment assistance. The legislation proposed in other states generally is similar in its provisions, although Ohio would require a two-year notice to be given. The establishments covered by the laws are those with over 50 employees in Massachusetts and those with over 100 employees in Connecticut and Rhode Island. Maine is the only New England state which has passed such a measure thus far. It provides for severance pay of one week's wages per year of employment but no notification or community assistance; all establishments employing over 100 workers are covered.

A Complex Set of Issues

Discussions of plant closings fall under three main concerns: job rights, economic efficiency, and regional competition. "Concerns" is a proper term here because, while it could be said that there is only one issue, that of the overall social and economic cost of a particular policy, different individuals and groups tend to focus on one of the three perspectives somewhat independently of the others. Thus one can worry about whether plant-closing laws will make New England less competitive with other regions while ignoring what these laws will do to overall economic efficiency, or can be concerned with job rights regardless of what they will do to regional competitiveness. It seems unlikely that anyone can provide an overall analysis quantifying all the benefits and costs of these

50

proposed policies, since they involve so many intangible and distributional issues.

Job Rights

The job rights concern involves two main areas: prior notification of dismissal and the "property" accumulated by job tenure. In the U.S. economy, contracts are entered into between management and labor (or, more abstractly, between capital and labor) subject to the body of laws governing such agreements. Labor unions have bargaining power to obtain, in most cases, benefits according to seniority and, in some cases, prior notification and negotiation with regard to dismissal or layoff. Nonunion workers rarely have these rights. Plant-closing laws seek to change the terms of employment contracts regarding these matters. This is the direction taken by West Germany, Sweden, and a number of other countries where the legal presumption is that it is not management's decision alone whether a firm may lay off workers, but rather a joint agreement by labor, management, and government. The legislation pending in the Northeast and North Central would not go so far. It would not take the closing decision out of the hands of management; rather it would impose monetary costs and notification requirements on employers in order to provide an incentive to postpone or reverse the shut-down decision.

The concept of the job as a property right has received growing attention. Pension benefits are the largest form of property accumulated by workers; in addition, the expanded rights of workers not to be dismissed without due cause constitute another form of intangible property. The advocates of mandatory severance pay and notification believe that a firm's decision to relocate production in order to take advantage of lower wages represents an unfair dismissal of workers; therefore, compensation should be paid to them in proportion to their years of service. Severance pay would be a claim against a bankrupt firm's assets in the same way as are the claims of taxing bodies, debt holders, and equity investors.

Economic Efficiency

The efficiency argument for restricting plant closings rests on an assumed difference between social and private cost, or in other words the difference between the cost to the whole economy compared to the cost as perceived by the individual firm. A firm will decide to close a plant if it expects that the operating costs will be

51

greater than the revenue received by continuing to do business (overhead or fixed cost does not enter the decision because it might be paid regardless of what course is taken). Alternatively, a firm will close a plant in one state and open one elsewhere if the total cost (operating and fixed) in the new location is less than the operating cost alone in the old location. In both of these cases only the costs actually borne by the firm ("private costs") are used to make the decision. But, say proponents of plant-closing laws, society bears additional costs as a direct result of the firm's decision to close the plant ("external costs"). As a result, the total cost of the decision to close may be greater from society's point of view than the benefit. . . .

Regional Competition

One of the major themes underlying the debate over plant-closing laws is that New England and the rest of the Frostbelt are losing employment in manufacturing to the Sunbelt, and especially to the South Atlantic, because wages are lower in the Sunbelt. This raises many questions with regard to manufacturing location decisions, union labor versus nonunion labor, push versus pull theories of location, and the preference of population groups for the various regions. In brief, the advocates of plant-closing laws see employers running away from unions in the North and relocating in states with right-to-work laws. This is the source of the terms "runaway plant" and "capital flight." This process refers to manufacturing alone, because service, trade, and other establishments rarely move from one region to another. And it includes only closings or layoffs which result in relocation of some production, not to bankruptcies or other permanent closings.

The opponents of plant-closing laws dispute the idea of capital flight. Their counterargument has two parts. First, they argue, the causation of the outmigration is reversed. Low wages in the South do not "pull" industrial employment out of the North, with the result that the North "loses" employment; rather wages in the North are being bid upward by competition from the fast-growing manufacturing sectors, so that manufacturing becomes uncompetitive and plants are "pushed" out to relocate in the South. This means the North does not "lose" the employment but experiences a redistribution of employment through competition for labor.

The other argument used against the idea of capital flight is to downgrade its importance. While it is true that manufacturing is growing more rapidly in the South than in the Northeast, this difference has many possible causes. Changes in manufacturing employment reflect expansions and contractions of existing plants, openings, permanent closings, and relocations. As will be seen below, it is very difficult to sort out the separate contributions of these different processes. By interpreting the available data in certain ways, relocations may be either a large or a small factor in employment changes. Those who would argue that they are a small factor say that the reason for the South's rapid growth is a higher rate of new openings. This could be due to population movement to the South or to the presence of a large labor supply available there rather than to a large number of relocations from the North to the South.

The Evidence on Plant Closings

A crucial need in the discussion of plant-closing legislation is knowledge of the extent of the problem of layoffs and closings. The federal government does not collect any data directly in this area, and state employment or local labor agencies do not organize their employment statistics in such a way that closings can be distinguished reliably from acquisitions or other changes in status. The only source of information on individual establishments for the entire country which attempts to identify firms moving or closing is *Dun's Market Identifiers*. Because it is the only source, it has been used by both proponents and opponents of plant-closing laws. Both sides have found comfort in the numbers—such are the possible interpretations. Basically, Dun's data show that very few establishments close up shop in the Frostbelt and move to the Sunbelt. But on the other hand they show a large absolute number of closings, which are subject to several interpretations.

The Arguments for Closing Laws

The principal study in support of plant-closing legislation is *Capital and Communities: The Causes and Consequences of Private Investment*, by Barry Bluestone and Bennett Harrison.[1] Relying mostly on Dun's data, they try to show that closings and layoffs have affected the Northeast and North Central severely. To a lesser extent they argue

---

[1]Barry Bluestone and Bennett Harrison, *Capital and Communities: The Causes and Consequences of Private Investment* (Washington, D.C.: The Progressive Alliance, 1980).

53

Table 4.1

INVESTMENT ACTIVITY OF SELECTED FORTUNE 500 TRANSPORTATION EQUIPMENT COMPANIES BY REGION DURING THE 1970s

Investment Activity	Total	New England	Middle Atlantic	North Central	South Atlantic	South Central	Mountain	Pacific
Existing Plants (Early 1970s)								
expanded	77	5	12	41	7	7	1	4
contracted	7	0	2	3	0	1	0	1
closed	18	1	1	7	2	2	1	4
divested	10	0	1	5	2	1	0	1
no change	219	16	27	108	18	17	1	32
Total	331	22	43	164	29	28	3	42
New Plants								
acquired	69	1	1	41	2	11	3	10
opened	57	1	3	20	6	18	4	5
moved in from another location	17	0	1	2	6	3	0	5
Total	143	2	5	63	14	32	7	20

SOURCE: Harvard-MIT Joint Center for Urban Studies, project directed by Roger W. Schmenner. Data sources included *Dun's Market Indentifiers*, company annual reports, 10-K statements, and *Moody's Industrial Manual*, and verification by many (but not all) firms.

Table 4.2

INVESTMENT ACTIVITY OF SELECTED TRANSPORTATION
EQUIPMENT COMPANIES BY GEOGRAPHIC AREA DURING THE
1970s

	Total	North	South and West
Number of Plants			
contracted	7	5	2
closed	18	9	9
expanded	77	58	19
Percent of Plants			
contracted	2.1	2.1	2.0
closed	5.4	3.9	8.8
expanded	23.3	25.3	18.6
Total Plants	331	229	102

SOURCE: Table 4.1.

that capital (as distinct from manufacturing establishments per se) is moving from the Frostbelt to the Sunbelt.

Table 4.1 presents some of the data used by Bluestone and Harrison; it shows the number of openings, closings, expansions, and contractions during the 1970s for a sample of Fortune 500 companies in the transportation equipment industry. These data are used to point out that more contractions occur in the North (Northeast and North Central regions) than in the South and West. To the authors this represents the movement of capital out of the North; they note that "every closing represents a potential capital shift, by freeing up at least some resources whose owners have the option of reinvesting them elsewhere."[2]

However, the data in table 4.1 do not show any capital shifting. Table 4.2 breaks out the main components from table 4.1 into a summary of the North versus the South and West. From this it appears that the proportion of establishments which contracted in the North, 2.1 percent, was virtually the same as that of the South and West, 2.0 percent. Surprisingly, the North had a smaller closing rate, 3.9 percent versus 8.8 percent, and a larger expansion rate, 25.3 percent versus 18.6 percent. The Bluestone-Harrison emphasis seems to be on the absolute number of contractions in the North—

[2]Ibid., p. 33.

55

Table 4.3
EMPLOYMENT GAINED OR LOST THROUGH START-UPS, CLOSINGS, AND RELOCATIONS OF PRIVATE BUSINESS ESTABLISHMENTS IN SELECTED STATES: 1969–1976

	Number of Jobs (thousands) 1974	1969–1976			
		Jobs Created (thousands)	Jobs Destroyed (thousands)	Ratio of Jobs Destroyed to Jobs Created	Net Employment Change (thousands)
Frostbelt					
New England					
Massachusetts	1,639	448	508	1.13	−60
Connecticut	828	211	238	1.13	−27
Mid-Atlantic					
New York	4,475	1,087	1,494	1.37	−407
Pennsylvania	3,071	827	865	1.05	−38
East North Central					
Michigan	2,080	639	552	0.86	87
Ohio	2,701	789	720	0.91	69
West North Central					
Minnesota	798	249	243	0.98	6
Missouri	1,041	321	305	0.95	16

Table 4.3 cont.

	Number of Jobs 1974 (thousands)	Jobs Created (thousands)	Jobs Destroyed (thousands)	Ratio of Jobs Destroyed to Jobs Created	Net Employment Change (thousands)
				1969–1976	
Sunbelt					
South Atlantic					
Georgia	1,258	594	416	0.70	178
North Carolina	1,299	372	374	1.01	– 2
East South Central					
Alabama	730	283	252	0.89	31
Tennessee	1,054	354	296	0.84	58
West South Central					
Louisiana	679	300	233	0.78	67
Texas	2,658	1,153	830	0.72	323
Mountain					
Arizona	363	141	125	0.89	16
Colorado	511	238	174	0.73	64
Pacific					
California	4,165	1,820	1,477	0.81	343
Washington	619	244	180	0.74	64

SOURCE: Bluestone and Harrison calculations from David Birch, *The Job Generation Process*, MIT Program on Neighborhood and Regional Change, Cambridge, Mass., 1979.

five out of the total of seven. In contrast, however, the North has the same absolute number of closings as the South and West, and the North also has three times as many expansions.

One industry cannot give a reliable picture of the extent of plant closings and contractions, especially since tables 4.1 and 4.2 include only Fortune 500 companies. So Bluestone and Harrison also present data aggregated for several states in each region. These are shown in table 4.3. Only start-ups, closings, and relocations are available here; expansions and contractions of existing firms are not included. The authors focus on the ratio of jobs destroyed to jobs created, and they point out that the ratio is generally greater than 1.0 for the Frostbelt and less than 1.0 for the Sunbelt.

Again, several interpretations of these data are possible. By the ratio of destroyed to created jobs, capital appears to be moving to the Sunbelt. However, total employment grew in all the states reported in table 4.3. As mentioned, expansions of existing establishments are not included here, and they more than make up for the net loss in start-ups and closings in the Frostbelt. From the point of view of plant-closing laws, we want to know whether jobs destroyed, including both unavoidable permanent closings and relocations, are higher in the Frostbelt. This can be obtained from table 4.3 by looking at the ratio of jobs destroyed over the entire period 1969–1976 to the total jobs in 1974, the last year for which they are given. This ratio is presented in table 4.4. The Frostbelt states on average and in most individual cases apparently have a lower rate of job loss than the Sunbelt states. The real difference between the two areas is in the rate of job creation. The Sunbelt is expanding faster than the Frostbelt, but not because firms are closing their doors in the Frostbelt at a faster rate. This naturally raises the question whether public policy should be more concerned with reducing closings or with encouraging openings.

Lastly, Bluestone and Harrison give a breakdown of closings by size of establishment. This is important because so many more establishments are small rather than large. Since the legislation being considered would only apply to establishments employing over 50 (or in some cases over 100) workers, the closing rates for these larger establishments are needed. Table 4.5 presents this size breakdown by region and industrial sector for a sample of establishments. The entries in the table represent the fraction of plants closed between 1969 and 1976 by type and location. There are distinct differences shown in the experience of the sectors, the

58

Table 4.4

RATIO OF JOBS LOST 1969–1976 TO TOTAL JOBS 1974, SELECTED STATES

Frostbelt States		Sunbelt States	
Massachusetts	.309	Georgia	.311
Connecticut	.287	North Carolina	.287
New York	.334	Alabama	.341
Pennsylvania	.282	Tennessee	.281
Michigan	.265	Louisiana	.343
Ohio	.267	Texas	.212
Minnesota	.305	Arizona	.344
Missouri	.293	Colorado	.341
		California	.355
		Washington	.291
Average Frostbelt	.296	Average Sunbelt	.327

SOURCE: Calculations from Barry Bluestone and Bennett Harrison, *Capital and Communities: The Causes and Consequences of Private Disinvestment* (Washington, D.C.: The Progressive Alliance, 1980).

regions, and the various sizes. Closing rates decline dramatically with the size of establishment, being from two to three times as high for the establishments with 0 to 20 employees as for those with over 500 workers. Much of the decline in closing rates comes between the smallest size class and the 21 to 50 class. Establishments with fewer than 20 employees in 1969 had, in every case but one, more than a 50 percent chance of closing by 1976. Yet the weighted average closing rate for each category is close to the high rate for the smallest size class, because there are far more small establishments than large ones. The size classes covered by plant-closing laws would be those with more than 50 employees, and the closing rates for these cluster around 30 percent.

Given all the publicity surrounding plant closings in the "old" Northeast and North Central, these regions would be expected to have the highest closing rate in this sample. It is surprising, therefore, to see in table 4.5 that in manufacturing the North Central has the lowest closing rate in the country in every size category. The Northeast has the highest closing rate for smaller establishments, but has a lower rate than the South for plants with over 100 workers. For the weighted average across size classes, the closing rates of

Table 4.5

PROPORTION OF FIRMS EXISTING IN 1969 THAT HAD CLOSED BY 1976, BY SIZE OF ESTABLISHMENT, REGION, AND INDUSTRIAL SECTOR

Region in 1969 and Industrial Sector	No. of 1969 Establishments in the Sample (thousands)	Ratio of Firms Closed by 1976 by Number of Employees					Weighted Average of the Size Class
		0–20	21–50	51–100	100–500	501 +	
Northeast							
Mfg.	76	.53	.40	.37	.33	.21	.48
Trade	295	.60	.35	.34	.36	.57	.59
Services	51	.61	.42	.43	.39	.29	.59
Total[a]	514	.59	.37	.36	.33	.26	.57
North Central							
Mfg.	63	.48	.30	.27	.27	.15	.43
Trade	296	.57	.33	.30	.28	.27	.56
Services	56	.60	.39	.38	.41	.30	.59
Total[a]	519	.56	.32	.28	.27	.17	.54

Table 4.5 cont.

Region in 1969 and Industrial Sector	No. of 1969 Establishments in the Sample (thousands)	Ratio of Firms Closed by 1976 by Number of Employees						Weighted Average of the Size Class
		0–20	21–50	51–100	100–500	501+	
South							
Mfg.	49	.53	.36	.36	.34	.28	.48
Trade	335	.59	.33	.30	.23	.23	.58
Services	63	.61	.41	.40	.39	.34	.60
Total[a]	565	.58	.35	.33	.32	.27	.57
West							
Mfg.	41	.53	.39	.36	.31	.16	.50
Trade	182	.60	.38	.34	.29	.33	.59
Services	35	.62	.41	.40	.42	.36	.60
Total[a]	318	.59	.38	.35	.32	.23	.57

SOURCE: David L. Birch, *The Job Generation Process*, M.I.T. Program on Neighborhood and Regional Change, Cambridge, Mass., 1979, Appendix D-2; based on Dun & Bradstreet Corporation records.
[a]Measures all private sector employment recorded by Dun & Bradstreet, manufacturing, trade, and services, plus other industries not recorded here (farming, mining, transportation, utilities, and finance). Total is a weighted averge of the industry probabilities.

the Northeast and North Central are less than or equal to those for the South and West. The Northeast ranks better on average than for its individual categories because it has relatively more larger plants, where its closing rates are lowest.

In trade and services the issue is somewhat different. On the one hand, closing rates should be the same everywhere because trade and services cannot be footloose but are tied to population. On the other hand, closing rates could be lower in the South and West because population is growing more rapidly there and with it the demand for these firms. Table 4.5 indicates that the North Central has the lowest closing rate in most of these categories, and the Northeast is again high in many individual rates but ranks well overall. No dramatic Frostbelt-Sunbelt difference is evident here; if anything, the Frostbelt has lower closing rates. *The impression of numerous closings may arise because the Northeast and North Central contain a disproportionate share of the country's manufacturing establishments.* While a number of "mature" industries such as steel and rubber have closed quite a few older plants, either this is not large enough to sway the overall closing rate in the Frostbelt, or else similar closing trends are occurring in the Sunbelt which have not been widely publicized.

The Argument against Plant-Closing Laws

Since the issue of plant-closing laws arose because of certain social and economic problems which were attributed to plant closings, the opposition to the legislation mainly takes the form of attacking the arguments and the evidence of the proponents. The most comprehensive treatment of the opposing arguments is *Restrictions on Business Mobility* by Richard B. McKenzie.[3] The main thrust of this book is that very little migration from the Frostbelt to the Sunbelt is taking place and that the proposed legislation on closings would be harmful to the economy.

McKenzie attempts to show that the reports of Frostbelt-Sunbelt migration of population and business are exaggerated. The population of the Northeast increased by only 0.1 percent per year between 1970 and 1976; this was the result of a 0.4 percent rate of natural increase and a 0.3 percent net outmigration rate. The South, in contrast, increased at 1.5 percent per year over this period, with a

---

[3]Richard B. McKenzie, *Restrictions on Business Mobility: A Study in Political Rhetoric and Economic Reality* (Washington, D.C.: American Enterprise Institute, 1979).

Table 4.6

NUMBER OF PERSONS LIVING IN THE SOUTH AND WEST IN 1975
WHO LIVED IN THE NORTHEAST AND NORTH CENTRAL REGIONS
IN 1970, BY AGE (IN THOUSANDS)

Region of Residence and Age in 1975	Region of Residence in 1970	
	Northeast	North Central
South		
5–17 years	360	460
18–34 years	577	709
35–64 years	386	376
65 years and over	184	93
Total	1,508	1,638
West		
5–17 years	124	247
18–34 years	225	440
35–64 years	133	201
65 years and over	30	88
Total	511	975

SOURCE: U.S. Bureau of the Census, *Current Population Reports* P-20, No. 285, October 1975, Table 30.

natural increase of 0.8 percent and net inmigration of 0.7 percent. The migration differential can be regarded as large or small depending on what is considered important. McKenzie points out that the fall in the Northeast's population growth rate after 1970 was due more to a decline in the birth rate than to an increase in outmigration. On the other hand, some people might consider it more significant that the Northeast changed from a region with net inmigration in the sixties to one with net outmigration in the seventies.

McKenzie argues that there has not been a large movement of workers from the North to the South and West. In addition, asserting that the observed migration numbers are not "large" (his interpretation of large), he suggests noneconomic reasons for the migration: "Furthermore, the overall population growth of the South in the first half of the 1970s was significantly affected by the nearly 25 percent population growth of one state, Florida. Much of the growth came . . . from retired people seeking Florida's sunshine."[4] Table

[4]Ibid., p. 13.

63

4.6, which presents migration figures for the movement of population from the Northeast and North Central to the South and West, refutes this claim. Between 1970 and 1975 about 1.5 million people moved from the Northeast to the South. Only 184,000 of these people, 12 percent, were over the age of 65. Similarly, only 5.7 percent of those moving from the North Central to the South were over 65. The remaining 88 percent and 94.3 percent, respectively, were of working age or were most likely the children of working-age parents. The same is true of those moving to the West.

The main purpose of the McKenzie book is to attempt to show that plant-closing laws are not needed because the problem of Frostbelt-Sunbelt migration of business is exaggerated. To this end he uses the same data source as Bluestone and Harrison—Dun's establishment listings. Between 1969 and 1972, the Dun's data record that only 1.5 percent of the employment loss in the Northeast–North Central region was due to firms migrating out of that area. The rest of the employment loss was due to the death of firms (53.8 percent of the total) and contraction of firms (44.7 percent). Apparently very few firms fled to the Sunbelt. In terms of the total labor force in the North, outmigration of firms caused only a 0.3 percent loss of employment.

The main problem with Dun's numbers is in the definition of deaths and outmigrants. Deaths are in reality "disappearances," not confirmed permanent closings. Conversely, outmigrants are only those which Dun & Bradstreet have confirmed. Some deaths may really be outmigrants. And a closing which is the end of one firm may result in an expansion elsewhere by another firm owned by the same conglomerate parent. So, as Bluestone and Harrison argue, some deaths and contractions of firms as well as conventional migrations represent capital shifts from one region to another. Thus the low rate of confirmed outmigration does not establish a case against plant-closing laws.

Alternative View of Sunbelt Manufacturing Growth

This section attempts to reconcile the conflicting theories, evidence, and impressions of the arguments for and against plant-closing laws. The proponents of plant-closing laws charge that capital is fleeing from the North because of a desire to run away from high wages and unions. Yet the evidence which has thus far been brought to bear on this charge does not show either a large outmigration of capital or a higher closing rate for plants in the

North. The opposing side argues that manufacturing is not fleeing from the North, but they cannot account for the higher growth rate of manufacturing employment in the Sunbelt due to more plant openings or for the net migration of population from Frostbelt to Sunbelt.

The central fact with which both sides of the plant-closing controversy have failed to deal is the historical regional imbalance in U.S. manufacturing. The Northeast and North Central regions have had a highly disproportionate share of manufacturing employment since the beginning of the country's industrial development. Much of this industry grew up in large urban concentrations whose growth paralleled that of the economy. Urbanization and industrialization have been similarly associated in other developed nations. The major reason for these urban-industrial concentrations is that they increase the productivity of individual firms through the proximity of many firms which do business together and use the same labor force and other resources. Higher productivity in the northern industrial centers has meant that wages, rents, and other costs could be higher in these areas while production remained competitive with the South and West.

The evidence, however, is growing that a turning point of sorts has been reached. The long trend of population and employment concentration appears to have been reversed both in the United States and in many other developed countries. Many nations which experienced net inmigration to their major industrial complexes since the beginning of economic development have recently seen a switch to net outmigration in favor of less densely populated regions. In general, the countries which industrialized first have been decentralized first. This group which is experiencing outmigration from established areas includes—besides the United States—Belgium, Denmark, France, Holland, and West Germany. Countries which have had a virtual cessation of inmigration are Canada, Finland, Iceland, Italy, Japan, Norway, Spain, Sweden, and the United Kingdom. And those countries which have begun industrializing recently, such as South Korea and Taiwan, are still in the stage of having inmigration to their urban complexes.[5]

With this perspective, the U.S. experience looks less like a flight

[5]For a study of these patterns, see Daniel R. Vining, Jr., "Population Dispersal from Core Regions," Working Paper in Regional Science and Transportation, University of Pennsylvania, February 1980.

from the Frostbelt to escape unions and taxes. The evidence points more toward a lessening of the economic attractions which originally caused firms to cluster. Those production processes which are relatively standardized and do not require highly skilled labor or specialized resources can be located in less industrially developed regions where wages and other costs are lower. Over time more and more processes become standardized, and automated production technology matures, in more industries.

This view of the redistribution of industry is more appealing than the capital flight idea because it explains not only the reason for the movement of industry but its timing of the movement as well. Wages have always been lower in outlying regions than in the industrial centers, yet the high-wage centers continued to attract industry until recently. But in the past two decades tremendous improvements have taken place in transportation and communication, which along with the adoption of mass production and automated technology have allowed establishments, especially branches of manufacturing concerns, to move out of the larger centers.

This movement can be termed "outward" as much as "sunward." Table 4.7 shows the gain or loss in manufacturing employment by state between 1968 and 1978. The big losers are in the Frostbelt, such as Connecticut, Massachusetts, the entire Middle Atlantic, Ohio, and Illinois. But some of the gainers are surprising. In New England, Vermont, New Hampshire, and Rhode Island gained. In the Midwest, Wisconsin, Indiana, Minnesota, Iowa, and Kansas were big winners. The West North Central region on a per capita basis gained roughly as much as California. Decentralization or outward movement can be seen also in an urban versus nonurban context. For example, the smaller labor market areas of New England gained in manufacturing employment relative to the large market areas.

The data examined above indicate that the overall closing rate of manufacturing establishments in the North as well as those by size category is in most cases as low as or lower than rates in the South and West. Yet the Northeast lost 750,000 manufacturing jobs from 1968 to 1978. The redistribution of manufacturing, then, took place by way of lower birth and expansion rates in the North. The South and West have not experienced completely autonomous growth controlled within those regions. In the South, 72 percent of new employment in manufacturing branch plants between 1969 and

Table 4.7

GAIN (LOSS) OF MANUFACTURING EMPLOYMENT, 1968–1978
(IN THOUSANDS OF FIRMS)

Northeast	(750.1)		**South Atlantic**	328.8
		DE		(2.8)
New England	(77.6)	MD		(36.1)
ME	(6.1)	VA		49.4
NH	7.1	WV		(5.2)
VT	4.3	NC		112.3
MA	(35.9)	SC		60.5
RI	11.3	GA		55.2
CT	(58.3)	FL		95.5
Middle Atlantic	(672.5)		**East South Central**	242.9
NY	(388.8)	KY		56.0
NJ	(90.4)	TN		75.1
PA	(193.3)	AL		51.5
East North Central	(110.2)	MS		60.3
OH	(45.7)		**West South Central**	378.1
IN	21.4	AR		59.0
IL	(140.5)	LA		27.6
MI	(3.2)	OK		47.9
WI	57.8	TX		243.6
West North Central	138.9		**Mountain**	181.2
MN	57.5	MT		4.2
IA	24.5	ID		22.1
MO	(7.8)	WY		2.2
ND	7.0	CO		58.1
SD	8.1	NM		16.6
NB	11.3	AZ		38.3
KS	38.3	UT		29.5
		NV		10.2
			Pacific	288.5
		WA		9.9
		OR		53.6
		CA		225.0
			U.S. Total	698.3

SOURCE: *Establishment Data, State and Area Employment,* Bureau of Labor Statistics.

1976 was created by firms headquartered in the North. For the West, this figure is 68 percent. So decentralization is taking place partly through the branch plant location decision.

The pattern of manufacturing employment growth in the Frostbelt and the Sunbelt is interrelated in several ways. Plant-closing laws assume that the connection comes through a reduction of manufacturing capacity in the Frostbelt and a corresponding expansion in the Sunbelt. If capacity can be held in the Frostbelt, it will not move South and West. But the evidence reviewed here does not support this view. Production is moving South and West mostly through a greater rate of plant openings in those areas. Plant-closing laws will affect not only the decision to move production facilities from the Frostbelt to the Sunbelt, but also the decision regarding where to open a facility and whether or not to close one permanently.

Closing laws provide a disincentive to relocate to the Sunbelt by raising the cost of such a move. But actual relocations are a minor factor in employment changes as far as we know. The laws also raise the cost of a permanent closing by lessening the benefit of liquidation. But this effect is likely to be quite small for two reasons. First, the laws do nothing to make a firm's operations more profitable. If revenue is less than operating cost, then production cannot continue indefinitely. Second, if firms can demonstrate that they are losing money, they will be exempt from most requirements of the proposed laws. The most important decision regarding regional redistribution of manufacturing, then, is where to locate a new facility, and this decision cannot be controlled by closing laws. In fact, the closing laws will act to discourage new openings in those states which have them. A national plant-closing law would neutralize this perverse effect, but it would not provide any positive incentive to locate in the Frostbelt.

The basic shortcoming of plant-closing laws is that they do not address directly the problem of unemployment due to closings. The laws are a kind of unwieldy instrument relative to the desired task. They influence business decisions that they are not meant to influence by discouraging some plant openings, and they do not reach a large proportion of the decisions they are meant to influence because they are aimed only at relocations of establishments employing over 50 or 100 workers. Most significantly, they are not targeted at the specific labor markets which experience the highest cost from closings—inner-city areas and smaller towns which are dependent on a few large establishments. The small labor market areas which have suffered a contraction of their employment base have large numbers of workers who do not find new jobs at levels comparable to their old ones or who choose early retirement because of a lack of new opportunities.

The problem for inner cities and small urban areas is one of labor immobility. Programs such as the Trade Adjustment Assistance Act have attempted to treat the problem with job training and allowances for moving costs, but the results have not been very encouraging. In the final section of this paper, Swedish labor mobility programs are analyzed as an example of a more comprehensive approach. When a firm in Sweden announces its intention to close or to lay off workers, a whole set of programs becomes available— subsidies to keep the firm operating, retraining, job referral, relocation assistance, and public-sector employment. All together, these policies come close to guaranteeing the workers their jobs, but the costs to the economy are only beginning to be realized.

Swedish Plant-Closing Policy

There are three major reasons for looking at the Swedish experience: the similarity of the Swedish and New England economies; the extensive array of Swedish policies related to plant closings; and the fact that much of the discussion surrounding plant-closing legislation in the United States refers to the European experience.

Sweden's economy is approximately the same size as New England's. The labor forces are roughly comparable, with structural composition markedly alike (see table 4.8). More important than similar size and composition, however, are the trends experienced by both New England and Sweden in recent years. Changes in several markets have created substantial structural problems for industry at the same time as the labor market displayed a growing disinclination for structural adjustment. Industry has been characterized by a shift from lower-skilled industrial goods production to advanced technology industries requiring skilled labor. The most precipitous declines in both New England and Sweden have been in the textile, clothing, and shoe industries. Growth in both economies has been concentrated in engineering activities (which include machinery, electronics, transportation, equipment, and instruments).In 1978, engineering provided 45 percent of Swedish industrial production and employment; similarly, engineering accounted for 45 percent of industrial employment and 53 percent of produc-

Table 4.8

COMPARISON OF NEW ENGLAND AND SWEDISH ECONOMIES

	Sweden	New England
Gross Product, 1978		
Total ($ millions)	89,661	109,366
Per Capita ($)	10,822	8,923
Size of Labor Force, 1978 (millions)	4.2	5.6
Percent Distribution of Employment by Economic Sector, 1977		
Agriculture, Forestry, Fishing	5.5	0.3
Mining and Manufacturing	25.8	34.9
Construction	7.9	3.6
Transportation, Communications, Utilities	7.4	5.1
Trade and Services	53.4	56.0
Other	0.0	0.1
Total	100.0	100.0
Percent Distribution of Manufacturing, Transportation, Communications, Utilities Employment by Sector, 1977		
Food, Drink, Tobacco	6.4	3.5
Textiles, Clothing, Leather	5.1	11.6
Wood Products	3.5	2.9
Pulp, Paper, Printing, Publishing	9.2	9.2
Chemicals, Petroleum, Rubber, Plastics	5.4	6.2
Stone, Clay and Glass	2.8	1.6
Metals	5.7	2.9
Engineering, Machinery, Fabrication	35.5	32.8
Transportation, Communications, Utilities (incl. SIC 37)	21.7	19.6
Miscellaneous	4.7	9.7
Total	100.0	100.0

tion in New England. Forecasts for both New England and Sweden point to continued growth in the high technology industries.

During the 1960s, Swedish labor market policy was developed in a variety of directions and was provided with greatly increased resources. Plant closings and job security were major concerns. Support of geographical and occupational mobility was linked with various methods of direct employment creation. As a result, Sweden has enacted most of the proposed American legislation. The relative size of Swedish labor market programs is shown in figure 4.1. It should be pointed out that individuals are often involved in more than one program; many workers are involved in different programs at different times. However, figure 4.1 attempts to correct for this duplication by presenting the size of each program in the beginning of 1978.

The American plant-closing debate has explicitly addressed the European experience with legislation. Swedish programs are repeatedly presented by proponents of closing legislation in the United States. Unfortunately, the discussion of Swedish plant-closing policy has focused on its existence and on a description of its extensiveness. Much less attention has been paid to assessing its effectiveness.

Overview of Swedish Policy

The achievement and maintenance of full employment are the cornerstones of Swedish economic policy. To this end, labor market expenditures have greatly increased in the past twenty years, and currently amount to slightly over $2 billion (almost 10 percent of total government expenditures and about 3 percent of GNP). The National Labor Market Board plays an aggressive role in the labor market. Policy can be classified in four categories: measures to promote adjustment; measures to support employment; measures to create employment; and measures for regional development.

Measures to Promote Adjustment

The keystone of labor adjustment programs is prior notification of layoffs. The length of notice required depends on the size of the dismissal, with a maximum of six months for layoffs of 100 or more workers. The firm must notify the employee, the trade union, and the Labor Market Board. Layoffs cannot begin until management has negotiated with union officials over terms of the dismissals. These negotiations introduce greater flexibility in plant-closing policy, as strategies can take into account specific firm and industry conditions. This flexibility also characterizes actions by the National Labor Market Board. The extent and composition of the measures taken are determined by the general economic situation, the

Figure 4.1
THE SWEDISH LABOR MARKET, 1978

Total Labor Force

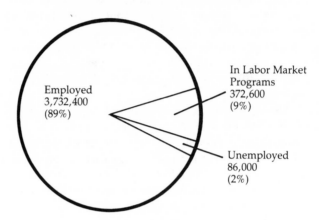

Persons in Labor Market Programs

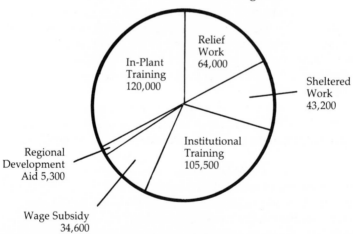

SOURCE: Swedish National Labor Market Board.

number of persons involved, the type of firm, and the conditions in the local labor market.

Labor market policy emphasizes providing information, vocational training, and relocation and retraining aid. Since 1977, registration of all job vacancies has been mandatory; thus the

Employment Service acts as a national labor exchange. Employment services are provided within the firm during the notice period, to reach as many affected workers as possible.

Labor market training involves educational programs, financial assistance, and placement services. Programs are especially geared to direct workers to industries with labor shortages. Such vocational training usually lasts a year, after which the Employment Service is responsible for finding jobs for the trainees or placing them in other programs. Substantial training allowances are supplemented by moving and relocation grants.

The Swedish economy has been sluggish in recent years, resulting in fewer alternative opportunities for unemployed workers—especially for older ones. As a result, early retirement has become common. The number of disability pensions has also multiplied, as the government has broadened eligibility to ease labor market problems.

Measures to Support Employment

Policies to support employment involve in-plant training, wage subsidies, and measures to spur investment.

In-plant training provides a labor subsidy for firms that arrange training programs for their employees instead of laying them off. Used extensively, this grant plays a central role in maintaining employment. Some 120,000 persons (3 percent of the labor force) took part in such training during FY 1977–78, compared with 91,000 in FY 1976–77.

Wage subsidies have also grown in importance. Bankrupt firms can receive a state grant to maintain production. Support amounts to half of total wage costs for six months, but the government has prolonged this period to one year in most cases. A 75 percent wage subsidy is available for troubled firms with a dominant position in their district; there is also a grant which wholly finances wage costs of elderly employees in the textile industry. (Wage subsidies were provided to 35,000 employees in 1978, an increase of 5,000 from 1977.)

The government provides production assistance to firms through targeted procurement, investment reserves, and inventory stockpiling programs. The investment reserve is designed to increase private investment during recessions. During boom years, firms may set aside tax-free reserves. When the government decides that economic conditions mandate increased investment, the reserves are released and may be used tax-free for investment purposes. In the late 1970s, the release of reserves coupled with advance government orders is credited with saving 20,000 jobs.

Measures to Create Employment

Two major policies are used for employment creation: relief work and sheltered workshops. Although supposed to be temporary, relief work has become an ongoing and expanding program. The goal of the program is permanent employment in the open market, but studies indicate that only about one-quarter of the participants obtained jobs after their initial period of relief work. As a result, the length and variety of relief work activities have greatly increased.

Sheltered employment programs were originally instituted to improve opportunities for the occupationally handicapped. As structural unemployment has increased, however, the definition of "handicapped" has been extended to include older workers and those with low skill levels. Sheltered employment subsidies were provided for 43,000 persons in 1978.

Measures for Regional Development

Regional policy is designed to increase employment in distressed areas. Financial support for plants locating in the northern tier of Sweden has been available since 1965; this aid has recently been extended to all regions where labor market imbalances have occurred. Programs include wage subsidies, site development, targeted procurement, and transport subsidies.

Effectiveness

During the 1970s, serious imbalances became visible in the Swedish economy. Swedish industry has experienced a shift from the traditional emphasis on two important raw materials—timber and iron ore—to increasingly advanced industries with a high technology content. Weak demand and international competition have resulted in substantial closings and layoffs in the older textile and shoe industries. This far-reaching structural adjustment has resulted in a major need for increased labor mobility.

Compared to the United States, Sweden has developed a comprehensive labor market policy aimed at maintaining employment during recessions and facilitating structural adjustment during growth periods. The primary approach has been through policies which increase the occupational and geographical mobility of workers.

Recently, however, the slow growth of the economy has affected the success of relocation and retraining programs. As a result, programs that create or subsidize employment have expanded dramatically.

Labor market measures have been successful, in that unemployment has been kept down at a low level by international standards. During 1977 and 1978, unemployment averaged between 1.8 percent and 2.2 percent of the labor force. However, unemployment totals understate the employment problems in the Swedish economy: The number of persons involved in labor market programs rose from 5 percent of the labor force in 1976 to almost 9 percent in 1978. The generally weak demand for labor in the open market has forced many displaced workers to remain in training or subsidy programs. Labor market training programs, unable to place workers, have been used to retain jobs. Temporary relief work has become an ongoing program. Many persons unable to reenter the market, have moved from one program to another.

A major concern is the expansion of wage subsidy programs in the 1970s. While originally intended as temporary subsidies to specific firms in financial trouble, wage allowances have become a primary means of keeping redundant workers from losing their jobs. The result has been a decrease in labor costs to the firm, causing other firms in the industry to demand the same subsidy. The outcome is a general industry subsidy, in which firms are not bearing the full cost of labor. A related concern is the rising cost of the wage subsidy programs. In practice, it has been impossible to remove or reduce subsidies even when mandated in legislation. With increased structural change, expenditures on labor market programs have skyrocketed, increasing 35 percent from 1977 to 1979. The rise in disability and early retirement pensions, the extension of sheltered employment to redundant workers, and the continuing wage subsidies have raised questions of ability to pay.

The inability of wage subsidies and industry aid to solve structural problems has resulted in a marked shift in industrial employment policy beginning in 1980. Labor market programs will now emphasize the development of competitive industries; only in special cases will programs be directed at maintaining activities in ailing firms. A defensive policy cannot solve any long-term problems and involves a risk of incurring large macroeconomic costs and delaying a necessary adjustment of industry to the world market. Budgetary costs are also large.

While recent economic conditions have reduced their effectiveness, the extensive retraining programs have created a high degree of preparedness for employment transition in the future. The programs have been successful in moving redundant workers into the growing engineering sector. A growing issue is who should pay. Current programs are financed out of general revenues plus a fee paid by *all* employers. The goal of income redistribution has been raised to defeat arguments that individuals should be made to pay for their own training. Also, there are many indications that redundant workers have high aversion to risk and thus would hesitate to place their own funds in labor market programs.

A central characteristic of Swedish labor market policy is flexibility. Swedish policy has adapted previously existing labor programs instead of creating programs specifically targeted at plant shutdowns. The Labor Market Board has available a range of instruments to deal with closings and layoffs. The centralized administrative structure has been able to adopt flexible strategies that may not have been possible if policy was established in a more restrictive legislative framework. Recent legislation strengthening job security provisions has hampered efforts to promote structural change.

For the most part, Sweden has rejected the most common provisions in the proposed U.S. plant-closing legislation. Notification requirements do exist, but for a shorter period than advocated in the United States. The required notice in Sweden is almost always superseded by negotiated agreement, so few conclusions about notification can be drawn.

Severance pay in Sweden is also determined through collective bargaining. The main purpose is to help older workers. Payments are made out of a jointly owned insurance company to which employers contribute 0.1 percent of their annual wage bill. Swedish legislation does *not* require further worker indemnity by the closing firm; according to one source, it was felt that those plants considering layoffs were those least able to afford the cost. (The additional expense may be the difference between solvency and bankruptcy.)

Community payments are not made by closing firms. Economic development programs (financed out of general revenues) and tax equalization grants are used to help municipalities affected by plant closings. The investment reserve and other development programs act to protect interindustry trading relationships, but otherwise Swedish policy doesn't attempt to deal with costs accruing to communities. Sweden's unsuccessful experience with industry and labor subsidies in the 1970s has resulted in a marked shift in policy. Sweden has rejected the place-oriented policies proposed in U.S. legislation. In their place is a strong mandate to negotiate closing provisions through collective bargaining, supplemented by a wide range of government programs aimed at developing new industry and increasing labor mobility.

Conclusion

Many people consider plant closings and layoffs in the Northeast and North Central regions important contributors to higher unemployment rates in some parts of these regions. Accordingly, plant-closing laws have been proposed in many states to prevent "capital flight" from the Frostbelt to the Sunbelt. This paper has examined the arguments and the evidence for such an approach to unemployment caused by closings. The evidence suggests that the number of relocations to the Sunbelt which have been positively identified is quite small relative to the total number of closings in the Frostbelt and relative to total employment change. The rate of plant closings does not differ much between regions. However, the rate of establishment openings in the Sunbelt is much higher than in the Frostbelt. Plant-closing laws would, if anything, tend to reduce the number of openings in states where they are enacted, while their impact on closings may be negligible, since most closings do not appear to be relocations.

Sweden's labor transition or "redundancy" programs would seem to offer a comprehensive approach to this problem. However, Sweden's experience indicates that these programs have diverted an increasing share of the labor force into subsidized work and public employment rather than assisting workers in making the desired transition to profitable industries. Notification of layoffs in Sweden does not seem to help workers find new jobs more efficiently as much as they lock workers into subsidized programs. One of the major problems in designing programs for labor mobility is a lack of knowledge regarding the process whereby jobs are generated. Until we know more about just what affects the formation of new jobs, plant-closing laws appear to be an inappropriate component of employment policy.

V. Where Have All the Firms Gone? An Analysis of the New England Economy

Carol L. Jusenius and Larry C. Ledebur

It is well known that the New England region presently confronts serious economic difficulties. With the exception of the decade 1910–20, the rate of employment growth in this region has lagged behind that of the United States since the turn of the century, indicating that these problems and their underlying causal factors are not of recent origin (table 5.1). Between 1950 and 1970, employment in the region increased by 33.6 percent, 4.4 percentage points less than the employment growth experienced by the nation as a whole (table 5.2). This was an average annual rate of 1.6 percent compared with 1.8 percent for the United States.

In more recent years, specifically during the recession years of the period 1970–75, the employment performance of the New England economy also diverged from that of the nation. The regional employment growth rate was again well below the national average, and the regional unemployment rate was well above the national average. In large measure, these two economic problems were responsible for the emergence of coalitions both among the northeastern governors and among members of the House of Representatives.[1]

"Where Have All the Firms Gone? An Analysis of the New England Economy" by Carol L. Jusenius and Larry C. Ledebur is reprinted from *Economic Development Research Report* (Washington, D.C.: U.S. Department of Commerce, September 1977).

Carol L. Jusenius is an economist with the National Commission for Employment Policy in Washington, D.C.; Larry C. Ledebur is the director of the Economic Development Program of the Urban Institute in Washington, D.C. When this essay was written, both authors were visiting scholars at the Office of Economic Research, Economic Development Administration, of the U.S. Department of Commerce.

[1]See "Regional Economic Trends: A Profile of Problems" from the Office of Congressman Michael J. Harrington (Mass.), August 1976. See also "The Northeast—Target for Action," Coalition of Northeastern Governors, undated; and Robert W. Rafuse, Jr., *The New Regional Debate: A National Overview*, prepared for the National Governors' Conference (at the Hall of the States in Washington, D.C.), April 1977.

Table 5.1

LEVEL AND GROWTH RATES OF THE CIVILIAN LABOR FORCE IN THE UNITED STATES AND NEW ENGLAND, 1900–1940[a]

Area	1900	1910	1920	1930	1940
United States: Number Employed	28,282,610	37,271,360	41,236,185	48,594,592	47,695,689
Percent Change		31.8	10.6	17.8	– 1.8
New England: Number Employed	2,368,996	2,910,290	3,231,393	3,429,870	3,232,235
Percent Change		22.9	11.0	6.1	– 5.8
Connecticut: Number Employed	384,713	489,783	589,257	676,917	702,766
Percent Change		27.3	20.3	14.9	3.8
Maine: Number Employed	275,364	304,601	309,525	308,512	291,343
Percent Change		10.6	1.6	– 0.3	– 5.6
Massachusetts: Number Employed	1,206,819	1,529,385	1,726,887	1,813,625	1,638,178
Percent Change		26.7	12.9	5.0	– 9.7
New Hampshire: Number Employed	177,790	191,386	192,633	192,609	185,666
Percent Change		7.7	0.7	– 0.01	– 3.6
Rhode Island: Number Employed	189,809	251,567	274,814	297,084	282,002
Percent Change		32.5	9.2	8.1	– 5.1
Vermont: Number Employed	134,501	143,568	138,277	141,134	131,280
Percent Change		6.7	– 3.7	2.1	– 7.0

SOURCES: U.S. Population Census of 1940. *The Labor Force*, Vol. III, Table 2; U.S. Population Census of 1940, *Characteristics of the Population*, Vol. II, Table 16.
[a]14 years and older.

Table 5.2
EMPLOYMENT GROWTH RATES, 1950–1975

Area	1950–60	1960–70	1950–70	1970–75
New England	13.0%	18.2%	33.6%	2.8%
Connecticut	22.6	25.0	53.2	3.2
Maine	10.3	9.5	20.7	2.8
Massachusetts	10.4	15.2	27.1	3.4
New Hampshire	18.5	25.5	48.8	10.8
Rhode Island	6.6	18.8	26.5	−9.7
Vermont	3.7	19.4	23.8	6.9
National Average	15.5	19.5	38.0	6.9

SOURCES: 1950–70 data from U.S. Department of Commerce, Bureau of Economic Analysis, *Regional Employment by Industry, 1940–1970*, p. XIII; 1975 data from U.S. Department of Labor, Bureau of Labor Statistics, "PWEDA Area Employment and Unemployment, 1975 Annual Averages," November 1976.

Between 1970 and 1975, employment increased 6.9 percent for the nation, while in New England employment grew by only 2.8 percent. The average annual rate of increase in employment for New England was 0.46 percent, 0.69 percentage points below the national average of 1.15 percent.

This slow growth in employment was reflected also by the high unemployment rates experienced by the New England states (table 5.3).[2] Between 1970 and 1974, the region averaged an unemployment rate almost one percentage point above the national average. In 1975, when 8.5 percent of the national labor force was unemployed, the unemployment rate in New England was 11.4 percent.

Although there is recognition of the New England region's severe employment problems, little is known about the changes in the

[2]While the region as a whole has been experiencing employment problems, there have been variations among the six states in the degree of economic difficulties experienced. New Hampshire's unemployment rate has been lower than the national average since 1970. This state also has experienced a higher than average growth rate in employment between both 1950 and 1970, and 1970 and 1975. Connecticut's economic problems appear to be of recent origins: While its employment growth rate was below that of the nation between 1970 and 1975, over the period 1950–1970 it was well above. The employment problems of the other four states are of long-standing duration: Each of these states has had a lower than average employment growth rate since at least 1950.

Table 5.3
UNEMPLOYMENT RATES IN NEW ENGLAND, 1970–1975

Area	Average 1970–74[a] Percent	1975[a] Percent	1975[b] Percent
New England	6.3	11.4	
Connecticut	6.9	10.1	9.1
Maine	6.6	10.2	
Massachusetts	6.3	12.5	11.2
New Hampshire	4.0	6.9	
Rhode Island	6.4	14.6	
Vermont	6.1	10.0	
National Average	5.4		8.5

SOURCES: *Employment & Training Report of the President, 1976,* Section 1, p. 15, and Appendix Table D-4, p. 312; *Geographic Profile of Employment and Unemployment, 1975,* U.S. Bureau of Labor Statistics Report 481, p. 2.
[a]Based on data supplied by state employment security agencies.
[b]Compiled from the *Current Population Surveys* by the U.S. Bureau of Labor Statistics. Data not strictly comparable with data in [a] above.

profile of the business firms of the region, changes that determine the direction and rates of employment change in the area. The information that does exist tends to be apocryphal and anecdotal, identifying, as the primary cause of the loss of employment opportunities, either the migration of firms out of the region or the preference of headquarters for opening branch operations in the South.[3]

This paper investigates recent changes in the composition of business enterprises in the region and the employment impacts of these changing configurations. The precise period covered is December 31, 1969, through December 31, 1974, the most recent for which data are available. Dun & Bradstreet data are used to identify those changes that have resulted from birth of new firms, deaths or closures of existing firms, expansion and contraction of firms, and the in- and outmigration of firms.

[3]See "The Second War between the States," *Business Week,* May 17, 1976, pp. 92–114; and "Northeast's Economic Health Is a Worry, Diagnosis by Conference Board Claims," *Wall Street Journal,* April 7, 1977, p. 8.

The Changing Status of Firms and Employment: An Overview

Between 1969 and 1974, New England lost 17,655 firms in the Dun & Bradstreet sample, a decline of 10.2 percent (table 5.4). Over the same period, employment in Dun & Bradstreet–rated firms decreased by 7.45 percent (tables 5.5 and 5.6).[4] Only two states, Vermont and New Hampshire, experienced an employment gain; Rhode Island's employment loss was the greatest in the region.

Of the firms lost to the region, 97.5 percent had fewer than 100 employees,[5] and the vast majority were in the Wholesale/Retail Trade industry. Many of these were small retail outlets, which traditionally have a high rate of attrition. They are dependent upon the vitality of the economic base of the region to generate incomes for retail purchases, and the recent, serious recession undoubtedly accelerated the rate at which these smaller firms were forced to close. Thus, the high rate of loss of firms in this industry reflects their traditional rates of attrition and the current economic problems of the New England economy.

Certainly the loss of manufacturing firms was the most serious blow to the economy of the region, since firms in this industry generate employment, not only directly but also indirectly, in other industries (such as Wholesale/Retail Trade) via the employment multiplier. Between 1969 and 1974, the region lost, on net balance, 3,740 manufacturing enterprises, a reduction of 14.4 percent of the firms in the industry in 1969.

In only two of the one-digit SIC (Standard Industrial Classification) industries did the number of firms increase over the period. In Finance, Insurance, and Real Estate, the number of firms increased by 52.6 percent (684 firms). In the Service industry, the number of firms increased by 7.6 percent (122 firms).

These changes may be indicative of a movement of the New England economy toward the long-anticipated "post industrial" economy—one in which the composition of the region's economic base shifts away from manufacturing and toward the provision of

[4]It should be noted that not all Dun & Bradstreet–rated firms reported their employment size. Furthermore, it is not possible to characterize those firms that did (did not) report. Thus the employment figures given here and elsewhere in this paper are underestimates of the total employment impact of changes in the number of firms in New England.

[5]Of the net reduction of firms in New England between 1969 and 1974, 98.5 percent had no employees; i.e., they were sole proprietorships.

Table 5.4

NUMBER OF FIRMS IN NEW ENGLAND BY STATUS AND SELECTED CHARACTERISTICS, 1969–1974

Characteristics	In New England 1969	Born between 1969 and 1974	Died between 1969 and 1974	Outmigrated from New England between 1969 and 1974	Inmigrated to New England between 1969 and 1974	In New England 1974	Net Change[c]
Total Number	163,328	36,162	54,026	144	353	145,673	−17,655
Subsidiary	2,913	857	1,262	28	94	2,957	44
Not Subsidiary	160,415	35,505	52,764	116	259	142,720	−17,695
Not Multiunit Affiliated	142,417	34,157	47,166	83	206	128,297	−14,120
Headquarters of Multiunit	10,144	1,940	2,788	58	147	10,434	290
Branch of Multiunit	10,767	65	4,072	3	0	6,942	−3,825
	(151,851)[b]	(35,645)[b]	(48,441)[b]	(143)[b]	(336)[b]	(142,246)[b]	
Number of Employees							
0[a]	19,780	8	7,696	9	1	2,395	−17,385
1–19	112,089	33,328	35,841	87	213	120,417	8,328
20–50	12,738	1,736	3,120	22	60	12,657	−81
51–99	3,013	318	780	5	11	3,017	4
100 or more	4,195	255	1,004		51	3,760	−435
	(163,289)[b]	(36,162)[b]	(54,022)[b]		(352)[b]	(145,635)[b]	

Table 5.4 cont.

Characteristics	In New England 1969	Born between 1969 and 1974	Died between 1969 and 1974	Outmigrated from New England between 1969 and 1974	Inmigrated to New England between 1969 and 1974	In New England 1974	Net Change[c]
Agriculture	1,871	291	499	2	0	1,611	−260
Mining	187	36	47	0	6	185	−2
Construction	20,183	5,666	5,880	11	15	19,871	−312
Manufacturing	26,051	4,369	7,999	54	137	22,311	−3,740
Transportation, Communications, and Public Utilities	5,427	1,165	1,494	5	15	5,146	−281
Wholesale/Retail Trade	92,064	19,701	33,156	42	126	78,264	−13,800
Finance, Insurance, and Real Estate	1,300	709	338	11	24	1,984	684
Services	15,956	4,219	4,522	19	29	16,078	122
Public Administration	31	4	8	0	0	26	−5
Unclassified	214	2	80	0	0	159	−55

SOURCE: Dun & Bradstreet data, 1969, 1974.
[a]Sole proprietorship.
[b]This total differs from that given at the top of the column because of differences in nonresponses on various items.
[c]Because of changes in the characteristics of firms (e.g., from subsidiary to nonsubsidiary status), the difference between the 1969 and 1974 figures does not equal the sum of the components of change.

Table 5.5

EMPLOYMENT CHANGE BETWEEN DECEMBER 31, 1969, AND DECEMBER 31, 1974, IN NEW ENGLAND

						Employment Change as a Percent of 1969 Employment—Attributable to:			
Area	Total Employment 1969	Percent Change 1969–74	Death of Firms[a]	Birth of Firms[b]	Expansion/ Contraction	Migration into New England[c]	Migration Out of New England[d]	Inmigration from Other New England States[d]	Outmigration to Other New England States[d]
New England	2,897,583	−7.45	21.91	9.37	4.52	0.80	0.23	—	—
Connecticut	856,903	−14.98	18.80	7.88	−5.66	1.75	0.21	0.07	0.02
Maine	179,314	−0.95	29.10	12.78	14.48	0.21	0.05	0.84	0.09
Massachusetts	1,366,556	−2.87	23.03	9.50	−10.70	0.41	0.31	0.09	0.21
New Hampshire	159,748	2.70	24.41	12.20	12.31	1.07	0.02	1.80	0.26
Rhode Island	256,468	−21.98	20.03	8.53	−10.39	0.05	0.20	0.30	0.24
Vermont	78,594	6.92	20.92	12.39	15.14	0.39	0.01	0.04	0.10

SOURCE: Dun & Bradstreet data, 1969, 1974.
[a]1969 employment.
[b]1974 employment.
[c]1974 employment; that is, after migration.
[d]1969 employment; that is, prior to migration.

services and financial and information expertise. However, it is clear that over the 1969-to-1974 period, the increase in the growth industries—Services, and Finance, Insurance, and Real Estate— was not sufficient to generate the employment opportunities necessary to offset those lost through the decline in manufacturing.

Disaggregation of these data reveals that the primary cause of the loss of firms to the region was closure or death of businesses.[6] In the five-year period under consideration, 54,026 firms died, 33 percent of those that had existed in 1969. In a growing economy, those firms that die are replaced by other, new firms or "births." However, in the case of New England, this replacement process was not complete. Only 36,162 new firms were born over this period, a rate of birth of 22.1 percent of the 1969 base. Thus, replacement by new firms fell short of deaths by 17,864 business enterprises. The net result of the birth/death process was a loss of over 360,000 jobs.

It is interesting to note that among the firms that were alive and located in New England in both 1969 and 1974, there was a net increase (expansion over contraction) in employment opportunities. This increase amounted to 4.52 percent of the 1969 employment level.

Recently, extensive publicity has been accorded the outmigration or relocation of firms from New England. While this topic is discussed in detail later, it must be noted at this point that the data do not support the view that a major source of employment loss in New England is the outmigration of industry. Between 1969 and 1974, 144 firms migrated out of New England. However, over the same period, more than twice that number (353 firms) migrated into the region, a net increase of 209 firms.

Moreover, outmigration accounted for relatively little of the total employment loss in the region. If only outmigration of firms had occurred, employment in 1974 would have been only 0.23 percent lower than in 1969. In fact, as a result of the in- and outmigration of firms, New England appears to have experienced a net increase

---

[6]A firm can "die" for one of several reasons. For example, bankruptcy can occur in spite of the intentions of the owners. Alternatively, bankruptcy could be "purposeful": An owner could run down the existing capital stock, declare bankruptcy, and reestablish related operations in a new firm and location. Additionally, a conglomerate could close a firm which was unprofitable relative to its alternative investment opportunities.

Table 5.6
Distribution of Employment by Status of New England Firms, 1969–1974, and Selected Characteristics

Characteristics	In New England 1969	In New England 1969 and 1974	Born between 1969 and 1974	Died between 1969 and 1974	Outmigrated from New England between 1969 and 1974[a]	Inmigrated to New England between 1969 and 1974[b]	In New England 1974
Total Number	2,897,583	2,256,157	271,401	634,797	6,629	23,089	2,681,660
Percent:							
Not Subsidiary	91.21	92.40	84.09	87.23	70.36	67.41	90.20
Subsidiary	8.79	7.60	15.91	12.77	29.64	32.59	9.80
Percent:							
Not Multiunit Affiliated	52.06	50.76	86.70	56.85	38.35	27.88	54.95
Headquarters of Multiunit	20.75	22.71	12.73	13.40	60.70	72.12	22.59
Branch of Multiunit	27.18	26.54	0.57	29.76	0.95	0.0	22.45
Percent:							
0 employees[c]	—	—	—	—	—	—	—
1–19	19.9	18.2	49.2	26.2	8.5	5.3	21.9
20–50	13.4	13.0	19.1	14.8	12.6	8.1	14.4
51–99	7.3	6.9	8.2	8.7	4.8	3.7	7.8
100 or more	59.4	61.9	23.5	50.4	74.2	82.5	55.9
					(6,634)[d]		(2,681,255)[d]
Percent:							
Agriculture	1.2	1.5	0.7	0.5	0.9	0.0	0.5
Mining	0.1	0.1	0.4	0.1	0.0	2.4	0.2
Construction	5.7	5.7	10.5	5.9	0.8	1.3	6.0

Table 5.6 cont.

Characteristics	In New England 1969	In New England 1969 and 1974	Born between 1969 and 1974	Died between 1969 and 1974	Outmigrated from New England between 1969 and 1974[a]	Inmigrated to New England between 1969 and 1974[b]	In New England 1974
Manufacturing	55.4	55.2	30.5	56.2	47.2	50.2	48.7
Transportation, Communications, and Public Utilities	3.9	4.1	3.0	3.1	4.1	5.4	3.7
Wholesale/Retail Trade	23.4	22.6	40.0	26.1	11.7	7.8	24.4
Finance, Insurance, and Real Estate	4.2	4.9	3.9	1.4	29.8	13.2	5.2
Services	5.7	5.6	11.1	6.2	5.4	19.7	10.0
Public Administration	0.2	0.3	0.1	0.0	0.0	0.0	1.2
Unclassified	0.01	e	e	0.03	0.0	0.0	e

SOURCE: Dun & Bradstreet data, 1969, 1974.

[a]1969 employment level.
[b]1974 employment level.
[c]Sole proprietorship, no employees.
[d]Base on which percent distribution by industry was calculated. This total differs from that given at the top of the column due to differences in nonresponses on various items.
[e]Less than 0.01 percent.

in employment: new jobs, resulting from inmigration seem to have exceeded the number lost due to outmigration.[7]

Perhaps the most startling finding of this study is that New England gained 290 headquarters of multiunit enterprises over the five-year period, an increase of 2.8 percent (table 5.7). At the same time, the region experienced a net reduction of 3,825 branches of multiunit affiliated businesses, a decrease of 35.5 percent from the number that existed in 1969. The number of non-multiunit affiliated firms also decreased between 1969 and 1974, by 14,120 firms or 9.9 percent.

That there was a net increase in the number of headquarters is explained by the patterns of change in multiunit affiliation among those firms that were in New England in both 1969 and 1974. The loss of headquarters resulting from their becoming branches of other multiunit organizations (− 79 firms) and from their assuming an independent status (− 2,536)[8] was offset by the number of branch and independent firms that became headquarters. Of the branch firms in 1969, 51 were headquarters by 1974; and 3,613 independent firms became headquarters by 1974.

Thus it is clear that a major reason for the increase in the number of headquarters in New England was the acquisition of other firms by previously unaffiliated businesses. The overall impact was that firms in New England became increasingly consolidated, with many firms that were previously independent moving to an affiliated status by 1974.[9]

The Birth and Death of Firms

Historically, New England has specialized in two industries relative to the nation as a whole—Finance, Insurance, and Real Estate,

[7]The employment loss due to outmigration of firms from the region was less than one-third of 1 percent in each of the six states. Only Rhode Island experienced a net loss of employment due to the migration of firms: 0.15 percent of its 1969 employment base.

See also "Tired Old Danbury Is Perking Up as Corporations Move into Town," *New York Times*, January 23, 1977, pp. 1 and 34.

[8]Assumption of an independent status implies closure or sale of branches. The finding that many of the headquarters in New England did lose their branch operations is discussed more fully in a later section of the paper.

[9]This is demonstrated also by the patterns of change of non-multiunit affiliated firms. While 2,687 firms became independent over the period, almost 4,000 firms that had been independent became either headquarters or branches by 1974.

Table 5.7

CHANGE IN MULTIUNIT AFFILIATION (M.U.A.) OF FIRMS IN NEW ENGLAND, 1969–1974[a]

Headquarters		
Status	Number	Percent of 1969 Base
Headquarters 1969	10,144	100.0
Born 1969–1974	1,940	19.1
Died 1969–1974	−2,788	−27.5
Outmigrated	−58	−0.6
Inmigrated	147	1.4
Headquarters 1969 and Branch 1974	−79	−0.8
Not M.U.A. 1974	−2,536	−25.0
Branch 1969 and Headquarters 1974	51	0.5
Not M.U.A. and Headquarters 1974	3,613	35.6
Headquarters 1974	10,434	—
Change 1969–1974	290	2.8

Branches		
Status	Number	Percent of 1969 Base
Branches 1969	10,767	100.0
Born	65	0.6
Died	−4,072	−37.8
Outmigrated	−3	−0.03
Inmigrated	0	0.0
Branch 1969 and Headquarters 1974	−51	−0.5
Not M.U.A. 1974	−151	−1.4
Headquarters 1969 and Branch 1974	79	0.7
Not M.U.A. 1969 and Branch 1974	308	2.9
Branches 1974	6,942	—
Change 1969–1974	−3,825	−35.5

Table 5.7 cont.

Not Multiunit Affiliated (M.U.A.)

Status	Number	Percent of 1969 Base
Not M.U.A. 1969	142,417	100.0
Born	34,157	24.0
Died	− 47,166	− 33.1
Outmigrated	− 83	− 0.06
Inmigrated	206	0.1
Not M.U.A. 1969 and Headquarters 1974	− 3,613	− 2.5
Branch 1974	− 308	− 0.2
Headquarters 1969 and Not M.U.A. 1974	2,536	1.8
Branch 1969 and Not M.U.A. 1974	151	0.1
Not M.U.A. 1974	128,297	—
Change 1969–1974	− 14,120	− 9.9

SOURCE: Dun & Bradstreet data, 1969, 1974.

[a]It is probable that some firms (headquarters, branches, and unaffiliated) were consolidated, absorbed, or merged with other firms and, by 1974, no longer existed as separate legal entities. In this situation, these firms would not appear in the Dun & Bradstreet data at the end of the period, but would appear as deaths in the tabulation of the data. To the extent that this occurs, the Dun & Bradstreet data overstate the number of "deaths." Given that in excess of 96 percent of the firms that died had no employees, and, in all possibility, did not represent mergers, the magnitude of this overstatement of deaths may be relatively small. However, in the case of headquarters and branches, the possible overstatement of closures is more critical, but the data do not permit identification of such mergers and consolidations.

and Manufacturing. Only in the former industry was the number of firm openings greater than the number of firm closures. Moreover, the growth of the Finance, Insurance, and Real Estate industry was quite rapid. The birth rate of firms was 2.5 times the average rate for all industries combined, 0.55 percent versus 0.22 percent (table 5.8).

In contrast, the Manufacturing industry experienced severe difficulties. Almost 8,000 firms closed while only 4,389 firms started up (table 5.4). This net shortfall occurred in every employment size

Table 5.8

RATES OF BIRTH BY INDUSTRY, NEW ENGLAND, 1969–1974[a]

Industry	Five-Year Period	Average Rate Per Year
Total	0.22	0.04
Agriculture	0.16	0.03
Mining	0.19	0.04
Construction	0.28	0.06
Manufacturing	0.17	0.03
Transportation, Communications, and Public Utilities	0.22	0.04
Wholesale/Retail Trade	0.21	0.04
Finance, Insurance, and Real Estate	0.55	0.11
Services	0.26	0.05
Public Administration	0.13	0.03
Unclassified	0.01	[b]

SOURCE: Dun & Bradstreet data, 1974.
[a]Openings divided by the number of firms in each industry in 1969.
[b]Less than 0.05 percent.

category. Most important, of the manufacturing firms that died, more than 200 had 300 or more employees, and slightly more than 100 had 500 or more workers (table 5.9). On the other hand, of the firms that opened, approximately 30 had 300 or more workers, and only 14 had 500 or more employees.

While it would appear that the problem confronting the New England economy is the substantial number of firm closures in Manufacturing, this conclusion would be somewhat misleading. Examination of birth and death rates in this industry reveals that the source of the difficulty lies in the relatively low birth rate (table 5.8). The death rate was slightly below average (0.31 versus 0.33 percent), but the birth rate was *well below* average (0.17 percent versus 0.22 percent).

Interest recently has been directed toward the birth, death, and migration behavior of branch firms.[10] In part, this interest undoubtedly stems from the fact that a change in the status of a branch firm

[10]See "Northeast's Economic Health."

Table 5.9

NUMBER OF MANUFACTURING FIRMS THAT DIED, WERE BORN,
BY EMPLOYMENT SIZE CATEGORY, NEW ENGLAND, 1969–1974

Number of Employees	Births		Deaths		Net Change (Births minus Deaths)
	Number	Percent	Number	Percent	
Total	4,318	100.0	6,706	100.0	−2,388
1–100	4,198	97.2	6,028	89.9	−1,830
101–200	69	1.6	322	4.8	−253
201–300	20	0.5	129	1.9	−109
301–400	16	0.4	67	1.0	−51
401–500	1	0.02	54	0.8	−53
501 or more	14	0.3	106	1.6	−92

SOURCE: Dun & Bradstreet data, 1969, 1974.

Table 5.10

CLOSURE RATES BY INDUSTRY, NEW ENGLAND, 1969–1974[a]

Industry	Five-Year Period	Average Rate Per Year
Total	0.33	0.07
Agriculture	0.27	0.05
Mining	0.25	0.05
Construction	0.29	0.06
Manufacturing	0.31	0.06
Transportation, Communications, and Public Utilities	0.28	0.06
Wholesale/Retail Trade	0.36	0.07
Finance, Insurance, and Real Estate	0.29	0.06
Services	0.28	0.06
Public Administration	0.26	0.05
Unclassified	0.39	0.08

SOURCE: Dun & Bradstreet data, 1969, 1974.
[a]Closures divided by the number of firms in each industry in 1969.

reflects comparative rates of return on investment opportunities available to the headquarters—a headquarters which may be in another state or region.

As a test of the proposition that decisions are being made by corporate headquarters to close and not to open branch firms in the Northeast, birth and death rates were calculated for firms according to their multiunit affiliation. The results indicate that branch firms had a higher than average death rate, but more important, their birth rate was considerably below the regional average for all firms combined (tables 5.11a and 5.11b). Over the five-year period, the

Table 5.11a

CLOSURE RATES BY MULTIUNIT AFFILIATION, NEW ENGLAND, 1969–1974[a]

Status	Five-Year Period	Average Rate Per Year
Total	0.331	0.066
Not Multiunit Affiliated	0.331	0.066
Headquarters	0.275	0.055
Branch	0.378	0.066

SOURCE: Dun & Bradstreet data, 1969, 1974.
[a]Closures divided by the number of firms in each category in 1969.

Table 5.11b

RATES OF BIRTH BY MULTIUNIT AFFILIATION, NEW ENGLAND, 1969–1974[a]

Status	Five-Year Period	Average Rate Per Year
Total	0.221	0.044
Not Multiunit Affiliated	0.240	0.048
Headquarters	0.191	0.038
Branch	0.006	[b]

SOURCE: Dun & Bradstreet data, 1969, 1974.
[a]Openings of firms divided by the number of firms in each category in 1969.
[b]Less than .05 percent.

birth rate among branch operations amounted to *less than 1 percent* of the 1969 base.

Headquarters Location of Branch Firms

For New England as a whole, the branches that closed were slightly more likely to have headquarters outside the region than the branches that opened (table 5.12). Approximately 30 percent of those that died and 25 percent of those that were born had headquarters located outside New England.

Nevertheless, for branches that closed, the vast majority of headquarters were within the region itself. In fact, more than 52 percent of the branch firms that died in Connecticut, Maine, Massachusetts, and Rhode Island had headquarters within their own states. For New Hampshire and Vermont, more than 50 percent of the headquarters were located either in the state itself or in Massachusetts.

Industry of Branch Firms

The branch firms that died were more likely to be in Manufacturing than in any other industry (table 5.13). Of these firms, slightly more than 50 percent had headquarters within the region; another 25 percent had headquarters within New York State. Connecticut was the only New England state to have more than 50 percent of the headquarters of its manufacturing branch firms located outside the region. For this state, decisions regarding the closure of branch operations were as likely to have been made in New York as in New England.

The small number of branch firms in Finance, Insurance, and Real Estate that died reflects the economic well-being of this industry, as has already been noted. Only 34 such branch operations were closed. A more interesting point here is that, in contrast to manufacturing branch firms, headquarters of these branches that closed were more likely to be outside than inside the region. Specifically, while one-third were located in New England, 41 percent were located in New York state alone.

Employment Size of Branch Firms

Examination of the size of branch firms that closed and their headquarters location reveals that the smaller the New England branch firm, the more likely it was to have its headquarters located in the region (table 5.14). While 76 percent of the small-size branches in New England that closed between 1969 and 1974 had headquarters in the region, this was true only for 38 percent of those with

100 or more employees. In fact, in Connecticut, Maine, Massachusetts, and Rhode Island, more than 55 percent of the small branch firms had headquarters in the same state. For New Hampshire and Vermont, more than 50 percent had headquarters either in their own state or in Massachusetts.

In contrast, for the region as a whole, branch firms with 100 or more employees that closed were as likely to have had headquarters within the Middle Atlantic states as within New England. For these large branch firms, the importance of New York shows up in each of the six New England states. For example, in Connecticut, New Hampshire, and Vermont, more of the branches of this employment size had headquarters in New York than in the states themselves. An extreme case was New Hampshire: While 3.8 percent of the branches had headquarters in the state, 30 percent were in New York.

The Migration of Firms

Much recent interest has focused on the migration of firms, particularly to states of the South and West, as a primary cause of the loss of employment in New England. The Dun & Bradstreet data do not support the contention either that migration of firms contributed significantly to the economic difficulties of the region or that the preponderance of those firms that did move out of New England went to states in the Sunbelt.

Interregional Flows

Between 1969 and 1974, more firms moved into New England than left the region, resulting in a net increase in employment due to migration: 144 firms outmigrated and 353 inmigrated, a net increase of 209 firms (tables 5.15 and 5.16).

Inmigration. Of the firms that entered the region, 72 percent (254) located in Connecticut and 20.1 percent (71) entered Massachusetts.[11] Thus, 92 percent of the firms entering New England between 1969 and 1974 located in these two states.

Almost 93 percent of the firms that entered New England came from the Middle Atlantic region; 83.9 percent came from New York alone. Of the 254 firms entering Connecticut, 90.2 percent had migrated from New York.

[11]This same point regarding the inmigration of firms to Connecticut was made in "Tired Old Danbury."

97

Table 5.12
LOCATION OF HEADQUARTERS OF BRANCH FIRMS THAT DIED AND WERE BORN, BY LOCATION OF HEADQUARTERS, 1969–1974

Headquarters Location	Location of Branch Firms That Died						
	New England	Connecticut	Maine	Massachusetts	New Hampshire	Rhode Island	Vermont
Total Number	4,053	1,067	422	1,828	267	352	117
New England	71.1%	64.3%	82.4%	69.9%	82.7%	75.1%	71.9%
Connecticut	18.1	56.1	2.1	4.2	6.4	7.1	6.0
Maine	7.3	—	60.2	0.8	8.2	0.3	2.6
Massachusetts	32.8	6.1	13.0	58.1	30.3	14.8	12.0
New Hampshire	3.7	—	5.2	1.7	31.1	0.6	9.4
Rhode Island	7.5	2.0	0.5	5.0	2.2	52.3	0.9
Vermont	1.7	0.1	1.4	0.1	4.5	—	41.0
Middle Atlantic	17.8	23.9	12.1	16.8	9.0	18.5	18.0
New Jersey	1.8	2.7	1.4	1.7	1.1	1.4	0.9
New York	14.2	19.4	10.0	12.9	7.5	14.8	16.2
Pennsylvania	1.8	1.8	0.7	2.2	0.4	2.3	0.9
East North Central	4.6	5.6	2.1	4.6	4.9	4.5	3.4
West North Central	1.1	0.7	0.9	1.6	0.7	0.6	0.9
South Atlantic	2.1	2.2	0.9	2.5	0.7	0.9	5.1
East South Central	0.4	0.4	0.2	0.5	—	0.3	—
West South Central	0.7	0.7	0.2	1.1	0.4	—	—
Mountain	0.2	0.3	—	0.3	0.4	—	—
Pacific	2.0	2.0	0.9	2.7	0.7	1.4	0.9

Table 5.12 cont.

Headquarters Location	Location of Branch Firms That Were Born						
	New England	Connecticut	Maine	Massa-chusetts	New Hampshire	Rhode Island	Vermont
Total Number	65	14	6	27	12	2	4
New England	76.9%	57.2%	100.0%	81.5%	75.0%	100.0%	75.0%
Connecticut	12.3	42.9	16.7	3.7	—	—	—
Maine	4.6	—	50.0	—	—	—	—
Massachusetts	38.5	14.3	16.7	74.1	16.7	—	—
New Hampshire	12.3	—	16.7	—	50.0	—	25.0
Rhode Island	7.7	—	—	3.7	8.3	100.0	25.0
Vermont	1.5	—	—	—	—	—	25.0
Middle Atlantic	4.6	7.1	—	3.7	—	—	25.0
New Jersey	—	—	—	—	—	—	—
New York	4.6	7.1	—	3.7	—	—	25.0
Pennsylvania	—	—	—	—	—	—	—
East North Central	3.1	14.3	—	—	—	—	—
West North Central	1.5	—	—	—	8.3	—	—
South Atlantic	1.5	—	—	—	8.3	—	—
East South Central	1.5	—	—	3.7	—	—	—
West South Central	3.1	14.3	—	—	—	—	—
Mountain	1.5	—	—	—	8.3	—	—
Pacific	6.2	7.1	—	11.1	—	—	—

SOURCE: Dun & Bradstreet data, 1969, 1974.

Table 5.13

LOCATION OF HEADQUARTERS OF BRANCH FIRMS THAT DIED, BY LOCATION OF BRANCH FIRMS AND SIC CODE, 1969

Headquarters Location 1969	Location of Branch Firm, 1969: Manufacturing						
	New England	Connecticut	Maine	Massachusetts	New Hampshire	Rhode Island	Vermont
Total Number	1,198	312	128	527	80	112	39
New England	51.4%	37.2%	68.6%	53.1%	63.8%	52.7%	79.1%
Connecticut	10.8	29.5	4.7	2.8	11.2	2.7	10.3
Maine	4.9	—	39.1	0.8	3.8	0.9	2.6
Massachusetts	27.4	5.1	21.1	45.2	37.5	10.7	12.8
New Hampshire	2.0	—	3.1	1.5	11.3	0.9	7.7
Rhode Island	5.5	2.6	—	2.8	—	37.5	2.6
Vermont	0.8	—	1.6	—	—	—	23.1
Middle Atlantic	31.5	43.2	21.1	27.7	21.3	36.7	28.3
New Jersey	3.7	5.1	3.1	3.4	1.3	3.6	2.6
New York	25.4	34.6	17.2	21.6	20.0	31.3	23.1
Pennsylvania	2.4	3.5	0.8	2.7	—	1.8	2.6
East North Central	8.3	11.5	3.9	8.0	8.8	8.0	5.1
West North Central	1.5	0.3	2.3	2.3	2.5	—	—
South Atlantic	2.7	2.2	1.6	3.6	1.3	0.9	7.7
East South Central	0.7	1.0	—	0.8	—	0.9	—
West South Central	0.8	0.6	—	1.1	1.3	—	—
Mountain	0.6	1.0	—	0.6	1.3	—	—
Pacific	2.6	2.9	1.6	3.0	1.3	1.8	2.6

Table 5.13 cont.

Headquarters Location 1969	Location of Branch Firm, 1969: Finance, Insurance, and Real Estate						
	New England	Connecticut	Maine	Massachusetts	New Hampshire	Rhode Island	Vermont
Total Number	34	11	2	15	2	3	1
New England	32.3%	36.4%	100.0%	6.7%	100.0%	66.7%	—
Connecticut	5.9	18.2	—	—	—	—	—
Maine	2.9	—	—	—	50.0	—	—
Massachusetts	14.7	18.2	—	6.7	—	66.7	—
New Hampshire	2.9	—	—	—	50.0	—	—
Rhode Island	—	—	—	—	—	—	—
Vermont	5.9	—	100.0	—	—	—	100.0%
Middle Atlantic	41.2	27.3	—	60.0	—	33.3	100.0%
New Jersey	—	—	—	—	—	—	—
New York	41.2	27.3	—	60.0	—	33.3	100.0
Pennsylvania	—	—	—	—	—	—	—
East North Central	8.8	9.1	—	13.3	—	—	—
West North Central	2.9	—	—	6.7	—	—	—
South Atlantic	11.8	27.3	—	6.7	—	—	—
East South Central	—	—	—	—	—	—	—
West South Central	—	—	—	—	—	—	—
Mountain	—	—	—	—	—	—	—
Pacific	2.9	—	—	6.7	—	—	—

Table 5.13 cont.

Headquarters Location 1969	New England	Connec-ticut	Maine	Massa-chusetts	New Hampshire	Rhode Island	Vermont
				Location of Branch Firm, 1969: All Other Industries			
Total Number	2,825	744	292	1,286	185	241	77
New England	79.8%	75.1%	86.3%	77.4%	91.3%	84.2%	74.0%
Connecticut	21.3	67.9	1.0	4.8	4.3	9.1	3.9
Maine	8.3	—	70.0	0.8	10.0	—	2.6
Massachusetts	35.2	6.3	7.9	64.0	27.6	15.8	11.7
New Hampshire	4.4	—	6.2	1.8	40.0	0.4	3.9
Rhode Island	8.5	1.7	0.7	5.9	3.2	58.9	—
Vermont	1.9	0.1	0.7	0.1	6.5	—	51.9
Middle Atlantic	11.8	15.6	8.2	11.8	3.8	9.5	11.7
New Jersey	1.1	1.6	0.7	1.0	1.1	0.4	—
New York	9.1	12.9	6.8	8.7	2.2	6.6	11.7
Pennsylvania	1.6	1.1	0.7	2.1	0.5	2.5	—
East North Central	2.9	3.1	1.4	3.2	3.2	3.3	2.6
West North Central	1.0	0.1	0.3	1.2	—	0.8	1.3
South Atlantic	1.7	13.7	0.7	2.2	1.1	0.8	3.9
East South Central	0.2	0.1	0.3	0.4	—	—	—
West South Central	0.7	0.7	0.3	1.1	—	—	—
Mountain	0.1	—	—	0.3	—	—	—
Pacific	1.8	1.6	0.7	2.5	0.5	1.2	—

SOURCE: Dun & Bradstreet data, 1969, 1974.

Outmigration. In contrast to much of the recent publicity, the number of firms that outmigrated from New England to the Sunbelt was relatively small. While the Middle Atlantic region was the recipient of 49 percent of the firms that left New England, 41.7 percent outmigrated to the combined states of the South Atlantic, East and West South Central, Mountain, and Pacific regions. Only 29.2 percent of the firms leaving the region went to the South Atlantic region. In fact, more firms moved to New York state than to the entire South Atlantic region.

The greatest exchange of firms occurred between the adjacent states of Connecticut and New York, with Connecticut experiencing a net increase in firms resulting from this interchange. This, undoubtedly, reflects the economic difficulties of New York City and the suburbanization of firms from this city to Connecticut.

Intraregional Flows

Over the period 1969 to 1974, substantial intraregional migration occurred: 195 firms relocated within the region (table 5.17). The net result of this internal migration was a loss of firms by Connecticut, Massachusetts, and Rhode Island. Despite this loss, Connecticut experienced a net increase in employment from this movement. Massachusetts and Rhode Island, however, lost jobs as well as firms.

Industry of Migrant Firms

Migration rates by industry reveal that firms in Finance, Insurance, and Real Estate are the most likely ones to be "footloose." Both their in- and outmigrant rates were above the regional average for all firms combined (table 5.18). The fact that the inmigrant rate was over twice the outmigrant rate demonstrates again the economic health and viability of this industry in New England.

Given the low *birth* rate of manufacturing firms in the region, it is interesting to note that more firms in this industry inmigrated than outmigrated. Indeed, the inmigrant rate was more than double the outmigrant rate. Moreover, on net balance, New England gained fifteen manufacturing firms with over 100 employees, eight of which firms had over 400 workers (table 5.19).

Multiunit Affiliation of Migrant Firms

Headquarters of multiunit operations were more likely to migrate than either independent firms or branch firms. Both the in- and outmigrant rates of headquarters were over six times greater than

Table 5.14

LOCATION OF BRANCH FIRMS THAT DIED, BY LOCATION OF HEADQUARTERS OF BRANCH FIRMS, BY SIZE, 1969–1974

Headquarters Location 1969	Location of Branch Firm, 1969: 1–50 Employees						
	New England	Connec- ticut	Maine	Massa- chusetts	New Hampshire	Rhode Island	Vermont
Total Number	2,129	502	249	1,039	127	139	73
New England	76.0%	68.1%	85.1%	75.4%	89.0%	81.3%	76.7%
Connecticut	17.8	59.1	1.6	5.0	8.7	7.2	8.2
Maine	8.9	—	65.9	1.1	8.7	—	—
Massachusetts	37.2	7.0	10.8	62.6	34.6	18.7	12.3
New Hampshire	3.8	—	4.8	2.0	31.5	—	9.6
Rhode Island	6.6	2.0	0.8	4.7	2.4	55.4	1.4
Vermont	1.7	—	1.2	—	3.1	—	41.1
Middle Atlantic	14.3	21.5	10.0	13.0	6.3	11.5	15.1
New Jersey	1.9	2.4	1.6	1.7	1.6	7.2	1.4
New York	11.1	18.1	8.0	9.5	3.9	8.6	12.3
Pennsylvania	1.3	1.0	0.4	1.8	0.8	0.7	1.4
East North Central	3.6	4.4	2.0	3.8	3.1	3.6	2.7
West North Central	0.9	0.8	0.8	1.2	—	0.7	1.4
South Atlantic	2.2	2.8	0.8	2.6	0.8	0.7	2.7
East South Central	0.3	—	0.4	0.5	—	—	—
West South Central	0.7	0.6	0.4	1.0	—	—	—
Mountain	0.2	0.2	—	0.3	—	—	—
Pacific	1.8	1.6	0.4	2.4	0.8	2.2	1.4

Table 5.14 cont.

Headquarters Location 1969	Location of Branch Firm, 1969: 51–99 Employees						
	New England	Connecticut	Maine	Massachusetts	New Hampshire	Rhode Island	Vermont
Total Number	179	42	10	91	12	19	5
New England	41.9%	38.1%	80.0%	41.8%	41.6%	26.4%	60.0%
Connecticut	9.5	33.3	10.0	2.2	—	—	—
Maine	2.8	—	50.0	—	—	—	—
Massachusetts	22.9	—	20.0	36.3	33.3	5.3	20.0
New Hampshire	2.2	—	—	1.1	8.3	5.3	20.0
Rhode Island	3.9	4.8	—	2.2	—	15.8	—
Vermont	0.6	—	20.0	—	—	—	20.0
Middle Atlantic	41.4	52.4	20.0	36.3	33.3	68.5	—
New Jersey	3.4	—	—	5.5	—	5.3	—
New York	35.8	47.6	20.0	28.6	33.3	63.2	—
Pennsylvania	2.2	4.8	—	2.2	—	—	—
East North Central	6.7	4.8	—	8.8	8.3	—	20.0
West North Central	1.7	—	—	2.2	8.3	—	—
South Atlantic	2.8	2.4	—	3.3	—	—	20.0
East South Central	—	—	—	—	—	—	—
West South Central	1.1	—	—	2.2	—	—	—
Mountain	—	—	—	—	—	—	—
Pacific	4.5	2.4	—	5.5	8.3	5.3	—

Table 5.14 cont.

Headquarters Location 1969	Location of Branch Firm, 1969: 100 or More Employees						
	New England	Connecticut	Maine	Massachusetts	New Hampshire	Rhode Island	Vermont
Total Number	392	99	37	184	26	38	8
New England	37.9%	24.1%	62.1%	38.6%	42.2%	47.4%	12.5%
Connecticut	5.6	14.1	5.4	2.2	—	5.3	—
Maine	2.6	—	27.0	0.0	—	—	—
Massachusetts	23.0	6.1	27.0	32.6	34.6	10.5	12.5
New Hampshire	0.8	—	2.7	0.5	3.8	—	—
Rhode Island	5.9	4.0	—	3.3	3.8	31.6	—
Vermont	—	—	—	0.0	—	—	—
Middle Atlantic	38.8	46.0	24.3	35.3	34.6	44.7	75.0
New Jersey	2.3	3.0	2.7	1.6	3.8	2.6	—
New York	31.9	33.0	21.6	30.4	30.8	36.8	75.0
Pennsylvania	4.6	10.1	—	3.3	—	5.3	—
East North Central	10.5	13.1	5.4	9.8	15.4	7.9	12.5
West North Central	2.3	—	2.7	3.8	3.8	—	—
South Atlantic	3.6	3.0	2.7	5.4	—	—	—
East South Central	1.5	3.0	—	1.6	—	—	—
West South Central	1.3	1.0	—	2.2	—	—	—
Mountain	1.3	2.0	—	1.1	3.8	—	—
Pacific	3.0	7.1	2.7	2.2	—	—	—

SOURCE: Dun & Bradstreet data, 1969, 1974.

Table 5.15

DISTRIBUTION OF FIRMS THAT MIGRATED INTO NEW ENGLAND BETWEEN 1969 AND 1974: PLACE OF DESTINATION BY PLACE OF ORIGIN

Place of Origin	Place of Destination						
	New England	Connec-ticut	Maine	Massa-chusetts	New Hampshire	Rhode Island	Vermont
Total Number	353	254	7	71	8	7	6
Middle Atlantic	92.4%	96.9%	71.4%	76.1%	100.0%	100.0%	100.0%
New York	83.9	90.2	14.3	70.4	75.0	71.4	83.3
New Jersey	5.9	5.1	42.9	2.8	25.0	0.0	16.7
Pennsylvania	2.5	1.6	14.3	2.8	0.0	28.6	100.0
East North Central	4.2	2.0	28.6	11.3	0.0	0.0	0.0
West North Central	0.0	0.0	0.0	0.0	0.0	0.0	0.0
South Atlantic	0.3	0.0	0.0	1.4	0.0	0.0	0.0
East South Central	0.6	0.4	0.0	1.4	0.0	0.0	0.0
West South Central	0.0	0.0	0.0	0.0	0.0	0.0	0.0
Mountain	0.3	0.0	0.0	1.4	0.0	0.0	0.0
Pacific	2.3	0.8	0.0	8.5	0.0	0.0	0.0

SOURCE: Dun & Bradstreet data, 1969, 1974.

Table 5.16

DISTRIBUTION OF FIRMS THAT MIGRATED OUT OF NEW ENGLAND BETWEEN 1969 AND 1974: PLACE OF DESTINATION BY PLACE OF ORIGIN

							Place of Destination						
Place of Origin	Total Number	Total Percent	Middle Atlantic	(New York)	(New Jersey)	(Pennsyl-vania)	East North Central	West North Central	South Atlantic	East South Central	West South Central	Moun-tain	Pacific
New England	144	100.0	49.3	(38.9)	(8.3)	(2.1)	8.3	0.7	29.2	0.7	2.8	0.7	8.3
Connecticut	69	100.0	59.4	(46.4)	(11.6)	(1.4)	7.2	1.4	24.6	0.0	4.3	0.0	2.9
Maine	3	100.0	66.7	(66.7)	(0.0)	(0.0)	0.0	0.0	33.3	0.0	0.0	0.0	0.0
Massachusetts	59	100.0	35.6	(30.5)	(3.4)	(1.7)	11.9	0.0	30.5	1.7	1.7	1.7	16.9
New Hampshire	3	100.0	66.7	(33.3)	(0.0)	(33.3)	0.0	0.0	0.0	33.3	0.0	0.0	0.0
Rhode Island	8	100.0	37.5	(25.0)	(12.5)	(0.0)	0.0	0.0	62.5	0.0	0.0	0.0	0.0
Vermont	2	100.0	100.0	(50.0)	(50.0)	(0.0)	0.0	0.0	0.0	0.0	0.0	0.0	0.0

SOURCE: Dun & Bradstreet data, 1969, 1974.

Table 5.17
INTRAREGIONAL MIGRATION OF FIRMS AND JOBS, 1969–1974

Area	Firms Percent Distribution of					Employment Percent Distribution of				
	Number 1969	Non-migrants	Out-migrants	In-migrants	Net Change (Number)	Level, 1969	Non-migrant Firms[a]	Firms That Outmigrated[b]	Firms That Inmigrated[c]	Net Change (Number)[d]
New England	163,328	108,963	195	195	—	2,681,660	2,251,745	4,412	6,926	—
Connecticut	24.3%	24.5%	13.3%	9.7%	-7	27.2%	30.8%	4.8%	8.4%	97
Maine	8.7	8.6	4.1	10.8	13	6.6	5.6	3.8	21.7	1,058
Massachusetts	47.9	48.4	47.7	31.3	-32	49.5	46.4	66.1	16.8	-3,306
New Hampshire	6.4	6.1	10.3	30.8	40	6.1	5.3	9.3	41.4	2,356
Rhode Island	8.4	8.4	21.5	13.3	-16	7.5	9.1	14.1	11.3	-168
Vermont	4.3	4.1	3.1	4.1	2	3.1	2.8	1.8	0.4	-37

SOURCE: Dun & Bradstreet data, 1969, 1974.

a 1969 employment.

b 1969 employment level prior to migration.

c 1974 employment level after migration.

d 1974 employment of firms that migrated to a state minus the 1974 employment of firms that had left the same state.

Table 5.18

MIGRATION RATES BY INDUSTRY, NEW ENGLAND, 1969–1974[a]

Industry	Inmigrant Rate	Outmigrant Rate
Regional Total	0.0022	0.0009
Agriculture	0.0000	0.0011
Mining	0.0321	0.0000
Construction	0.0007	0.0005
Manufacturing	0.0053	0.0021
Transportation, Communications, and Public Utilities	0.0028	0.0009
Wholesale/Retail Trade	0.0014	0.0005
Finance, Insurance, and Real Estate	0.0185	0.0085
Services	0.0018	0.0012
Public Administration	0.0000	0.0000
Unclassified	0.0000	0.0000

SOURCE: Dun & Bradstreet data, 1969, 1974.
[a]Number of in- or outmigrants divided by the number of firms in the industry in 1969.

Table 5.19

NUMBER OF MIGRANT MANUFACTURING FIRMS BY EMPLOYMENT SIZE CATEGORY, 1969–1974

Number of Employees	Outmigrants[a]		Inmigrants[b]		Net Change (Inmigrants minus Outmigrants)
	Number	Percent	Number	Percent	
Total	51	100.0	130	100.0	79
1–100	41	80.4	105	80.8	64
101–200	4	7.8	13	10.0	9
201–300	5	9.8	3	2.3	−2
301–400	1	2.0	1	0.8	0
401–500	0	0.0	4	3.1	4
501 or more	0	0.0	4	3.1	4

SOURCE: Dun & Bradstreet data, 1969, 1974.
[a]Employment size category in 1969 (before migration).
[b]Employment size category in 1974 (after migration).

Table 5.20

MIGRATION RATES BY MULTIUNIT AFFILIATION, NEW ENGLAND, 1969–1974[a]

Status	Inmigrant Rate	Outmigrant Rate
Total	0.0022	0.0009
Not Multiunit Affiliated	0.0014	0.0006
Headquarters	0.0145	0.0057
Branch	0.0000	0.0003

SOURCE: Dun & Bradstreet data, 1969, 1974.
[a]Number of in- or outmigrants divided by the number of firms in each category in 1969.

the average migrant rates (table 5.20). Furthermore, New England experienced a net increase in the number of headquarters through geographical movement. Over the five-year period 1969–1974, 147 headquarters inmigrated and 58 outmigrated, for a net increase of 89 headquarters in the region (tables 5.21 and 5.22).[12]

Connecticut, in particular, gained, with 24 firms leaving and 97 entering: a net increase of 73 headquarters. In the case of outmigrant as well as inmigrant headquarters, the state with which the largest exchange occurred was New York. Over 50 percent (13 firms) of the headquarters migrating out of Connecticut relocated in New York, and over 80 percent (82 firms) of the headquarters that relocated in Connecticut had moved from New York.

The only New England state that experienced a net loss of headquarters was Rhode Island. While six such operations left the state, only one entered.

Net inmigration of headquarters, in combination with the failure of branch firms to inmigrate or to open, reveals that, on the one hand, New England is perceived as a desirable location for headquarters but, on the other hand, is simultaneously perceived as a less desirable location for operational units. For instance, given the high death rate and low birth rate of branch firms in Manufacturing, it is interesting to note that New England experienced a net inmigration of 32 headquarters in this industry (tables 5.23 and 5.24).

[12]Additional data on the movement of headquarters are found in "Are There Discernible Trends in Corporate Headquarters Relocations?" *Site Selection Handbook, 1977* (Atlanta, Ga.: Conway Publications, 1977), pp. 87–96.

Table 5.21

LOCATION IN NEW ENGLAND IN 1969 OF HEADQUARTERS THAT OUTMIGRATED, BY LOCATION AFTER MIGRATION

Location in 1974	Location in 1969						
	New England	Connecticut	Maine	Massachusetts	New Hampshire	Rhode Island	Vermont
Total Number	58	24	2	26	0	6	0
Middle Atlantic							
New Jersey	3.4%	8.3%	—	—	—	—	—
New York	37.9	54.2	50.0%	23.1%	—	33.3%	—
Pennsylvania	1.7	—	—	3.8	—	—	—
East North Central	13.8	12.5	—	19.2	—	—	—
West North Central	1.7	4.2	—	—	—	—	—
South Atlantic	27.6	16.7	50.0	26.9	—	66.7	—
East South Central	—	—	—	—	—	—	—
West South Central	1.7	4.2	—	—	—	—	—
Mountain	—	—	—	—	—	—	—
Pacific	12.1	—	—	26.9	—	—	—

SOURCE: Dun & Bradstreet data, 1969, 1974.

Table 5.22

LOCATION IN NEW ENGLAND IN 1974 OF HEADQUARTERS THAT INMIGRATED, BY LOCATION PRIOR TO MIGRATION

Location in 1969	Location in 1974						
	New England	Connec-ticut	Maine	Massa-chusetts	New Hampshire	Rhode Island	Vermont
Total Number	147	97	2	41	4	1	2
Middle Atlantic							
New Jersey	6.8%	8.2%	50.0%	—	25.0%	—	—
New York	81.0	84.5	50.0	73.2%	75.0	100.0%	100.0%
Pennsylvania	4.1	4.1	—	4.9	—	—	—
East North Central	3.4	1.1	—	7.3	—	—	—
West North Central	—	—	—	—	—	—	—
South Atlantic	0.7	—	—	2.4	—	—	—
East South Central	0.7	—	—	2.4	—	—	—
West South Central	—	—	—	—	—	—	—
Mountain	—	—	—	—	—	—	—
Pacific	3.4	1.0	—	9.8	—	—	—

SOURCE: Dun & Bradstreet data, 1969, 1974.

Table 5.23

Location in New England in 1969 of Headquarters That Outmigrated, by Location After Migration and SIC Code

	Location in 1969								
	Manufacturing			Finance, Insurance, and Real Estate			All Other Industries		
	New England	Connecticut	Massachusetts	New England	Connecticut	Massachusetts	New England	Connecticut	Massachusetts
Total Number	26	8	13	6	2	4	26	14	9
Middle Atlantic									
New Jersey	3.8%	12.5%	—	—	—	—	3.8%	7.1%	—
New York	26.9	50.0	15.4%	33.3%	—	50.0%	50.0	64.3	22.2%
Pennsylvania	3.8	—	7.7	—	—	—	7.7	7.1	11.1
East North Central	23.1	25.0	30.8	—	—	—	3.8	7.1	—
West North Central	—	—	—	—	—	—	—	—	—
South Atlantic	23.1	12.5	7.7	33.3	50.0%	25.0	30.7	14.3	55.6
East South Central	—	—	—	16.7	50.0	—	—	—	—
West South Central	—	—	—	—	—	—	—	—	—
Mountain	—	—	—	—	—	—	—	—	—
Pacific	19.2	—	38.5	16.7	—	25.0	3.8	—	11.1

SOURCE: Dun & Bradstreet data, 1969, 1974.

Table 5.24

LOCATION IN NEW ENGLAND IN 1974 OF HEADQUARTERS THAT INMIGRATED, BY LOCATION PRIOR TO MIGRATION AND SIC CODE

	Location in 1969								
	Manufacturing			Finance, Insurance, and Real Estate			All Other Industries		
	New England	Connecticut	Massachusetts	New England	Connecticut	Massachusetts	New England	Connecticut	Massachusetts
Total Number	58	46	8	18	12	5	71	39	28
Middle Atlantic									
New Jersey	8.6%	8.7%	—	5.6%	8.3%	—	5.6%	7.7%	—
New York	75.8	82.6	37.5%	88.9	83.3	100.0%	83.1	87.2	78.6%
Pennsylvania	3.4	4.3	—	5.6	8.3	—	4.2	2.6	7.1
East North Central	8.6	4.3	37.5	—	—	—	—	—	—
West North Central	0.0	—	—	—	—	—	—	—	—
South Atlantic	0.0	—	—	—	—	—	1.4	—	3.6
East South Central	1.7	—	12.5	—	—	—	—	—	—
West South Central	0.0	—	—	—	—	—	—	—	—
Mountain	0.0	—	—	—	—	—	—	—	—
Pacific	1.7	—	12.5	—	—	—	5.6	2.6	10.7

SOURCE: Dun & Bradstreet data, 1969, 1974.

Of the headquarters of manufacturing firms that left the region, one-third went to the Middle Atlantic states. While Connecticut experienced a net inmigration of headquarters of firms in this industry, Massachusetts experienced a net outmigration. Of those that entered New England, 91 percent came from the three contiguous Middle Atlantic states.

In Finance, Insurance, and Real Estate, there was also a net inmigration of headquarters into the region. As in the case of Manufacturing, most of the headquarters that inmigrated went to Connecticut (12 out of 18) and had relocated from New York.

Conclusions

In contrast to widespread publicity, this paper has found that the recent employment problems of New England are not the result of significant outmigration of firms. Previous evidence to support the outmigration thesis has been, at best, anecdotal. Generalizations have been made—based on the identification of relatively few migrating firms—which are not supported in fact.

Indeed, the migration of firms in either direction has not been significant. To the extent that migration has occurred, New England was a net beneficiary between 1969 and 1974. As might be expected, the greatest interchange was among adjacent states; more firms moved from New England to the state of New York than to the entire South Atlantic region.

Both the increase in the number of headquarters in New England and the decrease in the number of branch firms are especially significant. The increase in headquarters may be the outcome of a maturing economy—the concentration of decision-making functions proximate to clusters of financial, informational, and analytical resources and expertise. On the other hand, the decrease in branch firms indicates that the region is now being perceived as a less ideal location for production operations. If this is a trend, and if it is played out over time, New England should retain or increase its national share of upper-level white-collar employment while simultaneously witnessing a diminution of its share of blue-collar employment, especially Manufacturing.

The longer-term economic implications of these shifts, if they continue, need to be studied carefully. The shift to white-collar employment—if it is accompanied by significant outmigration of workers in blue-collar occupations and continued decreases in fertility rates—should result in very high levels of per capita income.

116

However, if blue-collar workers prove to be relatively immobile (and it is known that low-income groups tend to have relatively high rates of fertility), the region could face serious unemployment and welfare problems in the future. Thus decision makers within the region must orient their concern, not toward the outmigration of workers (which may be a desirable adjustment for the region), but rather toward a consideration of the occupations and incomes of those who are migrating.

The primary manifestations of New England's economic problems in terms of employment loss appear to be a relatively low birth rate and a relatively high death rate among firms. This is a difficult problem to confront through regional political mechanisms. It necessitates a focus, not only on the attractiveness of other regions for the location of new firms, but also, and primarily, on the market dynamics, economic conditions, and institutional factors in New England itself—factors that may discourage the location of firms in the region and impact adversely on the ability of existing firms to operate profitably. In other words, this problem focus suggests that the basic cause of the region's economic difficulties must be confronted within the region. For example, issues such as capital stock aging, local tax structures, and the whole array of institutional factors that may create an adverse climate for business, warrant investigation.

This paper has provided much descriptive, empirical information about recent changes in the configuration of firms in New England. In many cases, the information and data are new; in many ways, the study has served to raise questions regarding the behavior of the region's firms. These questions should provide an agenda of issues to be researched to understand and address effectively the underlying problems of the New England economy.

VI. Labor Turnover and the Sunbelt/ Frostbelt Controversy: An Empirical Test

Robert Premus and Rudy Fichtenbaum

This study focuses on the relationship between growth disparities among the Frostbelt and Sunbelt states and labor turnover in the manufacturing sector. Alternative theories of regional development are presented and their implications for labor turnover are discussed and tested. A major hypothesis of the paper is that the willingness of workers to quit their jobs in the Frostbelt and move to the Sunbelt is a function of the economic circumstances confronting them in the regions. Are workers in the Frostbelt migrating to jobs in the Sunbelt because of location preferences, or are they being forced by economic circumstances to relocate? The answer has important implications for the public policy debate over policies aimed at stimulating growth in the Frostbelt versus relocation allowances and migration assistance.

The study plan is as follows. First, competing theories of regional economic development are presented. This discussion addresses the potential alternative causes of the relative demise of the Frostbelt region. Second, the implications of each of the competing theories of regional development for geographic differences in worker quit and firm layoff behavior are discussed. Regression analysis is used to provide a statistical test of the alternative labor turnover hypotheses in the third section. Both the results of time-series and cross-section analyses are presented. Finally, a summary and conclusions are presented.

"Labor Turnover and the Sunbelt/Frostbelt Controversy: An Empirical Test" by Robert Premus and Rudy Fichtenbaum is reprinted from *Economic Development Research Report* (Washington, D.C.: U.S. Department of Commerce, September 1977).

Robert Premus is a professor of economics at Wright State University in Dayton, Ohio, now on leave as economist on the Joint Economic Committee, U.S. Congress. Rudy Fichtenbaum is an assistant professor of economics at Wright State.

119

Alternative Theories of Regional Development

A "chicken or egg" controversy has emerged in the regional economic development literature. Do people migrate to regions experiencing economic expansion in pursuit of jobs or do population movements precede job expansion? Some analysts argue that population migration precedes regional economic development (i.e., jobs follow people). Migrants are viewed as selecting a location independently of employment opportunities, resulting in population expansion in amenity-rich regions. As the population grows, more people are looking for jobs, shifting the region's labor supply function to the right. This shift in the region's labor supply function results in a surplus which can only be eliminated by lowering wages. Of course, in inflationary times wages may fall only in a relative sense; i.e., in regions experiencing a net inmigration wages would not rise as quickly as in other regions. Lower relative factor costs, in turn, attract private and public investment, leading to job expansion. In the long run, a region's demand for labor is viewed as being horizontal, which implies that eventually enough jobs will be created to employ everyone in the region at the initial wage rate.

Other analysts argue that people primarily follow jobs. The migration literature is replete with studies that have found changes in income and employment opportunities to be significant determinants of interregional migration flows. This people-follow-jobs approach implies that regional change in relative factor prices, for example wages, cause capital to flow from relatively expensive to relatively cheap areas. This shift in capital investments leads to plant closings in regions experiencing a rise in relative factor prices and to plant additions and expansions in regions experiencing a fall in relative factor prices. In other words, the people-follow-jobs approach implies that the demand for labor in regions with relatively low factor prices shifts to the right, creating a temporary shortage of labor. As a result, wages rise temporarily, causing people to migrate in pursuit of higher paying jobs. In the long run, this view sees the supply of labor as being horizontal, meaning that it is population which responds to changes in job opportunities.

A third view of the regional economic development process, hereafter labeled the incubator approach, primarily views regional development as resulting from job gains from the expansion of existing businesses and the formation of new firms in excess of job losses from the contraction of existing businesses and business failures. Regional growth disparities, according to this view, occur primarily as a result of the interregional differentials in the factors that influence the expansion of existing businesses and the formation of new businesses, and not as a result of the migration of existing businesses. Capital investment *in place* is viewed as relatively immobile. Thus, according to this view, the formation of new businesses and the expansion of existing ones provide the impetus for growth in the Sunbelt; whereas, a decline in business starts and the reluctance of existing businesses to expand is viewed as the primary cause of economic stagnation in the Frostbelt. In general, plant closings and business migration account for very little of the growth disparity between the Sunbelt and the Frostbelt, according to this view.

Regional Development and Labor Turnover

In recent years, a growing literature on labor turnover (quits and layoffs) has emerged. Each of the competing theories mentioned above has testable implications for labor turnover behavior in the Frostbelt. The people-follow-jobs approach suggests that workers in the Frostbelt are involuntarily separating from their current jobs as a result of plant closings and moving to the Sunbelt. Thus industries with a large concentration of jobs in the Frostbelt should experience a higher rate of involuntary separations (layoffs) than industries that are geographically dispersed. Worker quit behavior is expected to be affected as well. In particular, this view hypothesizes that workers in the declining states will quit their current employment—in anticipation of future layoffs and inadequate wage increases—and migrate to the Sunbelt regions. Thus, if the people-follow-jobs approach is a valid explanation of regional development patterns, both layoffs and quit rates should be higher in industries more geographically concentrated in the Frostbelt, other things constant.

The jobs-follow-people approach suggests that quit rates in the Frostbelt should reflect workers' preferences for amenities in the Sunbelt. Thus industries with a high concentration of jobs in the Frostbelt should experience, other things equal, a higher quit rate than industries geographically concentrated in other regions. Also, business-initiated layoffs in the Frostbelt would be higher because as people leave the region the demand for goods and services declines. Thus, if this theory has empirical validity, quit rates and

121

layoff rates should be higher in industries that are geographically concentrated in the Frostbelt.

The implications of the incubator hypothesis for labor turnover are quite different. Regions suffering from economic decline due to a low business formation rate are expected to experience increasing competition among workers for the available jobs. When a worker decides to quit one job in order to search for another, he/she must take into account the availability of alternative economic opportunities as well as the cost of obtaining information about them. To the extent that the incubator hypothesis is valid, the relative decline of economic opportunities in the Frostbelt, coupled with imperfect worker knowledge of alternatives, is expected to reduce worker quit rates in industries that are geographically concentrated in the Frostbelt. Also, plant layoffs are expected to be unaffected by geographical concentration since, according to the incubator hypothesis, plant closings are not the primary cause of economic stagnation. However, a lower layoff rate would also support the incubator hypothesis since it would imply that the relative decline of the Frostbelt is not due to a loss of comparative cost advantage for existing industries.

The Results

In order to test the hypotheses enumerated in the previous section, we examined differences in quit rates and layoff rates between the Frostbelt and the rest of the country over time as well as differences between industries which are heavily concentrated in the Frostbelt. For the purposes of this study, the Frostbelt has been defined to include the following states: Michigan, Indiana, Illinois, Ohio, Pennsylvania, New York, New Hampshire, Rhode Island, Massachusetts, Connecticut, Maine, Vermont, and New Jersey.

Time Series

Our time-series analysis consisted of examining differences in average quit and layoff rates between the Frostbelt states and the rest of the country. In the Frostbelt, the average quit rate over a twenty-year period beginning in 1960 was 1.92 quits per hundred employees, compared to an average quit rate of 2.48 for the rest of the country. This result is consistent with the incubator hypothesis which predicts that quit rates should be lower in regions that are declining because there is more competition for jobs.

The same approach was used to examine regional differences in layoff rates. Over the same twenty-year period the average layoff rate in the Frostbelt was 1.45 per hundred employees compared to 1.60 for the rest of the country. This finding indicates that there is only a slight difference in layoff rates between the Frostbelt and the rest of the country. Again, this finding is consistent with the incubator hypothesis, suggesting that the demise of the Frostbelt economy is the result of a low business formation rate and not the relocation of existing businesses to other parts of the country.

Cross-Section

In order to compare differences in quit rates across industries to determine the effect of regional concentration, it is necessary to hold constant all other factors which might influence quit rates. To do this, we have used a multiple regression, including other variables which have been found in previous studies to be important determinants of quit rates, along with a variable to indicate whether or not an industry was heavily concentrated in the Frostbelt.

Firms that invest in human capital (i.e., pay to have their workers trained) are expected to offer higher wages to retain their workforce. Thus industries which pay higher wages should experience lower quit rates. Therefore, we have included a wage variable in our regression. If we had not included this variable, and industries which were highly concentrated in the Frostbelt paid high wages, it is possible that the effect we have attributed to regional concentration is in reality a wage effect. However, by including this variable in our model we are able to control for its influence. In addition, we have included several other variables in our regression to eliminate their possible influence. The probability of injury or illness on the job is expected to affect worker quit behavior. Industries with a high incidence of injuries and illnesses are expected to have higher quit rates. Also, unions may influence quit behavior. Presumably, unions confer benefits on workers by giving them recourse to arbitration and negotiations to resolve conflicts. Thus industries which are highly unionized should have lower quit rates. Establishment size is also expected to influence worker quit behavior. The organizational behavior literature suggests that the bureaucratic control mechanisms of large organizations result in job dissatisfaction and higher turnover. Finally, workers with brief tenure are more likely to quit. Therefore, if an industry has a high percentage of workers with brief tenure, it is likely that they will also have a higher quit rate.

123

The regression results from the quit equation are presented in the appendix to this chapter on page 125. All of the regression coefficients pass reasonable tests of statistical significance, and they display the expected signs. Over 89 percent of interindustry variation in quit rate is explained by the equation and the regression. The regression results show that industries which are concentrated in the Frostbelt have lower quit rates. Also, unions and high wage rates were found to reduce quits; whereas, industrial accidents, establishment size, and lack of work experience increased industry quit rates.

The layoff equation is also presented in the appendix to this chapter. This equation is structured to measure the effects of industry concentrated on layoff rates. To control for other factors that might influence layoff rates we include in our multiple regression a wage variable, an industry outlook variable, and a variable to capture changes in product demand. High wages increase labor costs, which can lead to layoffs. Therefore, we expect industries with high wages, other things equal, to have higher layoff rates. Industry outlook as measured by the percentage change in employment from 1971 to 1976 indicates whether an industry is experiencing secular growth or a decline. Since both 1971 and 1976 were one year into a recovery from a recession, taking into account employment changes over this period eliminates variation caused by the business cycle. Industries experiencing a secular decline (growth), other things equal, are expected to experience a higher (lower) layoff rate. Finally, current economic conditions in the industry will influence layoff behavior. The unemployment rate in each industry relative to the overall unemployment rate is used in this study to reflect product demand conditions. Industries experiencing a decline in product demand are expected to initiate layoffs. An unemployment rate lower than the unemployment rate for the economy as a whole would indicate strong product demand, resulting in a low layoff rate.

The test results show that the layoff rate is lower for industries concentrated in the Frostbelt, a result that supports the incubator hypothesis. The other results are interesting as well. With regard to layoffs, we found that industries which paid high wages had no higher incidence of layoffs than industries which paid lower wages. Thus it would appear that high wages cannot be cited as a reason for layoffs. In addition, we found that industries with weak demand in the product market had higher layoff rates and that industries where employment growth is lagging also had higher layoff rates.

Summary and Conclusion

The results obtained from our multiple regression indicate that industries which are concentrated in the Frostbelt, other things equal, have a significantly lower quit rate. This finding lends empirical support to the incubator hypothesis. In addition, we found that industries that are concentrated in the Frostbelt had a slightly lower layoff rate, other things equal. Apparently, the relative decline of the Frostbelt is not due to worker disenchantment with employment and environmental conditions or layoffs. If the Frostbelt states were experiencing a relative decline in comparative advantage for existing industries, or if they were lacking in amenity resources, higher quit and layoff rates would have been expected. Instead, the results of our study support the view that economic stagnation in the Frostbelt region is due to the inability of the region to stimulate business starts and expand existing businesses at a rate sufficient to absorb the growing labor force.

The findings of this study have implications for policies dealing with growth disparities between the regions. Apparently, the forces of the market are not sufficient (1) to cause people in the Frostbelt to migrate or (2) to provide the necessary incentives in that region to increase business formation rates. Also, our study suggests that plant-closing legislation designed to retard the movement of industry south would not be sufficient to overcome labor market problems due to economic stagnation of the industrial tier states.

APPENDIX

Formally, the quit equation used in the test is presented as follows (t values are in parentheses):

$$X_1 = 3.548 - 0.77X_3 - 0.526X_4 + 0.0293X_5$$
$$ (3.45) \quad\ (7.35) \qquad (3.03)$$
$$- 0.0091X_6 + 19.65X_7 + 0.29X_8$$
$$ (3.46) \qquad (2.86) \qquad (3.46)$$
$$(R^2 = .89) \qquad\qquad (F = 78.9) \qquad\qquad (N = 61)$$

where

X_1 = quits per 100 employees in the ith industry,

X_3 = percent of ith industry employment in the Frostbelt region,

X_4 = average hourly earnings per employee in the ith industry,

X_5 = the number of industrial injuries and illnesses per 100 workers in the ith industry,

X_6 = percent of workers in the ith industry that belong to a union,

X_7 = percent of establishments in the ith industry with 500 or more employees, and

X_8 = the ith industry accession rate per 100 employees (recalls and new hires) lagged one year.

The layoff equation used in this study is as follows (t values are in parentheses):

$$X_2 = 0.575 = 0.00287X_4 - 1.277X_9 = 0.957X_{10} - 0.651X_3$$
$$(0.36) \qquad (2.109) \qquad (4.53) \qquad (1.83)$$

$(R^2 = .30)$ $\qquad\qquad\qquad (F = 7.97)$ $\qquad\qquad\qquad (N = 79)$

where

X_2 = layoffs per 1,000 employers in the ith industry,[1]

X_3 = percent of ith industry employment in the Frostbelt region,

X_4 = average hourly earnings per employee in the ith industry in 1976,

X_9 = percent change in employment in the ith industry from 1971 to 1976, and

X_{10} = the unemployment rate in the ith industry relative to the unemployment rate for the manufacturing sector in 1976.

---

[1]The sample for the test consisted of quit and layoff data on 79 industries in the manufacturing sector for the year 1976. A technical discussion of the model development, data, and test results can be found in Robert Premus and Rudy Fichtenbaum, "Regional Development and Labor Turnover: More on the Frostbelt-Sunbelt Controversy," *Review of Regional Studies*, Vol. XI, N.1, Spring 1981, pp. 92–99.

VII. Plant Closings and Worker Dislocation

Daniel A. Littman and Myung-Hoon Lee

In any dynamic economy, capital investments must be retired at the end of their useful lives and replaced by more productive investments. The industrial structure and its geographic distribution respond to a variety of powerful economic forces, including changes in prices, consumer preferences, production technologies, and international trade competition. The opening of new plants and closing of obsolete plants are part of this vital process. An economy is efficient when productive resources are allowed to move freely in response to this ever-changing environment. It follows that some magnitude of capital turnover, reflected in part by plant openings and closings, may signify economic health, as it assists growth and competitiveness (see Schumpeter 1950). Permitting a relatively uninhibited flow of capital among firms, industries, and geographic locations therefore may lead to net economic benefits for society.

Plant closings also can impose tremendous adjustment costs on particular economic actors—laid-off workers (hereafter, *dislocated workers*) and their families, local governments, and local businesses linked to the closing plants. Plant closings are attracting increased media and public attention because of the problems that such closings cause or symbolize—socioeconomic hardships for dislocated workers, increased unemployment, decay of the local employment base, and fiscal distress. Public officials have begun to consider policy options to strengthen the social safety net and to moderate the pace of plant closings. Proposals include incentives for employee ownership of marginal plants (employee stock ownership plans, or

"Plant Closings and Worker Dislocation" by Daniel A. Littman and Myung-Hoon Lee is reprinted with permission from *Economic Review of the Federal Reserve Bank of Cleveland*, Fall 1983, pp. 2–18.

Daniel A. Littman is an economist with the Federal Reserve Bank of Cleveland. Myung-Hoon Lee is a researcher/consultant with the World Bank.

ESOPs), expanded use of industrial investment and employment/ wage incentives, and increased occupational training and income maintenance assistance. One popular and comprehensive policy option considered by state and local governments is plant-closing laws, which are examined in this article. Since 1975, five states (California, Maine, New Jersey, Rhode Island, and Wisconsin) and at least three municipalities (Philadelphia, Pittsburgh, and Vacaville, CA) have enacted plant-closing laws. During their 1981 and 1982 sessions, 21 state legislatures considered almost 60 proposals to alleviate the problems surrounding plant closings. State legislatures have found it difficult to weigh the merits of policy alternatives. Certainly one reason for this difficulty is that the existing literature does not embrace thorough economic analyses of the plant-closing problem.

In section I of this article, we review the characteristics of existing and proposed plant-closing laws. We also outline the major justifications for plant-closing laws, such as reducing unemployment, reducing hardships for dislocated workers, and alleviating fiscal distress of local governments. In section II we review the evidence on dislocated worker hardship and compare these hardships with the problems experienced by other unemployed workers. We conclude that dislocated workers as a group cannot be distinguished from other unemployed workers on the basis of the severity of their problems. In section III we examine whether, and to what extent, plant closings cause unemployment. Although plant closings are associated with the shrinking of local labor markets, such closings appear to be only a relatively small source of national unemployment. In section IV we analyze whether statutory provisions that inhibit plant closings would effectively reduce unemployment and the probability of fiscal distress. The analysis shows that plant-closing laws would not necessarily delay or otherwise inhibit closings. In section V we examine the effects of plant-closing laws on resource allocation, finding that the laws may unintentionally create incentives to reduce the size of the work force in affected plants, especially among high-seniority workers.

I. Plant-Closing Laws

Existing and proposed plant-closing laws are rather diverse with respect to comprehensiveness, coverage tests, and statutory obligations placed on public authorities and affected firms (see table 7.1). The proposed laws are more comprehensive and more ambitious

Table 7.1
TYPICAL PROVISIONS OF PLANT-CLOSING LAWS

Provisions	Number of plant-closing laws with provision
Prior notice of closing	20
Firm-paid severance benefits	14
"Good-faith" sale efforts, incentives for employee ownership and firm reimbursements for employee retraining	11
Continuation of health-insurance coverage for specified period after termination	10
Effects bargaining, or requirement for employer to discuss effects of plant-closing with workers	10
Employer payments to state of specified proportion of annual wage bill	9
Firm reimbursement for employee relocation expenses	8
Paid leave time for workers prior to shutdown	7
Preferential transfer rights for affected workers	6
Decision bargaining, or requirement for employer to discuss decision to close with workers	2

NOTE: Provisions of existing and proposed plant-closing laws are listed in order of descending frequency. The number of states having proposed or existing laws with such provisions is listed in the right column.

than existing statutes, in part because these laws have yet to run the gauntlet of legislative scrutiny. In Wisconsin, for example, firms that wish to close facilities employing more than a specified minimum number of workers must give employees and public officials at least a 60-day prior notice of such action. Maine's plant-closing law requires a 60-day prior notice of closing and severance pay to laid-off workers equivalent to their average weekly pay multiplied by their years of service. In marked contrast, the proposed plant-closing law in Hawaii would require employers to give a three-year prior notice of closing. Ohio's proposed law would require a one-year prior notice and severance pay, along with a variety of other obligations for public authorities and the firm that is planning to close a plant (see table 7.2).

Table 7.2
FEATURES OF OHIO'S PROPOSED PLANT-CLOSING LAW

Coverage tests for firm

Employs 100 or more workers

Cannot be political subdivision or nonprofit firm

Must have operated in state for 5 years or more; if affected facility was acquired from another firm, purchaser succeeds to seller's obligations

Affected by permanent shutdown for reasons other than bankruptcy

Affected if transferring operations an "unreasonable distance" and reducing work force by 10 percent or more

Affected if one or more parts of an operation are being phased out, resulting in an overall work force reduction of 50 percent or more over 2 years

Obligations of state authorities

Establish Employee and Community Readjustment Administration (ERCA)

Establish rules for severance payments and firm payments to Community Readjustment Fund

Receive employer notification of closing, relocation, or reduction in operations

Investigate failures to provide prior notice

Receive and evaluate economic impact statements

Have subpoena powers

Notify and coordinate activities of county authorities

Obligations of county authorities

Establish local citizens' council within 45 days of closing notice

Establish Community Readjustment Fund

Administer Community Readjustment Fund to provide or maintain local employment opportunities, job finding and job creation assistance, planning services, emergency tax relief, community development projects

Have subpoena powers

Obligations of firm closing plant

Submit 1-year prior notice of closing, relocation, or reduction in operations to ERCA, workers, union, and community officials

Prepare economic impact statement within 90 days of notice

Give lump-sum severance payment to all affected workers with over 5 years seniority equal to average weekly earnings over past 2 years multiplied by years and partial years of service

Allocate lump-sum payment to Community Readjustment Fund equal to 5 percent of annual payroll

Continue health insurance coverage for affected workers for a period not to exceed 6 months

Allow affected workers to transfer to other facilities

Allow adequate relocation reimbursement

130

Advocates of plant-closing laws justify such labor-market intervention on the grounds of reducing hardships for dislocated workers, reducing flows into national and local unemployment, and insulating local governments from fiscal distress that a plant closing could cause. Advocates of plant-closing laws recognize that plant closings impose severe socioeconomic hardships on dislocated workers and attempt to alleviate these hardships. It is argued that dislocated workers usually face more severe hardships than other unemployed workers, in terms of unemployment duration, income losses, and health and family difficulties. Advocates maintain that the existing policies to protect the unemployed in general do not address the particular difficulties experienced by dislocated workers. The features of plant-closing laws that specifically address dislocated worker hardships include cash-severance benefits, extra paid leave time, continuation of health insurance benefits after closing, occupational training, job counseling and placement, and income support.

Advocates of plant-closing laws maintain that plant shutdowns are a major source of local, regional, and national unemployment. It is argued that governments have a responsibility to inhibit or delay closings, thereby reducing the flow of workers into unemployment. The provisions of plant-closing laws aimed at this issue include discouraging closings through the threat of financial penalties for firms contemplating such action; providing incentives for employee ownership; and/or requiring firms that intend to close plants to offer preferential transfer rights and relocation assistance to affected workers.

Another reason for supporting plant-closing laws is that shutdown-related unemployment of dislocated workers can cause fiscal distress for local governments. Local tax revenues might be reduced through the loss of firm-paid property taxes, worker-paid local income and sales taxes, and reductions in property values. Simultaneously, a major closing could increase government outlays in such areas as General Assistance, Unemployment Insurance, and Aid to Families with Dependent Children.

II. Plant Closings and Hardships for Dislocated Workers

The existing literature on plant closings is filled with case studies that quantify the primary and secondary effects of permanent closings on workers and their families. Typical primary effects include extended unemployment, losses in income and occupational status, and failure to regain steady employment. Secondary effects include stress-related health and family difficulties.

Plants often experience a lengthy period of decline in output, productivity, capital investment, and employment prior to closing. As work forces decline in size, new hiring is curtailed and *pre-closing* layoffs tend to be concentrated among younger, lower-seniority workers. Case studies show that the typical dislocated worker is older (40 years to 55 years old), has higher seniority (15 years to 25 years) and occupational status, is less well-educated (7 years to 10 years of formal education), and has achieved relatively higher earnings than other workers in the labor pool. These five characteristics—age, seniority, occupational status, education, and earnings—often prove to be labor-market handicaps once such workers become unemployed and begin to search for new jobs. Employers tend to screen older and less-educated workers in the hiring process. Conversely, many dislocated workers tend to be more selective about the jobs they will accept, because they have become accustomed to higher occupational status and higher earnings. The labor-market difficulties of dislocated workers are sometimes compounded by the fact that they often are dislocated from a declining industry or during a recession; in addition, the dislocated worker often is reluctant to relocate to areas where job prospects are better.[1]

The case studies indicate that, among dislocated workers, 10 percent to 15 percent find new jobs immediately or accept interplant transfers, 10 percent to 25 percent permanently drop out of the labor force, and 60 percent to 80 percent tend to experience very long unemployment spells. Estimates of the mean duration of the initial spell vary widely (ranging from 10 weeks to 13 months), depending on the industry involved, demographic and occupational composition of the work force, plant location, and stage of the business cycle at which the plant closing occurred. Our research adjusts for time period and business cycle by comparing the average duration of unemployment for dislocated workers in each case study with the average length of unemployment spells for all workers in the nation for the reference year. We found that dislocated workers experience average unemployment spells that are 50

---

[1]While reluctance to relocate suggests a voluntary element in the unemployment of dislocated workers, it should be remembered that older workers are more likely to have stronger community roots, families, and homes—all of which explain their reluctance to move.

percent to 80 percent longer on average than the average for all workers.

Lengthy unemployment, combined with lower earnings in subsequent jobs, results in permanent earnings losses for dislocated workers. Jacobson and Thomason (1979) found earnings diverged from their preclosing trend by 11 percent to 46 percent during the first two years after closing, and 10 percent to 30 percent after three years. Holen, Jehn, and Trost (1981) estimated that dislocated workers' earnings were 27 percent below their projected earnings two years after layoff. These two studies, along with Holen (1976), also found that dislocated workers' earnings converged to the pre-closing trend within five years of closing, although such workers experienced a reduction in current income (see figure 7.1). In addition to lengthy unemployment and reduced earnings, dislocated workers

Figure 7.1

EARNINGS LOSSES OF DISLOCATED WORKERS

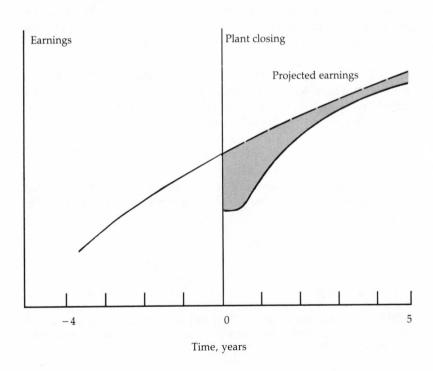

suffer a number of secondary effects. Shostak (1980) found higher incidence of physiological health problems, mental disorder, divorce, alcoholism, suicide attempts, and anomie among dislocated workers than he found among employed workers.

The identification of hardships for dislocated workers does not necessarily imply a need for new policies to address such hardships. Special help for dislocated workers, in addition to existing policies for the unemployed, can be justified only if the difficulties of dislocated workers are found to be decidedly more severe than those of other unemployed workers. While the case studies demonstrate significant differences between dislocated workers and the "average" unemployed worker, dislocated workers generally cannot, as a group, be distinguished from the long-term unemployed. Older, less educated workers with relatively high pre-termination earnings and occupational status are disproportionately represented among the long-term unemployed, just as they are among the dislocated. Consequently, the labor-market and income problems of dislocated workers would appear to be the same as the difficulties faced by many other individuals suffering relatively long unemployment spells. The social, personal, and family problems experienced by dislocated workers also have been shown to be pervasive among the long-term unemployed.[2] It follows that dislocated workers are served just as well or just as poorly by existing unemployment protections as are other long-term unemployed workers, and there is no strong justification for policy targeting of the select group of dislocated workers. The structure of existing unemployment measures, both public and private, provides a substantial amount and range of protection to the unemployed in general and to dislocated workers who are part of that population (see table 7.3). Dislocated workers are likely to benefit from unemployment-insurance coverage, as well as from other federal and state programs, the National Labor Relations Board, corporate personnel policies, and union contracts.

---

[2]See Barbara S. Dohrenwend and Bruce P. Dohrenwend, eds., *Stressful Life Events: Their Nature and Effects* (New York: John Wiley & Sons, 1974); Louis Ferman and Jeanne Gordus, *Mental Health and the Economy* (Kalamazoo, Mich.: W. E. Upjohn Institute for Employment Research, 1979); and Phyllis Moen, "Family Impacts of the 1975 Recession: Duration of Unemployment," *Journal of Marriage and the Family* 41 (August 1979): 561–72.

Table 7.3

EXISTING PROTECTION FOR DISLOCATED WORKERS

Protection	Coverage	Applicability
Federal and State		
Unemployment compensation	Income maintenance for unemployed	89% of U.S. workers in 1982
Comprehensive Employment and Training Act, Titles IIB, IIC, and VII	Employment, training, and counseling for structurally unemployed adults	In FY 1982, 835,234 individuals served by IIB and IIC; 125,994 served by VII
Trade Adjustment Assistance	Income maintenance and CETA-like services for workers adversely affected by imports	30,480 workers received first TAA payments in FY 1982
U.S. Employment Service	Job referral, counseling, and other supportive services	14.3 million workers served in FY 1982
Redwood National Park Act amendments of 1978	Income supplements for workers adversely affected by expansion of Redwood National Park	Primarily California-based lumber workers
Civil Aeronautics Board and Airline Deregulation Act of 1978	Income supplements and job guarantees for workers adversely affected by mergers and airline deregulation	Workers in air-transportation industry

Table 7.3 cont.

Protection	Coverage	Applicability
Regional Rail Reorganization Act of 1973, Urban Mass Transportation Act, and High Speed Ground Transportation Act of 1965	Income supplements to workers adversely affected by these pieces of legislation	Mainly railroad workers, especially with Amtrak, Conrail, and their predecessors
Employee stock ownership plans (ESOPs)	Internal Revenue Code and Treasury regulations offer very favorable tax treatment to ESOPs	ESOPs nationally; potential ESOPs in 6 states in 1982
Prior notice of separation	National Labor Relations Board (NLRB) decisions require that unions have sufficient time to bargain over the rights of workers affected by closings, out-sourcing, and subcontracting	Union workers
Effects bargaining	NLRB decisions require that unions be allowed to discuss effects of closing; usually upheld by courts	Union workers
Decision bargaining	NLRB decisions require that unions be given the opportunity to bargain over decision to close, out-source, or subcontract; usually overturned in courts	Union workers

(continued)

Table 7.3 cont.

Protection	Coverage	Applicability
Health insurance	Conversion to individual policy without waiting period or physical examination upon layoff	40 states in 1982
	Employer required to continue health insurance coverage for 3 months to 12 months after layoff	22 states in 1982
Corporate Personnel Policies		
Severance pay	Separation for economic cause, 2-week lump-sum payment to 2 weeks pay times years of service in lump sum	66% of companies and 56% of workers 1977
Supplemental unemployment benefits	Supplements to income after layoff	15% to 27% of workers in 1981
Relocation assistance and/or retraining	Reimbursement of relocation expenses; company-paid retraining	45% of companies in 1977
Outplacement counseling	Counseling, job referral, supportive services	53% of companies in 1977
Continuation of life and/or medical insurance	Company continues to pay insurance premiums for period of 1 month to 3 years	70% of companies in 1977

(continued)

Table 7.3 cont.

Protection	Coverage	Applicability
Advance notice of separation	1–6 months advance notice; mode of 2–4 weeks (47% of companies)	95% of companies in 1977
Collective Bargaining Agreements		
Prior notice of closing	2 weeks to 1 year prior notice	19.8% of union workers in 1980
Decision bargaining	Negotiations with union over decision to close	1.5% of union workers in 1982
Effects bargaining	Negotiations with union over effects of closing	10.1% of union workers in 1982
Supplemental unemployment benefits	Income supplements to laid-off workers	27.7% of union workers in 1980
Severance pay	Lump-sum payment upon termination	37.8% of union workers in 1980
Relocation assistance	Reimbursement for relocation expenses	32.0% of union workers in 1980
Transfer rights	Preferential transfer and bumping rights, with retention of seniority	49.2% of union workers in 1980

SOURCE: U.S. Department of Labor (1972, 1981a, 1981b, 1982); Scarry (1982); Miner (1978); Gorlin (1981); Industrial Union Department, AFL-CIO (1982); Gacek (1981); Millen (1979); Goldfarb (1980); and Freedman (1978).

III. Local and National Unemployment

Several researchers have examined the effects of plant closings on local labor markets. Bagshaw and Schnorbus (1980) and Aronson and McKersie (1980) found that plant closings increased local unemployment rates but that the increase vanished after 12 months. The local unemployment rate returns to trend levels as a result of re-employment, voluntary and involuntary labor-force dropouts (e.g., retirement vs. "discouraged workers"), and worker relocations. As a direct result of such adjustments, the local labor market tends to shrink as the unemployment rate once again approaches trend levels. The speed of adjustment and the decline in local employment levels may affect local government tax revenues and expenditures. Among three communities studied by Aronson and McKersie (1980), two experienced slight increases in real-estate tax delinquencies, and one suffered a slight decline in sales-tax revenues. In all three cases, the divergence from trend was evident only in the year of the plant shutdown. Neither declines in real-estate values nor increases in local outlays for social services were found in any of the communities (although one reported a marked increase in food-stamp distribution).

Plant closings are considered to be a major source of U.S. unemployment and a significant constraint on the expansion of U.S. employment. Appraisals of the magnitude of the plant-closing problem have been hampered by measurement difficulties and a lack of historical information. Since 1979, Conway Publications has tracked closings of U.S. manufacturing plants, and the California Employment Development Department (CEDD) has collected similar data for all industries in California. The Bureau of National Affairs (BNA) began to track the national private nonfarm business sector in 1982. Conway and BNA base their estimates on many bibliographic sources and an extensive network of contacts with trade associations and federal, state, and local public agencies. CEDD's estimates are based primarily on the state's ES-202 data collection program, conducted under the auspices of the national payroll survey of the Bureau of Labor Statistics.

These data sources are the basis for 1982 estimates of the number of jobs lost through plant closings. The estimates can be compared with measures of labor-market activity to determine the extent to which plant closings cause labor-market problems in the aggregate (see table 7.4). While the estimates differ in terms of geographic

139

Table 7.4

LOSSES FROM U.S. PLANT CLOSINGS, 1982

Measures	BNA[a]: U.S., all industries	BNA[a]: U.S. manu- facturers	Conway[a]: U.S. manu- facturers	CEDD[a]: California, all industries
Number of plant closings	619	424	72	304
Number of jobs affected	215,500	146,900	63,723	57,406
Annual Work Experience Supplement to Current Population Survey[b]				
Unemployment spells, %	0.64	na	na	na
Workers who experienced unemployment, %	0.96	2.49	1.08	na
Unemployment spells exceeding 6 months, %	4.27	11.30	4.90	na

Table 7.4 cont.

Measures	BNA: U.S., all industries	BNA: U.S. manufacturers	Conway: U.S. manufacturers	CEDD: California, all industries
Current Population Survey[b]				
Labor force, %[a]	0.20	0.64	0.28	0.47
Employment, %	0.22	0.72	0.31	0.52
Unemployment, adjusted %[c]	0.95	2.48	1.08	2.23
Unemployment exceeding 6 months, adjusted %[c]	5.07	11.96	5.19	15.76

[a] Alternative sources of dislocation data relative to measures of labor-market activity

[b] The percentages reflect the estimated contribution of dislocated workers to 1982 unemployment spells, workers experiencing unemployment, and unemployment spells of more than six months duration (from the *Annual Work Experience Supplement to Current Population Survey*, Bureau of Labor Statistics) and annual averages for labor force, employment, unemployment, and unemployment of more than six months duration (from the BLS *Current Population Survey*).

[c] To derive a more precise measure of the contribution of plant closings to the average monthly level of unemployment and the average monthly level of workers unemployed for at least six months, we have adjusted the number of dislocated workers to reflect case-study findings on the average duration of dislocated worker unemployment. Aronson and McKersie (1980) provided supplementary unpublished data that were particularly helpful in making these adjustments.

coverage, industry, and underlying definition, it is readily apparent that dislocated workers do not constitute a very large proportion of the national labor force, employment, and unemployment.

In 1982, for example, the BNA recorded 619 plant closings involving 215,500 jobs. Unemployment spells of workers dislocated by these closings accounted for less than 1 percent of the total unemployment spells experienced in the United States in 1982. Similarly, dislocated workers constituted less than 1 percent of the total number of workers who experienced unemployment spells in the year. Dislocated workers achieved a somewhat larger representation among the long-term unemployed and among unemployed manufacturing workers.[3] Based on the CEDD count, plant closings and worker dislocation would appear to be more common in California than in the nation as a whole. However, the CEDD defines plant closings and worker dislocation more broadly than the other sources. While BNA and Conway count only complete plant closings and the number of workers immediately affected by such actions, CEDD measures job losses from the plant's employment peak during the 24 months prior to closing and includes partial closings and "massive" permanent layoffs from continuing plants that affect at least 50 percent of a facility's work force.

The foregoing analysis demonstrates that dislocated worker hardships are not unique; indeed, such hardships are "special" only insofar as the dislocated constitute roughly 5 percent of the long-term unemployed. Plant-closing laws are intended to make our economic system fairer and more equitable, yet their narrow applicability creates inequities. If the existing structure of unemployment protection is inadequate to the needs of the dislocated worker, it is likewise inadequate for the much larger mass of long-term unemployed. It follows that the most appropriate response for public policy would involve the modification and expansion of the existing

[3]The empirical literature on plant relocations also suggests that the number of workers affected by intrastate moves is small relative to labor-market activity. David Birch found that emigration of entire facilities across state lines affected between 0.03 percent and 0.10 percent of the national labor force each year from 1969 to 1976. See Birch, *The Job Generation Process* (Cambridge, Mass.: MIT Program on Neighborhood and Regional Change, 1979). In chapter 3 of this volume, James P. Miller concludes that "relocations play a very minor role in reallocating manufacturing employment among regions . . . [and] that when relocations do occur, the majority involve short-distance, intrastate moves by non-corporate-affiliated employers" (p. 46).

structure of unemployment assistance that would more adequately address the needs of all long-term unemployed workers, including dislocated workers experiencing relatively lengthy unemployment spells.

IV. The Timing of Plant Closings

The existing and proposed plant-closing laws generally require firms to make a lump-sum severance payment to dislocated workers, equivalent to their most recent weekly earnings times the number of years of service for each worker. Firms with no severance-pay protection or with an existing arrangement less generous than required by law would be affected by this provision. Advocates of plant-closing legislation argue that such laws should discourage and/or delay closings, thereby maintaining local employment stability and helping local governments to avoid fiscal distress. Unfortunately, existing plant-closing laws are too recent, have little history of enforcement, and are not sufficiently widespread to facilitate an empirical analysis of their economic effects. Thus, the analysis in this article relies on theoretical tools to indicate the direction but not the magnitude of the economic effects of severance-pay requirements. In this section, we examine whether severance-pay requirements and resulting adjustments by firms would influence the timing of plant closings and, if so, in what direction.

We assume that firms would continue to operate a plant as long as the net present value of future returns from operation remains greater than the net present value of returns from closing, or, alternatively, as long as the internal rate of return (IRR) from operation is larger than the IRR from closing. Let

$$\sum_{t=s}^{T} P_t/(1 + r)^{T-s}$$

represent the net present value of an operating plant's profit stream over a period of $T - s + 1$ years, where the plant becomes obsolete at year T. The symbols P_t and r denote profit in the year t and the discount rate, respectively. The P_t stream is assumed to be nonnegative for simplicity. The net present value of returns from continuous operation of the plant as of year s $(NPVO_s)$ can be expressed as

(1) $$NPVO_s = \sum_{t=s}^{T}\frac{P_t}{(1 + r)^{t-s}} + \frac{SV_T - TSP_T}{(1 + r)^{T-s}},$$

where SV_T and TSP_T are the plant's scrap value and total severance payments at closing, respectively, in year T. The net present value of returns from immediate closing of the plant as of year s ($NPVC_s$) may be written as

(2) $$NPVC_s = SV_s - TSP_s.$$

Closing of the plant at year s rather than at year T makes the firm better off if, and only if, the following condition is satisfied:

(3) $$NPVC_s > NPVO_s,$$

or, equivalently,

(4) $$SV_s - TSP_s > \sum_{t=s}^{T} \frac{P_t}{(1 + r)^{t-s}} + \frac{SV_T - TSP_T}{(1 + r)^{T-s}}.$$

Changes in the severance-pay formula (TSP_s and TSP_T), as well as changes in scrap values (SV_s and SV_T), the profit stream (P_t), and the discount rate (r), can change a firm's decision on the optimal timing for closing by changing the direction of the inequality in equation 4. As an introduction to our main concern—the effects of changes in the severance-pay formula—let us first discuss the potential effects of changes in r, P_t, SV_s, and SV_T. First, $ceteris\ paribus$, an increase in the profit stream (P_t) or the scrap value at year T (SV_T) would delay the closing by increasing $NPVO_s$, while an increase in the scrap value at year s (SV_s) would accelerate the closing by increasing $NPVC_s$. Second, the effect of an increase in r on optimal timing of closing is uncertain, depending on the sign of $P_T + SV_T - TSP_T$. To describe this more clearly, we may rewrite equation 1 by moving $P_T/(1 + r)^{T-s}$ from its first term to its second term, as follows:

(5) $$NPVO_s = \sum_{t=s}^{T-1} \frac{P_t}{(1 + r)^{t-s}} + \frac{P_T + SV_T - TSP_T}{(1 + r)^{T-s}}.$$

Assuming the profit stream to be nonnegative ($P_t \geq O, t = s, \ldots, T-1$) and to be positive for at least one period, an increase in the discount rate (r) always decreases the first term of equation 5. The discount rate sensitivity of the second term of equation 5 depends on the sign of $P_T + SV_T - TSP_T$: an increase in r decreases, does not affect, or increases the second term of equation 5 as $P_T + SV_T - TSP_T$ is positive, zero, or negative, respectively. When the two terms are combined, an increase in r unambiguously decreases $NPVO_s$ and accelerates the closing as long as $P_T + SV_T - TSP_T$ is nonnegative. If the expression $P_T + SV_T - TSP_T$ is negative, an increase in the discount rate reduces the first term and increases the second term in equation 5, thereby making uncertain the effect of a discount rate increase on the sequence of closing-related events.

An increase in TSP_s alone, *ceteris paribus*, would delay closing by decreasing the value of $NPVC_s$; likewise, an increase in TSP_T alone would accelerate closing by decreasing $NPVO_s$. However, the effect of changes in the severance-pay requirement on the optimal timing of closing is uncertain when TSP_s and TSP_T change simultaneously, depending on the size of the discount rate (r) relative to the growth rate of TSP over time (expressed as m). Let us begin from a situation in which $NPVC_s$ equals $NPVO_s$, or, equivalently,

$$
(6) \quad SV_s - TSP_s = \sum_{t=s}^{T} \frac{P_t}{(1 + r)^{t-s}} + \frac{SV_T}{(1 + r)^{T-s}} - \frac{TSP_T}{(1 + r)^{T-s}}.
$$

Then the net present value of returns from closing is the same as that from remaining in operation until time T, and there is no incentive for a firm to advance its expected time of closing from T toward s. If concurrent changes in TSP_s and TSP_T are such that

$$
(7) \quad \Delta TSP_s = \Delta TSP_T/(1 + r)^{T-s},
$$

then the changes do not alter the equilibrium of equation 6, since both sides of equation 6 are simultaneously being changed by the same amount. However, closing would be accelerated if TSP_s and TSP_T change such that

$$
(8) \quad \Delta TSP_s < \Delta TSP_T/(1 + r)^{T-s},
$$

because $NPVC_s$ decreases less rapidly than $NPVO_s$. Equation 8 may be rewritten as

$$
(9) \quad \frac{1}{\Delta TSP_s} > \frac{(1 + r)^{T-s}}{\Delta TSP_T},
$$

or,

(10)
$$\frac{\Delta TSP_T}{\Delta TSP_s} > (1 + r)^{T-s}.$$

Assuming, for simplicity, that the total severance-pay obligation *(TSP)* changes over time at a constant annual rate of *m*, such that $TSP_T = TSP_s(1 + m)^{T-s}$, equation 10 may be rewritten as

(11)
$$\frac{\Delta TSP_s(1 + m)^{T-s}}{\Delta TSP_s} > (1 + r)^{T-s},$$

(12)
$$(1 + m)^{T-s} > (1 + r)^{T-s},$$

(13)
$$m > r.$$

Thus, the optimal time of closing can be accelerated by severance-pay requirements if employers observe that the growth rate of severance-pay liability *(m)* exceeds the discount rate *(r)*. The size of *m* depends on the structure of the laws and on technical and institutional constraints that each plant faces: *m* is likely to be larger for plants whose production functions allow less substitution between capital and labor and less substitution between skilled and unskilled labor. Likewise, plants will have greater difficulty in reducing *m* if their production functions are relatively inflexible, and if the work place is governed by relatively restrictive work and seniority rules. We therefore conclude that the severance-pay provision would not unambiguously delay or otherwise inhibit plant closing. Indeed, depending on institutional and technological conditions, severance-pay requirements may result in earlier closings than otherwise would be the case. Thus, it is possible that plant-closing laws could accelerate both flows into unemployment and the pace of local employment decay.[4]

---

[4]The foregoing analysis was restricted to the effects of severance-pay requirements on plants already located in a given state and effects on the local labor market. The analysis would not, however, be complete without brief comment on the effects of plant-closing laws on potential new investments in a given locality. The literature on this capital-flow question has been limited by the absence of empirical evidence. However, Richard McKenzie, among others, has argued that plant-closing laws reduce the attractiveness to new investment by increasing the cost of doing business in a place that enacts such a law. This assertion is supported by the literature on the effects of certain discretionary government policies, such as environmental protection. We have some reservations concerning the applicability of these examples to plant-closing laws, and we reserve judgment on the issue of plant-closing laws and capital inflows, leaving the question to further research.

V. Distortions of Resource Allocations

Having shown that the timing of a plant closing can be accelerated by plant-closing laws, we now shall show that severance-pay requirements can change the optimal mix of production inputs by changing the perceived prices of the inputs. In the framework of comparative static analysis, we assume that a single-plant firm maximizes its profits *(PRF)* subject to its production function

$$Q = Q (K,L),$$

where K and L denote capital and labor, respectively, and

(14) $$\max PRF = P \cdot Q (K,L) - WL - RK,$$

where P, W, and R represent prices of the product (Q), labor, and capital, respectively. In the short run, where capital is fixed and labor is assumed to be the only variable input, *PRF* is maximized when the wage rate equals the value of labor's marginal product.

Taking the partial derivative of *PRF* with respect to L yields the following first-order condition:

(15) $$W = P \cdot \frac{\partial Q}{\partial L},$$

where the second-order conditions are assumed to be satisfied. In the long run, when the capital stock is allowed to change, profit maximization requires that the price of capital equal the value of its marginal product:

(16) $$R = P \cdot \frac{\partial Q}{\partial K}.$$

In the long run, the profit-maximizing input combination $(K/L)^*$ before the imposition of the severance-pay requirement can be obtained from equation 17, which is derived by dividing equation 16 into equation 15:

(17) $$\frac{W}{R} = \frac{\partial Q/\partial L}{\partial Q/\partial K}.$$

That is, profits are maximized when the ratio of each factor's marginal product equals the ratio of each factor's price.

Suppose plant-closing laws would necessitate severance payments in the amount of *SP* per eligible employee. Although the amount of the severance pay does not increase the "actual" price of labor as long as the plant is in operation, it certainly would increase the "contingent" price of labor unless the firm's subjective probability of closing were zero. Consider a hypothetical situation where plant-closing laws allow voluntary transactions between employers and employees regarding the newly imposed severance-pay requirement and where the transactions costs are relatively low. The firm apparently is "worse off" than in the case of no severance payment, but the workers are "better off" because they can anticipate additional income should the plant be closed. Such an imbalance creates an environment conducive to trading between the employer and employees. Conceivably, the firm might prefer to increase the current level of workers' wages in exchange for the workers' voluntary releasing of the firm from the severance-pay obligation. Likewise, employees may prefer an increase in current wage levels in exchange for future contingent severance pay.

Such transactions would not occur if bargaining failed to achieve a wage increase satisfactory to both parties. Technically speaking, this would take place if the firm's maximum wage offer (FXW) remained below the minimum wage increase acceptable to workers (ENW). The optimal wage increase would, of course, lie between FXW and ENW, but the probability of satisfactory agreement depends on the relative bargaining strength of the parties and the structure of negotiations.

It is not our purpose to elaborate on the likelihood that such voluntary transactions would arise, or the actual determination of the equilibrium level of wage increases. It suffices, rather, to indicate that the subjective wage rate has increased from W to $W + FXW$, and the subjective input price ratio between L and K has increased from W/R to $(W + FXW)/R$ as a result of the severance-pay requirement.[5] The level of FXW would be higher if the firm were relatively risk averse and if the level of SP were relatively high. Excluding the extreme case of perfect factor substitution, the resulting increase in the subjective wage rate would raise the marginal cost of production, in turn reducing the profit-maximizing level of output. In the short run, the entire burden of the output reduction

[5]Another way to look at this is through the insurance concept. If a company could insure against the new liability of severance pay, assuming that no moral hazard prevailed, the insurance premium that the firm would like to pay to the insurance company per each employee would be equal to FXW, the amount of wage-rate increase offered by the firm.

is borne by labor: as the wage rate rises from W to $W + FXW$, the use of labor input would be curtailed to satisfy equation 15.

In the long run, the increase in the marginal cost of production would be smaller than in the short run, because the capital stock would no longer be fixed. Therefore, excluding the extreme cases of zero or infinite factor substitution, the profit-maximizing level of output would fall with the imposition of severance pay, but by less than in the short run. In contrast to the short-run effects, the burden of reduced output in the long run is shared by capital and labor. Nevertheless, labor still would shoulder a disproportionate share of the burden arising from reduced output and from the substitution effect: since the severance-pay requirement increases the subjective input price ratio, the right-hand part of equation 17 must increase to satisfy the profit-maximizing condition. With the assumption of decreasing marginal product, this implies that the optimal input combination $(K/L)^*$ must increase through a greater reduction in labor input (L) than in capital input (K). These would be perverse and unintended consequences of the severance-pay requirement—reduced production and reduced labor demand—considering that increased employment constitutes a key objective of plant-closing laws.

Just as severance pay can affect the quantity of labor used in production, it may also affect the quality of labor. For convenience, we define skilled labor as higher-wage and higher-seniority workers. Suppose the optimal input mix of capital and labor has been pre-determined with regard to the considerations discussed previously. Plant management may wish to manipulate labor quality and quantity to reduce the contingent liability associated with severance-pay requirements. Assuming a production function that allows substitution between the types of labor, plants could hire more skilled labor to keep overall labor productivity constant and reduce the number of workers. Let us suppose that the severance payment to employee h (SP^h) is a simple function of minimum-service years (MSY), years of seniority (SY^h), and current wage level (W^h), as follows:

(18) $$SP^h = a + b \cdot [(SY^h - MSY) \cdot W^h].$$

Total severance payments (TSP) for the plant may then be defined as

$$(19) \qquad TSP = \sum_{h=1}^{H} \{a + b \cdot [(SY^h - MSY) \cdot W^h]\}$$

$$= a \cdot H + b \cdot \sum_{h=1}^{H} (SY^h - MSY) \cdot W^h ,$$

where H is the total number of employees.

Consider three combinations of signs of a and b, as follows:

(a) $a > 0, b = 0$.

In this case, SP^h is a flat payment of equal amounts to employees regardless of years of service or wage level. Plants can reduce TSP by hiring more skilled labor and reducing their overall number of employees (H), while keeping total labor productivity constant.

(b) $a > 0, b > 0$.

In this case, SP^h is a flat payment of equal amounts to each employee, plus a variable payment that increases in accordance with W^h and SY^h (as long as SY^h is greater than MSY). The direction of employment impact is uncertain, because an increase in skilled labor and a reduction in total employment use reduces TSP by lowering the first term of equation 19, $a \cdot H$, but increases TSP by raising the second term (by increasing SY^h and/or W^h). Thus, the direction of change depends on the relative sizes of $a \cdot H$ on the one hand, and

$$b \cdot \sum_{h=1}^{H} (SY^h - MSY) \cdot W^h$$

on the other.

(c) $a = 0, b > 0$.

There is no flat payment in this case, and SP^h is a function solely of SY^h, MSY, and W^h. This severance-pay formula is more relevant than the previous two, since it closely resembles the formulas incorporated in existing and proposed plant-closing legislation. If there were a requirement for minimum years of service to be eligible for severance pay (five years in most laws), plants may wish to add new workers relative to high-seniority skilled workers, attempting to reduce TSP by decreasing $SY^h - MSY$ and W^h. Firms can unambiguously reduce TSP by deliberately hiring new, unskilled workers and letting them go before they have worked MSY years. Therefore, in the absence of effective worker opposition, plants have incentives

150

to increase work-force size, decrease average seniority and average wages, and increase employee turnover. Early retirement of high-seniority workers is one of many methods to reduce average seniority. As a result, high-skilled, high-seniority workers would tend to be worse off with this severance-pay formula.

VI. Policy Implications

Plant closings can result in serious hardship for dislocated workers and their families, including periods of extended unemployment, losses in income and occupational status, deterioration of health, and family difficulties. Yet, the foregoing analysis shows that such hardships (alone or in combination) are not unique to dislocated workers. The same kinds of hardships are prevalent among the long-term unemployed, of which dislocated workers constitute a relatively small part. Plant-closing laws are intended to make our economic system more fair and more equitable, by transferring scarce economic resources to the unemployed. It follows that plant-closing laws might help equalize the disparity *between* the employed and the unemployed members of our society. The laws have the opposite effect, however, *within* the pool of unemployed workers. Plant-closing laws are designed to benefit an arbitrarily defined subgroup of the unemployed: to qualify, a worker must have lost his/her job in a permanent facility shutdown. Dislocated workers receive additional benefits not available to other unemployed workers who share the hardships of unemployment.[6]

Plant-closing laws do not appear to be effective policy instruments. The laws are intended to inhibit closings, yet the standard severance-pay requirement, in many cases, would create incentives for plants to close earlier than they would otherwise. While the laws are intended to reduce the number of unemployed workers (especially high-seniority workers), they may create incentives to reduce overall labor use, increase employee turnover, and shed high-seniority workers more rapidly.[7]

---

[6]Indeed, given that the case-study evidence shows that some dislocated workers experience no unemployment or only brief spells of unemployment and still qualify for benefits, plant-closing laws may exacerbate the inequities between employed and unemployed workers.

[7]If plant-closing laws were more effective policy instruments, their implementation might harm national economic efficiency. Less capital and labor would be available for their most productive and profitable uses. Resources already located in the

The design of plant-closing laws could be modified to make them less ineffective policy instruments, although the adverse effects on within-group distributional equity would remain. The inherent bias against high-seniority workers might be eliminated by exchanging the severance benefit based on years of service and pay for a fixed severance payment per worker. This approach would not, however, eliminate the incentives to use less labor per unit of output. A second possibility would involve shifting the penalty for closing from a labor-based to an asset-based formula: if firms engaged in closings were required to pay a proportional tax on the plant's scrap value at closing, the laws might delay closings in the short run without causing distortions in the optimal mix of productive resources. This approach would not, however, provide much direct financial assistance to dislocated workers, and it might create incentives for firms to keep plants operating with only skeletal work crews.

A more comprehensive unemployment assistance policy, aimed at the structurally unemployed and financed by tax revenues and experience-rated employer payments, would avoid many of the equity, efficiency, and design problems associated with plant-closing laws. Such a policy would deliver general- and specific-skills training, income support, career and job-search planning services, and relocation assistance to the unemployed. It could also include additional incentives for the establishment of ESOPs. This proposal closely resembles the existing structure of unemployment protections, and it could be built on a well-developed administrative delivery system and substantial past program experience. While the existing framework of unemployment protection is by no means perfect (and could certainly benefit from increased coordination), both dislocated workers and the pool of unemployed workers probably would obtain greater benefit from a broad-based approach than from the selective intervention of plant-closing laws.

References

Aronson, Robert L., and Robert B. McKersie. *Final Report: Economic Consequences of Plant Shutdowns in New York State.* Albany, NY: State Employment and Training Council, 1980.

Bagshaw, Michael L., and Robert H. Schnorbus. "The Local Labor-Market Response

affected jurisdiction would be trapped in unproductive pursuits, and resources that might otherwise enter the jurisdiction would be discouraged by higher operating costs.

to a Plant Shutdown," *Economic Review*, Federal Reserve Bank of Cleveland, January 1980, pp. 16–24.

Birch, David. *The Job Generation Process*. Cambridge, MA: MIT Program on Neighborhood and Regional Change, 1979.

Bluestone, Barry, and Bennett Harrison. *The Deindustrialization of America*. New York, NY: Basic Books, 1982.

Bureau of National Affairs. *Layoffs, Plant Closings, and Concession Bargaining: Summary Report for 1982*. Washington, DC: BNA, 1983.

Carlisle, Rick, and Michael Redmond. *Community Costs of Plant Closings: Bibliography and Survey of the Literature*. Washington, DC: C&R Associates for the Federal Trade Commission, 1978.

Cropper, Maureen, and Louis Jacobson. *The Earnings and Compensation of Workers Receiving Trade Adjustment Assistance*. Alexandria, VA: Public Research Institute, 1983.

Dohrenwend, Barbara S., and Bruce P. Dohrenwend, Eds. *Stressful Life Events: Their Nature and Effects*. New York, NY: John Wiley & Sons, Inc., 1974.

Ferman, Louis, and Jeanne Gordus. *Mental Health and the Economy*. Kalamazoo, MI: W.E. Upjohn Institute for Employment Research, 1979.

Freedman, Audrey. *Security Bargains Reconsidered: SUB, Severance Pay, Guaranteed Work*. Report No. 736. New York, NY: Conference Board, 1978.

Gacek, Stanley A. "An Employer's Duty to Bargain on the Termination of Unit Work," *Labor Law Journal*, vol. 32, nos. 10 and 11 (October and November 1981), pp. 659–78, 699–724.

Goldfarb, Robert S. "Compensating Victims of Policy Change," *Regulation*, October 1980, pp. 22–30.

Gordus, Jeanne Prial, Paul Jarley, and Louis A. Ferman. *Plant Closings and Economic Dislocation*. Kalamazoo, MI: W.E Upjohn Institute for Employment Research, 1981.

Gorlin, Harriet. *Personnel Practices I: Recruitment, Placement, Training, Communication*. Bulletin 89, 1981; *Personnel Practices II: Hours of Work, Pay Practices, Relocation*. Bulletin 92, 1981; *Personnel Practices III: Employee Services, Work Rules*. Bulletin 95, Conference Board, 1981.

Hammerman, Herbert. "Five Case Studies of Displaced Workers," *Monthly Labor Review*, vol. 87, no. 6 (June 1964), pp. 663–70.

Harris, Candee S. *Small Business and Job Generation: A Changing Economy or Differing Methodologies*. Washington, DC: Brookings Institution, 1983.

Hekman, John S., and John S. Strong. "Is There a Case for Plant Closing Laws?" *New England Economic Review*, Federal Reserve Bank of Boston, July/August 1980, pp. 34–51, reprinted as Chapter 4 of this volume.

Holen, Arlene. *Losses to Workers Displaced by Plant Closures or Layoff: A Survey of the Literature*. Arlington, VA: Public Research Institute, 1976.

———, Christopher Jehn, and Robert D. Trost. *Earnings Losses of Workers Displaced by Plant Closings*. Alexandria, VA: Public Research Institute, 1981.

Industrial Union Department, AFL-CIO. *Comparative Survey of Major Collective Bargaining Agreements*. Washington, DC: AFL-CIO, 1982.

Jacobson, Louis. *Community-Wide Labor Adjustment to Declining Employment*. Alexandria, VA: Public Research Institute, 1982.

———, and Janet Thomason. *Earnings Losses Due to Displacement*. Alexandria, VA: Center for Naval Analyses, 1979.

Leighton, Julia C., Melissa R. Roderick, and Nancy R. Folbre. " 'Pick Up Your Tools and Leave—The Mill is Down,' Plant Closings in Maine, 1971–1981." Brunswick, ME: Bowdoin College, 1981.

Lipsky, David B. "Interplant Transfer and Terminated Workers: A Case Study," *Industrial and Labor Relations Review*, vol. 23, no. 2 (January 1970), pp. 191–206.

Mick, Stephen S. "Social and Personal Costs of Plant Shutdowns," *Industrial Relations*, vol. 14, no. 2 (May 1975), pp. 203–08.

Millen, Bruce H. "Providing Assistance to Displaced Workers," *Monthly Labor Review*, vol. 102, no. 5 (May 1979), pp. 17–22.

Miller, James P. *Nonmetro Job Growth and Locational Change in Manufacturing Firms.* Washington, DC: U.S. Department of Agriculture, 1980.

———. "Manufacturing Relocations in the United States, 1969–75." Chapter 3 of this volume.

Miner, Mary Green. *Separation Procedures & Severance Benefits, Personnel Policies Forum Survey No. 121.* Washington, DC: Bureau of National Affairs, 1978.

Moen, Phyllis. "Family Impacts of the 1975 Recession: Duration of Unemployment," *Journal of Marriage and the Family*, vol. 41, no. 3 (August 1979), pp. 561–72.

Palen, J. John, and Frank J. Fahey. "Unemployment and Reemployment Success: An Analysis of the Studebaker Shutdown," *Industrial and Labor Relations Review*, vol. 21, no. 2 (January 1968), pp. 234–50.

Scarry, Donald M. *Employee Stock Ownership Plans: A Program for New Jersey.* Trenton, NJ: New Jersey Department of Labor, 1982.

Schumpeter, Joseph A. *Capitalism, Socialism and Democracy.* New York, NY: Harper & Row Publishers, Inc., 1950, pp. 81–6.

Senia, Al. "A Dark Cloud of Plant Closings Hangs over Sunny California," *Iron Age*, vol. 226, no. 8 (March 16, 1983), pp. 28–31.

Sheppard, Harold L., Louis A. Ferman, and Seymour Faber. *Too Old to Work—Too Young to Retire: A Case Study of a Permanent Plant Shutdown.* Washington, DC: Government Printing Office, 1960.

Shostak, Arthur B. "The Human Cost of Plant Closings," *AFL-CIO American Federationist*, vol. 87, no. 8 (August 1980), pp. 22–5.

Site Report, vol. 2, nos. 1–6, Atlanta, GA: Conway Publications, Inc., 1982.

Stern, James. "Evolution of Private Manpower Planning in Armour's Plant Closings," *Monthly Labor Review*, vol. 92, no. 12 (December 1969), pp. 21–8.

———. "The Consequences of Plant Closure," *Journal of Human Resources*, vol. 7, no. 1 (Winter 1972), pp. 3–25.

U.S. Department of Labor, Bureau of Labor Statistics. *Employee Benefits in Industry, 1980.* Bulletin 2107, 1981; *Employee Benefits in Medium and Large Firms.* Bulletin 2140, 1982; *Layoff, Recall and Worksharing Procedures.* Bulletin 1425-13, 1972; *Plant Movement, Interplant Transfer and Relocation Allowances.* Bulletin 1425-20, 1981.

Weiss, Marc A., and Philip Shapira. *Series of Briefing Papers on Assembly Bill 2839,* nos. 1–5. Berkeley, CA: University of California, 1982.

Wilcock, Richard C. "Employment Effects of a Plant Shutdown in a Depressed Area," *Monthly Labor Review*, vol. 80, no. 9 (September 1957), pp. 1047–52.

VIII. Industrial Policy: A Dissent

Charles L. Schultze

The last ten years have been a time of troubles for most of the world's industrial economies. The growth of output and productivity has slowed. Both inflation and unemployment have averaged substantially higher than in earlier postwar years. And the decade has produced the two worst recessions of the postwar period.

In the United States, this experience has spawned two new economic doctrines, each purporting to explain the source of at least some of our economic ills and offering a plan of action to deal with them. These economic theories originated outside of the mainstream of professional economic thought. The first of them is supply-side economics, which is based on a vast exaggeration of the incentive effects of lower taxes. It has had a spectacular political success, and was installed in early 1981 as official U.S. government policy.

The second of these new theories—and the latest entry in the competition for the hearts and minds of political candidates—is a set of economic ideas and policy recommendations that goes by the name "industrial policy." It has been the subject of a growing stream of books and articles; it has been endorsed as a concept by the AFL-CIO; its precepts have been incorporated in a number of bills now before the Congress; and it is receiving a sympathetic hearing from many of the candidates for the 1984 Democratic presidential nomination.

The phrase "industrial policy" means somewhat different things to different people; it refers not so much to a single theory as to a loose collection of similar diagnoses and proposals. The diagnoses generally cluster around two basic propositions:

First, the United States has been "de-industrializing." The share of

"Industrial Policy: A Dissent" by Charles L. Schultze is from *The Brookings Review*, Fall 1983, pp. 3–12. Copyright © 1983 by The Brookings Institution, Washington, D.C.

Charles L. Schultze is a senior fellow at the Brookings Institution and was chairman of the Council of Economic Advisors from 1977 to 1980.

national output generated by manufacturing has been falling in recent years while the share attributable to services has been growing. Within manufacturing a number of essential heavy industries are in absolute decline, and the United States is no longer at the cutting edge of technological advance in the newer, high-tech industries. We are becoming increasingly uncompetitive in world markets. These are the symptoms of deep-seated structural problems; they will not be cured by macroeconomic measures aimed at overall economic growth. The private market is not directing investment to the right places; older manufacturing industries cannot find the funds they need to rehabilitate themselves, and promising new firms in the advancing sectors are often unable to secure as much venture capital as they need for growth. American labor finds it difficult to make the necessary transition from older, declining industries to newer ones with good growth potential and high value-added per worker; this is partly because investment is being directed to the wrong industries and partly because laid-off workers do not have the skills needed or are not in the right locations. And when these dislocated workers eventually do get reemployed it is often in low-skill jobs paying low wages. We are in danger of becoming a nation of hamburger joints and boutique shops.

Second, some other countries—Japan being the preeminent example— have developed governmental policies that successfully promote vigorous industrial growth. The Japanese government identifies potential winners in the competition for world markets and encourages their growth, while simultaneously protecting and easing the burden of adjustment for older but essential heavy industries. Farsighted officials in the Japanese Ministry of International Trade and Industry (MITI), working closely with cooperative Japanese business leaders and bankers, plan and organize, years in advance, such industrial achievements as the penetration of world automobile markets, the development of automated steel mills producing at water's edge for exports, the 256K memory chip, and now the ultimate supercomputer.

The various proponents of industrial policy offer a wide range of suggestions to deal with the structural problems they identify. Many of their proposals involve new or modified federal initiatives in traditional areas: expanded support for technical education; research and development; and programs to retrain workers. Whatever the merits of these ideas, they do not constitute a major new thrust in economic policy. What is new, however, is the proposal

156

that government deliberately set out to plan and create an industrial structure, and a pattern of output and investment, significantly different from what the market would have produced. Two leading advocates of industrial policy, Ira Magaziner and Robert Reich, put the matter this way: "We suggest that U.S. companies and the government develop a coherent and coordinated industrial policy whose aim is to raise the real income of our citizens by improving the patterns of our investments rather than by focusing only on aggregate investment levels."[1]

Industrial policy thus aims to channel the flow of private investment towards some firms and industries—and necessarily, therefore, away from others. The government develops, at least in broad outline, an explicit conception of the direction in which industrial structure ought to be evolving, and then adopts a set of tax, loan, trade, regulatory, and other policies to lead economic activity along the desired path.

Industrial policy typically has two aspects—"picking the winners" and "protecting the losers"—and proponents sometimes disagree as to the relative emphasis to be placed on each. "Picking the winners" involves identifying industries that are at the cutting edge of economic progress, with such characteristics as high growth potential and high value-added per worker, and then providing investment subsidies, research support, and other assistance to existing firms and new entrants in those industries. "Protecting the losers," on the other hand, involves supporting and presumably helping to rehabilitate major declining industries. The government measures that would be deployed for this purpose include creation of barriers against competition from imports, special tax breaks, subsidized loans, and selectively favorable regulatory treatment. In most versions of industrial policy, the government, in a switch from current practice, would require that labor and management in these declining industries accept major reforms—wage restraint, reduction of featherbedding rules, and improved managerial practices—as preconditions for assistance.

In addition to the two explicit propositions noted above—that America has been de-industrializing and that the government of Japan has successfully managed industrial adjustment—there are two *implicit* premises on which the case for a U.S. industrial policy

---

[1]Ira Magaziner and Robert Reich, *Minding America's Business* (New York: Harcourt Brace Jovanovich, 1982), p. 4.

rests. The first of these is that the government has the analytical capability to determine with greater success than market forces what industrial structure is appropriate, who the potential winners are, which of the losers should be saved, and how they should be restructured. The second is that the American political system would (or could) make such critical choices among firms, individuals, and regions on the basis of economic criteria rather than political pressures.

In fact, as we shall see, reality does not square with any of the four premises on which the advocates of industrial policy rest their case. America is *not* de-industrializing. Japan does *not* owe its industrial success to its industrial policy. Government is *not* able to devise a "winning" industrial structure. Finally, it is *not* possible in the American political system to pick and choose among individual firms and regions in the substantive, efficiency-driven way envisaged by advocates of industrial policy.

De-industrialization: A Nonexistent Trend

America has not been de-industrializing. Throughout the industrial world, economic performance in the 1970s did fall behind the record of the 1960s. But relative to the industries of other countries, American industry performed quite well by almost all standards.[2]

During the decade of the 1970s, before the current recession began, the United States was vastly superior to the major European countries and to Japan in the generation of new jobs. Total employment grew by 24 percent in the United States during that decade. The next best performer was Japan, with a 9 percent increase. Other countries were far behind; in Germany, for example, employment actually fell. Moreover, the United States was one of only three major industrial countries—Italy and Canada having been the others—with any increase in *manufacturing* employment. According to OECD data, manufacturing production in the United States, while rising less rapidly than production in Japan, grew faster than the European average and outstripped the gains made in Germany, a

---

[2]In a forthcoming Brookings book, Robert Z. Lawrence documents in substantial detail the absence of any trend toward de-industrialization in the United States during the 1970s and, in particular, the fallacy of the proposition that international trade has contributed to depressing output and employment in American manufacturing. This section of the paper owes much to his work.

country that is usually mentioned, along with Japan, as a leading example of industrial strength.[3]

Manufacturing production in the United States typically rises more in business cycle expansions, and falls further in contractions, than does total GNP. After adjustment for the regular cyclical pattern—and contrary to popular impression—the share of private domestic GNP produced by manufacturing industries did not decline significantly in the 1970s.[4] The proportion of total U.S. employment accounted for by manufacturing has been falling throughout the postwar period, but this principally reflects the fact that productivity growth (output per person) has continued to grow faster in manufacturing than in most other parts of the economy.

The relatively good performance of the industrial sector in the 1970s was partly due to a very large increase during the decade— in fact, a doubling—in exports of American manufactured goods. This was a good bit less than the rise in Japanese exports, but substantially higher than the increase experienced by Europe. America's export strength was aided by a decline in the real exchange value of the dollar, from an overvalued level at the beginning of the decade to what many people believed was a somewhat undervalued level at the end. Since it is unlikely that the value of the dollar will fall steadily over the long run, the share of U.S. economic activity accounted for by the manufacturing sector could conceivably decline very slowly. That would be a natural development,

[3]To reduce distortions caused by cyclical influences (U.S. recessions in 1970 and 1980), average output in 1969–70 and 1979–80 was used to make the decade output comparisons. The European average was held down by the very poor performance of the United Kingdom, but even if the United Kingdom is excluded from these calculations, the growth of manufacturing output in the United States still exceeded that of the rest of Europe as reported by the OECD data. The U.S. Bureau of Labor Statistics produces an alternative set of manufacturing output measures for selected countries; according to these data, the United States outperformed Germany and the average of eight European countries, but grew less than the European average (33.5 versus 36 percent) if the United Kingdom is excluded.

[4]During the cyclical peak of the Vietnam war boom, 1965–69, the constant-dollar manufacturing share averaged slightly higher (30 percent) than it did in both the early years of that decade (28.2 percent) and the last years of the 1970s (28.6 percent), but by no more than can be explained by the strength of the boom. In a regression equation fit to data from 1955–80 that linked the manufacturing share to a cyclical variable and a time trend, the time trend did have a very small negative coefficient of marginal statistical significance. The trend was so slight that it would require some thirty years to reduce the share by one percentage point. There was no evidence that the trend became larger in the 1970s.

159

however, in no way reflecting a structural malaise requiring new governmental policies.

The United States does have some old-line heavy industries with deep-seated structural problems—especially the steel and automobile industries. But they are not typical of American industry generally. There is no evidence that in periods of reasonably normal prosperity American labor and capital are incapable of making the gradual transitions that are always required in a dynamic economy, as demand and output shift from older industries to newer ones at the forefront of technological advances.

Indeed, American industry successfully made some important and desirable structural adjustments in the 1970s, even though that was a decade of economic difficulties throughout the world. Thus, Robert Lawrence of Brookings reports that the U.S. international trade *surplus* in the products of high-tech industries grew from $12 billion in 1972 to $40 billion in 1979, while the trade *deficit* in other manufactured products rose from $15 billion to $35 billion over the same period. Yet, according to a study done for the National Commission for Employment Policy, dislocated workers—defined as unemployed people whose last jobs were in declining industries and who had been out of work for more than eight weeks—amounted to only 0.4 percent of the labor force in March, 1980.[5] In addition, although the total unemployment rate was higher in the United States than in most large European countries as the 1970s drew to a close, long-term unemployment was substantially lower.[6]

But even if it is true that the United States was not de-industrializing in the 1970s, has not the industrial sector performed very much worse than the economy in general during the past several years? Yes, it has. From 1981 through the fourth quarter of 1982—the trough of the recession—GNP declined by 2.2 percent while manufacturing production fell by 10.6 percent. But the outsized

[5]Marc Bendick, Jr., and Judith Radlinski, "Workers Dislocated by Economic Change: Do They Need Federal Employment and Training Assistance?" National Commission for Employment Policy, *Seventh Annual Report*, Appendix B.

[6]Long-term unemployment rates (percent of the labor force) in 1979 were: United States (1.14), United Kingdom (1.92), France (4.41), Germany (3.35). The long-term unemployment definition—fifteen weeks or longer for the U.S., fourteen weeks for the U.K., and three months for France and Germany—does bias the U.S. rate down relative to the others, but not by enough to account for those differences. *Economic Review of the President* (January 1981), p. 127. These findings were confirmed by a later OECD analysis reported in *Economic Outlook* (July 1983), p. 46 (table 15).

drop in manufacturing production occurred for two reasons having nothing to do with de-industrialization. First, as noted above, manufacturing production *always* falls faster than GNP during recessions, and rises faster during booms. In the first half of 1983, for example, as GNP began to recover at a 5.9 percent annual rate, manufacturing production jumped up at a 16.2 percent rate. Second, the huge rise in the real exchange value of the dollar over the last two years discouraged U.S. exports and encouraged foreign imports—a development that had an especially depressing effect on American manufacturing industries. But the overvaluation of the dollar was obviously not caused by structural deficiencies in American industry; it was principally the result of the combination of tight money and loose budgetary policy that gave us unprecedentedly high interest rates. What is needed is a better mix of macroeconomic policies, not a new government agency to influence the pattern of industrial investment.

What about the dramatic fall in the rate of productivity growth in the United States during the 1970s? Does that not reflect, at least in part, a major structural problem in the U.S. manufacturing sector? The pace of productivity growth did, indeed, decrease. While the reasons for this decline are still something of a mystery, a few things are known. First, the decline was worldwide—and its magnitude in the United States was about midway down the list of industrial countries. Second, the decline was not concentrated in manufacturing industries; in fact, by most estimates it was somewhat smaller there than in the other sectors of the economy, and productivity growth has continued to be higher in manufacturing than in most sectors. Third, the decline was not caused by a shift in production away from high-productivity manufacturing industries to low-productivity service industries.[7]

Productivity growth is the source of rising living standards. The sharp decline in that growth, in manufacturing and elsewhere, is the most serious long-run problem facing the U.S. economy. But there is no evidence that this decline stems from a tendency for the private market system to allocate investment to the "wrong" places—away from the manufacturing sector or, within manufacturing, to

[7]Martin Neil Baily estimated, more generally, that none of the slowdown in American productivity growth since 1973 can be explained by a shifting composition of output among major American industries. Baily, "The Productivity Growth Slowdown by Industry," *Brookings Papers on Economic Activity*, 2:1982, pp. 445–51.

the wrong firms or industries. The decrease in productivity growth in no way bolsters the case for an industrial policy.

A Closer Look at the Japanese Success

The postwar flourishing of Japan's economy is frequently cited as the premier example of how successful an industrial policy can be. The Japanese do have a way of working cooperatively towards national economic objectives without getting strangled in bureaucratic red tape or dulling competition among business firms. But the contributions of MITI and of industrial policy to Japan's postwar success have been far overstated. Other factors were primarily responsible for the phenomenal growth that the Japanese economy enjoyed until very recently.

First, over the past two decades, the Japanese saved and invested some 30 to 35 percent of their GNP, compared to 17 to 20 percent in the United States.[8] Second, with an industrial plant technologically far behind those of the United States and Western Europe, Japanese business firms were able to put the huge savings to work at moderate risk and with good returns by upgrading their capital stock with known technologies. Countries that were much nearer to the technological frontier, like the United States, had to depend more heavily for their economic growth on the gradual advance of technical knowledge. Third, the Japanese appear to have developed a unique set of cooperative labor-management relationships that promote high quality work and rapid productivity growth.

Throughout the postwar period, the Japanese government in general, and MITI in specific, did act on a broad view of what was required for rapid economic growth in the particular circumstances facing Japan. For example, private savings and investment were encouraged by tax laws and other measures. Up through the early 1970s, macroeconomic policies were highly expansive, but with a combination of very stimulative monetary policies and large budget surpluses. Thus, the government endeavored to encourage the rapid expansion of both demand and supply. Since it needed to import virtually all of its fuel and raw materials, Japan discouraged the import of manufactured goods. Especially in the earlier part of

---

[8]Based on OECD estimates of gross fixed capital formation as a percent of gross domestic product (GDP). *Economic Outlook 1960–1980*, Table R-3. The difference between GDP and GNP is small and does not affect the basic comparison between the United States and Japan.

162

postwar history, when it was still lagging behind other major countries in industrial technology, Japan protected large segments of its home market against import competition.

But while a broad strategy along these lines did guide Japanese economic policy during the postwar period, that strategy did not dictate the detailed structure of Japanese industry. The major decisions about where funds would be invested were made by Japanese business leaders, not by MITI. Hugh Patrick, professor of Far Eastern economics at Yale, has put forward this assessment:

> Indeed, looking at Japanese industrial development as a whole in the postwar period, I think the predominant source of its success was the entrepreneurial vigor of private enterprises that invested a good deal and took a lot of risks. The main role of the government was to provide an accommodating and supportive environment for the market, rather than providing leadership or direction. Unquestionably government planning bodies were important in a few industrial sectors, but not in many others, which flourished on their own.[9]

The Japanese government, through its Fiscal Investment and Loan Program (FILP), does control substantial investment sums, amounting in 1980 to some $80 billion in direct investments, subsidized loans, and loan guarantees. Such a large investment budget does seem to offer potential leverage for carrying out an industrial policy. In fact, however, as Brookings' Philip Trezise carefully documented in the Spring, 1983, issue of the *Review*, the government's investment portfolio is spread across a wide range of enterprises in response to regional, political, and special interest pressures. In 1979, the FILP budget was allocated among some fifty separate agencies, plus a number of local governments. The local governments, together with four agencies (a housing loan corporation, two small business financing entities, and the Japanese National Railways), got a total of 60 percent of the funds. Another 27 percent went to such entities as the Ex-Im Bank; the Japan Highway Corporation; the Japan Housing Corporation; the Agriculture, Forestry, and Fisheries Corporation; and the Japan Development Bank.

The Japan Development Bank (JDB), in turn, seems a likely candidate for the role of financing an industrial policy aimed at building

[9]Interview in *Manhattan Report on Economic Policy*, Manhattan Institute for Policy Research, vol. II, no. 7 (October 1982).

up major growth industries. The facts belie this conjecture, too. In the first twenty years of the JDB's life, according to Trezise, three-quarters of its funds went to merchant shipping, electric utilities, and regional and urban development. The burgeoning steel industry, on the other hand, received during these two decades less than one percent ($110 million) of the JDB's financing. Since 1972, in Japan as in the United States, public investment has emphasized energy and pollution control—and the JDB budget reflects this trend. But JDB investment in the development of new technologies outside of the energy industry has averaged only $313 million a year over the past decade.

Thus, in Japan as in any other democratic country, the public investment budget has been divvied up in response to diverse political pressures. It has not been a major instrument for concentrating investment resources in carefully selected growth industries. Indeed, if one changed the institutional labels, the Japanese government's investment budget looks remarkably like what might have emerged from a House and Senate conference committee on public works in the United States Congress.

All of this is not to suggest that MITI had no influence on the direction of Japanese industrial investment. For example, MITI is widely, and probably quite correctly, cited as having played a major role in organizing the very successful Japanese penetration of the memory chip segment of the world semiconductor markets. As Paul Krugman has pointed out, however, the relevant question is whether this particular use of Japanese savings generated a higher return for the nation than would have been earned had the market allocated the funds.[10] It may have done so, but we do not yet know the answer.

MITI has also had some major failures. For instance, MITI tried very hard—and, as is evident, to no avail—to keep Honda out of the automobile business and to consolidate Japanese auto production into a few giant companies. MITI also attempted to get a major commercial aircraft industry going in Japan, but the banks failed to follow MITI's lead and would not provide the necessary capital. Those who attribute Japan's economic success principally to MITI's industrial policy seem to be suggesting that without MITI the huge

[10]Paul Krugman, "Targeted Industrial Policies: Theory and Evidence," a paper prepared for the Conference on Industrial Change and Public Policy, sponsored by the Federal Reserve Bank of Kansas City, August 25–26, 1983, pp. 46–49.

30 to 35 percent of GNP that the Japanese invested in the past several decades would have gone mainly into such industries as textiles, shoes, plastic souvenirs, and fisheries. This is sheer nonsense. Given the quality of Japanese business executives, those massive investment funds probably would have wound up roughly where they actually did. And to the extent that there would have been differences, there is no reason to believe that MITI's influence, on balance, improved the choices in any major way.

The combination that worked so well for Japan—a huge saving rate, aggressive business leaders, and a backlog of modern technology waiting to be exploited—may now be faltering. In particular, as Japan has caught up to the technological frontier of other Western countries, the potential for large returns from investment in known technologies has been reduced. The propensity to save remains high, but investment opportunities appear to have dwindled. Partly for this reason, Japanese economic growth, while still above that in other advanced countries, fell from an average of 9.9 percent a year between 1960 and 1973 to 3.5 percent a year between 1973 and 1983.[11]

Identifying the "Right" Industrial Structure

Despite the lack of evidence that the United States has been deindustrializing or that the key to Japan's economic success has been its industrial policy, advocates of an industrial policy for the United States nevertheless propose that the federal government play a much enlarged role in determining the structure of American industry. The centerpiece of an industrial policy is some kind of a development bank—a new Reconstruction Finance Corporation—with authority to do some or all of the following: provide loans, loan guarantees, and subsidies to business firms and regional development bodies; certify firms as being eligible for special tax breaks; recommend measures to protect domestic industries against competition from imports; and negotiate restructuring agreements with labor and management in firms and industries that are in trouble and are candidates for assistance. In many versions of industrial policy, the new RFC would be governed, or at least be advised, by a tripartite body made up of representatives from business, labor, and government. The powers of the Corporation would be exercised in pursuit of explicit industrial objectives designed to achieve

[11]1983 growth as forecast by the OECD, *Economic Outlook*, July 1983.

165

some combination of the two broad goals—stimulating the emergence and growth of new high-tech industries and protecting and rehabilitating older industries.

The first problem for the government in carrying out an industrial policy is that we actually know precious little about identifying, before the fact, a "winning" industrial structure. There does not exist a set of economic criteria that determine what gives different countries preeminence in particular lines of business. Nor is it at all clear what the substantive criteria would be for deciding which older industries to protect or restructure.

Originally, comparative advantage and international specialization among countries were thought to derive principally from the relative abundance or scarcity of the factors of production—labor, capital, and various natural resources. The United States and other advanced industrial countries do in fact have a broad advantage in the production of those goods that are research-based and technologically sophisticated, and that require for their production an educated labor force. It is also demonstrably the case that the availability of certain kinds of natural resources can play an important role in determining comparative advantage. But beyond these very broad principles, there are no general criteria that allow one to predict the industries in which a country will be particularly successful.

Advanced industrial countries both export and import a wide range of goods that covers almost the entire spectrum of their manufacturing industries. Exports are not concentrated in one set of selected industries and imports in another. One study has shown, for example, that in major countries very few industries, classified at a medium (three digit) level of detail, had less than 30 percent of their international trade as *intra*-industry trade—i.e., in most categories of industrial goods, international trade involved significant volumes of *both* exports and imports, rather than exclusively one or the other. The distribution among advanced nations of the production of various manufactured products is not principally a function of some broad set of national characteristics, but arises in large part from quite different causes.

In an insightful article on industrial policy, Assar Lindbeck of the University of Stockholm has analyzed the origins of industrial specialization among advanced countries.[12] He argues that what a country

[12]Assar Lindbeck, "Industrial Policy as an Issue in the Economic Environment," *The World Economy*, December 1981, pp. 391–405.

will specialize in is determined by a combination of historical coincidence and momentum. Individual entrepreneurs search for a niche in the market. Once one or more firms in a country successfully establish a foothold in the market for some special product, forces come into play that can heighten, at least for a while, that country's comparative advantage in the manufacture of that product. A growing market leads to economies of scale for the original producers. Ancillary firms spring up to supply the new industry's special needs. Workers and managers acquire skills and know-how. Success tends to breed success.

In short, the winners emerge from a very individualistic search process, only loosely governed by broad national advantages in relative labor, capital, or natural resource costs. The competence, knowledge, and specific attributes that go with successful entrepreneurship and export capability are so narrowly defined and so fine-grained that they cannot be assigned to any particular nation. The "winners" come from a highly decentralized search process, the results of which cannot be identified on the basis of abstract criteria. As Lindbeck points out, there is nothing in Swedish natural resources or national character that would have foreordained that Sweden would be preeminent in the production of ball bearings, safety matches, cream separators, and automatic lighthouses. Nor, it might be added, is there a basis in observable national characteristics to have predicted Japanese dominance in the motorcycle industry or the American success in pharmaceuticals and the export of construction management and design.

There are, of course, overall policies that government can pursue to create the kind of environment in which a decentralized search process is most likely to be fruitful. What government cannot do—except perhaps in a country that is far behind the leaders and simply trying to catch up by imitating them—is to identify in advance the particular lines and products in which its country will be successful.

Some have argued that a new industrial policy should particularly seek to reallocate investment towards industries with high value-added per worker and away from those with low value-added. The argument for such a reallocation implicitly assumes (1) that there are large numbers of skilled American workers trapped in low-paying jobs in industries with low value-added per worker; (2) that there are large untapped markets for the products of high value-added industries employing skilled workers; and (3) that this situation exists because of a propensity on the part of American business to invest too much in the low value-added, and too little in the high value-added, industries. Government policies designed to improve the skills of the labor force make good sense. But given the current mix of skills in the labor pool, there is no evidence that market forces in the United States have tended to ignore potentially large returns in industries with high value-added per worker and to channel excessive investment to those with low value-added. Indeed, as Krugman points out, government redistribution of a fixed aggregate investment from low value-added to high value-added industries would tend to lower employment and output, since capital-labor and capital-output ratios are higher in the latter industries.[13]

There are equally formidable barriers to designing substantively defensible criteria to govern a systematic government policy of trade protection and investment assistance for declining older industries. No one seriously suggests a policy of indiscriminate aid to *all* such industries, so some criteria for choice are necessary. One litmus test that is proposed is the importance of an industry to the national defense; that, however, is almost always a red herring. The national defense/essential industry argument is usually presented in an all-or-nothing mode, as though, in the absence of import protection, the affected industry would disappear. In fact, what is almost always at stake is a much less dramatic change in the industry's fortunes, of a magnitude that is irrelevant to national defense. Whether, for example, the domestic steel industry meets 80 percent of the nation's peacetime needs, as it does now, or only 60 percent is of no significance to the nation's security.

It has also been suggested that we assist those particular older and troubled industries that other governments are heavily subsidizing. The industries we would end up supporting under this decision rule would most likely be those with worldwide excess capacity, in which the returns to investment are unusually low, since those are the ones most apt to be getting help from other governments. A systematic reallocation of investment away from other American industries towards these would lower the growth of national output and real wages.

Ironically, the systematic provision of import protection to various industries, in an effort to "restructure" them, would indirectly weaken the most dynamic and progressive sector of American

---

[13]Krugman, "Targeted Industrial Policies," pp. 6–8.

industry. Import protection would initially worsen the trade balances of the countries against whom it was directed. As a result, their currencies would tend to depreciate against the dollar. In turn, this would impair the competitive position of American export industries, which, by their very nature, are likely to be at the leading edge of economic progress. We would trade jobs and output in the leading sectors for jobs and output in the losing sectors.

In practice, the motivation behind most existing efforts to protect the losers is not so much to improve economic performance as to lessen the pains of economic change. Almost by definition, a dynamic economy is one in which change is continually at work—change in technology, in tastes, and in world markets. And while change creates new opportunities, it also forces some firms, workers, and communities to make painful adjustments.

A decent concern for the human costs imposed by economic change is one hallmark of a compassionate society. But society can act to reduce those costs in two quite different ways. First, it can short-circuit market forces and try to slow the pace of change through subsidies, trade protection, and regulations designed to prop up declining firms. Second, it can attempt to accommodate and ease the transitions dictated by changing economic conditions through the provision of reasonable unemployment compensation, relocation assistance, and generous training opportunities to those facing major adjustment problems. Neither approach will fully insulate workers and communities from the pains of economic change. But systematic application of the first approach, while preventing some pain for some people, will over time sap the economy of dynamism and hold down growth in living standards. The second option is far from perfect, but it offers the potential of reducing transition costs with much less impairment of the dynamism that generates economic growth.

Industrial Policy and the American Political System

Not only would it be impossible for the government to pick a winning industrial combination in advance, but its attempts to do so would almost surely inflict much harm.

There are many important tasks that only governments can do—and, with constant effort and watchfulness, they can do those tasks passably well. But the one that most democratic political systems—and especially the American one—cannot do well at all is to make critical choices among particular firms, municipalities, or

169

regions, determining cold-bloodedly which shall prosper and which shall not. Yet such choices are precisely the kind that would have to be made—and made explicitly—for an industrial policy to become more than a political pork barrel.

The government can, and continually does, adopt policies that have the indirect consequence of harming particular individuals or groups. But a cardinal principle of American government is "never be seen to do direct harm." The formal and informal institutions of the political system are designed to hinder government from making hard choices among specific individuals, rewarding some and penalizing others. So it is, for example, that we have an Economic Development Administration, created to help "depressed areas," that has eligibility criteria so broad that they encompass over 80 percent of the counties in the United States. The same pattern—that of obviating the necessity of choice—is evident in the evolution of the Model Cities Program. Two decades ago, planners in the Johnson administration set out to test the proposition that a very comprehensive assistance program—directed at physical capital, education, retraining, social services, and so on—that concentrated large investment in a few areas could overcome the inertial force and vicious cycle of inner city poverty and decay. A demonstration of this approach was initially designed to be carried out in a very limited number of cities; hence the name "Model Cities Program." By the time the concept had made its way through the political thickets of the administration and the Congress, the Model Cities Program encompassed one hundred and fifty cities, each receiving only a fraction of the funding needed.

It is not surprising that the American political system is seldom capable of making express choices among individuals, firms, or regions. The American government, after all, was not established to bring order and authority out of social chaos. Quite to the contrary, it originated in an effort to reduce what was seen as too much authority on the part of the British king and parliament. Its founders were principally concerned to constrain legislative and executive authorities so that they could not make arbitrary and invidious choices among individuals. In the American system, most decisions that discriminate among specific citizens and firms are reached through litigation in the courts, where "fairness," rather than "efficiency," is the major criterion for settling disputes. When it is necessary to permit executive officials to make such decisions, their exercise of discretion is hedged about by complex procedural safeguards, including the right of appeal to the courts. The Administrative Procedures Act, which governs the exercise of regulatory authority, is a prime example of this approach.

The governmental choices that an industrial policy contemplates have little to do with fairness and much to do, at least ostensibly, with exacting economic criteria. As we have seen, these are precisely the sorts of decisions that the American political system makes very poorly. A new RFC would do no better. For every twenty new entrants into the high-tech race, nineteen will probably perish and only one succeed. But the federal government's portfolio would likely carry all twenty forever.

To be anything more than a universal protector of inefficiency, a systematic program of assistance to declining industries would have to call for some very hard-headed decisions among particular firms, cities, and groups of workers—that the Youngstown plant can live but the Weirton one must close, for example, or that the cotton textile industry has a reasonable chance to rehabilitate itself but the wool textile industry is a hopeless case and must die. Or that in order for the steel industry to compete successfully in world markets, the large increases over the last fifteen years in its wages and fringe benefits relative to those of the rest of industry must be eliminated. Quite apart from the inability of any staff to make such substantive calls correctly, can anyone seriously imagine an American RFC being left alone to make such decisions, with its authorizations and appropriations controlled by the Congress and its policies supervised by a president interested in his own and his party's political success? Rather, we can expect a combination of patterns to emerge: Some assistance would be made available, on a formula basis, to all industries that were in trouble; the wheels with the loudest squeaks might get a bit of extra financial grease; and protectionist interests would have a new and highly vulnerable pressure point to exploit. In the process, resources would be misallocated, incentives for industrial efficiency reduced, and competitive forces blunted.

The False Allure of "Coordination"

One of the most frequently heard arguments for industrial policy is that it would bring a much-needed coordination to government policy-making. Those who make this argument begin by pointing out that the government already has in place many individual policies that affect the industrial structure, often in illogical, contradictory, or harmful ways. They go on to ask why we do not, therefore, adopt a positive and coherent industrial policy in place of the current ad hoc array. These advocates often cite examples of the foolishness that ad hoc assistance decisions lead to:

- The U.S. government now spends five times more on research and development for commercial fishing than for steel.
- The U.S. tax code provides almost $750 million a year in tax breaks for the timber industry, but only a small fraction of that amount for semiconductors.
- We now provide substantial import protection for the carbon and specialty steel industries (an illustration presumably adduced on the grounds that with an industrial policy we would be able to extract more competition-oriented reforms from labor and management in the favored industries).

In fact, this argument makes little sense—even if the examples cited are indeed blunders. It might very well be bad policy to spend five times more on R&D for commercial fishing than for steel (although what is relevant is total R&D, private as well as government, and even then it is not self-evident that the payoff from R&D in commercial fishing is less than from R&D in steel). Tax experts long ago concluded that the special treatment of the timber industry was excessively generous. And virtually all economists would argue that the steel protectionist measures are bad for the country. But these conclusions would all be true even if the term "industrial policy" had never been invented, and regardless of whether industrial production was an increasing or a decreasing share of GNP. Indeed, it is curious logic to cite examples of how the American industrial structure has been distorted by political pressures—in support of an argument for entrusting even more economic decisions to the same political system. One does not have to be a cynic to forecast that the surest way to multiply unwarranted subsidies and protectionist measures is to legitimze their existence under the rubric of industrial policy. The likely outcome of an industrial policy that encompassed some elements of both "protecting the losers" and "picking the winners" is that the losers would back subsidies for the winners in return for the latter's support on issues of trade protection.[14]

[14]The chief executive of a firm producing semiconductors has recently argued that his industry does not need special government help—only a "Buy America" provision for its products.

172

The argument is also made that we do provide assistance to individual firms, on occasion and in a very ad hoc way; the Chrysler and Lockheed bailouts are usually cited as examples. Should we not, therefore, regularize and rationalize this procedure, rather than making these assistance decisions on a case-by-case basis? In fact, the ad hoc approach is precisely the right approach. To every rule there are exceptions. It may very occasionally be in the public interest to supersede the market's judgment and to prevent the bankruptcy of some major firm. But it is a virtue that a special law is now needed for each case. It is a virtue that each case is, in fact, treated as an exception. Only very exceptional cases are likely to muster the support needed to enact a special law, and the government's bargaining power, to impose needed and painful reforms on management and labor, is consequently enhanced. Should this process of decision by exception be supplanted by an ongoing authority to initiate bailouts, the result would almost surely be a politically vulnerable fund, available to help avoid or delay politically sensitive plant closings.

Some Real Problems

To say that industrial policy is a dangerous solution for an imaginary problem is not to say that the United States has no serious economic difficulties. It has a number of them.

Our most immediate set of problems is macroeconomic in nature. Recovery from the deepest recession of the postwar period has just begun. Having paid a very high price for partially wringing out a stubborn inflation fifteen years in the making, we—along with every other industrial country—will have to walk a very fine line to sustain an economic recovery vigorous enough to make substantial inroads on unemployment, but not so buoyant as to risk a resurgence of inflationary pressures or inflationary expectations.

In addition, we in the United States face the special problem of a political impasse that threatens to perpetuate very sizeable federal budget deficits even as the economy recovers towards full utilization of its resources. Since the Federal Reserve is most unlikely to accommodate these high budget deficits with large and inflationary increases in the money supply, failure to break the impasse with tax increases and spending cuts would extend today's high real interest rates—or, more likely, even higher ones—into the indefinite future. This outcome would have particularly serious consequences for the health of America's industrial structure. High interest rates would tend to perpetuate overvaluation of the U.S. dollar, and would continue to penalize American exports and encourage imports. At home, the high interest rates would especially depress purchases of durable manufactured goods. Finally, the ability of new and young enterprises, at the frontiers of technological advance, to raise new capital could be seriously impaired to the extent that the actuality and the expectation of continued high interest rates depressed stock market values.

Getting America's monetary and fiscal policies in order is far more important for the health of the nation's industrial structure than any conceivable set of new industrial policies. What now seem to be serious problems of industrial structure would quickly shrink and become far more manageable with a few years of balanced economic recovery at lower real interest rates.

After the achievement of a sustained and balanced recovery, the prospects for which depend heavily on how the government uses its macroeconomic tools, the next most important factors influencing industrial performance are mainly beyond the government's control—such things as the pace of technological progress, the course of labor-management relationships, and the stability of world markets. There is, however, a variety of governmental microeconomic policies that can affect, favorably or unfavorably, the vigor and adaptability of American industry. Choices among alternatives in this area sometimes pose very difficult tradeoffs between economic efficiency and other social goals. For example, environmental considerations compete with the objective of keeping industrial costs low. The provision of generous tax incentives for risk bearing has to be balanced with the objective of a more equal distribution of income. Additional federal support for scientific and technical education would conflict with the goal of budget expenditure control. In other cases, what is at issue is not a tradeoff among competing national objectives, but the reform or elimination of provisions in tax or regulatory codes that distort the pattern of investment among different industries. The 1981 liberalization of depreciation allowances, for example, was desirable in the aggregate but very arbitrary as among investments of different types. It sharply skewed rates of return and distorted investment incentives among industries. Determining the federal government's stance on these and other thorny issues will continue to provide grist for the legislative and political mills in the years ahead. How they are settled will

174

have an important, even if not overwhelming, influence on the behavior of American industries.

The most critical and vexing structural problems that American society will have to face in the coming decade have little to do with the issues raised by industrial policy. Even with a return to prosperity, unemployment among America's black youth will remain scandalously high. Large parts of American central cities will continue to be afflicted by serious financial constraints, social problems, and physical decay. And, if recent studies are to be believed, the quality of American education has been deteriorating for a number of years. Unfortunately, no one yet seems to have a very clear idea of exactly how the federal government can best play a constructive role in fundamentally reversing these very troubling structural trends. But we must keep searching for solutions—and where federal outlays are required to experiment with promising approaches, these are the areas, unlike most others, where the benefit of the doubt ought to be given a little more rather than a little less funding.

In sum, there are changes in federal fiscal and monetary policies that could help the economy generally, and industry in particular, attain a more satisfactory level of economic prosperity. There are microeconomic policies that we know could contribute to an environment that is favorable to the creation of new and rapidly expanding lines of business and to the adaptability of American industry. In many cases, formulating these policies requires making some very difficult choices among competing national objectives.

In addition, there are a few very important structural problems for which, at the moment, no convincing solutions are in sight. Yet it is absolutely essential that we keep searching and experimenting to try to solve them.

One structural problem, however, that does *not* exist is the deindustrialization of American industry. And one set of government measures that we do *not* need is an industrial policy under which the federal government tries to play an important role in determining the allocation of resources to individual firms and industries.

We have enough real problems without creating new ones.

175

IX. The Myth of Deindustrialization
William H. Branson

Discussion of industrial policy is heard everywhere in Washington today, as political campaigners gear up for 1984. Deindustrialization theorists present an image of an American economy so muscle-bound that it cannot cope with instability and structural change in the world economy and is inevitably losing its presence in basic industries. For some unknown reason, McDonald's ubiquitous hamburgers are a favorite illustration of the problem. A May (1983) issue of *Time* magazine, for example, quotes the chairman of Firestone Tire and Rubber as saying, "It is utter nonsense that we are going to become a high-tech and service economy. The high-tech companies have more manufacturing offshore than here. The idea that we can have an economy by selling hamburgers to each other is absurd." Hamburgers aside, the comment reflects the widely felt fear that basic industries will "disappear" due to foreign competition, leaving the United States with no manufacturing capacity or jobs. To survive, it is argued, the economy needs an industrial policy, as well as some sort of protection against outside shocks.

The data on the changes in the composition of U.S. trade since World War II, however, tell just the opposite story. They show a flexible economy that is moving labor and capital resources into sectors where the U.S. performs best in a world of increasing economic integration and competitive pressure.

This flexibility has costs, which are emphasized by the deindustrialization theorists. Plants close or move, labor requires retraining, equipment becomes obsolete, towns and cities shrink or grow. The declining industries lobby Congress for protection and try to convince the public that the United States is losing out in international trade. But the movement of resources away from declining, low-

"The Myth of Deindustrialization" by William H. Branson is reprinted with permission from *Regulation,* September/October 1983.

William H. Branson is a professor of economics and international affairs, Woodrow Wilson School, Princeton University.

productivity industries is a movement toward high-productivity areas of expansion. The flexibility of our economy permits, even encourages, adjustment to the changing world economy and the changing U.S. position in it. Rather than an industrial policy aimed at supporting declining industries or subsidizing already profitable ones, we need an adjustment policy that minimizes the costs of flexibility.

Since World War II, U.S. trade has gone through two major adjustment periods. First came the erosion in our temporary post-war position of being net exporters of nearly everything. As the economies of Europe, Japan, and the newly industrializing countries gained strength, U.S. trade moved back to its pre-war pattern. The second adjustment followed the oil price increases of 1973–74 — which raised our net oil import bill by $65 billion between 1973 and 1981. The changes that enabled us to pay that bill were dramatic. Our trade surplus in capital goods alone, for example, rose by $32 billion.

The economic strength that those adjustments reflect is based on a productive agricultural sector and on an educated and flexible labor force. Growth in manufacturing exports comes in sectors that use intensively the skills embodied in the labor force, while imports squeeze industries that are older, more capital-intensive, and based on routine operations. As industries such as autos, textiles, and steel became internationalized during the seventies, the U.S. retained its comparative advantage in the high-skill, high-technology ends of those industries, and lost only the lower-skill manufactures to the developing countries.

Since 1981, high real interest rates and an overvalued dollar have temporarily (it is to be hoped) halted this successful process of structural adjustment in the U.S. economy. They have produced a doubly depressing effect on the industries that manufacture durable, tradeable goods: autos, steel, equipment. This, in turn, has added to pressures for industrial policy or for protection—because a *macroeconomic* problem is misdiagnosed as a trade problem. The basic problem in these industries since 1981 has been caused by fiscal and monetary policy, and will not be rectified by trade or adjustment policies.

A Pocket History of U.S. Postwar Trade

During the years just after World War II, the United States was a net exporter of all kinds of manufactures that it would normally import. This artificial situation could not last. The adjustment back to a "normal" competitive position, which was largely completed in the 1960s, is summarized in table 9.1.

The broad outlines of the "normal" position can be seen as early as 1930. The United States was a major net exporter of fuel, capital goods, and autos—the latter two being the high-technology industries of the time—and an importer of consumer goods and industrial inputs other than fuel or chemicals. Trade in agricultural goods was roughly balanced, and the chemical and arms industries were just developing. This pattern held even after the full force of the Great Depression hit the U.S. economy in the 1930s, with two exceptions. The midwestern drought and depopulation led to large imports and trade deficits in agriculture from 1935 to 1939, and the growing chemical industry was providing a rapidly increasing surplus. These trends are reflected in the 1937 trade figures. The high-skill, high-technology basis for our comparative advantage in trade was well established before World War II.

The 1947 data in table 9.1 show clearly the effect of World War II. The United States had substantial surpluses in all categories that year, including nearly $1 billion in each of its traditional import fields of consumer goods and other industrial materials. And the overall trade surplus reached a post-war peak of $9.5 billion, compared with $0.3 billion in 1937. In those years, we were, indeed, a supplier of all goods to the world. This sudden expansion in world demand for American manufactures gave birth to plants and industries that could not possibly survive when international competition was reestablished. It was the pressure on these noncompetitive industries during the 1950s that helped create the post-war impression that the United States was losing out in trade. Actually, our trade was just moving back to its pre-war basis of comparative advantage.

Comparison of the data for 1930, 1937, and 1960 is convincing on this point. In all categories except agriculture, the *pattern* of surpluses and deficits was the same in 1960 as in 1930 and 1937—although the surpluses and deficits were generally larger, reflecting the overall expansion of world trade. We had also become a major exporter of farm products.

During the decade of the 1960s, the dollar was increasingly overvalued, and that led to a shrinkage in the United States' shares of world manufacturing exports and in its overall trade surplus, from $5.5 billion in 1960 to $3.3 billion in 1970. This was also partly due

Table 9.1

TRENDS IN THE U.S. TRADE BALANCE, 1930–81
(millions of dollars)

Year	Agricultural Goods	Industrial Supplies and Materials			Capital Goods	Consumer Goods	Automotive Products	Military Goods	Total[a]
		Fuels and Lubricants	Chemicals	Other					
1930	15	433	3	−271	518	−92	282	7	782
1937	−459	395	22	−184	486	−38	353	22	265
1947	1,604	1,013	553	890	3,144	958	1,147	174	9,530
1960	857	−739	1,128	−1,226	4,949	−505	633	804	5,528
1970	558	−1,384	2,216	−3,163	10,557	−4,834	−2,242	1,230	3,303
1973	8,023	−6,369	3,137	−5,854	13,928	−8,481	−4,543	1,385	1,863
1981	24,308	−71,333	11,995	−13,325	45,680	−22,864	−11,750	3,608	−27,566

SOURCE: Department of Commerce, *Highlights of U.S. Export and Import Trade*, FT-990.

[a]Total figures reflect two categories that are not included in the table and that showed a surplus of $6.2 billion in 1981.

to the overheating of the economy during the expansion phase of the Vietnam War, 1965–68. As much of the automobile industry lost its high-technology character and production became routinized, activity moved abroad to low-wage areas—shifting U.S. trade in autos from a surplus to a deficit of $2.2 billion. In addition, as the growth in fuel demand outpaced supply and major sources were developed in the Arab world, our small fuel deficit grew to $1.4 billion. But the biggest change in trade during the decade came in capital equipment, where the surplus increased by $5.5 billion. By 1970, even with an overvalued dollar and deficits in fuel and autos, net exports in capital goods, chemicals, and military equipment were big enough to provide a trade surplus of $3.3 billion.

The pattern of trade in 1973 was much the same as in 1970. The main differences are in agriculture, where major strength was developing, and in fuel, where the deficit increased by $5 billion in response to the first signs of the collapse in the oil companies' power and the rise in OPEC's. The real devaluation of the dollar had stabilized the U.S. share of world manufactures exports.

The year 1973 marked the end of the U.S. post-war adjustment. Trade was roughly balanced. We had large and growing export surpluses in our areas of comparative advantage—agriculture, capital and military equipment, chemicals—along with corresponding deficits in lower-technology areas such as consumer goods, autos, industrial supplies, and in fuel. Growth in these deficits and surpluses signaled a continuing transfer of capital and labor resources from declining low-productivity to expanding high-productivity industries. The United States was set for a resurgence of expansion after the Vietnam debacle and the devaluations of 1971–73.

Then came the oil price shock of 1974, which set off a series of oil price increases that hiked U.S. net imports of fuel from $6.4 billion in 1973 to $71 billion in 1981. Yet, over that period, our total trade deficit increased by only $29 billion. This means that enough resources were transferred from production for domestic use to production for export to produce an additional $36 billion in net exports. The growth in U.S. exports is the real economic news of the 1970s.

Which sectors were expanding net exports to pay for the additional fuel bill, and pulling resources away from domestic consumption? The answers are summarized in table 9.2. Agriculture, capital goods, and chemicals led the way. Between 1973 and 1981, these three areas of U.S. comparative advantage *increased* their net

Table 9.2

CHANGES IN U.S. TRADE BALANCES, 1973–81
(billions of dollars)

Surplus categories	
Agricultural goods	16.3
Capital goods	31.8
Chemicals	8.8
Military equipment	2.2
Other	5.6
Deficit categories	
Other industrial supplies	−7.5
Consumer goods	−14.4
Automotive products	−7.2
Fuel	−65.0
Net change	−29.4

export surplus by $57 billion! The deficit sectors also showed significant increases. These increasing import deficits release resources from low-productivity sectors, freeing them to move to a higher-productivity employment.

The adjustment of the 1970s, then, had two aspects. First, there was a massive increase in exports in agriculture and relatively high-technology capital goods and chemicals, helping to pay for the rising oil bill imposed by the oil price increases. Second, there was a continuation of the 1960s trend toward specialization along lines of comparative advantage, with rising surpluses in areas of relative strength and increasing deficits in areas characterized by lower technology, low-skill requirements, and routinized operations. In short, the record shows that the U.S. economy is not a noncompetitive producer in manufactures, but rather has undergone a structural adjustment toward areas of comparative advantage. This adjustment process must be nurtured and eased by policy, not stifled by protection of low-productivity jobs.

Sources of U.S. Comparative Advantage

Any voluntary trade, whether between nations or persons, is based in some way on *relative*, or *comparative*, advantage. This is so obvious at the personal level that we usually do not even notice it. In all but the most backward economies, individuals specialize in their work on what they do best and then exchange their incomes for a whole range of goods that others produce. Our sales of labor services are our exports, and our purchases of consumer goods are our imports. This specialization along lines of comparative advantage depends on kinds and amounts of education and training, personal factors like strength, speed, manual skills, our preferences for kinds of work, and luck. The point is that there is a basis for the specialization and we all gain from trade. We would all be worse off if we could not specialize in production and trade the results.

In *international* trade, countries also specialize in production, and then trade for the broad range of consumer and investment goods their economies require. The basis for comparative advantage is obvious in the case of some countries, especially those with heavy endowments of natural resources. The comparative advantages of Kuwait in oil, South Africa in diamonds, Chile in copper, and Brazil in coffee are pretty easy to understand. Less clear is the source of comparative advantage between the industrialized countries of Europe, Japan, North America, and the newly industrializing countries.

The very stable *pattern* of trade that the United States has had since the late 1960s is based on our relative advantage in land and highly trained and skilled labor. In agriculture, the two combine in an extremely productive and low-cost sector that produces an export surplus of some $25 billion a year, even in the face of highly protected agriculture in Europe and Japan. In manufacturing, the U.S. comparative advantage in a skilled, educated, and mobile labor force permits U.S. industry to concentrate on production that requires high-skill inputs and uses the latest technology. These products tend to be new and to be produced in nonroutine ways that require thought and initiative in the workplace. These are the capital goods and military equipment industries, chemicals, and the innovative and high-technology end of basic industries.

Economists combine all kinds of marketable skills that are embodied in the work force in the concept of "human capital." This is the capital accumulated through years of education, on-the-job training, and experience, and embodied in the individual worker. The difference between the unskilled worker's wage of around $5 an hour and the aircraft mechanic's wage of over $20 is the return on the latter's investment in human capital.

U.S. industry increasingly concentrates on goods that intensively use human capital in production. This pulls resources—labor and "ordinary" capital—from goods that use unskilled labor more intensively in production, and the production of these goods moves to countries with a comparative surplus of literate and disciplined but unskilled labor. The unskilled labor-intensive operations tend to be repetitive, disciplined processes and production lines. They produce the U.S. imports.

The correlation of human-capital intensity in U.S. exports and unskilled labor in imports is conventional wisdom among researchers on U.S. trade. In my study with Nicholas Monoyios, human capital consistently had the highest positive correlation with net exports, and unskilled labor the highest negative correlation (*Journal of International Economics*, 1977). Keith Maskus and Robert Stern studied data for each year from 1958 to 1976 and obtained the same results (*Journal of International Economics*, 1981). Clearly the United States should look after its trade advantage in a skilled and mobile labor force.

A trade advantage in skilled labor also shows up in the use of frontier industrial technology in our export industries. The way an industry best uses skilled labor is in producing new and developing goods or using new and evolving processes. This is the basis of the concept of the "product cycle" pioneered by Raymond Vernon. High-technology countries innovate and produce high-technology products, gradually developing export markets. When the products become standardized and production routinized, manufacture shifts to areas with lower-skilled workers and lower wages; and the products become imports for the high-technology countries, whose industries move on to new frontiers. This is the story of trade in basic U.S. industries, as told below.

The very strong correlation of U.S. exports and high technology, as well as of U.S. imports and low or routine technology, is shown in figure 9.1. (High-technology industries are defined as those having high R&D expenditures relative to total sales and a high proportion of skilled labor in their work force; the low-technology industries have low R&D expenditures and a low proportion of skilled workers.) The difference in trade patterns is striking. U.S. low-technology products show a deficit that has been growing exponentially since the early 1960s, reaching about $35 billion in 1980. Over the same period, the U.S. high-technology *export* surplus grew first steadily and then explosively, climbing from $12 billion to $40 billion in the last seven years. Again the economy's adjustment to the oil price shock is apparent. U.S. exports of high-technology

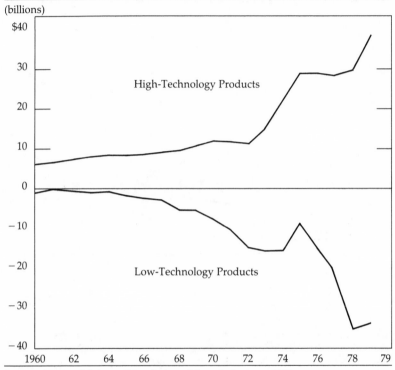

Figure 9.1

U.S. TRADE BALANCE IN HIGH-TECHNOLOGY
AND LOW-TECHNOLOGY PRODUCTS, 1960–79

(billions)

High-Technology Products

Low-Technology Products

1960 62 64 66 68 70 72 74 76 78 79

SOURCE: National Science Foundation, *Science Indicators—1980.*

goods, which tend to be capital goods and chemicals, increased rapidly as the economy moved resources into these sectors.

Most of that increase after 1973, as figure 9.2 shows, was in exports to the developing countries. The U.S. high-technology surplus with these countries increased from $6 billion in 1973 to $25 billion by 1980. Our high-tech trade with Western Europe as a whole also showed a surplus that was growing but not nearly so fast. (This slowly increasing U.S. surplus, at least until 1980, reflects the tendency for industry in Western Europe to fall behind in high-technology manufacturing.) In contrast, our high-tech trade with Germany has remained roughly balanced, while that with Japan has shown an increasing deficit since the mid-1970s.

185

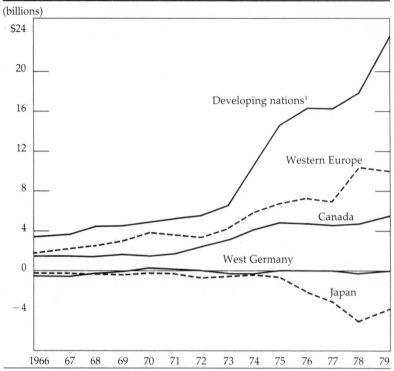

Figure 9.2

U.S. TRADE BALANCES IN HIGH-TECHNOLOGY PRODUCTS

SOURCE: National Science Foundation, *Science Indicators—1980.*
[1]Includes the Republic of South Africa in 1966 and 1967.

The data of figure 9.2 signal two points. First, the developing countries are an increasingly important market for U.S. manufactured exports, probably because our advantage in the goods that are produced with skilled labor is greatest *relative* to these countries. Second, Japan is our major competitor. The picture is one of our competing with Japan for developing-country markets in the years to come.

Will Basic Low-Technology Industry "Disappear"?

The increasing trade deficits in the low-technology sectors mean a loss of jobs in these sectors. But the fear that whole industries will disappear stems from the misconception that these large basic

186

industries—autos, steel, and textiles—are big, homogeneous, backward sectors. The truth is that they are made up of many subsectors. Some of the subsectors are very high-technology and skill-intensive, and in these the United States will become more competitive and will even expand its share. Other subsectors produce standard products using standard methods and a lower level of skills, and here we will become less competitive over time. These are the shrinking subsectors of the basic industries. The U.S. steel and textile industries will not "disappear." Rather they will concentrate on the advanced end of the industry, allowing the routine and lower-skill end to move abroad.

A few details will show how this process works. The iron and steel industry trade data can be broken down into three subsectors—basic materials for iron and steel, iron and steel products *except* advanced manufactures, and finished metal shapes *and* advanced manufactures. Basic materials have high transportation costs and therefore, as would be expected, show a small trade balance. Standard products, whose production is routinized and capital-intensive, show a growing deficit as manufacturing has moved abroad. Finished products, especially advanced manufactures, have remained competitive and have turned in a small surplus since the early 1970s. Far from vanishing, the American steel industry is being transformed through trade into a relatively high-technology industry!

The same is true in textiles. This industry's trade data can be broken into two subsectors. At the low-technology, low-skill end are consumer textiles, the imported clothes and fabrics that are familiar to us all. At the high-technology end are "industrial textiles," synthetic fibers that are used as industrial inputs and that are frequently produced with highly automated, computer-controlled processing equipment. The new technology began to take hold around 1970, stimulating a wave of investment and creating for the United States a comparative advantage in this end of the industry. Since 1974 we have run a surplus in industrial textiles. Here again, trade is transforming an industry's base from low skills and routine operations to high skills and technology.

A final example is provided by the auto industry, whose death has been proclaimed by so many of its own executives and union leaders. In fact, however, the auto industry has become a world industry, with worldwide rationalization of production. Assembly is done near the consuming market, with parts coming from many areas. Each country will fit into this world picture, depending on which sector it provides best. To quote from Marina Whitman, distinguished economist and vice-president of General Motors:

> Under the "world car" concept, automobiles little differentiated in size and design among different geographic areas are assembled from parts and components that are to a large extent standardized and interchangeable. The expanded production takes advantage of economies of scale and the allocative efficiencies generated by differences in factor endowments and therefore in production costs. . . . One of the implications of these developments for the automotive trade is that the strategy of direct exports of finished vehicles will be replaced gradually by more complex trading relationships involving vehicles and parts. [Princeton Essays in International Finance, no. 143, 1981]

In the rationalized world auto industry, the United States will provide parts that require skill, innovation, and technology data. The increasing total deficit in auto trade since the 1960s is due to imports of passenger cars. But since the mid-1950s, the United States has had a *surplus* in trade in auto *parts* running at about $1–2 billion. The U.S. auto industry will probably shrink some more, but it will not disappear. It will be integrated into a world system in which the United States will maintain its competitiveness in the subsectors where it performs best.

Our Competitive Position Threatened, 1981–83

In 1981 a shadow was cast over this bright picture of competitiveness and continuing adjustment toward high-productivity sectors. The shadow was the combination of the massive multi-year tax cut and the phased increase in defense spending prescribed in the 1981 budget, and the monetary tightness needed to restrain inflation in the face of the resulting budget deficits. This raised U.S. interest rates and the value of the dollar. Indeed, the 25 percent real increase in the dollar from 1980 to 1983 gave back to the world *all* of the competitive gains that had been achieved from 1971 to 1980. By making U.S. manufactures that much less competitive across the board, the dollar's appreciation threatens to weaken the entire U.S. industrial structure. In a March 1983 speech, Chairman Martin Feldstein of the President's Council of Economic Advisers stated the problem clearly:

> The prospect of large future deficits in the second half of the 1980s and beyond would keep long-term interest rates high in the next

few years and thereby depress spending on investment in plant and equipment and in housing. The higher real long-term interest rate would also keep the exchange value of the dollar very high, thus encouraging imports and weakening the competitive position of U.S. exports in the world economy. In short, the prospect of large budget deficits would mean a very lopsided and unhealthy recovery in which several key industries fail to share in the economic recovery.

The source of the problem, of course, is the Reagan administration's own budget. There is no way that adjustment and flexibility can offset the effects of high interest rates and a highly overvalued dollar in undermining the U.S. competitive position. A macroeconomic policy that permits realistic levels of U.S. exchange rates and interest rates is essential if our "high-tech" industries are to be competitive and continue to grow.

The Moral of the Story: Adjustment to Competition

When the economy is adjusting smoothly, jobs lost in declining industries are lost to firms, but not to *workers*—who move on to other jobs that are opening in expanding industries. While the movement can be painful and costly, especially if we do not have an effective policy for training and relocation, the new jobs are likely to have higher productivity and perhaps higher pay than the old jobs. Nevertheless, the old jobs are surely "lost" to the shrinking basic low-technology industries, which creates serious problems for the firms, the communities, and the unions entrenched in those industries.

With plants closing or cutting back, workers having to search for new jobs, and the local tax base contracting, it is little consolation to the particular workers, unions, and towns that growth is rapid in another industry on the other side of the country. The gains from trade and adjustment go to *all* the consumer/taxpayers in the country, while the losses are concentrated on the few who are in the shrinking industries. Thus, it is entirely appropriate that the federal government use general tax revenues to minimize the costs of adjustment and speed the process. By and large, the capital markets move resources in the right direction, so there is no need for an industrial policy that directs the allocation of resources. What we do need, however, is a program that provides retraining and relocation assistance for workers who have to adjust and some sort of interim support for the affected communities. Designing an effective program of this kind should be a high priority for policy makers and researchers today. For it is an essential part of a policy package to keep the U.S. economy flexible and competitive.

A policy of encouraging open trade and resource reallocation can stand only as one leg of the stool. An effective assistance policy that smooths the course of adjustment and a macroeconomic policy that ends the misalignment of the dollar are the other two legs. Without any one of the three, the gains from a competitive economy will be lost.

THE CONCEPTUAL ISSUES

X. Sunbelt/Frostbelt Confrontation?

Bernard L. Weinstein and John Rees

A few years ago Kevin Phillips wrote an intriguing article entitled "The Balkanization of America," observing that severe symptoms of decomposition have begun to appear throughout America's body politic—in the economic, geographic, ethnic, religious, cultural, and biological sectors of society. He further suggested that this trend, unless stopped, will bring about a fundamental reversal in the American experience. This Balkanization is perhaps best exemplified by the growing regional confrontation that is sometimes referred to as "The Second War between the States" or the "Sunbelt-Frostbelt" conflict. Ironically, the background to this new confrontation is very much like that of the first: sharp differences in regional economic interests. This conflict may prove just as divisive as the first Civil War, because it is being fought over jobs, people, income, and capital.

A host of political coalitions has formed to do economic battle for new industry and federal dollars. In 1976 the governors of seven northeastern states (Connecticut, Massachusetts, New Jersey, New York, Pennsylvania, Rhode Island, and Vermont) formed the Coalition of Northeastern Governors (CONEG) "to establish mechanisms to reactivate and rebuild the depressed economy of the Northeast." One of CONEG's expressed aims is to "present a united front before the Congress and the national administration in an effort to redress the current federal expenditure imbalances." Also in 1976, a new congressional caucus was formed called the

"Sunbelt/Frostbelt Confrontation?" by Bernard L. Weinstein and John Rees is reprinted with the permission of the authors and published by permission of Transaction, Inc., from *Society*, vol. 17, no. 4. Copyright © May/June 1980 by Transaction, Inc.

Bernard L. Weinstein is a professor of economics at the University of Texas at Dallas. John Rees is an associate professor of geography and political economy at the University of Texas at Dallas and an associate director of the Center for Policy Studies there.

Northeast-Midwest Congressional Coalition. Composed of 204 representatives from sixteen states (New England, the three mid-Atlantic states, plus Illinois, Ohio, Michigan, Indiana, Wisconsin, Iowa, and Minnesota), this bipartisan group seeks to direct a higher proportion of public and private money to the northern states. The caucus is fed ammunition by the Northeast-Midwest Research Institute, conveniently housed on Capitol Hill, which conducts studies designed to show that the North is short-changed when it comes to federal aid and federal procurement. The Sunbelt has countered with several coalitions of its own. In the forefront is the Southern Growth Policies Board, a thirteen-state organization established in 1972 to conduct research and shape public policies on economic growth management in the South. Increasingly, the board's efforts have been directed toward monitoring northern attempts to change federal funding formulas and initate new legislation that could be detrimental to the economy of the South. To this end, the board has established a well-staffed Washington office within two blocks of the Capitol. In another development, over twenty municipal leagues from non-northeastern states have funded a National Economic Research Institute to provide documentation for counterattacks against the Frostbelt coalitions.

The Real Issue

The resurgence of sectionalism in the Untied States can be best understood by looking at recent changes in the distribution of people and economic activity among the various geographic regions of the nation. Between 1950 and 1977, the U.S. population increased by 43 percent; but this growth has not been spread evenly across regions. The West has been the fastest growing region since 1950, having nearly doubled its population. In absolute numbers, the South has gained more people than any other region over this 27-year period. By contrast, the northeast and north central regions have posted population gains well below the national average in recent decades (24.8 percent and 30.3 percent, respectively), and since 1970 population growth has nearly come to a standstill in these two regions.

With declining birthrates throughout the nation, interregional migration has become the most important factor in population redistribution. For example, in the 1955–60 period, net inmigration was responsible for a mere 6 percent of the population change in the South. During the 1965–70 period, migration accounted for 12

194

percent of the South's population growth; from 1970 to 1977, migration accounted for 49 percent of the growth. During 1977 alone, the four southwestern states (Arkansas, Louisiana, Oklahoma, Texas) received 306,000 migrants net. A similar pattern is observed in the western region where net migration accounted for about 50 percent of the population growth between 1950 and 1977. Net outmigration has been primarily responsible for the slow population growth of the northeast and north central regions. As early as 1955, the north central region was experiencing net outmigration while the Northeast has been a net outmigratory region since 1970. In the 1970–77 period, two-and-a-half million more people moved out of the North than moved into it.

With slow population growth and net outmigration from the North, it is not surprising that its employment gains in recent years have lagged behind the rest of the nation's. Between 1950 and 1977, total nonagricultural employment grew 70 percent nationwide but only 45 percent in New England, 28 percent in the mid-Atlantic states, and 53 percent in the Great Lakes region. The other regions of the nation, by contrast, scored employment gains well above the national average—186 percent for the mountain states, 155 percent for the Pacific states, and 133 percent for the south central states. Since 1970, the differential employment growth rates have become even more pronounced. Total employment in the mid-Atlantic states has actually declined, owing to huge job losses in New York, while expansion in New England and the Great Lakes region has been consistently below the national growth rate. At the same time, employment gains have accelerated in the south central and mountain states. By other measures of economic performance—industrial expansion, personal income, retail sales, bank deposits, construction starts, etc.—the northeast and north central regions have also lagged behind the rest of the nation in recent years. And, perhaps most significantly, these regions stand to lose congressional seats after the 1982 reapportionment based on this year's [the 1980] census.

Federal Spending

Before World War II, economic growth in the various regions depended almost entirely on private-sector activities. The postwar era has seen a tremendous increase in the size and scope of federal government, and federal spending has become a major force in shaping regional economic activity. Much of the ongoing public

195

debate about regional growth and decline has focused on the differential impacts of federal taxing and spending policies. Many northern politicians—such as Senator Daniel P. Moynihan of New York—have alleged that favorable federal spending policies have been instrumental in bringing about the rapid growth of the Sunbelt while accelerating the decline of the industrial North—especially New York State. Such assertions are often backed up by statistical computations showing that the northeastern and midwestern states are running "balance of payments" deficits with the federal government; i.e., they are sending more to Washington in the form of taxes than they are receiving back in federal outlays. A study by the *National Journal* calculated that the five Great Lakes states ran a $20.1 billion deficit with Washington in fiscal 1976 while the mid-Atlantic states ran a $12.6 billion deficit. By contrast, according to the study, the South ran a "surplus" with Washington of some $12.6 billion while the West came out $10.4 billion ahead.

The New England, mid-Atlantic, and Great Lakes regions all show spending-tax ratios less than one on a per capita basis, while the other regions show ratios greater than one. Such ratios do not, by themselves, support northern claims of regional discrimination. An *a priori* expectation of regional balances between spending and taxes would totally ignore the significant distributional aspects of federal fiscal policy. For example, progressive income taxes take more from wealthy persons (and states) than they do from poor persons (and states). Similarly, many federal expenditure and transfer programs have been specifically designed to raise the incomes of the nation's lowest socioeconomic groups. Per capita incomes in the south Atlantic, south central, and mountain regions are well below the national average, while the New England, mid-Atlantic, and Great Lakes regions show per capita incomes above the national average. Thus the average tax payment per person is lower in the South and the mountain states than it is in the North. The tax differentials simply reflect the relative income positions of the regions. Though growing rapidly, the south central region is still the poorest in the nation. Yet per capita federal spending in this region was $1,447—considerably below the national average of $1,524 in 1976.

State-by-state or region-by-region comparisons of federal taxes and expenditures are misleading on other grounds as well. For example, a number of federal spending programs are channeled to individuals rather than local governments or private contractors. Social Security payments, federal retirement, military pensions, and welfare payments are received by highly mobile people. The fact that many retirees are moving to the Sunbelt, and bringing their Social Security, military, and federal pensions with them, is not a matter of discretionary fiscal policy.

The importance of federal spending to the economic development of the Sunbelt has been overstated. The North has been losing people, jobs, and investment to the Southeast and Southwest for over two decades. To a large extent, the migration of population and employment opportunities is occurring in response to economic forces affecting the cost and efficiency of production. Lower living costs, taxes, energy costs, and land costs in many parts of the Sunbelt have facilitated the economic development of the region and, at the same time, improved the overall efficiency and productivity of the national economy. Growing markets and a broadening industrial base have made economic growth in the Sunbelt self-sustaining. Given the present diversity and dynamism of the Sunbelt's economy, it is unlikely that a redirection of federal funds to the North would stem the southerly flow of people, investment, and jobs.

Sunbelt Prosperity/Northern Decline

Although interregional shifts in population and industry have only recently emerged as a major public policy issue, such movements have been occurring since the early days of the Republic. Most historians and demographers cite three major phases of internal migration prior to the Sunbelt surge of the late 1960s. The first and longest phase began after the Revolutionary War and ended with the closing of the western frontier around 1880, a period during which America remained a predominantly agricultural society. The second phase of internal migration coincided with the industrialization and urbanization of the American economy, the period from around 1890 to 1920. The third significant phase of internal migration occurred between 1920 and 1960 when net black outmigration from the 16 southern states exceeded three-and-a-half million persons. A common thread to all the mass migrations in U.S. history has been the search for economic opportunity. People left the areas where they were living because they perceived better opportunities for themselves and their families elsewhere. This was true of the nineteenth-century pioneers and the southern blacks of the 1920s, and is also true of the educated, middle-income whites who migrated in increasing numbers to the Sunbelt during the 1970s. Migration is perhaps best defined as one form of human response to the uneven spatial distribution of opportunities and resources.

There is a strong relationship between migration and regional economic development. Migration affects personal income, employment, investment, and the demand for public services in both growing and declining areas. Typically, regions receiving large numbers of migrants show per capita income growth above the national average, while those areas losing population show slower than average income growth. Rapidly growing regions often require heavy public expenditures for roads, schools, and utilities, while declining regions find themselves faced with heavy public outlays for unemployment, welfare, and other social services.

While federal fiscal flows have obviously had some impact on regional development, the rise of the Sunbelt and the relative decline of the North can be best understood in the context of convergence toward regional equality in a major economic system—that system being the United States as a whole. Neoclassical economic growth theory would predict such a convergence. In its simplest form, neoclassical growth theory posits that factors of production—labor, capital, entrepreneurship, etc.—are free to move within an economic space to seek their "opportunity costs" or highest returns. Eventually, an equilibrium is reached where returns to factors (income) are equalized among regions. In short, the theory suggests that any differences in income levels among regions are temporary and will disappear over time.

Differential growth rates in per capita income over the past half century indicate that factor price equalization is indeed occurring among the regions of the United States. In 1929, per capita income in the Southeast was only 53 percent of the U.S. average and 38 percent of the mid-Atlantic average. Per capita income in South Carolina, the lowest state in 1929, was only 23 percent of that in New York, the highest state. By 1976, however, per capita income in the Southeast had reached 84 percent of the U.S. average and 74 percent of the mid-Atlantic average. Per capita income in Mississippi, the lowest state in 1976, was 62 percent of that in Illinois, the highest state (excluding Alaska). With the exceptions of Indiana and Wisconsin, all of the states of the northeast-midwest manufacturing belt showed relative declines in per capita income between 1929 and 1966; in some states, such as New York, Connecticut, and Delaware, the declines were dramatic. In contrast, all of the southeastern and southwestern states posted substantial gains in relative per capita income. These two regions have also been the largest recipients of immigrants in recent years, suggesting that individuals are, in fact, seeking their "opportunity costs" and thereby bringing about income convergence among regions.

There is also growing evidence that rapid economic development is helping to reduce the longstanding poverty levels so endemic to the South. In 1969, 16.2 percent of all families in the South were classified as poor, compared to 10.7 percent for the nation as a whole. By 1975, however, poverty status in the South had dropped to 12.1 percent of all families compared to 9.0 percent for the United States. This translated into a 14.7 percent decline in the number of poor families living in the South, compared to only a 7.5 percent decline in the number of poor families nationwide. The region's poorest states posted the sharpest reductions in poverty. Mississippi saw its poverty population drop from 28.9 percent of all families in 1969 to 20.4 percent in 1975, while Arkansas's poor dropped from 22.8 percent to 14.1 percent of all families. At the same time the Northeast, which showed little economic growth during the 1969–1975 period, posted only a modest 1.6 percent decline in the number of poor families. In fact, the number of poor families actually increased in New England (by 4.6 percent).

Another explanation of Sunbelt prosperity and northern decline may perhaps be found in Joseph A. Schumpeter's theory of capitalist development. In Schumpeter's view, the process of economic development emerges from the fiercely competitive environment of the capitalist system. He called this competitive struggle "creative destruction." Capitalism grows by destroying old economic structures and creating new ones. Old firms and products are driven out of business by more efficient and innovative producers. Schumpeter predicted that the very success of capitalism would sow the seeds of its eventual demise for three reasons. Investment opportunities, so critical to the process of creative destruction, would vanish as human wants were increasingly satisfied. The entrepreneurial function would become obsolete. The capitalist system would generate growing social hostility among intellectuals and laborers that would lead to a decomposition of the political framework on which capitalism rests.

While Schumpeter did not have a spatial context in mind when discussing the process of creative destruction, it is easy to visualize the Sunbelt and the Northeast as rising and declining systems of entrepreneurial capitalism. Because of industrial obsolescence and slow population growth, investment opportunities have diminished in the Northeast. The Sunbelt, by contrast, offers a wide range of new investment opportunities as migrants and industry flow to the South. At the same time, the entrepreneurial spirit seems to be alive and well throughout much of the South. Sunbelters have not succumbed to the lofty, postindustrial attitudes so prevalent in the North. Moneymaking, trade, salesmanship, and economic growth have a positive connotation. Opportunities for financial aggrandizement and the application of entrepreneurial acumen have helped to attract risk-takers to the region. Similarly, the politically conservative environment of most southern states reinforces the institutional setting for competitive capitalism. Taxes are low, and labor unions are generally weak. This near absence of union influence reflects both a cultural anti-union bias and the existence of restrictive labor legislation in many southern states. In the Northeast, by contrast, Schumpeter's predictions of social hostility to capitalism have been realized. High taxes for individuals and businesses, liberal social welfare legislation, strong union pressures, and the coalescence of organized interest groups have stifled the atmosphere in which competitive capitalism can thrive. To use Mancur Olson's phrase, "institutional arthritis" has retarded the economy of the North while the Sunbelt is not yet afflicted with the disease.

Several other factors are stimulating the growth of the Sunbelt. In general, it is still cheaper to live in the South than the North. For example, in 1976 a family of four at a middle-income budget level required 36 percent more income in the Boston metropolitan area than in Austin to maintain the same standard of living. Recent census data on migration to and from metropolitan areas show that all of the high-cost areas experienced net outmigration during the 1970–74 period, while all of the low-cost metropolitan areas, located primarily in the Sunbelt, had considerable net inmigration. While it is likely that cost of living differentials between regions will narrow significantly over the next several decades, for the immediate future lower living costs in the Sunbelt will continue to be an inducement to southerly migration. The promise of a better quality of life has also contributed to the rapid growth of the Sunbelt and mountain states. Though concepts such as *quality of life* and *environmental quality* are subjective and difficult to quantify, they are clearly strong influences on migratory decisions. The perceived amenities of the rapidly growing southern and western regions— less environmental degradation, lower population densities, more moderate climates, ease of transportation, access to recreational activities, lower crime rates, etc.—are apparently striking a responsive chord with many residents of the older, congested areas of the Northeast and Midwest. The most cogent explanation of Sunbelt prosperity and northern stagnation stems from the rapidly disappearing structural differences between the South and the rest of the nation. The South was late in moving into sustained, diversified industrialization and agricultural modernization; but once the process took hold, the region moved ahead faster than the older industrial areas because of its larger backlog of modern technologies. The rapid rise of income and employment in the South is simply a manifestation of this transition to a modern, urbanized, industrialized society.

In recent years, a number of major firms have moved their corporate headquarters from northern to southern cities. This movement has helped to create the notion that industrial migration is playing a major role in the economic growth of the Sunbelt. In fact, migration of firms accounts for a very small percentage of employment growth in the South and West and a similarly small percentage of employment losses in the North. Peter Allaman and David Birch of MIT, working with data from the Dun & Bradstreet files, have tabulated and analyzed employment changes for 3.5 million firms between 1969 and 1972. They found that outmigration of firms accounted for only one-half of one percent of employment losses for the Northeast and only one-fifth of one percent of employment losses in the Midwest. Similarly, less than one-half of one percent of employment gains in the South and West were attributable to inmigration of firms during the 1969–72 period. Births of new firms, deaths of old ones, and expansions by existing firms, by contrast, varied significantly among regions and were the major causes of differential regional employment growth.

More recent studies conducted at the Southwest Center for Economic and Community Development, focusing on the southwestern region, have come to similar conclusions. Since the Southwest is the most dynamic industrial growth zone in the United States, one would expect to find that firms from the northeastern manufacturing belt were expanding into the region to capture sources of supply and new markets. In fact, locally based firms and new firms, as opposed to external sources, accounted for most of the manufacturing employment growth during the 1960–75 period. This phenomenon suggests that economic growth in regions peripheral to the main core of the American manufacturing economy is no longer initiated by the core and that parts of the Sunbelt have become industrial seedbeds in their own right.

At the same time our research has found that southwestern industries still rely on the manufacturing belt and California for nearly half of their inputs. Just as America's industrial heartland once reached out to the peripheral regions for raw materials, now the maturing Sunbelt depends on that same heartland for manufactured goods for its own industries. An important implication of these findings, of course, is that *economic growth in the South and West does not necessarily imply a decline in the North.*

Transregional Concerns

At present, the United States has no national policies dealing with population growth, population distribution, or balanced economic development. While numerous federal programs, from military procurement to FHA mortgage insurance, have undoubtedly had differential regional impacts, these programs are not specifically designed to influence the regional distribution of economic activity. The recent growth of the Sunbelt, coupled with economic stagnation in parts of the North, has led some observers to suggest that balanced regional economic development be incorporated as a major objective of federal economic policies and actions. Such an approach would probably be counterproductive. The basic issue is whether market forces are creating an optimal spatial distribution of economic activity over time. Since the United States is an open economy with different regional endowments and specializations, regional growth rates should vary as technology, aggregate demand, and factor endowments change over time.

Much of the ongoing debate about regional growth and decline has intimated that the rapid economic development of some areas while others stagnate or decline is somehow "unfair." But regional change and adjustment are not primarily issues of equity. The growth of the Sunbelt can be viewed mainly in terms of long-run income convergence within a major economic and political system, that system being the United States as a whole. To a large extent, migration of people and jobs is occurring in response to real economic forces affecting the costs of production and service delivery. The result has been to improve overall economic efficiency in the national economy. Furthermore, the dramatic declines in poverty rates in the fast-growing southern states suggest that *rapid economic development may provide the best hope for achieving social equity policy goals.*

The redirection of federal aid and procurement to northern states and cities, so vociferously advocated by many northern politicians, would probably be ineffective in spurring economic recovery of the region. It would also represent a serious misallocation of national resources. More than a decade ago, a special study for the Economic Development Administration concluded that federal procurement was not an appropriate tool for influencing regional development, since production undertaken to meet procurement needs should most logically occur where labor productivity, skills, and regional industrial capabilities were most adapted for the purpose.

Though the North has become a lagging region in recent years, in the sense that per capita income is growing more slowly than in other parts of the country, by no means can it be called a "distressed" region. Indeed, high unemployment rates are a relatively new phenomenon for the heavily industrialized states of the North. For the most part, the unusually high rates can be attributed to the major recession of 1973–75, the most severe economic downturn since the Great Depression. Given its high degree of industrial specialization, it is not surprising that the North was hit more heavily than other regions. In any case, subsequent national economic recovery has helped to bring down northern unemployment rates to more tolerable levels. In fact, New England's overall unemployment rate is now below the U.S. average, and Illinois currently posts one of the lowest rates in the nation among major industrial states.

The most unfortunate side effect of regional confrontation is that it has diverted public attention from many of the basic, long-term structural problems facing the U.S economy. For instance, a return to full employment and high economic growth rates would aid the lagging regions of the nation much more than any geographically targeted federal assistance or spending program. It would also help to relieve some of the intense pressure on state and local governments by increasing their tax receipts and reducing demands for welfare and other social services. Central city decay is another example of a critical structural problem that cuts across regional boundaries. While the old, industrial cities of the Northeast are in the worst shape, there is growing evidence that many supposedly healthy Sunbelt cities are beginning to show signs of economic and fiscal erosion.

XI. The Case for Plant Closures

Richard B. McKenzie

When he introduced the National Employment Priorities Act of 1977,[1] Rep. William Ford (D-Mich.) was concerned mainly with restricting the movement of business from the "frost belt" to the "sun belt." He called the industrial shift "the runaway plant phenomenon." For 1979, he expanded his vision and introduced legislation (a substantial revision of the earlier bill but under the same title)[2] that will severely penalize firms that want to cease operations for *any* reason. And the legislation is not limited to the "corporate giants," the favorite whipping boy of the new left; it applies to any firm that has as little as $250,000 in annual sales.

In 1977, Congressman Ford was content to penalize firms that moved "without adequate justification" by denying them tax benefits associated with moves and requiring them to give a two-year notice of their intention to relocate. In 1979 he proposed that any firm that shuts down must (1) effectively give its employees fifty-two weeks of severance pay; (2) pay the community an amount equal to 85 percent of one year's taxes; (3) offer the affected employees jobs at other plant locations with no cut in either wages or fringe benefits and pay moving expenses for a period of three years; and (4) if it decides to move abroad, pay the federal government an amount equal to 300 percent of one year's total lost taxes. As in earlier proposed legislation, the new Ford bill requires an advance notice of plant closings (up to two years) and provides for a variety

"The Case for Plant Closures" by Richard B. McKenzie is reprinted with the permission of the Heritage Foundation, Inc., from *Policy Review*, Winter 1981, pp.119–33.

[1]U.S. Congress, *National Employment Priorities Act of 1977* (H.R. 76). For a summary of the major provisions of the act, see Richard B. McKenzie, *Restrictions on Business Mobility: A Study in Political Rhetoric and Economic Reality* (Washington, D.C.: American Enterprise Institute for Public Policy Research, 1979), pp. 1–6.

[2]U.S. Congress, *National Employment Priorities Act of 1979* (H.R. 5040 and S. 2400).

of governmental aid to affected workers and communities and, if closings can be prevented, to firms.[3]

Once concerned primarily with the economic harm caused by the movement of firms, Congressman Ford and his followers have now broadened their case, and the political appeal of their legislation, by stressing the economic *and* social costs of all plant closings. In introducing his 1979 bill, Congressman Ford notes that workers displaced by plant closings have a suicide rate thirty times the national average and "suffer a far higher incidence of heart disease and hypertension, diabetes, peptic ulcers, gout, and joint swelling than the general population. They also incur serious psychological problems, including extreme depression, insecurity, anxiety, and the loss of self-esteem."[4] Barry Bluestone and Bennett Harrison, in their study for the Progressive Alliance, echo Congressman Ford's sentiments and conclude: "Unplanned, uncoordinated growth without adequate attention to national development leads to many of the same problems that we see in the emerging ghost towns— growing inequality in income and wealth, loss of local control over resources, congestion and pollution, and skyrocketing crime."[5]

Arguments offered three years ago in favor of restrictions on business movements had only flimsy and misleading empirical support. Proponents apparently found that arguments pitting the North against the South had (120 years after the Civil War) little emotional and political appeal. Virtually anyone could see that restrictions designed to retard the economic development of the South would work to the detriment of the North. This year, by tugging on the heartstrings of all workers and communities that have experienced plant closings, the movement has veered sharply into new political waters, and the empirical support has become somewhat more sophisticated. However, the statistical claims still grossly distort economic reality, and the arguments offered in

---

[3]See Appendix for statements Congressman Ford made in support of his 1974, 1979, and 1983 legislative proposals.

[4]Rep. William Ford, "National Employment Priorities Act of 1979," *Congressional Record—House*, August 2, 1979, p. H-7240. See Appendix.

[5]Barry Bluestone and Bennett Harrison, *Capital and Communities: The Causes and Consequences of Private Disinvestment* (Washington, D.C.: The Progressive Alliance, 1980), p. 103.

support of the restrictions remain inane, thin veils for the socialist's dream of strong central control of the economy.[6]

Unemployment and Corporate "Social Duties"

In the past, proponents of restrictions on business movements focused attention on the loss of more than a million northern manufacturing jobs in the previous ten years or so. Now that those job losses have evaporated with the resurgence of manufacturing employment, especially in the North, their attention has switched to the total number of jobs *destroyed* by plant closings nationwide. Hearing the proponents' claim that over 15 million jobs have been lost from plant closings during the last decade,[7] one gets the impression that employment is actually falling nationwide—*which it is not.* Indeed, between 1969 and 1979 total employment rose by about 20 million, or by 25 percent, meaning that the number of jobs *created* during the period was in the neighborhood of 35 million (or about 44 percent of the total number of jobs in existence in 1969).[8] The point is simple: The free market economy that advocates of restrictive legislation disparage as destructive of the social good and harmful to the interests of workers has done reasonably well in providing people with the working opportunities they need. The proponents' myopic concentration on job losses is on par with an evaluation of the banking industry by focusing solely on withdrawals. Such an evaluation leads inexorably to the conclusion that all banks will eventually close.

Backers of the new restrictive legislation fervently contend that firms have a social responsibility to their workers and to the

[6]For a detailed statement of the type of ideology that underpins the movement for restrictions, see Bluestone and Harrison, *Capital and Communities.* For additional views of the supporters of restrictive legislation, see Edward Kelly, "The Industrial Exodus: Public Strategies for Control of Runaway Plants," Washington, D.C.: Conference/Alternative State and Local Public Policies and the Ohio Public Interest Campaign, 1977; U.S. House Subcommittee on Labor Standards of the Committee on Education and Labor (95th Cong., 2d sess.), "National Employment Priorities Act of 1977" (H.R. 76), 1978; and U.S. Senate Committee on Labor and Human Resources, (96th Cong., 1st sess.), Hearings on "Employee Protection and Community Stabilization Act of 1979" (S. 1609), October 19, 1979, and on "Plant Closings and Relocations," January 22, 1979.

[7]Bluestone and Harrison, *Capital and Communities,* especially chapter 2.

[8]Bluestone and Harrison stress that their estimate of 15 million jobs lost is very "conservative." That simply implies that the number of jobs created during the 1970s is greater than 35 million.

communities in which they exist, a responsibility that extends beyond the labor contract and the shutting of a plant's doors. They point to the social disruption caused by plant closings (and ignore the good that is done): the loss of tax base, idle workers and plants, impairment of community services because of lower tax revenues, and higher taxes imposed on others, because of higher unemployment and social welfare expenditures. Dayton—a moderate-sized manufacturing city in western Ohio—is, to the proponents, a grand example of what plant closings can mean. In a relatively short period during early 1980, three medium-sized employers, including Dayton Tire Company, a subsidiary of Firestone, announced their intentions to close. Eighteen hundred jobs were lost at the Dayton Tire plant alone. Workers and town officials, interviewed for television, recounted the personal hardship the closings had imposed on themselves, their families, and the communities; and several denounced the company for giving them little notice of the intended closings and for being socially irresponsible.[9] No one can seriously contend that firms are totally unconcerned about their communities, but it is hard to accept the assumption that entrepreneurs and their management teams are any less socially responsible than their workers. If nothing else, the development of good community relationships is sensible strictly from a profit perspective. Rather than enlightening listeners and readers, such public stances only camouflage basic underlying issues: Where does a firm's social responsibility end, who is at fault in plant closings, and what are the alternatives open to workers and communities for dealing with the problems encountered when a plant shuts down? Admittedly, plant closings create hardships for some people. The important question to ask, however, is whether the remedy—Congressman Ford's proposed restrictions—is more damaging to social and economic progress than the disease. Further, should a firm's social responsibility remain a moral obligation or be made a legal liability? For any society that wishes to retain the remnants of individual freedom, a sharp but important distinction must be recognized between voluntary

[9]A program on plant closings was broadcast on "The MacNeil/Lehrer Report," Public Broadcasting System, June 18, 1980. During the week of June 18, 1980, the "Today" program, National Broadcasting Company, ran a series of programs on plant closings, focusing on the closing of Ford Motor Company's plant in Mahwah, N.J. Not all workers interviewed appraised the closings in the same manner; a few viewed the closings as an opportunity to take other jobs.

acceptance of social responsibility and forced compliance with a government edict.

Through wages and an array of taxes—from property to sales to income taxes—businesses contribute directly to the welfare of a community.[10] Through personal saving, workers can secure their own individual futures against job displacement. Indeed, wages tend to reflect the risk of plant closings: The greater the risk—everything else equal—the higher the wages. The proposed restrictive legislation will, if proponents are correct, reduce the risks of job displacement for some (but by no means all or even most) workers. The reduced risk will lead to a reduction in their wages. These workers will, in effect, be forced to buy a social insurance policy that, because of its national coverage, will not be suitable to many of their individual needs—but may be suitable to the limited number of people orchestrating the legislative drive.

Proponents of the plant-closing legislation seem to imagine that in the absence of government restrictions, workers will be exploited and, as a consequence, would be unable to prepare in a precautionary way for their own futures. They also imagine that the risk of job displacement will somehow disappear with government restrictions and that the costs of the restrictions, which are either overlooked or presumed to be trivial, will be borne fully by the "firm." However, for a firm like Dayton Tire, employing 1,800 workers and paying the average wage in Dayton in 1979, the costs of the two-year notice, plus the one-year severance pay (at 85 percent of the previous year's pay), plus the fringe benefits, plus the community payments, are anything but trivial; they can easily exceed $110 million! If the National Employment Priorities Act had recently been enacted and Firestone had been prevented from closing the Dayton plant (along with four others scattered around the country) the company would have possibly had to incur more than half a trillion dollars in production costs over the next three years, for which it would have been unprepared. Very likely, the financial solvency of the entire company and the jobs of the tens of thousands of other Firestone workers would have been placed in jeopardy.

[10]It is not at all clear that businesses use more community resources than they pay for. In the intense competition for plants, many communities effectively "pay" plants to locate in their areas through below-cost sewage and wage facilities and interest rates. Whether or not the competition that now exists among communities is socially beneficial is a question that needs careful attention.

To operate in a financially sound manner under such a law over the long run, a company must prepare for the eventual expenditure associated with closing: It can establish its own contingency fund or buy insurance against the risk that it must assume. Either way, the cost will be recovered from wages that would otherwise have been paid, or from higher prices charged consumers, in which case the purchasing power of workers' incomes is reduced. Owners of companies will be hurt by the legislation—no question about it— but that is not the point that needs emphasis. Workers will not escape paying for the benefits received under the restrictions.[11]

Instead of restricting business rights, communities could set aside funds from their taxes, and these funds could be used to alleviate social problems created by plant closings. In the absence of national legislation, communities could set up their contingency fund to meet local needs and to account for the trade-offs that people in the community are willing and able to make. If taxes are not sufficient to set up a contingency fund, then tax rates could be raised. Of course, such an increase would discourage firms from setting up or expanding their operations. But the proposed restrictions have the same effect. They are a subtle form of business taxation that, like all taxes, would deter investment and, thereby, further erode growth in productivity and worker wages. Contrary, perhaps, to the good intentions of its advocates, the new restrictive legislation increases the "social cost" associated with business operations.

Mobility: A Key Economic Liberty

Still, proponents of restrictions insist that firms draw on the resources of the communities and have an obligation to recompense the community for all of the benefits they received over the years. Proponents are particularly concerned when companies use their profits made in one place to expand elsewhere. Does not the company owe the community a "fair share" of any future expansion? Messrs. Bluestone and Harrison describe with some eloquence how northern firms are "disinvesting" themselves of their plants in the

[11]In the narrow case in which a plant is prevented from moving by government restrictions, the workers in the plant may be "better off." However, if all firms are prevented from moving to locations where costs of production are lower, then the workers at any given plant must pay higher prices for the many goods they buy. Further, they will not then have the opportunity of having higher paying plants moving into their areas. On balance and over time, the real incomes of most workers should be reduced by the restrictions.

North by earning a profit and then expanding their operations in the South and West.[12] A principal problem with such a line of argument is that it is perfectly applicable to employees: They also draw on a community's services and the resources of their plant. When they decide to resign their employment and move elsewhere, do they not owe a social debt to their community, and should they not compensate their employers (as restrictive legislation proposes that firms repay their employees and communities)? Through wages received and purchases made on household goods, employees send their incomes out of the community. To be consistent, shouldn't proponents propose that the "public interest" dictates that employees spend a "fair share" of their incomes in the community? Shouldn't employees (and their unions) be told how much of their incomes must be invested back in their companies?

These questions are not intended to make the case for restrictions on employee earnings and expenditures. Rather, the point is that we allow individuals the freedom to do what they wish with their incomes and to move when and where they please for very good reasons. First, a worker's income is only one half of a *quid pro quo*, a contractual agreement between the employer and employee that is freely struck and presumably mutually beneficial. Second, freedom gives workers the opportunity to seek out the lowest-priced and highest-quality goods compatible with their preferences; that very same freedom forces sellers to compete for the purchases of the workers and provides workers with the security of having alternative places to work and buy the goods they want. Third, but foremost, there is the firm belief—call it faith—that people are indeed created with certain "unalienable rights." Individuals know, within tolerable limits, what is best for them in their individual circumstances, and they are the ones best qualified to say what they should do and where they should live—how and where they should invest their resources, labor *and* financial capital. The right of entrepreneurs to use their capital assets is part and parcel of a

[12]As indicated in the text above, proponents of restrictions were originally interested in retarding the movement of businesses from the North to the South and only incidentally concerned with the more general problem of plant closings. Now that plant closings have become the focus of the legislation, the movement shows every sign of shifting its attention to controlling and directing the *expansion* plans of companies. The Bluestone-Harrison study *Capital and Communities* seriously questions the right of a firm to make a profit in one community and expand in another community.

truly free society; the centralization of authority to determine where and under what circumstances firms should invest leads to the concentration of economic power in the hands of the people who run government. Private rights to move, to invest, to buy, to sell are social devices for the dispersion of economic power.

There are those who think that the case made against this restrictive legislation is obviously an apology for the "corporate giants." Not so. Embedded in the proposed legislation are provisions that effectively institutionalize the Chrysler bailout of 1979 and 1980. The government is given broad discretionary authority to provide unspecified forms of aid to companies that get into financial straits.[13] Effectively, the bill could swing the doors of the federal treasury wide open to any firm sufficiently large and with sufficient political muscle to enlist the attention and sympathies of the secretary of labor. The bill destroys, in part, the incentive firms now have to watch their costs and avoid going broke. Because votes are what count in politics, under the proposed law the incentive firms have to avoid losses diminishes as the size of the firm (meaning number of employees) grows.

Large rather than small companies will be most likely to secure access to the discretionary authority of government. Chrysler was "bailed out" in 1979, not because it was the only firm that went broke that year (there were hundreds of thousands of others), but because it was large and had—through its employees, stockholders, and suppliers—the necessary political clout. We can only imagine what this bill portends.

Visible and Invisible Effects of Restriction

Supporters of the legislation frequently point to the emotional and physical difficulties of those who suffer job displacement. These problems can be serious; there is no debate on that point. However, the political attractiveness of restrictive legislation can be appraised by the *visibility* of the harm done by plant closings and the *invisibility* of the harm done by restrictions on closings. The hardship associated with closings is easily observed. The media can take pictures of idle plants and interview unemployed workers; researchers can identify and study the psychological effects of job displacement. *On the other hand, restrictions on plant closings are also restrictions on*

---

[13]U.S. House of Representatives, *National Employment Priorities Act of 1979* (H.R. 5040), pp. 34–36.

plant openings. They reduce the competitive drive of business, deter investment, and reduce the growth in truly productive employment—in general, retard the efficiency of the economy. However, it is impossible for the media to photograph plants not opened because of the restrictions on plant closings, or to interview workers not able to find employment (who, as a consequence, develop hypertension, peptic ulcers, and severe depression) because of the inability (or lack of incentive) of firms to open or expand plants.

Proponents contend that they support the "little person," the low-income, uneducated worker, as well as the relatively highly paid, skilled worker, who may otherwise be exploited by the "system." The fact of the matter is that the proposed protective legislation will work to the detriment of some of the lower-income, uneducated, and "trapped" workers in our midst. The legislation imposes a severe penalty on entrepreneurs who seek to establish production facilities where the chance of success is just above the risk of failure. Plants that would otherwise be built will, with this law, not be constructed. The law would, therefore, work to the detriment of workers in low-income neighborhoods in the inner cities, because that is where the chance of success is often lowest. Furthermore, if the law were ever put on the books, it would freeze in place for a period of at least three years many of the production facilities of the country. Relatively depressed areas like Dayton, Ohio, would lose one of their best opportunities for recovering from the recent loss of jobs: The recruitment of plants from other parts of the country.

With tunnel vision, limited by the size of the TV screen and fostered by the need to make news accounts "hard-hitting" and "dramatic," television coverage often fails to consider the widespread economic growth occurring over time in a particular area. Dayton Tire shut down in 1980; manufacturing employment in the Dayton area was down slightly from what it was in 1970. These are the stories we hear repeatedly. What we do not hear is that total employment in Dayton and in Ohio rose during the 1970s by 10 and 16 percent, respectively; that the average weekly wage in Dayton is 50 percent higher than what it is in Greenville, South Carolina;[14] and that earnings during the 1970s, after adjusting for inflation, rose modestly but several times faster than the earnings in the

[14]Greenville, South Carolina, is a city near a plant opened by one of the firms that left Dayton.

213

rest of the country. These are the good things brought about, to a significant extent, by the ability of firms to adjust—by closings and openings—to changing economic conditions.

It is difficult to measure the value of goods that are never produced because of the greater (government imposed) cost of capital. Nonetheless, if the legislation is passed, goods will go unproduced and many of the goods produced will be things consumers do not want. Firestone closed Dayton Tire because it produced bias-ply tires. The tire market had, only months prior to the announced closing of Dayton Tire, gone sour; domestic car sales plummeted with the general downturn in the economy due to higher automobile prices (brought on partially by safety and environmental regulations), higher fuel prices, and the shift in consumer tastes to smaller, imported cars. In addition, consumers revealed through their purchases that they wanted safer, more fuel-efficient, and more reliable radial tires. If Firestone had been required to keep the Dayton plant open, along with five others scheduled for closing, Firestone would have been forced to produce tires that consumers did not buy, or consumers would have been forced to purchase bias tires that they did not want.

If either Congressman Ford's bill or the Senate version of Senator Donald Riegle (D-Mich.) is ever passed, its victims will be largely invisible. Disenchanted consumers and unemployed workers may very well not realize they have been victimized; and if they do realize it, they will probably be unable to determine who is at fault. Therein lies the political appeal of restrictive legislation; Congressman Ford and others can champion this cause of the political left without ever confronting those harmed by it.

Congressman Ford, Mr. Bluestone, Mr. Harrison, and others dislike the fact that in the American economic system, businesses strive for profit. They fear that without government rules and regulations, employees and communities will be left without "protection." They seem to imagine businesses as giant, voracious octopuses, totally unconcerned about their community and workers, willing to do anything for a buck. To Congressman Ford and his supporters profit is a four-letter word. Although it is hard to argue that businesses are any less socially concerned than the government bureaucrats who run control programs, we must acknowledge that profit is the basic driving force behind the business system—*and it should be.* It is the motivating force that gives rise to competition, to new and better products for consumers, and to cost savings. And the drive for profits provides workers and communities with the primary means of keeping the businesses they have, and expanding their business tax base. By holding taxes and wages in line with the competition, workers and communities can induce firms to stay and expand—to buy out and to put back in operation those plants that are closed. Contrary to what is so often written and heard, profit provides protection.[15] Unfortunately, many of the advocates of the restrictive legislation—including unions—don't want to meet the competition. Proponents Bluestone and Harrison say as much:

> Trade unionists are especially concerned with how firms use capital mobility to keep labor off guard, to play off workers in one region against those in another, and how the threat of capital relocation is used to weaken labor's ability to resist corporate attacks on the social wage itself.[16]

What advocates of restrictions seem to want is protection from competition and from the threat of pricing themselves out of the market. Consumers and taxpayers should be gravely concerned about plant-closing restrictions. As the bill is now written, it hands over to unions the power to price labor out of the market—to turn a profitable concern into a losing proposition—and then gives them access to the coffers of the federal government for a "bailout" or "buyout."

Limitations on Reinvestment

Proponents point out that many plants are closed not because they are losing money, but because they can make more money elsewhere. The defect in the argument is obvious. No profit-making firm will intentionally shut down a plant that is truly profitable— one that is actually more than covering the risks of doing business

---

[15]On "The MacNeil/Lehrer Report" (see note 9, page 208) workers expressed dismay that Firestone was asking $20 million for a plant it felt compelled to close. Actually, the workers should have been elated with the "high" price tag. A high asking price tends to indicate that the plant has a market value, an alternative use to some other firm willing to pay the price for the facility. A selling price approximating zero would tend to indicate that the plant has no alternative use and that the plant and workers will tend to remain idle.

[16]Bluestone and Harrison, *Capital and Communities*, p. 7.

and what Peter Drucker calls the cost of staying in business.[17] It is a blatant contradiction to suggest "money-grubbing capitalists" will deny themselves profits by shutting down profitable plants. Of course, firms must always keep an eye on their competition, and must constantly look to the future. At times, a firm may close a plant because of cost savings and greater profits at another location. It knows that if it does not take advantage of lower production costs elsewhere, someone else surely will; and this someone else will be able to undersell and outcompete other producers.

Dayton Tire was, at the time of its closing, making a paper profit. Using an accounting system common in large companies, Firestone on paper "bought" tires from the Dayton plant at a price above plant costs. However, after adding in warehousing and marketing costs, the total cost of the tires produced exceeded the price that could be charged in the market. In short, the production of this tire was really not profitable.

Granted, as proponents of restrictions contend, there are companies that use plants as "cash cows"—a means of securing a flow of funds through the depreciation of buildings and equipment. Again, however, no plant will be intentionally "depreciated away" if, in the long run, its operation is expected to be profitable. Plants are allowed to depreciate to oblivion for one overriding reason: Replacement of buildings and equipment at current prices and continued operations will mean future company losses. From this perspective, a company that operates a "cash cow" is, if anything, extending the life of the plant, *not* cutting it short. The company is using the buildings and equipment (both of which are scarce resources) to their fullest—the economical thing to do. (From a social perspective, is it better to have equipment that is no longer economical to replace sit idle, or be used until it is no longer productive?)

---

[17]Peter Drucker, *Managing in Turbulent Times* (New York: Harper & Row, 1979). Modern inflation tends to mislead people into thinking that businesses are more profitable than they actually are. Because costs of plants and equipment used on profit and loss statements tend to be based on their historical purchase prices, and not on their higher replacement prices, and because revenues are computed from current sales at current prices, profits of businesses tend to be substantially overstated, perhaps by as much as 30 to 40 percent. Some businesses reporting profits during these inflationary times are actually losing money. See Richard B. McKenzie, "What We Have Learned from Inflation: Ten Short Lessons" (Clemson, S.C.: Economics Department, Clemson University, 1980.)

Proponents of restrictions are especially concerned about the foreign investments of domestic firms. As Messrs. Bluestone and Harrison have written, "Dollars invested abroad are unavailable for economic development at home."[18] The deduction all too readily (and incorrectly) drawn is that foreign investment denies Americans jobs. On the contrary, foreign investments and production actually allow Americans to take higher-paying jobs created by trade. And what is the probable effect of Congressman Ford's bill on foreign investment? It seems clear that American companies will have one more reason to set up production facilities in countries that do not have similar restrictions. Foreign firms will have less of an incentive to invest in our domestic economy. Finally, when firms do invest in this country, they will, because of the severance pay requirements, be inclined to substitute capital for labor, to establish more automated plants than would otherwise be economically desirable. We must never forget that restrictions on plant closings in the United States are equivalent to an excise tax businesses must pay on their use of labor in the domestic economy. Such a tax can only reduce the demand for labor.

Finally, the proposed law authorizes the secretary of labor to provide financial aid to displaced employees who would like to buy a closed plant and continue its operations. This provision is based on the presumption that many profitable plants are closed. If that is true, then the employees really don't need the aid; private investors should be willing to provide the necessary financial capital. Indeed, employees and their unions should be able to raise the money among themselves. After all, working people do save and invest. Private pension funds have hundreds of billions of dollars in assets, and a profitable plant should be a good investment.[19] If funds cannot be raised privately, this would indicate that the plant is not potentially profitable, and taxpayers, who then must foot the bill for the purchase, will be taken for another welfare ride.

Furthermore, without government aid, the proposed restrictions

[18]Bluestone and Harrison, *Capital and Communities*, p. 27.

[19]Many of the proponents of restrictions seem to think that businesses are almost totally owned by higher-income groups, not people of the working class, and that the costs of the restrictions borne by the businesses will inevitably be imposed on higher-income groups. However, through the investments of their pension funds, workers and their unions have a substantial stake in the profitability of businesses. Restrictions on plant closings can seriously affect the retirement incomes of present and future members of all income classes.

on firms very likely will reduce the chance that employee-owned and -managed businesses might be financially successful. If this bill is enacted, the employees—as the owners—will then be the ones who have to assume the risks and costs that the proposed restrictions impose on the firm. *They* will be the ones who will be responsible for giving the two-year notice, fifty-two weeks of severance pay, and restitution to the community. *They* will be the ones who might see their savings go up in the smoke of a lost cause and the extended period of time they must wait before they could close their doors. The chances, for example, of the Dayton Tire workers making their plant a going and profitable concern are very slim at best, especially without the management skills, the licenses and patents, the warehousing and distribution capabilities, and marketing talents that would probably not be sold with the plant but would be retained by Firestone. The workers, if they own the plant, would have to look squarely and soberly at the stark facts of the bias tire market faced by Firestone and ask whether they are willing to take the implied market- and government-imposed risks. With the proposed restrictions on the books, it appears that, without government aid, the employees will be less willing to put their money where their hearts are. Certainly, if they take the time to reflect on their job opportunities, they will have second thoughts about investing in their own firm.

Regardless of how inane the proponents' arguments are, they are blessed with tremendous emotional appeal. Still, the expanded scope of the proposed restrictive laws guarantees that, if they are enacted, domestic plants and equipment will become economic hostages of the state. Opponents of the legislation must keep that basic fact before the public and the Congress and must assert over and over the beneficial effects of the free flow of domestic resources. They must also stress the one constructive means by which employees and communities can prevent and overcome problems created by plant closings: Meet the competition. Those communities, especially in the North, that are having difficulties keeping and expanding their industrial base should search for ways to attract industries and induce them to stay. There are many areas of the country, like Spartanburg and Anderson, South Carolina, that are having tremendous success in building a solid industrial base. Other communities should take a look at what they are doing, and duplicate (and expand upon) their efforts. Through appropriate, competitive positioning of wages and taxes, workers and communities can ensure that firms can cover their costs of doing and staying in business. This is not intended to be a probusiness position. Rather, it is a propeople and profreedom argument. Appeals to the private interests of entrepreneurs *and* workers (and not to the restrictive, coercive powers of government) will remain the hallmark of a free society.

XII. Reindustrialization Policy: Atari Mercantilism?

James C. Miller III

Like many other industrial nations, the United States has experienced a period of rampant inflation, intolerably high levels of unemployment, significant dislocation of economic activity, and inadequate growth. Some industries and some areas of the country have been harder hit than others. We in Washington are acutely aware that the basic industries in the Midwest have been hit particularly hard in recent years. We believe that government must do its part to ease hardships and place economic policy on a firmer foundation.

Periods of economic stress often produce new ideas, new approaches. During the past year or so we have witnessed a plethora of proposals designed to rekindle the nation's industrial might and return its economy to the high-growth track of the 1960s. These proposals vary across the lot. As Robert Kaus recently pointed out, some are intended to preserve industries in decline; others would accelerate the adjustment process and focus the government's aid on so-called industrial winners.[1]

On the whole, debate over "industrial policy," "reindustrialization," or even "reindustrialization policy" is healthy, and I frankly welcome it. Progress is seldom served by turning a deaf ear to new ideas. But I want to raise certain questions about some of the more seductive proposals one hears and about the predicate on which they are based. Specifically, I want to caution against the simplistic notion that economic salvation lies in governmental intervention to promote high technology on the one hand and erect barriers to

James C. Miller III is chairman of the Federal Trade Commission. The views expressed are those of Chairman Miller and do not necessarily reflect those of the other Commissioners. This chapter is based on a speech delivered before the Economic Club of Detroit (April 18, 1983).

[1]Robert Kaus, "Can Creeping Socialism Cure Creaking Capitalism?" *Harper's*, (February 1983), pp. 17–21.

competition in basic industries on the other—a policy I call "Atari mercantilism."

Any discussion of industrial policy should begin with a recognition that we already have one. The issue is what type. For example, should the government be more or less involved? Should it be a "planner" or a "catalyst" for market forces? For reasons that will soon become clear, I am skeptical about government programs to achieve industrial growth through special subsidies, protective regulations, and grants of monopoly privilege.

Such proposals bother me for at least three reasons. First, the nation's recent economic troubles are themselves partly the result of ill-conceived government attempts at "guided free enterprise." Second, as Adam Smith and David Hume demonstrated in exposing the fallacies of 18th-century mercantilism, many of the programs now being advanced are bound to fail. Finally, efforts to achieve industrial growth through heightened governmental intervention raise troublesome questions about equity and individual liberty.

Industrial growth and productivity are complex matters, but economists have identified several key determinants. They include demographic factors. They include investment in physical capital—plant and equipment. They include investment in research and development. They include investment in what we call human capital—education and training.

In the 1970s the rate of industrial growth slowed dramatically. One of the founders of productivity studies, Professor John Kendrick, has compared the period from 1960 to 1973 with the post-oil-embargo years of 1973 through 1979. He finds that in the latter period growth in industrial output fell by one-third. And growth in labor productivity fell by nearly two-thirds.[2] Kendrick attributes part of the slowdown to factors beyond government influence—the oil shock and certain cyclical and demographic factors. But he also concludes that much of the decline was the result of an adverse investment climate, created by accelerating inflation, high taxes, income policies, and other regulations. Such policies reduced return on investment and increased risks. According to Kendrick, the decline in the rate of capital accumulation explains over one-third of the slowdown in economic growth. Another 20 percent is explained

[2]John W. Kendrick, "International Comparisons of Recent Productivity Trends," in Essays in Contemporary Economic Problems, ed. William Fellner (Washington, D.C.: American Enterprise Institute for Public Policy Research, 1981), pp. 125–70.

by a reduced rate of increase in outlays for research and development. And 15 percent is attributed directly to increased regulation.[3]

Is there anyone who believes that the decade of the 1970s saw anything but active intervention on the part of our federal government? Can anyone seriously contend that two protracted periods of wage/price restraints—first under President Nixon and then under President Carter—were anything but an exercise in "guided free enterprise"? Surely, such programs, together with escalating taxes and unstable monetary policy, wreaked havoc with business planning.

Over the whole decade of the 1970s, the pretax real rate of return on three-month U.S. Treasury obligations was *minus* 0.8 percent! For the median income family, in the 30 percent marginal tax bracket, that amounted to a minus 2.7 percent return on their hard-earned savings.[4] No wonder the savings rate declined, and so did the rate of capital accumulation, one of the important determinants of industrial growth.

For the decade, the United States ranked dead last among six major Western industrial nations in both capital formation as a percent of gross domestic product and in productivity growth.[5] By 1981 overall expenditures for pollution control had grown to $60 billion per year—an amount greater than last year's revenues from the corporate income tax.[6]

Another major experiment with guided free enterprise was the energy program, which Herbert Stein has referred to as "a plan under which low-cost energy [was] taxed and high-cost energy [was] subsidized, thus discouraging production of low-cost energy and encouraging production of high-cost energy."[7]

It is instructive to look at the predicate which guided that experiment. Retired Central Intelligence Agency analyst Donald Jameson recently discussed the study that formed the basis for the government's

[3]Ibid. See also Gregory B. Christiansen and Robert H. Haveman, "Public Regulations and the Slowdown in Productivity Growth," *American Economic Review* (May 1981), pp. 320–25.

[4]See, for example, *Economic Report of The President, 1983* (Washington, D.C.: Government Printing Office, February 1983), p. 87.

[5]Ibid., p. 81.

[6]Gary L. Rutledge and Suzan Lease-Trevathan, "Pollution Abatement and Control Expenditures, 1972–81," *Survey of Current Business* (February 1983), pp. 15–23; *Economic Report of The President*, p. 257.

[7]Herbert Stein, "Verbal Windfall," *AEI Economist* (September 1979), p. 7.

then-apocalyptic view of the energy market. The 1977 CIA report predicted, for example, that by 1985 the Soviet bloc would "require a minimum of 3.5 million barrels of imported oil every day" and that 1983 production by OPEC countries would be over 40 million barrels per day. In sharp contrast, today the Soviets are exporting well over a million barrels a day, and OPEC production is about 13 million barrels daily—one-third the CIA estimate.[8] The CIA study also projected total free-world demand at 55 million barrels per day in 1980 and 70 million by 1985. Actual 1980 daily consumption was about 45 million barrels and, partly due to the worldwide recession, it is running even lower today.[9]

Yet, such doomsday forecasts were the basis for preempting the free market. We went barreling ahead, imposing price controls and excise taxes on fossil fuels, providing special subsidies for the development of exotic new energy sources, and enacting a potpourri of specific measures to restrict industrial and consumer use of energy supplies. At a time when the flexibility of the free market was most needed, the economy was put in a straitjacket from which it is only now beginning to recover.

The intellectual basis for that program holds that managers, workers, and consumers are too shortsighted or uninformed to assess prospective future events. But a recent study by economists George Daly and Thomas Mayor questions that logic.[10] They conclude that automotive consumers were no less rational than the planners themselves. Indeed, they find that

> [c]onsumers [did not] ignore the energy crisis, that they were [not] inherently wasteful in the use of energy, that they were [not] psychologically unable to give up large automobiles, and that such policies as mandatory efficiency standards for appliances and automobiles were [not] the only way to prevent excessive dependence on imported fuel.[11]

Today, the effects of President Reagan's decision to deregulate energy are firmly taking hold. Real as well as nominal prices for

[8]Donald F. B. Jameson, "CIA Petroleum Prophecy," *Washington Post*, April 6, 1983, p. A-19.

[9]Ibid.

[10]George G. Daly and Thomas H. Mayor, "Reason and Rationality during Energy Crises," *Journal of Political Economy* (1983), pp. 168–81.

[11]Ibid., p. 180.

gasoline continue to fall. Yet, many of the interventionists are now calling for programs to enforce conservation, lest people be deluded into thinking energy prices will fall forever. It seems to me that, having seriously underestimated the intelligence of consumers and producers, the prospective planners would better keep silent for awhile.

Now don't get me wrong. I am not saying that every problem the economy has experienced was made in Washington. Or that there were no "market failures" that required governmental intervention. But to blame the nation's lagging growth in output and productivity on a lack of industrial policy is simply straining credulity. Again, the question is not *whether* to have an industrial policy, but what *kind*. If anything, the decade of the 1970s has taught us what kind *not* to have!

Those who would ignore the lessons of the 1970s can scarcely find solace in more ancient history. As Adam Smith and David Hume demonstrated in their scathing attacks on the British and French mercantilists—the central planners of their time—government attempts to pick winners and protect losers were inherently self-defeating. This was not only because such programs allowed special interests to capture the bureaucrats of the day, but in Smith's view it was also because of the tendency of central planners to view individuals mechanically, without regard to their divergent interests. Said Smith of the mercantilist planner:

> [H]e seems to imagine that he can arrange the different members of a great society with as much ease as the hand arranges the different pieces upon a chessboard; he does not consider . . . that, in the great chess-board of human society, every single piece has a principle of motion of its own, altogether different from that which the legislature might choose to impress upon it.[12]

It is remarkable that the first test of Smith's thesis—that economic growth is maximized in a free economy—began in the very year his classic treatise was published, 1776. That, of course, was the year of the American Revolution. Subsequently, as Milton and Rose Friedman have observed, from 1800 to 1929, aside from periods of major wars, government expenditures were never more than about 12 percent of national income. And two-thirds of that amount was

[12]Adam Smith, *The Theory of Moral Sentiments* (Indianapolis: Liberty Classics, 1976), pp. 380–81.

at state and local levels.[13] The results of that "test" were unparalleled economic growth and expansions in human freedom.

Despite the demonstrable superiority of free markets, there are those who point to the contemporary Japanese economy as illustrating the need for an interventionist industrial policy. Frankly, it is time to shatter a few myths about the Japanese success story. Let me emphasize that I do not condone restrictive Japanese trade policies. I support efforts by the administration to achieve greater access for U.S. firms to their markets. But Japanese industrial policy is not all it's cracked up to be.

First, among major industrial nations, from 1950 to 1973 Japan consistently maintained the *lowest* ratio of government expenditures to national income. In 1973, for example, 29 percent of Japan's national income was spent by government, versus 40 percent for the United States.[14]

Second, according to Brookings Senior Fellow Philip Trezise, the Japanese are spending an "almost trivial" amount of public funds on special subsidies for prospective high-growth industries. And he says the same thing is true for their program of tax incentives. Moreover, Trezise finds no evidence that Japanese import policy has singled out "winning" industries. In fact, today such protection is directed to the weakest sectors in the Japanese economy, such as apparel and agriculture.[15]

Third, some of Japan's so-called success stories seem to have occurred in spite of, not because of, governmental intervention. Consider, for example, the auto industry. Neither Toyota nor Nissan were established at the government's initiative. Both were started before the Second World War. Following the war, the Japanese government did impose trade protection and provide for minimal reconstruction loans. But its efforts to keep the industry in the hands of a few producers failed because of intense rivalry among Japanese auto firms.

Finally, there is the myth of the invulnerable Japanese basic industry. In that regard, the U.S. public should know that the value

[13]Milton and Rose Friedman, *Free to Choose* (New York: Harcourt Brace Jovanovich, 1980), p. 37.

[14]See G. Warren Nutter, *Growth of Government in the West* (Washington: American Enterprise Institute for Public Policy Research, 1978), pp. 6 and 58–73.

[15]Philip H. Trezise, "Industrial Policy is Not the Major Reason for Japan's Success," *The Brookings Review* (Spring 1983), pp. 13–18.

of Japanese merchandise exports actually fell by eight percent in the last half of 1982. Excess capacity has hit many of their heavy industries, including autos, steel, aluminum, plywood, and petrochemicals. The Japanese steel industry recently called for an "update" of their government's never-used antidumping laws. Japanese petrochemical companies–now operating at an average of 50 percent of capacity–are claiming that U.S. and Canadian companies are, in effect, "dumping" in the Japanese market. Many Japanese firms are said to require government rescue programs.

Thus, the idea that the industrial leadership of U.S. firms is about to be surpassed *en masse* by Japan is dubious at best. It reminds me of the nationwide concern over high Soviet growth rates in the late 1950s. Diminishing returns inevitably set in. My professor, G. Warren Nutter, a noted scholar of Soviet economic growth, made the point with the following kind of analogy: Each year my younger brother grows older by a greater fraction of his age than I do; of course, he'll never catch me.

And, as Santayana observed, those who would ignore history are condemned to repeat its mistakes. Let's recall our own brief experience with industrial planning during the Great Depression. It included the Smoot-Hawley tariff and the National Recovery Administration. Under the NRA, the federal government relaxed antitrust enforcement, fostered business/government coordination, developed codes of so-called ethical business behavior, and otherwise tried to pick "winners." Rather than expand industrial output, the short-lived NRA's major effects were to restrict production and raise prices. In short, active industrial planning policies did not work in this country in the 1930s. They are not responsible for the Japanese successes of the 1960s and 1970s. And they are not the answer for the United States in the 1980s. As my good friend Fred Kahn, noted deregulator and President Carter's "inflation czar," observed, we should:

> Cast a skeptical eye on glib references to the alleged success of government intervention in other countries in picking and supporting industrial winners, arguments that are being used to justify setting up monstrous Reconstruction Finance Corporations to speed the process of industrial revitalization.[16]

[16]Alfred E. Kahn, "The Relevance of Industrial Organization," in *Industrial Organization, Antitrust, and Public Policy*, ed. John V. Craven (Boston: Kluwer-Nijhoff Publishing, 1983), p. 15.

Let's now put aside for a moment questions about the efficacy of government planning strategies in raising productivity and increasing industrial output. Let's think of the impact on equity and individual freedom. How many of us liked having the government set and enforce minimum and maximum temperatures in commercial buildings? Or the mileage new automobiles must attain? How many of us would tolerate policies that discouraged small businesses and fostered collusion among their larger competitors? And who wants to subsidize so-called winner firms chosen by elite planning boards at the expense of taxpayers, including those who work in the hard-pressed industries? In our quest for increased economic growth, we must not ignore such questions. What price increased productivity if purchased through loss of freedom and dignity for the individual?

I submit that if we want to foster increased economic growth in a way that will be sustained in the long run and that will enhance, not restrain, individual liberty, we should stay with the president's program of reducing taxes, restraining the growth of government spending, relieving the economy of excessive regulation, and stabilizing monetary aggregates. Moreover, we should challenge those actions by our major trading partners that are incompatible with free trade and open markets. And we should show compassion for and aid those who are disadvantaged. Instead of developing grandiose, impossible schemes to pick winners and protect losers, we should redouble our efforts to help those whom the president observes, "pay the price of economic adjustment." For displaced workers, the Job Training Partnership Act that President Reagan signed last October is not just another "bureaucratic boondoggle." It is a solid effort to retrain up to a million unemployed Americans each year in new, marketable skills. And the recent package of proposals the president has sent to Congress will provide further incentives for businesses to hire and retrain the long-term unemployed.

If this is the kind of program that proponents of reindustrialization policy have in mind, I invite them to join the rest of us in moving America forward. If not, I ask them to reassess their positions. To quote again my friend, Herb Stein:

> We have a system that for two hundred years picked winners successfully. That system is the free market, the free enterprise

system, in which people bet their own money on who the winners are going to be.[17]

There is much room in our society for a constructive discussion of the problems we face—consumers, workers, managers, and government administrators. But, 220 million individuals are not like so many pieces on a chessboard. We will not improve economic progress and maintain our precious freedoms by turning the clock back to defunct mercantilist policies of a bygone era. Without the dynamic of open, competitive market processes, without significant freedom and flexibility for businesses, consumers, and workers to make decisions according to their own priorities, we will be condemned to repeat the failures of history.

Today, we face a critical choice. We can travel the dead-end route of Atari mercantilism. Or, we can build on the progress of the past two years, take note of the current resurgence in economic activity, help those who are disadvantaged through significant "hard times," and look confidently toward the future. Which is it going to be?

---

[17]Herbert Stein, in *Reindustrialization: Boon or Bane?* (Washington: American Enterprise Institute for Public Policy Research, 1980), p. 9.

THE LEGAL ISSUES

XIII. Plant Relocations and Transfers of Work: The NLRB's "Inherently Destructive" Approach

John S. Irving, Jr.

The rights of management and labor under the National Labor Relations Act develop and are clarified very slowly by the National Labor Relations Board and the courts. It was not until 1965 that it became clear that an employer has the right to close his business for any reason, even an antiunion reason, so long as there is no attempt to "chill" unionism at another of his facilities.[1] It was not until the same year that it became clear that an employer can lock out employees in order to put economic pressure on them to agree to the employer's contract proposal.[2] Also in 1965, the Supreme Court made it clear that nonstruck employers in a multiemployer association may hire temporary replacements.[3] It was not until 1981 that the Court made it clear that an employer need not bargain collectively about the decision to partially close his business.[4]

In all of these cases the NLRB's view was that the employers had violated the NLRA by taking these actions. *Darlington, American Ship Building*, and *Brown*[5] involved alleged antiunion conduct in violation of Section 8(a)(3) of the Act. In *Darlington*, the Board unsuccessfully argued that an employer could not exercise the

---

"Plant Relocations and Transfers of Work: The NLRB's 'Inherently Destructive' Approach" by John S. Irving, Jr., is reprinted with permission from *Labor Law Journal*, September 1983, pp. 549–62.

John S. Irving, Jr., is a partner in the Washington, D.C., office of Kirkland and Ellis.

[1] *Textile Workers Union of America v. Darlington Mfg. Co.*, 380 US 263 (US SCt, 1965), 51 LC ¶19,590.

[2] *American Ship Building Co. v. NLRB*, 380 US 300 (US SCt, 1965), 51 LC ¶19,594.

[3] *NLRB v. Brown*, 380 US 278 (US SCt, 1965), 51 LC ¶19,592.

[4] *First National Maintenance Corp. v. NLRB*, 452 US 666 (US SCt, 1981), 91 LC ¶12,805.

[5] Cited at notes 1, 2, and 3, respectively.

fundamental right to go out of business if he was motivated in doing so by antiunion reasons. In *American Ship* and *Brown*, the Board unsuccessfully argued that the employers' conduct was so destructive of employee Section 7 rights that no independent evidence of unlawful antiunion motive was necessary to support the finding of a Section 8(a)(3) violation. In *First National Maintenance*,[6] a Section 8(a)(5) refusal to bargain case, the Board argued unsuccessfully that employers must bargain in good faith *before* they decide to partially close.

In all of these cases the Supreme Court viewed the management right involved as fundamental to the employer, a right to which the union had no veto and which the Board could not fetter under the guise of protecting employee rights. In fact, in *First National Maintenance,* the Court made it clear that a union is not an "equal partner in the running of the business enterprise."

The *First National Maintenance* case and others discussed below form a backdrop for the latest misguided effort of the Board. During the difficult economic times of the past two years, the Board and the NLRB General Counsel have been faced with many cases involving plant relocations and transfers of work from one place to another. Such relocations have become the latest fertile field for the Board[7] and the General Counsel to sow confusion under the pretext of protecting employee rights. Hopefully, the agency's latest meddlesome efforts to bar relocations have seen their high-water mark.

The First Hurdle

Some prohibitions against plant and work relocations are easier for the Board to apply than others. For instance, the law is clear that an employer may not relocate his operations merely to "escape" the union. This is as much an unlawful "runaway shop" today as ever.[8]

The tricky area for the Board and the General Counsel has been relocations for purely economic reasons, i.e., where there is no

---

[6]Cited at note 4.

[7]Unless otherwise indicated, references herein to the "Board" are to the Board which until recently has been dominated by its "liberal" members, e.g., Members Fanning, Jenkins, and Zimmerman. Hopefully, with the recent appointments of a new Chairman, Donald Dotson, and a new Member, Patricia Diaz Dennis, the excesses of this old majority will change rapidly.

[8]*Darlington,* cited at note 1.

independent evidence of employer antiunion motive. Rather, such moves are based on one or more legitimate business considerations, frequently including labor costs.

The first hurdle that the General Counsel and the Board had to get over was the *First National Maintenance* holding that an employer need not bargain about the decision to partially close. The maneuver was easy. The General Counsel simply instructed his staff to construe *First National Maintenance* very narrowly.[9] That is, said the General Counsel, *First National Maintenance* deals with *closings*, and relocations of unit work are not closings because the work is still being performed elsewhere.[10] Like magic, *First National Maintenance* seemingly was removed as an obstacle and a defense in relocation cases.

From here, relocation problems have broken down into two distinct areas for the Board: relocations *during* the term of a labor agreement and those *after* a contract has expired. This discussion does not deal at length with the second situation. There, in the Board's view, it is clear that an employer must bargain in good faith (presumably to impasse) before relocating unit work after a contract has expired, at least when labor costs are a motivating factor.[11]

The real activity at the NLRB during the past two years has been in the first area: plant or work relocations which occur *during* the term of a collective bargaining agreement and are occasioned at least in part by labor cost considerations.[12] It is in this area that the General Counsel and the Board have been most "innovative" and incorrect.

[9]William A. Lubbers, NLRB General Counsel, Memorandum, No. 81-57, November 30, 1981, *Daily Labor Report* (Bureau of National Affairs, July 27, 1981), p. F1.

[10]John Irving, "Closings and Sales of Business: A Settled Area?" *Labor Law Journal*, Vol. 33, No. 4 (April 1982), p. 218.

[11]Even this post-contract expiration area is trickier for employers than it might appear. Whether or not he has bargained in "good faith" may become an issue for the Board to decide. The Board has attempted in recent cases to place the determination of when there is an impasse into the *union's* hands. See, e.g., *Saunders House*, 265 NLRB No. 207 (1982), 1982–83 CCH NLRB ¶15.469.

[12]Neither the Board nor the General Counsel has taken the position that midcontract relocations for reasons other than labor costs are unlawful. Such circumstances include moves at the insistence of a major customer or in order to be closer to the supply of raw materials. However, the more labor costs are even *a* factor, the more the Board gets into the act. Moreover, an employer risks demonstrating that labor costs *are* a factor as soon as he goes to the union to seek concessions which might avert a move.

Antirelocation Theories

The Board has fashioned more than one attack against midcontract relocations. The first centers on Section 8(a)(3) of the Act. Here, the Board resurrects the "inherently destructive doctrine" as a convenient substitute for evidence. Under this theory, there is no need for the General Counsel to develop independent evidence of unlawful antiunion motivation if the employer's action can be characterized as "inherently destructive." As one might imagine, this doctrine fits well in relocation situations where the employer justifications are purely economic for, without this doctrine, there would be no Section 8(a)(3) violation.

The "inherently destructive" doctrine is clearly explicated in a variety of cases and agency memoranda.[13] Briefly, the theory states that the relocation of unit work during the term of a labor agreement and without union consent so fundamentally undermines employee Section 7 rights that it is "inherently destructive" of these rights and, therefore, constitutes a violation of Section 8(a)(3).

At first, the Board was not even interested in looking at what the labor contract might have said about relocations. In *Brown Co. v. NLRB,* the Board argued to the Ninth Circuit that a midterm relocation violates Section 8(a)(3) *irrespective* of the contract.[14] As the Board now has refined its theory, however, it has begun to pay lipservice to the labor contract but has found a way to avoid the contract, as discussed below. The Ninth Circuit in *Brown* refused to enforce the Board's Section 8(a)(3) order and remanded the case with instructions to the Board that it consider the labor contract. Although the Board has not to date issued a supplementary decision in *Brown,* recently issued cases such as *Milwaukee Spring* and *Bob's Big Boy*[15] make it clear that the Board now concedes that the contract is relevant.

---

[13]*Los Angeles Marine Hardware Co., a Division of Mission Marine Associates, Inc.,* 235 NLRB 720 (1978) CCH NLRB ¶19,215, enf'd 602 F2d 1302 (CA-9, 1979), 87 LC ¶11,628; *Brown Co. v. NLRB,* No. 79-7380 (CA-9, September 2, 1981) (memorandum opinion), final disposition reported (CA-9, 1981), 663 F2d 1078; *Milwaukee Spring Division of Illinois Coil Spring Co.,* 265 NLRB No. 28 (1982), 1982–83 CCH NLRB ¶15,317; *Bob's Big Boy Family Restaurants,* 264 NLRB No. 178 (1982), 1982–83 CCH NLRB ¶15,629; and Quarterly Report of the NLRB General Counsel, January 6, 1983.

[14]Cited at note 13. See also *Zipp v. Bohn Heat Transfer Group* (DC Ill, 1982), 110 LRRM 3013, a relocation case in which the Board's brief to the district court did not *even mention* the contract.

[15]Cited at note 13.

As indicated, however, the Board has developed another convenient strategy for dealing with the contract which ensures that it rarely, if ever, will stand in the way of the Board's prohibition against midcontract relocations. Handily, that strategy invokes the "clear and unequivocal waiver" doctrine to dispose of contract issues in Section 8(a)(3) and 8(a)(5) cases.

The "clear and unequivocal waiver" doctrine can be summarized as follows. A variety of "statutory rights" can be waived by a labor agreement. However, the waiver of a statutory right must be clear and unequivocal. If it is no, there is no waiver. Since Section 8(d) of the Act forbids the unilateral modification of a labor contract, "statutory rights" are violated if the contract is unilaterally "modified" before it expires. Any waiver of the union's "right to object" to a midterm modification, therefore, must be clear and unequivocal. If it is not, the union may "object" to the relocation and, in the Board's view, may *veto* the move.

The rest is easy. The Board and the General Counsel rarely, if ever, conclude that a contractual waiver is clear and unequivocal. For instance, in *National Metalcrafters, Inc.*,[16] the General Counsel issued a Section 8(a)(3) and (5) complaint where a labor contract actually contained a *relocation clause* which reads as follows: "(B) in the event the Company contemplates the relocation of *any* of its operations conducted at its present divisions in Rockford, Illinois, the Company agrees to *discuss* such relocation in advance and to *negotiate* with the Union concerning the effect of such relocation on employees" [emphasis supplied]. The company not only discussed the proposed relocation months in advance with the union, but it offered to negotiate with the union about concessions and allowed the union's accountant access to its books.

What is clear, then, is that the Board will rarely concede that a contractual waiver is sufficiently clear and unequivocal to avoid a Section 8(a)(3) or Section 8(a)(5) violation. Even more clear from *Metalcrafters* is the fact that the General Counsel apparently *never* will find a waiver unless the waiver *expressly* singles out and permits relocations motivated by labor cost considerations.

Implications for Employers

By manipulating the inherently destructive and clear and unequivocal waiver theories, the Board has discovered a way to

[16]33-CA-6157, complaint has issued.

thrust itself into the middle of midterm plant relocation controversies and a rationale for siding with the objecting union in virtually all relocation cases. The practical implications for employers, of course, are enormous whether or not they are in dire economic straits. The fact that the employer may be charged with an unfair labor practice is hardly the most serious part of his predicament. If it were, the relocation could be implemented and the Board fought in court with a good chance of the employer prevailing.

However, the consequences for the employer of Board involvement are much more serious, particularly where a business may fail if it cannot be relocated quickly. This is because the Board has developed a practice of seeking injunctions against relocations under Section 10(j) and, indeed, may require the employer to bring relocated operations back to the original site. Such injunctions, or the threat of them, have become commonplace at the Board. For instance, in *Zipp v. Bohn*, the Board obtained an injunction against an employer who sought to relocate unit work from one of his plants to another, even though the same international union represented employees at *both* plants.[17]

The practical choices, then, for the employer who must relocate or fail are not pleasant. The relocation can be postponed until the end of a contract and after "good faith" bargaining, in which case the employer may go bankrupt; or the employer may relocate and incur substantial legal fees fighting the Board, with the possibility that at least the Board may prevail and that the employer may be required to move back and/or pay backpay to adversely affected employees at the old location. Suffice it to say that the Board is not unaware of the practical pressures its new stance places on employers contemplating relocation, and neither are the unions unaware that they have gained the Board as an ally.

Misuse of the Inherently Destructive Doctrine

The Board has sought to use the inherently destructive doctrine not only as a substitute for evidence but as a convenient way of avoiding any controversy over inherent *management* rights. Thus, if a plant relocation is inherently destructive, that is the end of the matter for the Board. Citing *Erie* and *Great Dane*,[18] the Board need

---

[17]Cited at note 14. See also *Kobell v. Cameron Mfg. Co.* (DC Pa, 1982), 112 LRRM 2397.

[18]*NLRB v. Erie Register Corp.*, 373 US 221 (US SCt, 1963), 47 LC ¶18,249; *NLRB v. Great Dane Trailers, Inc.*, 388 US 26 (US SCt, 1967), 55 LC ¶11,973.

only *declare* plant relocations inherently destructive of employee Section 7 rights, and no "independent evidence" of unlawful, anti-union motive is needed. A Section 8(a)(3) violation is made out because of the inherently destructive nature of the employer's conduct, i.e., the relocation. The strategy is convenient but improperly invoked by the Board in connection with relocations.

The major problem with the Board's analysis is that it starts at the wrong point. The Board assumes, improperly, that collective bargaining agreements are, in effect, job guarantees. That is, employees have a "Section 7 right" not to have "their work" relocated during the term of the labor agreement. In fact, there is *no such right*.

Employees have no right, Section 7 or otherwise, to job guarantees. Instead, quite the opposite is true. As the Seventh Circuit stated, citing *Fibreboard*,[19] in a Board case involving the University of Chicago[20]: "As we read the cases, unless transfers are specifically prohibited by the bargaining agreement, an employer is free to transfer work out of the bargaining unit if: (1) the employer complies with *Fibreboard* . . . by bargaining in good faith to impasse; and (2) the employer is not motivated by antiunion animus."[21]

What the Board has conveniently forgotten are inherent *management* rights. That is, unless management contractually waives its rights to relocate, it reserves the right to do so.

The basic issue, then, is one of contract interpretation, not employee Section 7 rights. If the employer has not waived his right to subcontract for economic reasons, subject only to the *Fibreboard* obligation to bargain, that right is *retained* by the employer. If the employer has retained the right to relocate his operations, his exercise of that right can hardly be viewed as an invasion of employee rights, "inherent" or otherwise. The Board's assertion that relocations are "inherently destructive" of employee Section 7 rights begs the question.

[19]*Fibreboard Paper Products Corp. v. NLRB*, 379 US 203 (US SCt, 1964), 50 LC ¶19,384.

[20]*University of Chicago v. NLRB*, 514 F2d 942 (CA-7, 1975), 76 LC ¶10,825.

[21]Indeed, the Board seems to have forgotten what it said *itself* in that case, 210 NLRB 190 (1974), 1974 CCH NLRB ¶26,442: "It is well-established that an employer may, after the necessary bargaining, terminate work done by the union's members at a particular location and subcontract it, transfer it elsewhere, or introduce different methods of operation at the same location, even though such action is taken during the contract term and results in the elimination or reduction of size of the unit involved [footnotes omitted]."

Moreover, if the Board's analysis were correct it would extend far beyond midcontract relocations. It would apply to *all midterm* actions taken by an employer and motivated in part by labor cost considerations, which arguably relate to *any* mandatory bargaining subject, e.g., subcontracting, automation, robotization, etc. In the Board's view, unions would retain the same kind of midterm "veto" that they "retain" with respect to relocations.

The flaw in the Board's reasoning, then, is obvious. No wonder the Board feels obliged simply to *declare* that relocations are inherently destructive of employee Section 7 rights. This declaration allows the Board to arrive at the result it prefers without having to enunciate with any precision the Section 7 right which, allegedly, is "inherently destroyed."

Even if the Board's analysis were correct, and it is not, the Board misapplies the very test it purports to apply. The inherently destructive doctrine as enunciated by the Supreme Court in cases like *Erie* and *Great Dane* requires a two-step application. The Board, on the other hand, resorts to a one-step analysis.

Thus, as the Supreme Court recently restated the inherently destructive doctrine in *Metropolitan Edison Co. v. NLRB:* "Determining that . . . conduct adversely affects protected employee interests does not conclude the inquiry. If the employer comes forward with a legitimate explanation for its conduct, the Board *must* 'strike the *proper* balance between the asserted business justifications and the invasion of employee rights' " [emphasis supplied].[22]

The Board simply ignores any obligation to balance competing interests. In the Board's view, it seems that its work is complete and a violation found as soon as it *declares* a relocation to be inherently destructive of Section 7 rights. As discussed above, this declaration is inaccurate and misleading in the first place. However, the Board compounds its mistake by failing to balance competing interests. This *required* balancing must be done with reason, not mirrors.

Thus, for instance, even if it could be said that a midterm relocation by a failing employer "destroys" Section 7 rights, the Board must balance between the interests of employees and the interests

[22]51 USLW 4350 (US SCt, 1983), 92 LC ¶13,110.

of employers.[23] Even assuming arguendo that employees have a Section 7 right to jobs, and they do not, an employer's fundamental interest in survival outweighs employee interests. To conclude otherwise does little to "protect" employee Section 7 interests since *all* employment will terminate if the business fails. Of course, business failure is the most inherently destructive of the interests of *all* concerned.

By the time the question of the permissibility of midterm relocations reaches the Supreme Court, and undoubtedly it will, the Court will reject the Board's ignorance of reserved employer rights just as it did in *Darlington* where the Board argued that an employer can be ordered to stay in business if his motive for going out of business is impure. Moreover, the Board's total failure to objectively balance competing interests will not escape the Court's attention.

Finally, plant relocation issues are fundamentally matters of contract interpretation. As such, they should be resolved not by NLRB intervention but by the private dispute resolution procedures agreed upon by the parties. Relocation disputes are perfectly susceptible to resolution under contractual grievance-arbitration procedures, procedures which are preferred by well-developed national labor policies[24] and the NLRB itself.[25]

Misapplication of the Clear and Unequivocal Waiver Doctrine

The Board's misapplication of the clear and unequivocal waiver doctrine to plant relocation cases is a device used to construe labor contracts to suit the Board's ends and in ways *never* intended by the parties. That doctrine as applied by the Board requires the contractual waiver of a "statutory right" to be clear and

---

[23]To date, the Board majority and the General Counsel appear totally disinterested in whether the relocating employer is in dire economic straits. In *Milwaukee Spring*, only then-Chairman Van de Water seemed concerned about such circumstances (see case note 7). In *Metalcrafters*, cited at note 16, even the union accountant agreed that the employer was on the verge of failure.

[24]*United Steelworkers of America v. Warrior & Gulf Navigation Co.*, 363 US 574 (US SCt, 1960), 40 LC ¶66,629.

[25]Section 203(d) of the NLRA, as amended, states: "Final adjustment by a method agreed upon by the parties is declared to be the desirable method for settlement of grievance disputes arising over the application or interpretation of an existing collective-bargaining agreement."

unequivocal.[26] This gives the Board license to find some ambiguity in the contract or even the bargaining history which casts "doubt" on the "clarity" of the waiver. The practical effect is that no contract is ever clear enough for the Board or the General Counsel. Once the Board can declare the contract silent or less than clear on the subject of relocation, it need not be bothered with the contract again, for it has been eliminated as a legal obstacle (or so the Board believes).

This approach ignores the realities of the very collective bargaining the Board is charged with fostering and completely ignores any concept of reserved management rights. Traditionally, management and labor have viewed the bargaining process as labor winning rights from management with the fruits of collective bargaining reflected in the contract.

Under the Board's theory, all rights with respect to mandatory bargaining subjects are reserved *to the union* unless those rights are "clearly and unequivocally" waived by the union. Therefore, if a contract is silent or less than clear with respect to plant relocations, the union reserves the "right" to "veto" relocations during the term of the agreement.

The Board's approach turns traditional bargaining on its head. That is, management has no right to relocate midterm unless the contract clearly and unequivocally gives management that right. Managers across the country are awakening to the reality that, at least in the Board's view, their labor contracts mean much more than they say.

The same reasoning, of course, applies with respect to other management actions as well. Thus, as discussed above, if a contract does not give an employer the clear and unequivocal right to introduce new machinery during the term of an agreement in order to save labor costs, the Board would say the union has a right to

---

[26]Where *employer* statutory rights are concerned, the Board's analysis is not so demanding. Thus, for instance, contractual "after acquired" facilities or "accretion" clauses require an employer to recognize a union if the union establishes that it represents a majority of the employees to be added to the existing unit. In such situations, the Board's analysis reaches an opposite result. That is, although the employer has a statutory right to insist that the union demonstrate its majority in election, that statutory right is deemed waived by the Board unless it is specifically reserved by the employer. Instead, the union need only demonstrate a majority based on authorization cards. *Houston Division of the Kroger Co.*, 219 NLRB 388 (1975), 1974–75 CCH NLRB ¶16,032.

"veto" the introduction. The same is true of work rule changes.[27] This is because the union has the "statutory right" to insist that the contract not be "modified" during its term, and the union has no obligation to bargain about the "change" during this period.[28] The same reasoning, then, applies to *all* midterm employer actions which involve *any* mandatory bargaining subject.

The Board's approach fails to recognize the true dynamics of collective bargaining. It completely eliminates management's opportunity to know what it is agreeing to and to demand something in return for the rights and compensation it agrees to yield. For, under the Board's view, even contractual silence results in the acquisition of "rights" for the *union*, i.e., the union "retains" all it does not clearly and unmistakably "yield." Whether the employer realizes it or not, this can result in job guarantees for the life of the agreement, unless, of course, the employer clearly and unmistakably specifies that job guarantees are not intended or he opts to go out of business altogether. Either there is something fundamentally wrong with the Board's approach, or there is something fundamentally wrong with the traditional assumptions of the parties when they undertake to bargain collectively.

Labor contracts, as with contracts generally, are for arbitrators and ultimately for the *courts* to construe.[29] While the Board is permitted to construe labor contracts in deciding unfair labor practice issues, it should not be permitted to construe them in a manner which is inconsistent with the way they would be construed by the courts.

In order to avoid an interpretive clash with the courts, the Board merely bends contract analysis into a form which focuses on whether "statutory rights" are "clearly and unequivocally waived." Again, as if by magic, the Board seeks to take contract interpretion out of the hands of the courts and, for that matter, out of the hands of the contracting parties. By applying its own brand of misguided logic, the Board can achieve the result it prefers. The Board can then argue

---

[27]*Pet, Inc.*, 264 NLRB No. 166 (1982), 1982–83 CCH NLRB ¶15,272.

[28]*Abbey Medical*, 264 NLRB No. 129 (1982), 1982–83 CCH NLRB ¶15,328.

[29]"The strong policy favoring judicial enforcement of collective bargaining contracts [is] sufficiently powerful to sustain the jurisdiction of the district courts over enforcement suits even though the conduct involved [is] arguably or would amount to an unfair labor practice within the jurisdiction of the National Labor Relations Board." *Hines v. Anchor Motor Freight, Inc.*, 424 US 554 (US SCt, 1976), 78 LC ¶11,284.

to the courts that its "judgment" about the waiver of statutory rights is entitled to great "deference" because the Board is the agency charged by Congress with the authority to defend Section 7 rights of employees.

The Board's whole approach to interpreting labor contracts is so distorted that it defies reality and reason. Nevertheless, by diverting courts from their proper role, the Board has been amazingly successful in accomplishing the results it desires.[30]

One of these days the courts will awaken to what the Board is doing and will put the interpretation of labor contracts back into proper perspective. This will be done when the courts reassert their authority to interpret labor contracts in ways that make sense.[31] When they do this, the current destructive uncertainties about plant relocations will be put to rest. Once again, labor contracts will become important for what they say rather than what they do not say, and employers will not be left to wonder about what prerogative they may have unintentionally yielded.

Practical Consequences

As a practical matter, the approach of the Board and the General Counsel stacks the deck against the employer in virtually *every* relocation case. A union can almost guarantee that the General Counsel will issue a complaint against the employer. Moreover, the union stands a better than 50–50 chance of persuading the Board to seek an injunction, all of which can be accomplished at little or no cost to the union.

The results become clear when the dynamics of an unfair labor practice proceeding are examined closely. Thus, a typical situation is where an employer is feeling the economic pinch of the current recession. He has cut costs in virtually all areas except his labor contract costs, and the contract has many months or even years to run. The employer reviews his labor contract and decides that it gives him the authority to relocate his operations.[32]

---

[30]*Zipp v. Bohn; Kobell v. Cameron,* cited at note 17; *Tocco Division of Park-Ohio Industries, Inc. v. NLRB,* 257 NLRB 413 (1981), 1980–81 CCH NLRB ¶18,270, enf'd (CA-6, 1983), 96 LC ¶14,122.

[31]*Milwaukee Spring* may be the first opportunity. The case has been argued and is pending in the Seventh Circuit.

[32]In *Metalcrafters,* the contract gave the employer the right to relocate provided that he *discussed* the relocation with the union and bargained about its effects.

Armed with a perceived right to relocate, the employer approaches the union to bargain concessions. Conscious of the Board's view that it need not bargain at all, the union wants no part of concessions. The frustrated employer announces that he intends to finalize and implement relocation plans.

The union then files Section 8(a)(3) and (5) charges with the nearest NLRB regional office. The regional director investigates the charges on behalf of the General Counsel but considers himself "bound" by Board law and case handling instructions of the General Counsel. These instructions say in effect that if the "waiver" of the union's "right to veto" the move is "less than clear and unequivocal," complaint should issue against the employer.

If the contract language seems fairly clear, the region will look at "bargaining history" and other conduct of the parties which may "cast light" on the "real" intentions of the parties. Because the case is in the investigative stage, the regional director (i.e., the General Counsel) will not make "credibility resolutions." Hence, where the employer and union disagree about the meaning of the contract or give conflicting accounts of the bargaining history or the way the contract has been applied, the evidence will be viewed most favorably *to the union* for purposes of determining whether a complaint should issue.

Keep in mind that all that is needed for the issuance of a complaint is *"reasonable cause"* for the General Counsel *"to believe"* that there has been a violation. Put another way, all the General Counsel needs is "reasonable cause" to believe that a waiver of the union's veto right is not "clear and unequivocal."

In most cases, then, a complaint against the employer will be authorized "absent settlement." For settlement purposes, the General Counsel seeks virtually everything to which he thinks he may be entitled after litigation. That is, if the employer has not yet relocated, the General Counsel will seek the employer's agreement not to relocate until after the contract has expired and the employer has "bargained in good faith." If the employer has relocated, the General Counsel will want to "settle" on the basis that the employer will move back to the old location and/or pay backpay for

---

Moreover, the contract's recognition clause recognized the union only at the present plant location. In addition, employees had been displaced by relocations in the past without objection from the union, which had acknowledged that it was powerless to prevent relocations.

"adversely affected" employees. Needless to say, most of these alternatives will be unattractive to all but the most cooperative, and passive, employers.

If there is no settlement, complaint is publicly "authorized" and then "issued." The union meanwhile is busy announcing to employees and the public about how the "NLRB" has "determined" that the employer is a law violator. Temporarily, anyway, the union is excused by its constituents because it at least looks as if the union is doing something.

The union's next step, if it has not already done so by then, is to insist that the General Counsel seek authority from the Board in Washington to petition a federal district court for an injunction under Section 10(j) of the Act. Since the General Counsel has already decided a complaint should issue, he has already determined that there is "reasonable cause to believe" that the employer has violated the Act, one of the two key elements necessary for a Section 10(j) injunction.

All the General Counsel need do now is look to see whether an injunction would be "just and proper." As a practical matter this entails an examination to see whether there are any "practical difficulties" with the case which make it a "bad candidate" for an injunction and, thus, whether the Board is likely to disagree with his Section 10(j) recommendation.

Receiving enormous pressure by this time from the so far successful union to speed an injunction "before all is lost," the General Counsel satisfies himself that there are no obvious obstacles in his path. He makes his recommendation to the Board.

Authorization Process

The authorization process is interesting in itself. Since the General Counsel is the Board's lawyer for purposes of initially determining the appropriateness of a Section 10(j) injunction, the parties are forbidden from communicating directly with the Board and must, instead, communicate with the Board only "through" the General Counsel. Because the General Counsel under the statute has "final authority" with respect to whether "reasonable cause" exists, and since he has already made the determination that it does, most of what the General Counsel passes on to the Board is evidence which for prosecutorial purposes is viewed *most favorably to the union*. This is done so that the Board is not "compromised" by being asked "prematurely" to "resolve factual matters."

The net result, as one might expect, is that the General Counsel's request for injunction authority is rarely denied, for the Board "relies on the General Counsel" to make "reasonable cause determinations." And all this is accomplished without the parties, which have so much at stake, having any opportunity to communicate their views directly to the Board. Instead, they must rely on the General Counsel to summarize their respective positions, positions which, presumably, the General Counsel has already rejected in authorizing the complaint.

Once the injunction is authorized by the Board, based essentially upon the General Counsel's reasonable cause determination of which the Board's understanding may be less than complete, the General Counsel will petition the district court for an injunction, again "absent settlement." Many employers as a practical matter, and if they can afford to, capitulate at this stage rather than risk an injunction. Those who can afford the litigation costs or who cannot afford to capitulate, do not.

Before the court, the agency argument advanced by the General Counsel takes on an interesting cast. "On behalf of the Board," the General Counsel argues that the Board "is entitled" to an injunction if reasonable cause exists and if an injunction would be "just and proper."

As to the reasonable cause determination, the court is told that the Board "is entitled to great deference" even though it was the General Counsel, not the Board, who made the reasonable cause determination (on the basis of evidence viewed most favorably to the union). In any event, the court is referred to cases which hold that, for the court's purposes, reasonable cause exists as long as the agency's legal theory is "substantial and not frivolous."[33] Of course, the court is urged to draw all inferences most favorably to the Board.[34]

As for the requirement that the injunction be "just and proper," the General Counsel argues, of course, that absent an injunction employees who lose their jobs will be "irreparably harmed." Moreover, the Board's processes will be "frustrated," the General Counsel

---

[33]See *Wilson v. Liberty Homes, Inc.*, 664 F2d 620 (CA-7, 1981), 108 LRRM 2699.

[34]See the General Counsel's brief to the district court in *Zipp v. Bohn* [citing *Hirsch v. Trim Lean Meat Products*, 479 FSupp 1351 (DC Del, 1979), 88 LC ¶12,024].

argues. Of course, the court should conclude that the Board's processes will be frustrated when the Board says they will be.[35]

By this time, all but the most astute court will have completely lost sight of the fact that the whole case really turns on *contract interpretation*, as to which the *court* has greater competence than the Board. Moreover, any suggestion by the court about the relevance of the labor contract will be diverted with a flurry of arguments about the need for a "clear and unequivocal waiver of statutory rights." At this point, the court gives up, defers to the "educated" judgment of the "expert labor agency," and issues an injunction against the employer. All this, mind you, is based in actuality upon the General Counsel's reasonable cause determination which in turn is based upon evidence viewed most favorably to the union.

A Nightmare

The consequences for the employer are disastrous, particularly if the court "defers" to the Board's request for a move back order, assuming it seeks one. By this time, the union is again bragging to all who will listen about how the *union* has stopped the employer in its tracks and saved the jobs of employees. And while the union has been prodding the General Counsel and the Board, and proclaiming its successes, there has been *no* meaningful bargaining which might help the employer to survive and provide employment opportunities in the future.

Meanwhile, the employer is reassessing the damage and by this time may be close to contract expiration and may postpone relocation efforts if he can afford to. However, without remedying the outstanding unfair labor practice case to the General Counsel's satisfaction, assuming no Board decision by the time the contract expires, it is far from clear that the employer may proceed with the relocation upon expiration. Thus, "good faith bargaining to impasse" is required after contract expiration *before* labor cost saving relocation can be implemented over the union's objection. How, the General Counsel is bound to ask, can the employer bargain in good faith while an "unsettled" bad faith bargaining complaint is outstanding and unremedied?

This is all to say that the Board's plant relocation doctrine has created a nightmare for even the best intentioned employer. No

[35]See the General Counsel's brief to the district court in *Zipp v. Bohn* [citing *Angle v. Sacks*, 382 F2d 655 (CA-10, 1967), 56 LC ¶12,151].

matter how right he might be about the meaning of his labor contract, the Board and the General Counsel make it impossible for him to assert any lawful rights he may have by erecting a "house of cards" designed to cast simple contract interpretation issues into issues only the Board can understand and is competent to decide.

It is easy to see, then, how the current odds are stacked against the employer. It is also easy to see why some employers might opt for bankruptcy rather than spend limited cash on legal fees to fight what could be a losing battle with the Board.

The legal analysis and procedures devised by the Board for plant relocation cases are "inherently destructive" of the employer's right to due process, particularly the employer who is in serious economic difficulty. The employer is finished before he can begin to fight, even assuming a fight is affordable. The union's, the General Counsel's, and the Board's case leading ultimately, and sometimes swiftly, to an injunction is based upon a series of assumptions.

The General Counsel's "reasonable cause" determination is built on evidence viewed most favorably to the union with all credibility conflicts resolved, without testing, in the union's favor. The General Counsel applies inherently destructive and clear and unequivocal doctrines constructed by himself and the Board which, in turn, point to a violation based on ambiguity instead of evidence. The Board's injunction authorization is based on the General Counsel's reasonable cause determination. The district court issues an injunction in reliance upon the determinations made by the Board and the General Counsel.

Once an injunction issues, if not before, that is the end of the case for the employer for all practical purposes. He has been prohibited from relocating by a federal injunction without *any* opportunity to test credibility or the merits of the General Counsel's case, let alone his interpretation of the contract. Faced with an injunction, it makes little sense for the employer to test the General Counsel's case in a Board proceeding where the answer even if favorable is many months or even years away—long after the labor contract has expired and after which he may be able to relocate with or without the union's blessing if he is careful.

This entire "house of cards," of course, is erected at little or no cost to the union, which simply files a charge and allows the government to pursue its claim at taxpayer expense. The dynamics are so lopsided and stacked against the employer from the outset that he can ill afford to fight even if he could ultimately win in court.

The result, therefore, is inherently unfair to an employer who acts in good faith reliance on what he believes to be his rights under his labor contract and whose motives are undisputedly economic and *not* antiunion.

Further Criticism

The wisdom of the Board's approach to relocation is susceptible to further criticism. Of course, one question, as indicated above, is whether it is wise federal labor policy for the Board to force itself into relocation situations at all. At least in most relocations during the term of a labor agreement, the question of whether the employer has the right to relocate is more logically a matter of *contract interpretation.*

Such questions are the kind that are resolved many times daily under agreed-upon grievance and arbitration procedures. By short-circuiting contractual dispute resolution procedures, the Board undermines the very collective bargaining process it professes to "protect." Arbitrators duly selected by the parties are every bit as capable of interpreting labor contracts as the Board and it is private dispute resolution and arbitration that are the favored cornerstones of national labor policy, not federal intervention.

The only available explanation for the apparently urgent need the General Counsel and the Board feel to inject themselves into relocation cases is that they perceive that they can tip the scales in most cases against the move. Thus, by applying inherently destructive and clear and unequivocal waiver doctrines, the Board can block relocations which arbitrators construing the contract might permit.

What must lie at the heart of the Board's approach, an approach which turns labor contracts on their head, is a conscious or unconscious desire to tip the relocation balance in favor of unit employees and unions. No consideration is given by the Board to the economic predicament of the employer, let alone the stockholder-owners of the company whose rights (and fortunes) are completely overlooked. Indeed, these stockholder-owners could even be employees themselves or their pension funds. It does not seem to matter to the Board that these other important rights may be sacrificed by the Board's single-minded desire to "protect" the Section 7 "rights" (i.e., short-term interests) of employees.

A federal judge has aptly criticized the Board's myopic approach recently in another context, but his words are equally applicable here. "The NLRB seems to use only its private knothole to view these issues and sees nothing except its own labor goals. I think this court instead of peering through the NLRB's knothole should look over the fence for a better understanding of the whole problem.[36]

When wading into such complex currents, the Board's approach should be buoyed by more than the narrow and perhaps short-lived interests of current employees. For all the Board knows, this group of employees may in substantial measure be responsible for their employer's threatened failure due to the quality of their work, their work habits or, for that matter, the excesses of their union contract. If so, the Board should take such considerations into account, but of course it does not.

Furthermore, the Board's approach actually discourages bargaining and fosters deceit. Thus, an employer is encouraged to construct reasons for a relocation which appear to be unrelated to labor costs in order to avoid Board involvement. In such situations, the employer must avoid offering to bargain *at all* for fear the Board may say that his willingness to do so is "proof" that he was motivated by the desire to lower labor costs.

Even when reasons unrelated to labor costs are real and not constructed for the purposes of legal defense, an employer is discouraged from seeking to bargain reductions in labor costs which might offset other reasons for the move. Here too, the employer is fearful that bargaining overtures to the union will be counted against him and used as "proof" by the Board of his "real," labor-related, reasons for the move.

Conclusion

How does the Board's policy encourage unions to negotiate solutions to employer economic problems which may threaten the long-range economic well-being of employees? The fact is the Board's approach *discourages* union cooperation. Why should a union bargain, indeed how can it bargain, when the Board allows it to simply refuse to bargain?

What is a union to tell its members if it "volunteers" to bargain about economic concessions in the absence of any obligation to do

---

[36]Dissenting opinion of Judge Wood in *NLRB v. Sure-Tan, Inc.*, 677 F2d 584 (CA-7, 1982), 94 LC ¶13,573. See also *Southern Steamship Co. v. NLRB*, 316 US 31 (US SCt, 1942), 5 LC ¶51,139.

so? Political organizations that they are, unions would have to be concerned about the perpetuation of their representational status if they were to volunteer concessions when all the Board requires them to do is remain closed-mouthed during the term of the agreement. Indeed, any risk inherent in refusing to cooperate with the employer is eliminated by the Board's willingness to back up its relocation prohibition with an injunction. The Board's approach, then, like wage and price controls, provides only a temporary moratorium at the expense of long-range labor stability.

The Board's approach undercuts the very system of collective bargaining all Board Members would swear they are bound to protect and promote. It is difficult to see how the Board's current view promotes anything but short-run interests.

What is needed is for a newly reconstituted Board to reexamine the mischief the current Board approach has wrought, not only on employers but on shareholder-owners, the long-term interests of employees, and the nation's economy. A broader, more realistic approach, one which allows labor and management to bargain contracts that they can understand, would do more to encourage mature collective bargaining than Board intervention. Nor would employees thereby be left unprotected. That is, they would be protected by the very agreement their representative has struck for them, no more and no less, and they would be able to resolve relocation disputes with grievance-arbitration procedures they have agreed upon.

The long-run interests of national labor policy are not served by the Board's approach to plant and work relocations. Only when the Board finally realizes that it is meddling in an area where it does not belong will sound national labor policy prevail. Until then, however, many employers have contracts which do not mean what they say, many unions and employees have contractual rights they never knew they had, many owners own businesses which are worth much less than they think, and many lawyers are guaranteed full employment for the foreseeable future.

XIV. Economically Motivated Relocations of Work and an Employer's Duties Under Section 8(d) of the National Labor Relations Act: A Three-Step Analysis

Edward P. O'Keefe and Seamus M. Tuohey

I. Introduction

Over the past decade the continued rapid development of industrial technology, the rise of a global marketplace and an unsteady worldwide economy have forced American businesses in increasing numbers to implement major structural changes in order to attract capital, resources and customers.[1] Changes such as automation, partial or total plant closures and even complete termination and subsequent reorganization of employing enterprises have become commonplace.[2] These phenomena are most pronounced and have

---

"Economically Motivated Relocations of Work and an Employer's Duties Under Section 8(d) of the National Labor Relations Act: A Three-Step Analysis" by Edward P. O'Keefe and Seamus M. Tuohey is reprinted with permission from *Fordham Urban Law Journal*, 1983, pp. 795–843.

Edward P. O'Keefe is an associate with Cadwalader, Wickersham & Taft in New York.

Seamus M. Tuohey is an associate with Grotta, Glassman, and Hoffman in Roseland, New Jersey.

[1]*See* B. Bluestone, B. Harrison & L. Baker, Corporate Flight 38 (1981); J. Gordus, P. Jarley & L. Ferman, Plant Closings and Economic Dislocations 18 (1981).

[2]*See generally Labor Relations in an Economic Recession,* 110 Lab. Rel. Rep. (BNA) (special report) (July 19, 1982) [hereinafter cited as BNA Report] (job losses and concession bargaining); J. Gordus, P. Jarley & L. Ferman, *supra* note 1 (comprehensive review of plant closings).

had the most devastating effect in urban industrialized areas of the United States.[3]

The implementation of such entrepreneurial decisions often has a direct and adverse effect on employees involved by generally causing relocations, layoffs and terminations.[4] Consequently, employees and their unions,[5] state and local officials,[6] and federal

[3]*See* Rees, *Regional Industrial Shifts in the U.S. and the Internal Generation of Manufacturing Growth Centers in the Southwest,* in Interregional Movements and Regional Growth 51–71 (W. Wheaton ed. 1979); BNA Report, *supra* note 2, at 23–54; *Another Steel Town at the Crossroads,* Industry Week, Sept. 1, 1980, at 21; *Actions Taken to Aid Auto Industry,* Monthly Lab. Rev., Sept. 1980, at 59–60; *Firestone to Close Six Plants,* Monthly Lab. Rev., May 1980, at 55–56; *Where Job Layoffs Will Strike Next,* U.S. News and World Rep., Nov. 16, 1981, at 87–88. The United States Congressional Budget Office estimates that there could be as many as 2.1 million dislocated workers in 1983, and that they will be mostly older, experienced workers. *Union Advised to Develop Programs to Assist Laid-Off or Displaced Workers,* Daily Lab. Rep. (BNA) A-9 (Dec. 15, 1982) (quoting AFL-CIO Human Resources Development Institute).

[4]*See* B. Bluestone, B. Harrison & L. Baker, *supra* note 1, at 24–27; B. Bluestone & B. Harrison, The Deindustrialization of America 18 (1982). Employee concessions of wages and benefits have rapidly become the mechanism through which employees try to cooperate with their industrial employers to prevent adverse effects caused by major structural changes. With depressed economic circumstances causing workers to join the jobless ranks, news items recounting labor concessions appear daily. *See Teamsters Agree to Tentative Pact With Concessions,* N.Y. Times, Jan. 16, 1982, at A1, col. 5; *Ford Calls for Sacrifices by Union to Gain Protection of Auto Jobs,* N.Y. Times, Jan. 16, 1982, at A10, col. 1; *G.M. and Auto Workers to Link Cut in Wages to Lower Car Prices,* N.Y. Times, Jan. 13, 1982, at A1, col. 4; *Teamsters, Truckers, Begin Talks Early; Some Assistance Seen for Ailing Industry,* Wall St. J., Dec. 2, 1981, at 3, col. 3.

[5]BNA Report, *supra* note 2, at 9–14, 20–21. As a reaction to the growing number of major business changes, the amount of contractual protection against layoffs has grown. *See Basic Patterns in Layoff, Rehiring and Work Sharing Provisions,* Daily Lab. Rep. (BNA) E-1 (March 9, 1983); *Job Security Playing More Crucial Role in 1982 Bargaining Than in Any Prior Negotiating Round,* Daily Lab. Rep. (BNA) C-1 (Jan. 25, 1982); *Contracts Offer More Relocations Aid for Transferred Workers, BLS Study Finds,* Daily Lab. Rep. (BNA) A-1 (Aug. 31, 1981); *Plant Transfer Rights Available to Half of Those Covered by Major Bargaining Pacts, BLS Survey Shows,* Daily Lab. Rep. (BNA) A-4 (Aug. 28, 1981).

[6]Boland, *Unholy Alliance: Church Groups, Legal Services Corp. Launch Attack on U.S Steel,* Barron's, June 2, 1980, at 9, col. 1. At least two states have enacted legislation limiting an employer's right to implement certain structural changes in its business organization such as transfer of work. *See* Me. Rev. Stat. Ann. tit. 26, § 625-B (Supp. 1982–1983); Wis. Stat. Ann. § 109.07 (West Supp. 1982–1983). In addition, many states have such legislation pending. *See* McKenzie, chapter 2; Miller, chapter 3, in this volume; BNA Report, *supra* note 2, at 57–64.

legislative[7] and administrative bodies[8] have attempted to restrict the increasing number of business closings and other reinvestment decisions which result in employee dislocation.

Some of the most strident resistance to major organizational business alterations has come from the National Labor Relations Board.[9] In a series of administrative decisions[10] and federal court actions,[11] the Board has sought to limit employer attempts to implement sweeping changes in their operations without prior consultation, and in certain circumstances prior agreement, with bargaining representatives of affected employees.

The most recent development in this series of decisions is the case of *Milwaukee Spring Division of Illinois Coil Spring Co.*[12] In *Milwaukee Spring*, the Board held that the employer unlawfully trans-

---

[7]BNA Report, *supra* note 2, at 55.

[8]*See* notes 115–20, 124–30, 165–78, 186–200 & 203–19 *infra* and accompanying text.

[9]The National Labor Relations Board (NLRB or Board) was created by the National Labor Relations Act, Pub. L. No. 74–198, 49 Stat. 449 (1935) (codified at 29 U.S.C. §§ 151–167 (1976)). *See* note 18 *infra*. In 1947, the Board's size and authority was expanded by the Taft-Hartley Act, Pub. L. No. 80–101, 61 Stat. 136 (1947) (codified at 29 U.S.C. §§ 141–144, 151–167. 171–187 (1976)). *See* note 18 *infra*. The Board is composed of five members, each of whom is appointed by the President, with approval by the Senate, and serves a five-year term. 29 U.S.C. § 153(a) (1976). The duties of the Board are two-fold: to conduct secret ballot elections among employees in units appropriate for collective bargaining for the purpose of determining whether the employees desire representation by a labor organization, 29 U.S.C. § 153(d) (1976), and to prevent unfair labor practices. *Id.* § 159(b), (c). A General Counsel is also appointed by the President, with the approval of the Senate, and serves for a term of four years. The General Counsel supervises all attorneys employed by the Board, except those attorneys on the immediate staffs and under the direction of Board Members. He also supervises the officers and employees in the Board's regional offices. By statute, he has final authority to investigate unfair labor practice charges and to issue or refuse to issue complaints and to prosecute them. *Id.* § 153(d). The Board appoints an executive secretary and such attorneys, field examiners, regional directors, and other employees as it deems necessary for the proper performance of its duties. *Id.* § 154(a). A regional director is an agent designated by the Board to manage a region. 29 C.F.R. § 102.5 (1980). There are 33 regions throughout the United States. *Areas Served by Regional and Subregional Offices,* NLRB Case Handling Manual (CCH) ¶ 28,991 (July 1980).

[10]*See* notes 165–78, 186–200 & 203–19 *infra* and accompanying text.

[11]*See* notes 132, 140, 179–85 & 201–02 *infra* and accompanying text.

[12]265 N.L.R.B. No. 28, 111 L.R.R.M. 1486 (1982), *petition for review filed,* No. 82-2736 (7th Cir. October 27, 1982).

ferred work during the term of its collective bargaining agreement[13] without the prior consent of its employees' collective bargaining agent.[14] The most disturbing element of this decision is the Board's unequivocal reaffirmance of prior holdings[15] that implementation of an employer's unilateral decision to relocate all or part of a business operation, regardless of prior bargaining, constitutes an unlawful modification of an existing collective bargaining agreement, in violation of sections 8(d)[16] and 8(a)(5)[17] of the National

[13]265 N.L.R.B. No. 28, 111 L.R.R.M. at 1490. Collective bargaining agreements are contracts or mutual understandings between a labor organization representing an employer's employees and the employer. Such agreements generally set forth the employees' terms and conditions of employment such as wages, hours, working conditions, discipline, health and accident insurance, retirement, pensions, promotions, layoffs, technical changes, and a host of minor items. H. Roberts, Roberts' Dictionary of Industrial Relations 15 (2d ed. 1971). Nearly all agreements contain procedures for resolving disputes concerning the interpretation and application of the contract, usually culminating in binding arbitration. A. Cox, D. Bok & R. Gorman, Cases and Materials on Labor Law 515 (9th ed. 1981).

[14]265 N.L.R.B. No. 28, 111 L.R.R.M. at 1490. Collective bargaining agents are the exclusive representatives of the employees in the bargaining unit with respect to wages, hours and other terms and conditions of employment. 29 U.S.C. § 159(a) (1976). Collective bargaining agents are selected by a majority of the employees in a bargaining unit. *Id.* § 159. Such agents are either recognized voluntarily by an employer or certified by the Board after a Board-conducted election. *Id.*

[15]*See* notes 165–78 & 186–200 *infra* and accompanying text.

[16]Section 8(d) of the Act, 29 U.S.C. § 158(d) (1976), provides in relevant part as follows:

For the purposes of this section, to bargain collectively is the performance of the mutual obligation of the employer and the representative of the employees to meet at reasonable times and confer in good faith with respect to wages, hours, and other terms and conditions of employment, or the negotiation of an agreement, or any question arising thereunder, and the execution of a written contract incorporating any agreement reached if requested by either party, but such obligation does not compel either party to agree to a proposal or require the making of a concession: *Provided,* that where there is in effect a collective-bargaining contract covering employees in an industry affecting commerce, the duty to bargain collectively shall also mean that no party to such contract shall terminate or modify such contract, unless the party desiring such termination or modification . . . (8) continues in full force and effect, without resorting to strike or lock-out, all the terms and conditions of the existing contract for a period of sixty days after such notice is given or until the expiration of such contract, whichever occurs later.

Id.

[17]Section 8(a)(5) provides that "[i]t shall be an unfair labor practice for an employer . . . [t]o refuse to bargain collectively with the representatives of his employees. . . ." *Id.* § 158(a)(5).

Labor Relations Act.[18] *Milwaukee Spring* takes on particular importance because the Board adopted a sweeping analysis, easily adaptable to a broad range of fundamental managerial decisions.

This Article will address the legal and practical issues which arise under the Act in connection with fundamental alterations of a business enterprise. Initially, the Article will review relevant Board and judicial precedent and the general principles which have developed concerning management's right to implement a variety of changes in operation. Thereafter, it will discuss the current application of these principles to Board and court decisions concerning one type of fundamental business change: relocation of bargaining unit work,[19] and the restrictions imposed by the Act upon an employer who is contemplating such action. Finally, the authors will propose a three-step analysis which the Board and courts should consider when faced with questions concerning an employer's duty in future

---

[18]The National Labor Relations Act (NLRA or Act) is comprised of the National Labor Relations (Wagner) Act of 1935, Pub. L. No. 74-198, 49 Stat. 449 (codified at 29 U.S.C. §§ 151–167 (1976)), the Labor-Management Relations (Taft-Hartley) Act of 1947, Pub. L. No. 80-101, 61 Stat. 136 (codified at 29 U.S.C. §§ 141–144, 151–167, 171–187 (1976)), and the Labor Management Reporting and Disclosure (Landrum-Griffin) Act of 1959, Pub. L. No. 86-257, Tit. VII, 73 Stat. 519 (codified at 29 U.S.C. §§ 153, 158–160, 164, 186–187 (1976)). Section 7 of the Act provides that "[e]mployees shall have the right to self-organization, to form, join, or assist labor organizations, to bargain collectively through representatives of their own choosing, and to engage in other concerted activities for the purpose of collective bargaining . . ." 29 U.S.C. § 157 (1976). In addition, it places duties upon both employers and labor organizations to bargain in good faith with respect to terms and conditions of employment. *Id.* § 158(d). Violation of this duty is an unfair labor practice under § 8(a)(5) of the Act. *Id.* § 158(a), (b). The Board initially determines whether an action constitutes an unfair labor practice. *Id.* § 160(a). The United States Circuit Courts have the power to review the Board's decision. *Id.* § 160(e), (f).

[19]Relocation is a term of art which has no precise legal meaning. In relocation, essentially identical jobs are available at the new site and employees of the old facility are either transferred or discharged. Relocation includes three distinct categories: (1) an employer abandons an existing plant and transfers the entire business to a new location, *see* McLoughlin Mfg. Corp., 182 N.L.R.B. 958 (1970), *enforced as modified sub nom.* International Ladies Garment Workers Union, 463 F.2d 907 (D.C. Cir. 1972); (2) a particular operation of an employer's plant is transferred to a new facility while continuing other operations at the old location, *see* Tennessee-Carolina Transp., Inc., 108 N.L.R.B. 1369, 1370 (1954), *enforcement denied and remanded,* 226 F.2d 743 (6th Cir. 1955); (3) a multi-plant employer simply transfers production contracts from one plant to another, *see* Industrial Fabricating, Inc., 119 N.L.R.B. 162, 164 (1957), *enforced,* 272 F.2d 184 (6th Cir. 1959). Murphy, *Plant Relocation and the Collective Bargaining Obligation,* 59 N.C.L. Rev. 5, 13 n.53 (1980).

relocation cases, particularly those cases which present factual and legal considerations different from those presented in *Milwaukee Spring*.[20]

II. The Statute: A Mandate for Collective Bargaining

Through the National Labor Relations Act,[21] Congress sought to "protect interstate commerce from the paralyzing consequences of industrial war"[22] by imposing an enforceable duty on labor and management to meet and confer in good faith with respect to "wages, hours, and other terms and conditions of employment."[23] This Congressionally mandated system of collective bargaining is the hallmark and central concern of the Act.[24] The Act seeks to promote

[20]For the reasons stated at note 244 *infra*, it is submitted that the Board's decision in *Milwaukee Spring* is unsupported by well-reasoned precedent and contrary to longstanding legal principles. Therefore, to the extent the decision is allowed to stand, it should be strictly limited to its facts.

[21]29 U.S.C. §§ 141–187 (1976).

[22]NLRB v. Jones & Laughlin Steel Corp., 301 U.S. 1, 41 (1937). The fundamental legislative policy underlying the Act is set forth in the Act itself. Congress sought "to eliminate the causes of certain substantial obstructions to the free flow of commerce and to mitigate and eliminate these obstructions . . . by encouraging the practice and procedure of collective bargaining. . . ." 29 U.S.C. § 151 (1976). This policy was cited by the Supreme Court in Sears, Roebuck & Co. v. Carpenters, 436 U.S. 180, 190 (1978). For the Board's comments on this policy, *see* United Aircraft Corp., 192 N.L.R.B. 382, 387 (1971), *modified on other grounds*, 534 F.2d 422 (2d Cir. 1975).

[23]29 U.S.C. § 158(d). As originally enacted in 1935, the Act set forth an employer's duty to bargain in very general terms and did not state specifically the scope of that duty. National Labor Relations Act of 1935, Pub. L. No. 74-198, 49 Stat. 449. To clarify the extent of the obligation established in § 8(a)(5), Congress, in 1947, enacted § 8(d) which explicitly defined the duty of both labor and management to bargain collectively and set forth in very general terms the subjects within the scope of the duty to bargain. Labor Management Relations Act of 1947, Pub. L. No. 80-101, 61 Stat. 136. The original House bill contained a specific listing of the issues subject to mandatory bargaining. H.R. 3020, 80th Cong., 1st Sess. § 2(11) (1947), *published in* H. R. Rep. No. 245, 80th Cong., 1st Sess. 48–49 (1947). Congress, however, rejected this attempt to "strait-jacket" and to "limit narrowly the subject matters appropriate for collective bargaining," *id.* at 71 (minority report), in favor of the more generalized listing of "wages, hours, and other terms and conditions of employment" now found in § 8(d), 29 U.S.C. § 158(d) (1976).

[24]*See* note 22 *supra*. *See also* § 1 of the Act in which Congress further recognized that "the refusal by some employers to accept the procedure of collective bargaining led to strikes. . . ." 29 U.S.C. § 151 (1976). This principle has long been recognized by the Supreme Court. *See Jones & Laughlin Steel Corp.*, 301 U.S. at 42; Carey v.

industrial peace by mandating that the conflicting interests of labor and management subject themselves to the mediatory influence of face-to-face collective bargaining concerning their differences as to terms and conditions of employment.[25]

A. Scope of the Duty

The duty imposed on labor and management by the Act to bargain collectively applies only to *"terms and conditions of employment,"*[26] a phrase which is contained, yet undefined in the Act.[27] The Board and the courts have sought to define an employer's duty in terms of whether a subject of bargaining is mandatory, permissive or illegal.[28] For subjects encompassed within the phrase "terms and conditions of employment, bargaining is mandatory."[29] As to all

---

Westinghouse Elec. Corp., 375 U.S. 261, 271 (1964) (the Act "is primarily designed to promote industrial peace and stability by encouraging the practice and procedure of collective bargaining . . .") (quoting International Harvester Co., 138 N.L.R.B. 923, 925–26 (1962), aff'd, 327 F.2d 784 (7th Cir. 1964)). *See also* First Nat'l Maintenance Corp. v. NLRB, 452 U.S. 666, 674 (1981) (purpose of the Act "is the promotion of collective bargaining as a method of defusing . . . conflict between labor and management"); Fibreboard Paper Prods. Corp. v. NLRB, 379 U.S. 203, 211 (1964) (purpose "of the Act is to promote peaceful settlement of industrial disputes by subjecting . . . controversies to . . . negotiation").

[25]29 U.S.C. § 158(d) (1976). *See* note 22 *supra.*

[26]NLRB v. Wooster Div. of Borg-Warner Corp., 356 U.S. 342, 349 (1958).

[27]*See* note 23 *supra.*

[28]*Wooster Div. of Borg-Warner Corp.*, 356 U.S. at 348–49. Reading §§ 8(a)(5) and 8(d) together, the Court declared that

these provisions establish the obligation of the employer and the representative of its employees to bargain with each other in good faith with respect to "wages, hours, and other terms and conditions of employment. . . ." The duty is limited to those subjects, and within that area neither party is legally obligated to yield. . . . As to other matters, however, each party is free to bargain or not to bargain, and to agree or not to agree.

Id. at 349 (citing NLRB v. American Nat'l Ins. Co., 343 U.S. 395 (1952)).

[29]356 U.S. at 349. The range of subjects which have been found to be mandatory subjects of bargaining is quite broad and includes such diverse matters as compensation, Oughton v. NLRB, 118 F.2d 486, 498 (3d Cir. 1941), *cert. denied*, 315 U.S. 797 (1942); pensions, Inland Steel Co. v. NLRB, 170 F.2d 247, 251 (7th Cir. 1948), *cert. denied*, 336 U.S. 960 (1949); profit-sharing plans, Winn-Dixie Stores v. NLRB, 567 F.2d 1343 (5th Cir. 1977), *cert. denied*, 439 U.S. 985 (1978); bonuses, Singer Mfg. Co. v. NLRB, 119 F.2d 131, 136–37 (7th Cir.), *cert. denied*, 313 U.S. 595 (1941); stock purchase arrangements, Richfield Oil Corp. v. NLRB, 231 F.2d 717, 724 (D.C. Cir. 1956); merit wage increases, NLRB v. J. H. Allison & Co., 165 F.2d 766, 768–69 (6th Cir.), *cert. denied*, 335 U.S. 814 (1948); insurance schemes, W. W. Cross & Co. v.

others, bargaining is either permissive[30] or illegal.[31] Although bargaining is required with respect to mandatory subjects, concession or agreement is not.[32] Consequently, either party may take a position fairly held on a mandatory subject and bargain to impasse.[33] This right, however, does not extend to permissive subjects.[34] Parties to negotiations may not bargain to impasse over, and thus condition agreement upon, a permissive subject of bargaining.[35]

NLRB, 174 F.2d 875, 878 (1st Cir. 1949); company housing, American Smelting & Ref. Co. v. NLRB, 406 F.2d 552, 554–55 (9th Cir.), *cert. denied*, 395 U.S. 935 (1969); hiring practices, NLRB v. Houston Chapter, Assoc. Gen. Contractors of Am., Inc., 349 F.2d 449, 451 (5th Cir. 1965); layoffs and recalls, Awrey Bakeries, Inc. v. NLRB, 548 F.2d 138 (6th Cir. 1976); operation of employer's seniority program, Industrial Union of Marine & Shipbuilding Workers v. NLRB, 320 F.2d 615, 620 (3rd Cir. 1963); "most favored nation" clauses, Dolly Madison Indus., Inc., 182 N.L.R.B. 1037 (1970); and even the price of food in company cafeterias, Ford Motor Co. v. NLRB, 441 U.S. 488, 494–95 (1979).

[30]Permissive subjects include, *inter alia*, the scope of a bargaining unit, Douds v. International Longshoremen's Ass'n, 241 F.2d 278, 282 (2d Cir. 1957), and including supervisors in a bargaining unit, NLRB v. Retail Clerks Int'l Ass'n, 203 F.2d 165 (9th Cir. 1953).

[31]Certain subjects may not be agreed upon by any party under the Act. *See, e.g.,* NLRB v. National Maritime Union, 175 F.2d 686 (2d Cir. 1949), *cert. denied,* 338 U.S. 954 (1950) (hiring hall provision which gives preference to union members); Penello v. United Mine Workers, 88 F. Supp. 935 (D.D.C. 1950) (closed shop); Amalgamated Lithographers, Local 17, 130 N.L.R.B. 985 (1961) (hot cargo clause in violation of § 8(e) of the Act), *enforced,* 309 F.2d 31 (9th Cir. 1962).

[32]29 U.S.C. § 158(d) (1976).

[33]*Wooster Div. of Borg-Warner Corp.,* 356 U.S. at 349. Impasse has been defined as a deadlock in negotiations between the employer and the collective bargaining agent of the employees. H. Roberts, *supra* note 13, at 193. Whether an impasse exists is a matter of judgment. In Taft Broadcasting Co. v. AFTRA, 163 N.L.R.B. 475 (1967), the Board explained:

The bargaining history, the good faith of the parties in negotiations, the length of the negotiations, the importance of the issue or issues as to which there is disagreement, the contemporaneous understanding of the parties as to the state of the negotiations, are all relevant factors to be considered in deciding whether an impasse in bargaining existed.

Id. at 478.

[34]356 U.S. at 349.

[35]*Id.* While parties to negotiations may choose to bargain over a permissive subject of bargaining, no amount of bargaining will transform a permissive subject into a mandatory subject of bargaining. *Id.* In NLRB v. Davidson, 318 F.2d 550 (4th Cir. 1963), the court stated:

A determination that a subject which is non-mandatory at the outset may become mandatory merely because a party had exercised this freedom [to bargain or not

The Act also requires that where the parties have reached agreement, the terms of which are embodied in a contract for a particular period, each must maintain "in full force and effect . . . all the terms and conditions of the existing contract . . . until the expiration date of the contract.[36] Moreover, the Act expressly provides that:

> the duties so imposed shall not be construed as requiring either party to discuss or agree to any modification of the terms and conditions contained in a contract for a fixed period, if such modification is to become effective before such terms and conditions can be reopened under the provisions of the contract.[37]

Thus, section 8(d) of the Act has a dual nature: it mandates a system by which labor and management may resolve their differences with respect to terms and conditions of employment and, upon resolution of those differences, prohibits unilateral modification of that agreement by any party for its full term.

B. Enforcement of the Duty

The dual mandates of section 8(d) are enforced by sections 8(a) and (b) of the Act.[38] The primary enforcer of section 8(d) as to employers is section 8(a)(5),[39] which renders unlawful an employer's refusal to bargain in good faith with its employees' representative.[40] Refusals by an employer to bargain in good faith

---

to bargain] by not rejecting the proposal at once, or sufficiently early, might unduly discourage free bargaining on non-mandatory matters. Parties might feel compelled to reject non-mandatory proposals out of hand to avoid risking waiver of the right to reject.
Id. at 558.

[36]29 U.S.C. § 158(d) (1976). Section 8(d) states that the parties must maintain all of the "terms and conditions of the contract." *Id.* The Supreme Court, however, has limited this requirement to maintaining only those terms of a contract which constitute mandatory subjects of bargaining. *See* Allied Chem. & Alkali Workers of Am., Local Union No. 1 v. Pittsburgh Plate Glass Co., Chem. Div., 404 U.S. 157 (1971).

[37]29 U.S.C. § 158(d) (1976).

[38]Section 8(a) of the Act prohibits unfair labor practices by an employer. *Id.* § 158(a). *See* notes 39–50 *infra* and accompanying text. Section 8(b), on the other hand, prohibits union unfair labor practices, including restraint or coercion of employees in the exercise of rights guaranteed under § 7, 29 U.S.C. § 158(b)(1) (1976), and "refus[ing] to bargain collectively with an employer. . . ." *Id.* § 158(b)(3).

[39]29 U.S.C. § 158(a)(5) (1976).

[40]*Id.* Section 8(b)(3) of the Act extends a similar prohibition to unions. *See* note 38 *supra*.

under section 8(a)(5) include not only direct refusals to bargain over terms and conditions of employment,[41] but also any unilateral actions[42] which alter such terms and conditions, even absent an existing agreement.[43] Section 8(a)(5) also prohibits unilateral modifications of the terms of a labor agreement during its effective period.[44]

Section 8(a)(1) of the Act[45] further regulates employer action by prohibiting an employer from interfering with, restraining or coerc-

---

[41]*See, e.g.,* NLRB v. Highland Park Mfg. Co., 110 F.2d 632 (4th Cir. 1940) (refusal to enter into any agreement with union); General Elec. Co., 150 N.L.R.B. 192 (presentation of a single, acceptable comprehensive offer as final in conjunction with extensive attempt to sell the package directly to the employees held to be a refusal to bargain in good faith), *vacated and remanded,* 382 U.S. (1966), *enforced,* 418 F.2d 736 (2d Cir. 1969), *cert. denied,* 397 U.S. 965 (1970); NLRB v. Truitt Mfg., 351 U.S. 149 (1956) (refusal to provide information necessary to conduct collective bargaining).

[42]Unilateral action is action by one of the parties to a collective bargaining agreement independent of the desires or wishes of the other, often without prior notice or consultation. H. Roberts, *supra* note 13, at 549.

[43]Generally, in determining whether an unlawful refusal to bargain has occurred, all the relevant facts of a case are studied in determining whether the employer or the union is bargaining in good or bad faith, i.e., the "totality of conduct" is the standard through which the "quality" of negotiations is tested. NLRB v. Stevenson Brick & Block Co., 393 F.2d 234 (4th Cir. 1968); B. F. Diamond Construction Co., 163 N.L.R.B. 161 (1967), *enforced,* 410 F.2d 462 (5th Cir. 1969). In Rhodes-Holland Chevrolet Co., 146 N.L.R.B. 1304 (1964), the Board stated:

In finding that Respondent violated its obligation to bargain in good faith, we, like the Trial Examiner, have not relied solely on the position taken by Respondent on substantive contract terms, a factor which, standing alone . . . might not have provided sufficient basis for the violation found, but have considered that factor as simply one item in the totality of circumstances reflecting Respondent's bargaining frame of mind.

Id. at 1304–05. The "totality of conduct" doctrine, generally, stems from NLRB v. Virginia Elec. & Power Co., 314 U.S. 469 (1941). Certain types of conduct, such as unilateral action, however, have been viewed as per se refusals to bargain, without regard to any considerations of good or bad faith. *See* NLRB v. Katz, 369 U.S. 736 (1962); NLRB v. American Mfg. Co., 351 F.2d 74 (5th Cir. 1965) (unilateral grant of wage increase); McLean v. NLRB, 333 F.2d 84 (6th Cir. 1964) (unilateral grant of health insurance). Of course, unilateral changes are permissible where there is no contract in effect and the parties have reached a legitimate impasse, or the union has waived its right to contest a unilateral change. *See* Almeida Bus Lines, Inc., 333 F.2d 729 (1st Cir. 1964); U.S. Lingerie Corp., 170 N.L.R.B. 750 (1968).

[44]Nassau County Health Care Facilities Ass'n, 227 N.L.R.B. 1680, 1683 (1977); C & S Indus. Inc., 158 N.L.R.B. 454, 457 (1966).

[45]29 U.S.C. § 158(a)(1) (1976).

ing employees in the exercise of their rights under section 7.[46] As a refusal to bargain necessarily interferes with employees' rights to collectively bargain concerning terms and conditions of employment, violations of section 8(a)(5) derivatively violate section 8(a)(1).[47]

Section 8(a)(3) prohibits an employer from engaging in discrimination with regard to any term and condition of employment to discourage membership in any labor organization.[48] Violations of section 8(a)(3) generally do not involve violations of the duty to bargain under sections 8(d) and 8(a)(5). However, certain unilateral employer actions which violate section 8(a)(5) have been held to be so inimical to employee rights to engage in concerted activities that they constitute not only refusals to bargain in good faith, but also violations of section 8(a)(3).[49] The Board and courts have reasoned that such acts are "inherently destructive" of employees' statutory rights and thus violate section 8(a)(3).[50]

In sum, the Act places two types of restrictions upon an employer's decision to implement substantial alterations in its operations. First, to the extent a substantial alteration changes mandatory terms and conditions of employment, section 8(d) imposes upon an employer a duty to bargain concerning the decision to implement the alteration.[51] Second, where there is a collective bargaining

---

[46]*Id.*

[47]The Board has noted since its inception that "a violation by an employer of any of the four subdivisions of section 8 . . . is also a violation of subdivision (1)." 3 N.L.R.B. Ann. Rep. 52 (1939). The employer's motive generally is not considered in determining whether it has violated § 8(a)(1). Cooper Thermometer Co., 154 N.L.R.B. 502, 503 n.2 (1965).

[48]Section 8(a)(3) provides that it is an unfair labor practice for an employer "by discrimination in regard to hire or tenure of employment or any term or condition of employment to encourage or discourage membership in any labor organization." 29 U.S.C. § 158(a)(3) (1976). Thus, violations of § 8(a)(3) generally require a showing of an employer's intention to discourage union membership. *See* American Ship Bldg. Co. v. NLRB, 380 U.S. 300, 311 (1965); Republic Aviation Corp. v. NLRB, 324 U.S. 793, 805 (1945).

[49]NLRB v. Great Dane Trailers, Inc., 388 U.S. 26, 34 (1967).

[50]*Id.* See note 250 *infra* for further discussion of the Board's application of the "inherently destructive" doctrine in the context of relocations of bargaining unit work.

[51]*See* notes 26–37 *supra* and accompanying text. Section 8(d) does not require either party to make concessions, if agreement cannot be made. 29 U.S.C. § 158(d) (1976). Once impasse in negotiations is reached, an employer is free to implement its decision. American Ship Bldg. Co. v. NLRB 380 U.S. 300, 318 (1965); Newspaper Printing Corp. v. NLRB, 692 F.2d 615, 620 (6th Cir. 1982). *See* notes 29–35 *supra* and

agreement in effect, section 8(d) prohibits employer action which modifies or otherwise changes any mandatory term or condition of employment contained in the agreement.[52]

Although the Board and the courts have issued numerous decisions defining the scope of an employer's duty under section 8(d),[53] considerable disagreement remains as to the extent to which certain employer actions, such as plant relocation, constitute unlawful conduct.[54] This disagreement is best understood by reviewing the Board and court decisions which concern an employer's bargaining duties with respect to a variety of substantial business alterations.

III. Judicial and Administrative Construction of the Duty to Bargain

The Board has long held that the decision to implement certain substantial alterations of a business which result in the termination of bargaining unit work is subject to the collective bargaining proc-

---

accompanying text. It is important to note, however, that the right to unilaterally implement a change in terms and conditions of employment only extends to implementing an employer's last proposal. Eddie's Chop Shop, 165 N.L.R.B. 861 (1967). No greater benefits or change may be implemented. *Id.*

Regardless of whether an employer is obligated to bargain concerning the decision to implement a substantial alteration in its operations, it will, in any event, be obligated to bargain over the effects or impact that such a decision will have on bargaining unit employees under § 8(d) and (a)(5) of the Act. *See, e.g.,* First Nat'l Maintenance Corp. v. NLRB, 452 U.S. 666, 681 (1981) (employer under duty to bargain over effects of partial closing); NLRB v. Royal Plating & Publishing Co., 350 F.2d at 191, 196 (3d Cir. 1965) (employer must bargain over effects of plant closing); Otis Elevator Co., 255 N.L.R.B. 235 (1981) (same); American Needle & Novelty Co., 206 N.L.R.B. 534 (1979) (duty to bargain over effects of plant relocation); Ozark Trailers, Inc., 161 N.L.R.B. 561 (1966) (same). Bargainable issues may include severance pay, seniority, pensions, and transfer rights, among others. *See* NLRB v. Royal Plating & Publishing Co., 350 F.2d at 191.

[52]*See* note 36 *supra* and accompanying text.

[53]*See* Continental Ins. Co. v. NLRB, 495 F.2d 44 (2d Cir. 1974), *enforcing,* 204 N.L.R.B. 1013 (1973); Underwriters Adjusting Co., 214 N.L.R.B. 388 (1974); Ramona's Mexican Food Prods., Inc., 203 N.L.R.B. 663 (1973), *aff'd,* 531 F.2d 390 (9th Cir. 1975).

[54]*See* Harper, *Leveling the Road from* Borg-Warner *to* First National Maintenance: *The Scope of Mandatory Bargaining,* 68 Va. L. Rev. 1447 (1982); Murphy, *Plant Relocation and the Collective Bargaining Obligation,* 59 N.C.L. Rev. 5 (1980); Comment, First National Maintenance Corp. v. NLRB: *Partial Closings and the Duty to Bargain,* 48 Brooklyn L. Rev. 307 (1982).

ess.[55] As early as 1946, the Board held that an employer must bargain prior to making a decision to subcontract work performed by its employees.[56] In 1962, the Board reaffirmed its position concerning subcontracting decisions in *Town & Country Manufacturing Co.*[57] Significantly, the Board read the mandate of section 8(d) broadly, stating that "the elimination of unit jobs, albeit for economic reasons, is a matter within statutory phrase 'other terms and conditions of employment' and is a mandatory subject of collective bargaining within the meaning of Section 8(a)(5) of the Act."[58] The Board reasoned that, although the Act does not require an employer to yield to a union's demand that a subcontract not be made, "experience has shown . . . that candid discussion of mutual problems by labor and management frequently results in their resolution with attendant benefits to both sides."[59] The emphasis in *Town & Country* upon utilization of the collective bargaining process for the presentation and discussion of the parties' respective positions concerning major business decisions[60] laid the foundation for the Supreme Court's landmark decision in *Fibreboard Paper Products Corp. v. NLRB.*[61]

A. Fibreboard

In *Fibreboard*, the Supreme Court confronted the issue of whether an employer's purely economic decision to subcontract bargaining unit work was a "term and condition of employment" rendering it

---

[55]Fibreboard Paper Prods. Corp., 130 N.L.R.B. 1558 (1961) (subcontracting), *supplemented*, 138 N.L.R.B. 550 (1962), *enforced*, 322 F.2d 411 (D.C. Cir. 1963), *aff'd*, 379 U.S. 203 (1964); Cooper Thermometer Co., 160 N.L.R.B. 1902 (1966) (transfer of employees), *enforced*, 376 F.2d 684 (2d Cir. 1967); Dixie Ohio Express Co., 167 N.L.R.B. 573 (1967) (reorganization of operations), *enforcement denied*, 409 F.2d 10 (6th Cir. 1969); Renton News Record, 136 N.L.R.B. 1294 (1962) (automation). *See* Fastiff, *Changes in Business Operations: The Effects of the National Labor Relations Act and Contract Language on Employer Authority*, 14 Santa Clara Law. 281 (1974); Tiballi, *Mandatory Subjects of Bargaining-Operational Changes*, 17 Fla. L. Rev. 109 (1964); Note, *Application of the Mandatory-Permissive Dichotomy to the Duty to Bargain and Unilateral Action: A Review and Reevaluation*, 15 Wm. & Mary L. Rev. 918 (1974).

[56]Timken Roller Bearing Co., 70 N.L.R.B. 500 (1946), *enforcement denied on other grounds*, 161 F.2d 949 (6th Cir. 1947).

[57]136 N.L.R.B. 1022 (1962), *enforced*, 316 F.2d 846 (5th Cir. 1963).

[58]136 N.L.R.B. at 1027.

[59]*Id.*

[60]*Id.*

[61]379 U.S. 203 (1964), *aff'g*, 138 N.L.R.B. 550 (1963).

a mandatory subject of bargaining.[62] Consistent with the Board's focus in *Town & Country*, the Court analyzed the employer's bargaining duty in terms of whether the subject at issue "was a problem of [such] vital concern to labor and management"[63] that it should

[62]379 U.S. at 209. In *Fibreboard*, the employer operated a plant in which its unionized employees provided maintenance services. Upon determining that substantial cost savings were possible if it utilized outside contractors to perform maintenance work, the employer engaged the services of an outside contractor and laid off its maintenance workers without prior bargaining with their union. *Id.* at 206. The Board found that, although the employer was not motivated by union animus in its decision to subcontract out the plant's maintenance work, it had violated § 8(a)(5) of the Act by its failure to negotiate with the union with regard to its decision to subcontract its maintenance work. 130 N.L.R.B. 1558 (1961), *supplemented*, 138 N.L.R.B. 550 (1962). The District of Columbia Circuit court affirmed the Board's finding and enforced the Board order that the employer bargain with the union in good faith concerning its decision to subcontract. 322 F.2d 411 (D.C. Cir. 1963).

[63]379 U.S. at 211. The Board has broad authority to fashion appropriate remedial sanctions for an employer's unlawful failure to bargain over a change in its business operations. Section 10 of the NLRA stipulates that the Board, upon finding that an unfair labor practice has been committed, "shall issue . . . an order requiring such person to cease and desist from such unfair labor practice, and to take such affirmative action including reinstatement of employees with or without back pay, as will effectuate the policies of [the Act]. . . ." 29 U.S.C. § 160(c) (1976). In Fibreboard Paper Prods. Corp., 379 U.S. 203, 216 (1964), the Supreme Court stated:

[Section 10(c)] "charges the Board with the task of devising remedies to effectuate the policies of the Act." The Board's power is a broad discretionary one, subject to limited judicial review. The Board's order will not be disturbed unless it can be shown that the order is a patent attempt to achieve ends other than those which can fairly be said to effectuate the policies of the Act.

Id. at 216 (citations omitted).

Generally, where the Board has found a violation of the Act based upon an employer's unlawful unilateral action, it has ordered the employer to bargain in good faith with the union, to cease and desist from further actions which have been deemed to be unlawful, to restore the status quo through reinstatement with back pay of all terminated employees, and even to reestablish its operations. *See, e.g.,* Jay's Foods, Inc., 228 N.L.R.B. 423 (1977) (unlawful subcontracted resulting in Board order requiring reinstatement with back pay plus interest and a complete abrogation of all subcontracts which were entered into prior to negotiations with the union), *enforced in part*, 573 F.2d 438 (7th Cir. 1978); Ohio Brake & Clutch Corp., 244 N.L.R.B. 35 (1979) (Board ordered the employer to bargain over decision and effects of a relocation); Local 57, Int'l Ladies Garment Workers Union v. NLRB, 374 F.2d 295 (D.C. Cir.) (following employer's unlawful plant relocation, Board ordered full reinstatement of employees, compensation for lost earnings and employer bargaining irrespective of union majority, following the relocation), *cert. denied*, 387 U.S. 942 (1967). Section 10(j) of the Act authorizes the Board, "upon issuance of a complaint . . . charging that any person has engaged in or is engaging in an unfair labor practice, to petition any United States district court . . . for appropriate temporary

be brought "within the framework [of collective bargaining] established by Congress as the most conducive to industrial peace."[64]

The Court held that the employer's decision to subcontract unit work constituted the type of activity which could benefit from collective bargaining. It reasoned that the employer's decision was suitable for collective bargaining because industrial experience had demonstrated that such decisions could generally be amicably resolved, and the employer had merely replaced one group of employees with another without substantial change in his investment.[65]

B. Darlington

In 1965, the Supreme Court issued its second major decision concerning an employer's duty under the Act with regard to substantial alterations in its enterprise: *Textile Workers Union of America v. Darlington Manufacturing Co.*[66] Unlike *Fibreboard*, which involved an employer's obligation under section 8(a)(5) of the Act in the context of a well-established bargaining relationship, *Darlington* arose under section 8(a)(3)[67] in the course of a union's drive to organize the employees at one of the employer's plants.[68] Because of its section 8(a)(5) implications, however, the *Darlington* case warrants more than passing consideration.

In 1956, the Textile Workers Union commenced organizational

---

relief or restraining order." 29 U.S.C. § 160(j) (1976). The Board has sought and obtained such relief in the context of cases involving relocations of bargaining unit work. *See* note 199 *infra*.

[64]379 U.S. at 211.

[65]*Id.* at 213. Justice Stewart, joined by Justices Douglas and Harlan, filed a concurring opinion. *Id.* at 217. Justice Stewart sought to limit the scope of the majority opinion. He stated that the majority opinion did not decide that every managerial decision which terminates an individual's employment would be necessarily held to be a mandatory subject of bargaining. *Id.* at 218. In particular, he remarked:

Nothing the Court holds today should be understood as imposing a duty to bargain collectively regarding such managerial decisions which lie at the core of entrepreneurial control. Decisions concerning the commitment of investment capital and the basic scope of the enterprise are not in themselves primarily about conditions of employment, though the effect of the decision may be necessarily to terminate employment.

Id. at 223.

[66]380 U.S. 263 (1965).

[67]29 U.S.C. § 158(a)(3) (1976). *See* notes 48–50 *supra* and accompanying text for a discussion of § 8(a)(3).

[68]380 U.S. at 266–67.

activity among the Darlington mill employees.[69] The employer responded in various ways, including alleged threats to close its facility should the union be successful in an NLRB election.[70] When the union won the election, Darlington closed the mill in November, 1956, and sold the plant's machinery and equipment in its entirety one month later.[71] The union countered by filing unfair labor practice charges alleging violations of sections 8(a)(1), (3) and (5) of the National Labor Relations Act.[72]

The Board found that Darlington was part of a single integrated enterprise, Deering Milliken & Co.[73] By closing an entire facility in response to the union's victory in the representation election, Deering Milliken was found to have violated sections 8(a)(1), (3), and (5).[74] The Fourth Circuit, however, denied enforcement of the Board's Decision and Order, holding that the employer had an absolute right to close all or part of its business regardless of its motivation for doing so.[75]

Before the Supreme Court, the union contended that an employer who goes completely out of business to avoid unionization violates the Act.[76] Rejecting the union's argument, the Court observed:

> A proposition that a single businessman cannot choose to go out of business if he wants to, would represent such a startling inno-

[69]*Id.* at 265.

[70]*Id.*

[71]*Id.* at 266.

[72]*Id.* at 266–67. Pursuant to § 10(b) of the NLRA, 29 U.S.C. § 160(b) (1976), an unfair labor practice case is initiated when a private party files a "charge" with the appropriate NLRB regional office that an unfair labor practice has been committed. 29 C.F.R. § 102.9 (1982). The regional office investigates the charge, and the regional director decides whether to issue a complaint. *Id.* § 102.15. If a complaint is issued, a Board attorney from the regional office prosecutes the case, which is tried in a formal hearing before an administrative law judge (ALJ). *Id.* § 102.35. The ALJ makes findings of fact and then issues a recommended decision and order either indicating the appropriate remedy or suggesting that the complaint be dismissed. *Id.* § 102.45. The charging party, respondent, or General Counsel of the NLRB in Washington, D.C., may file exceptions to this recommended order. *Id.* § 102.46. If no exceptions are filed, the order automatically becomes final as an order issued by the Board. *Id.* If timely exceptions are filed, the case is transferred to the NLRB, which then issues its own final decision and order. *Id.; see,* Comment, *supra* note 54, at 315–16.

[73]139 N.L.R.B. 241, 252 (1962).

[74]*Id.* at 244–53.

[75]325 F.2d 682 (4th Cir. 1963).

[76]380 U.S. at 269–70.

vation that it should not be entertained without the clearest manifestation of legislative intent or unequivocal judicial precedent so construing the Labor Relations Act. We find neither.[77]

It is important to note that since *Darlington* is a section 8(a)(3) case,[78] it did not raise the question of whether section 8(a)(5) requires an employer to bargain concerning a purely business decision to terminate its enterprise in its entirety.[79] However, the case has been relied upon repeatedly for the proposition that an employer's decision to terminate his entire enterprise is beyond the legitimate reach of sections 8(d) and 8(a)(5).[80]

C. First National Maintenance

After *Darlington*, the Board attempted to place further limitations on an employer's right to implement alterations in its business operations.[81] Although the Board did continue to provide lip service[82] to Justice Stewart's admonition in *Fibreboard* that the duty to bargain does not reach to managerial "decisions concerning the commitment

---

[77]*Id.* at 270.

[78]*Id.* at 268. Section 8(a)(3) prohibits an employer from engaging in discrimination in regard to any term or condition of employment so as to discourage labor organization membership. 29 U.S.C. § 158(a)(3) (1976).

[79]380 U.S. at 268. *See* Rabin, Fibreboard *and the Termination of the Bargaining Unit Work: The Search for Standards in Defining the Scope of the Duty to Bargain,* 71 Colum. L. Rev. 803, 818 (1971); Schwarz, *Plant Relocation or Partial Termination—The Duty to Decision Bargain,* 39 Fordham L. Rev. 81, 85–86 (1970).

[80]*See* Brockway Motor Trucks, Div. of Mack Trucks v. NLRB, 582 F.2d 720 (3d Cir. 1978); Morrison Cafeterias Consol., Inc. v. NLRB, 431 F.2d 254, 257 (8th Cir. 1970); NLRB v. Royal Plating & Polishing Co., 350 F.2d 191, 196 (3d Cir. 1965); NLRB v. Burns Int'l Detective Agency, 346 F.2d 897, 902 (8th Cir. 1965).

[81]Metro Transp. Servs. Co. 218 N.L.R.B. 534 (1975) (employer has duty to bargain over partial plant closing); Ozark Trailers, Inc., 161 N.L.R.B. 561 (1966) (same); L. E. Davis, 237 N.L.R.B. 1042 (1978) (economically motivated decision to convert restaurant into cafeteria held to be mandatory bargaining subject), *enforced sub nom.* Davis v. NLRB, 617 F.2d 1264 (7th Cir. 1980); McLoughlin Mfg. Corp., 182 N.L.R.B. 958 (1970) (duty to bargain over relocation), *supplementing* 164 N.L.R.B. 140 (1967), *enforced as modified sub nom.* International Ladies' Garment Workers Union v. NLRB, 493 F.2d 907 (D.C. Cir. 1972); Morco Indus., Inc., 255 N.L.R.B. 146 (1981) (same). *Cf.* Summit Tooling Co., 195 N.L.R.B. 497 (1972) (employer under no duty to terminate distinct line of business), *enforced sub nom.,* United Auto. Workers v. NLRB, 470 F.2d 422 (D.C. Cir. 1973).

[82]*See* Otis Elevator Co., 255 N.L.R.B. 235, 246 (1981); Brockway Motor Trucks, Div. of Mack Trucks, 230 N.L.R.B. 1002, 1003 (1977), *rev'd,* 582 F.2d 720 (3d Cir. 1978).

of capital and the basic scope of the enterprise,"[83] the Board continued to strictly limit various employer actions.[84] The Board's restriction on one such major business change reached its apex and was overruled by the Supreme Court in *NLRB v. First National Maintenance Corp.*[85] The facts before the Court in *First National Maintenance* presented the middle ground between *Fibreboard* and *Darlington*—the partial closure of a business for economic reasons.[86]

The issue before the Supreme Court was whether an employer's decision to partially close its business solely for economic reasons was within the scope of its duty to bargain under section 8(d). As in *Fibreboard*,[87] the Court emphasized that "[c]entral to the achievement of [creating industrial peace] is the promotion of collective bargaining as a method of defusing and channeling conflict between labor and management."[88] Building upon, and indeed quoting from,

---

[83]379 U.S. at 223.

[84]*See* Otis Elevator Co., 255 N.L.R.B. 235 (1981); Brockway Motor Trucks, Div. of Mack Trucks, 230 N.L.R.B. 1002 (1977), *rev'd*, 582 F.2d 720 (3d Cir. 1978); Royal Typewriter Co., 209 N.L.R.B. 1006 (1974), *enforcement denied*, 533 F.2d 1030 (3d Cir. 1976); Acme Indus. Prods., 180 N.L.R.B. 114 (1969), *enforcement denied*, 439 F.2d 40 (6th Cir. 1971).

[85]452 U.S. 666 (1981).

[86]In *First Nat'l Maintenance,* the employer provided cleaning and maintenance services for commercial customers, including several nursing homes. One of its nursing homes, Greenpark, paid First National Maintenance (FNM) a fixed professional service fee and also reimbursed its labor costs. 452 U.S. at 668. In 1976, Greenpark announced that it would pay FNM only half of its original service fee. *Id.* at 668. After determining that it was losing money at the lower service fee, FNM discontinued its operations at Greenpark without notifying or consulting with the union certified to represent its employees there. *Id.* at 669. In response to FNM's unilateral action, the union filed unfair labor practice charges alleging failure to bargain concerning the decision to discontinue servicing Greenpark. *Id.* at 670. The Board held that the company was under an obligation to bargain with the union concerning its decision to cease services at Greenpark. First Nat'l Maintenance Corp., 242 N.L.R.B. 462 (1979). The Second Circuit affirmed the Board's decision and enforced its order that the company bargain in good faith over its decision to partially close. 627 F.2d 596 (2d Cir. 1980). The Supreme Court reversed. 452 U.S. 666 (1981). The Court held that, while an employer is obligated to bargain over the effects of a partial closing decision, it is under no duty to bargain with respect to the decision itself. *Id.* at 681, 686.

[87]Fibreboard Paper Prods. Corp. v. NLRB, 379 U.S. 203 (1964) (discussed at notes 60–61 *supra* and accompanying text).

[88]452 U.S. at 674.

the analysis previously applied in *Fibreboard*,[89] the Court set forth a balancing test to determine whether a particular subject constitutes a mandatory subject of bargaining: *"bargaining over management decisions which have a substantial impact on the availability of employment should be required only if the benefit, for labor-management relations and the collective bargaining process, outweighs the burden placed on the conduct of the business."*[90] The Court underscored that the proper focus when determining an employer's bargaining duty with respect to a particular managerial decision is whether the decision is "suitable for resolution within the collective bargaining framework."[91]

Applying its test to the facts before it, the Court held that the employer's decision to partially close its business operation was not amenable to collective bargaining and, therefore, "[was] *not* part of Section 8(d)'s 'terms and conditions' over which Congress has mandated bargaining."[92]

While the Supreme Court in *First National Maintenance* appeared to limit the scope of its holding to cases involving partial closures,[93] the Board's General Counsel[94] has instructed the Board's Regional Directors to analyze cases involving employer decisions to substantially alter business operations, including but not limited to partial closures, to determine whether each decision is "amenable to resolution through the collective bargaining process."[95] The General

---

[89] 379 U.S. at 203.

[90] 452 U.S. at 679 (emphasis added).

[91] *Id.* at 680 (quoting *Fibreboard*, 379 U.S. at 214).

[92] *Id.* at 686. The Supreme Court noted that "under § 8(a)(5) bargaining over the effects of a [partial closing] decision must be conducted in a meaningful manner and at a meaningful time, and the Board may impose sanctions to insure its adequacy." *Id.* at 681–82.

[93] 452 U.S. at 686 n.22. The Court noted that it "intimate[d] no view as to other types of management decisions, such as plant relocations, sales, other kinds of subcontracting, automation, etc., which are to be considered on their particular facts." *Id.*

[94] NLRB General Counsel Memorandum 81-57, 1981 Lab. Rel. Yearbook (BNA) 315 (November 30, 1981) [hereinafter cited as General Counsel's Memorandum].

[95] *Id.* at 316. In many cases, however, the Board and the circuit courts have seemingly ignored *First Nat'l Maintenance* in determining whether an employer has an obligation to bargain concerning certain managerial decisions other than partial closures. *See* Tocco Div. of Park-Ohio Indus., Inc., 257 N.L.R.B. 413 (1981) (employer failed to bargain over decision to relocate), *enforced*, 112 L.R.R.M. (BNA) 3089 (6th Cir. 1983); General Motors Corp., Inland Div., 257 N.L.R.B. 820 (1981) (employer did not violate § 8(a)(5) by subcontracting without first bargaining since decision

Counsel's approach provides some indication that the Board, and perhaps the courts, will read *First National Maintenance* broadly and apply it as a general test by which to determine mandatory subjects of bargaining.

IV. The Duty to Maintain Terms of a Collective Bargaining Agreement Under Section 8(d)

Although an employer which is party to a collective bargaining agreement satisfies its duty to bargain with respect to a decision to change its operations, the Act may still prohibit unilateral implementation of that decision by the employer during the effective term of its agreement.[96] Section 8(d) of the Act prohibits midterm repudiation or modification by one party of the terms of a collective bargaining agreement covering mandatory subjects of bargaining, absent the consent of the other.[97] Moreover, violations of section 8(d) are also held to violate the good faith bargaining requirement of section 8(a)(5) of the Act.[98] Thus, in *Nassau County Health Facilities Association*,[99] an employer's refusal to grant wage increases required

---

was economically motivated, employer had past practice of subcontracting, and there were minimal adverse effects on bargaining unit employees); Olinkraft, Inc., 252 N.L.R.B. 1329 (1980) (no per se duty to decision bargain over subcontracting, absent evidence of substantial adverse impact on employees), *enforced in part and remanded*, 666 F.2d 302 (5th Cir. 1982). *But see* Bob's Big Boy Family Restaurants, Div. Marriott Corp., 264 N.L.R.B. No. 178, 111 L.R.R.M. 1354 (1982) (Board distinguished *First Nat'l Maintenance* in case concerning employer's decision to subcontract).

[96]29 U.S.C. § 158(d). *See* note 102 *infra* and accompanying text.

[97]*Id.* Section 8(d)'s protection of collective bargaining agreements has been described as "convoluted." Summers, *Labor Law Decisions of the Supreme Court, 1961 Term*, ABA Lab. Rel. Law Proc. 51, 67 (1962), and "mysterious," *The Developing Labor Law*, in ABA Sec. Lab. Rel. Law 477 (C. Morris ed. 1971). Indeed, one commentator has gone so far as to predict that the Supreme Court "may be even more puzzled than was Alice in the queen's croquet game" when it attempts to interpret section 8(d). Summers, *supra*, at 67.

[98]Allied Chem. & Alkali Workers of Am., Local Union No. 1 v. Pittsburgh Plate Glass Co., Chem. Div., 404 U.S. 157, 159, 183–88 (1971) (citing with approval NLRB v. Scam Instrument Corp., 394 F.2d 884, 886–87 (7th Cir.), *cert. denied*, 393 U.S. 980 (1968)); NLRB v. C & C Plywood Corp., 385 U.S. 421, 425 (1967). *See* NLRB v. Hyde's Supermarket, 339 U.S. 568, 571–72 (9th Cir. 1964); Teamsters Local Union No. 574, 259 N.L.R.B. 344, 350 (1981); KCW Furniture Co., 247 N.L.R.B. 541 (1979), *enforced*, 634 F.2d 436 (9th Cir. 1980); Oak Cliff-Golman Baking Co., 207 N.L.R.B. 1063 (1973), *enforced*, 505 F.2d 1302, *cert. denied*, 423 U.S. 826 (1975); Milk Drivers Local 783, 147 N.L.R.B. 264 (1964); Proctor Mfg. Corp., 131 N.L.R.B. 1166 (1961).

[99]227 N.L.R.B. 1680 (1977).

by a collective bargaining agreement[100] was deemed a violation of sections 8(d) and 8(a)(5). Despite the employer's assertion that it was unable to pay the contractual wage, the Board found that the employer unilaterally modified the terms of its contract.[101] The Board explained that:

> An employer acts in derogation of his bargaining obligation under Section 8(d) of the Act, which was designated to stabilize during a contract term agreed-upon conditions of employment, and hence violates Section 8(a)(5), when without consent of the union, he modifies terms and conditions of employment contained in a contract between the employer and the union, or otherwise repudiates his undertakings under the contract before the term of the contract has run its course—*and this even though he has previously offered to bargain with the union on the subject and the union has refused.*[102]

Section 8(d), however, insulates only those contract terms embodied in an agreement which concern mandatory subjects of bargaining.[103] In *Allied Chemical & Alkali Workers of America v. Pittsburgh Plate Glass Co., Chemical Division,*[104] the Supreme Court reversed a Board decision[105] that an employer's unilateral change in the benefits of retirees set forth in an existing collective agreement constituted a midterm modification in violation of section 8(d).[106] The Court reasoned that section 8(d) protects only those contract terms which

---

[100]*Id.* at 1680–81.

[101]*Id.* at 1686.

[102]*Id.* at 1683 (citing C & S Indus., Inc., 158 N.L.R.B. 454, 456–58 (1966)) (emphasis added). Nor is it any defense to an employer's modification or repudiation of such a contract during midterm that it has bargained to impasse concerning the terms it wishes to modify or abandon, since such terms are "frozen as . . . term[s] or condition[s] of employment for the contract period involved *absent mutual consent of the contracting parties to their alteration or qualification. . . .*" NLRB v. Scam Instrument Corp., 394 F.2d at 887 (emphasis added). *Accord* N.L. Indus., Inc. v. NLRB, 536 F.2d 786, 790 (8th Cir. 1976); Oak Cliff-Golman Baking Co., 207 N.L.R.B. at 1064.

[103]Allied Chem. & Alkali Workers of Am., Local Union No. 1 v. Pittsburgh Plate Glass Co., Chem. Div., 404 U.S. 157 (1971).

[104]*Id.*

[105]177 N.L.R.B. 911 (1969).

[106]404 U.S. at 183–86.

concern mandatory subjects of bargaining.[107] Since retirement benefits were deemed to be permissive subjects of bargaining,[108] the employer was not obligated under section 8(d) to maintain such benefits, even while the parties' contract was still in effect.[109] Accordingly, under *Pittsburgh Plate Glass*, if a contract term constitutes a permissive subject of bargaining, section 8(d) does not prohibit unilateral termination or modification thereof during the effective term of that agreement.[110]

The principles discussed in the foregoing section have been recently applied by the courts[111] and the Board in the context of relocations of bargaining unit work.[112]

V. An Employer's Right to Relocate Bargaining Unit Work: NLRB and Court Decisions

A. *The Duty to Bargain*

1. Before *First National Maintenance*. In a series of decisions after *Fibreboard*, and prior to *First National Maintenance*, the Board consistently held that an employer must bargain over its decision to terminate operations at one facility and transfer bargaining unit

---

[107]*Id.* at 186–87. In particular, the Court reasoned: "Accordingly, just as § 8(d) defines the obligation to bargain to be with respect to mandatory terms alone, so it prescribes the duty to maintain only mandatory terms without unilateral modification for the duration of the collective-bargaining agreement." *Id.* at 185–86. Thus, as with the duty to bargain, the force of the Act does not extend to the maintenance of permissive subjects even where those subjects are contained in a contract. *Id.*

[108]*Id.* at 188.

[109]*Id.* at 186–87.

[110]The repudiation or modification of a contract term which constitutes a permissive subject of bargaining may, however, be a breach of contract for which the injured party might have another remedy, such as a suit for damages under § 301 of the Act. 29 U.S.C. § 185 (1976). *See Pittsburgh Plate Glass*, 404 U.S. at 186–87 ("[o]nce parties have made a collective bargaining contract the enforcement of that contract should be left to the usual processes of the law and not to the National Labor Relations Board").

[111]*See* notes 179–185, 201 *infra* and accompanying text.

[112]*See* notes 162–227 *infra* and accompanying text.

work to another facility.[113] The Board has applied the same standard concerning the requirement to bargain whether such transfers are to be conducted before, during or after the effective period of a collective bargaining agreement.[114]

In one of its first decisions after *Fibreboard* concerning relocation, the Board held that an employer must bargain over the decision to relocate bargaining unit work.[115] In *Standard Handkerchief Co.*,[116] the

[113]Whitehall Packing Co., 257 N.L.R.B. 193 (1981); Otis Elevator Co., 255 N.L.R.B. 235 (1981); Ohio Brake & Clutch Corp., 244 N.L.R.B. 35 (1979); Coated Prod., Inc., 237 N.L.R.B. 159 (1978), *enforced*, 106 L.R.R.M. 2364 (3d Cir. 1980); P. B. Mutrie Motor Transp., Inc., 226 N.L.R.B. 1325 (1976); Stone & Thomas, 221 N.L.R.B. 573 (1975); Burroughs Corp., 214 N.L.R.B. 571 (1974); R. L. Sweet Lumber Co., 207 N.L.R.B. 529 (1973), *enforced*, 515 F.2d 285 (10th Cir.), *cert. denied*, 423 U.S. 986 (1975); American Needle & Novelty Co., 206 N.L.R.B. 534 (1973); Regal Aluminum, Inc., 190 N.L.R.B. 468 (1971); McLoughlin Mfg. Corp., 182 N.L.R.B. 958 (1970), *enforced as modified sub nom*. International Ladies Garment Workers Union v. NLRB, 463 F.2d 907 (D.C. Cir. 1972); Plymouth Indus., Inc., 177 N.L.R.B. 607 (1969), *enforced*, 435 F.2d 558 (6th Cir. 1970); Weltronic Co., 173 N.L.R.B. 235 (1968), *enforced*, 419 F.2d 1120 (6th Cir. 1969); Standard Handkerchief Co., 151 N.L.R.B. 15 (1965).

[114]*See, e.g.*, Tocco Div. of Park-Ohio Indus., 257 N.L.R.B. at 415 (employer required to bargain over decision to relocate after expiration of contract); Otis Elevator Co., 255 N.L.R.B. at 235 (employer required to bargain over decision to relocate during term of contract); Stone & Thomas, 221 N.L.R.B. at 577 (employer required to bargain over decision to relocate after certification of union as employees' collective bargaining representative but before contract negotiated).

[115]Standard Handkerchief Co., 151 N.L.R.B. 15 (1965). The Board's approach concerning an employer's duty to bargain over relocation had developed over a number of years. The initial trend was to require bargaining over the decision to relocate. *See* Gerity Whitaker Co., 33 N.L.R.B. 393 (1941), *enforced as modified per curiam*, 137 F.2d 198 (6th Cir. 1942); Brown-McLaren Mfg. Co., 34 N.L.R.B. 984 (1941); California Portland Cement Co., 101 N.L.R.B. 1436 (1952), *supplemented*, 103 N.L.R.B. 1375 (1953). *But see* Brown Truck & Trailer Mfg. Co., 106 N.L.R.B. 999 (1953) (duty to bargain limited to effects of decision to relocate). The Board's position was eventually clarified in Town & Country Mfg. Co., 136 N.L.R.B. 1022 (1962), *enforced*, 316 F.2d 846 (5th Cir. 1963), and Fibreboard Paper Corp., 138 N.L.R.B. 550 (1962), *enforced*, 322 F.2d 411 (D.C. Cir. 1963), *aff'd*, 379 U.S. 203 (1964). For a detailed discussion of the evolution of the Board's policy in this area, *see* Note, *Duty to Bargain: Subcontracting, Relocation and Partial Termination*, 55 Geo. L. J. 879, 901–08 (1967).

[116]151 N.L.R.B. at 15. The Board has held that an employer must notify and offer to commence bargaining with the union representing its employees concerning a decision to relocate "once he has reached the point of thinking seriously about taking such an extraordinary step. . . ." Ozark Trailers, Inc., 161 N.L.R.B. 561, 569 (1966); *see also* McLoughlin Mfg. Corp., 182 N.L.R.B. 958 (1970). However, an employer is relieved of its obligation to notify and bargain with a union over a decision to relocate all or part of its operations where the relocation does not detrimentally impact on

275

employer operated a plant in New York City. For strictly economic reasons, the employer moved its plant elsewhere in New York State without notifying or bargaining with the union representing its employees.[117] The Board held that "by proceeding unilaterally, and without notice to the Union to move its plant . . . Respondent failed and refused to bargain in good faith with the collective bargaining representative of its employees."[118] Consistent with this decision, a three-member panel of the Board in *American Needle & Novelty Co.*[119] proclaimed that "[i]t is well-settled that an employer has an obligation to bargain concerning a decision to relocate unit work."[120]

---

bargaining unit employees. *See* Morco Indus. Inc., 255 N.L.R.B. 146 (1981) (employer relieved of its obligation to bargain over economically motivated decision to relocate work from plant in Tampa, Florida, to a new plant in Long Beach, Mississippi, since Tampa facility continued to operate at full capacity and no layoffs of bargaining unit employees required); Rochester Tel. Corp., 190 N.L.R.B. 161 (1971) (employer did not unlawfully fail to bargain over decision to implement time measurement plan where union's evidence failed to establish impact on bargaining unit); Westinghouse Elec. Corp., 153 N.L.R.B. 443 (1965) (employer not required to bargain over decision to subcontract bargaining unit work). In the context of the employer's decision to subcontract bargaining unit work, the Board in *Westinghouse* stated:

[A]n employer's obligation to give prior notice, and an opportunity to bargain concerning particular instances of subcontracting, does not normally arise unless the subcontracting will effect some change in the terms and conditions of employment of the employees involved. Consistent with this view, the Board has refused to find a violation of Section 8(a)(5) where the employer's allegedly unlawful unilateral action resulted in no "significant detriment" to employees in the appropriate unit.

Id. at 446.

[117]151 N.L.R.B. at 17. The General Counsel conceded that Respondent's decision to move its plant from New York City to Amsterdam was not discriminatorily motivated, and was made only for economic reasons. *Id.* Nevertheless, the General Counsel contended that the employer unlawfully failed to bargain in good faith with the union over its decision to move its plant. *Id.*

[118]*Id.* at 18 (relying on Town & Country Mfg. Co., 136 N.L.R.B. 1022, *enforced on other grounds*, 316 F.2d 846 (5th Cir. 1963)). *See* Fibreboard Paper Prods. Corp., 138 N.L.R.B. 550 (1962), *enforced*, 322 F.2d 411 (D.C. Cir 1963), *aff'd*, 379 U.S. 203 (1964).

[119]206 N.L.R.B. 534 (1973).

[120]*Id.* A union may waive its statutory right to bargain concerning an employer's relocation of bargaining unit work. Tocco Div. of Park-Ohio Indus., 257 N.L.R.B. 413 (1981), *enforced*, 112 L.R.R.M. 3089 (BNA) (6th Cir. 1983). However, the Board and the courts require that a waiver of bargaining rights must be "clear and unmistakable." Tocco Div. of Park-Ohio Indus., 257 N.L.R.B. at 414; NLRB v. Pepsi-Cola Distrib. Co., 646 F.2d 1173 (6th Cir. 1981), *cert. denied*, 102 S. Ct. 1993 (1982); Beacon

Employers, relying upon Justice Stewart's oft-cited concurrence in *Fibreboard*,[121] have attempted to justify their failure to bargain over a decision to relocate bargaining unit work on the grounds that an economically motivated decision to terminate operations at one plant and transfer the work to another plant is not a mandatory subject of bargaining.[122] They have argued that such a decision is removed from the realm of mandatory bargaining because it involves a significant withdrawal of capital affecting the scope and ultimate direction of the enterprise and lies at the very core of entrepreneurial control.[123]

Illustrative of the Board's reaction to these employer arguments

---

Journal Publishing Co. v. NLRB, 401 F.2d 366 (6th Cir. 1968); C & C Plywood, 148 N.L.R.B. 414, 416, *enforcement denied*, 351 F.2d 224 (9th Cir. 1965), *rev'd and remanded,* 385 U.S. 421 (1967). *See* Walter B. Cooke, Inc., 262 N.L.R.B. No. 74 (1982), 111 L.R.R.M. 1152 (1982) (where contract expressly permitted subcontracting, unilateral exercise of employer's right found to be lawful); Amoco Prod. Co., 233 N.L.R.B. 290 (1977) (contract reserved to employer the right to make changes in the scope of the bargaining unit). Consolidated Foods Corp., 183 N.L.R.B. 832 (1970) (contract provided that "the employer shall have the exclusive right to at all times change, modify, or cease its operation, processes, or production. . . ."); International Shoe Co., 151 N.L.R.B. 693 (1965) (the employer retained the "sole" right to decide who and how many employees to hire and how to sell and distribute the company's product). *But see* AFC Indus., Inc., 231 N.L.R.B. 83 (1977) (absence of contractual restriction on subcontracting does not constitute waiver of union's right to bargain over decision), *enforced,* 592 F.2d 422 (8th Cir 1979); Universal Sec. Instruments, Inc. v. NLRB, 649 F.2d 247 (4th Cir. 1981) (no waiver of right to bargain over closing even though contract contained broad management rights clause), *cert. denied,* 454 U.S. 965 (1981).

A union may also waive its right to bargain over an employer's decision to relocate by its failure to request bargaining once it has been notified of the impending decision. *See* Reiter's Dairy, Inc., 9 N.L.R.B. Advice Memo Rep. ¶ 19,102 (June 15, 1982) (union's business agent, once having learned of employer's impending decision to relocate, failed to request decision bargaining); Harnischfeger Corp., 8 N.L.R.B. Advice Memo. Rep. ¶ 18,197 (July 31, 1981) (union waived right to decision bargain); Allen Materials, Inc., 8 N.L.R.B. Advice Memo. Rep. ¶ 18,233 (Sept. 30, 1981) (no timely demand for decision bargaining); *cf.* Kimberly Clark Corp., 8 N.L.R.B. Advice Memo. Rep. ¶ 18,235 (Sept. 30, 1981) (opportunity to bargain rejected). For a further discussion of the Board's application of these waiver doctrines, see note 244 *infra.*

[121] 379 U.S. at 223 (Stewart, J., concurring).

[122] *See* Otis Elevator Co., 255 N.L.R.B. 235 (1981); International Harvester Co., 227 N.L.R.B. 85 (1976), *enforcement denied,* 618 F.2d 85 (9th Cir. 1980); Transmarine Navigation Corp., 152 N.L.R.B. 998 (1965), *enforcement denied and remanded for reconsideration on the merits,* 380 F.2d 933 (9th Cir. 1967), *on remand,* 170 N.L.R.B. 389 (1968).

[123] *See* cases cited at note 122 *supra.*

is *Otis Elevator Co.*[124] In *Otis Elevator,* the employer operated a unionized plant in New Jersey.[125] As part of a plan to restructure its entire research and development operations, the employer spent in excess of three million dollars to construct a new research and development center in Connecticut.[126] Thereafter, during the term of its collective bargaining agreement and without first bargaining with the union over its decision, the company relocated 17 of its 350 bargaining unit employees and its research and development operations to the new facility in Connecticut.[127] The Board held that Otis' actions violated section 8(a)(5) of the Act.[128]

Otis had contended that the magnitude of its corporate reorganization and capital expenditure made the decision to transfer work

[124]255 N.L.R.B. 235 (1981).

[125]Otis, a wholly owned subsidiary of United Technologies, is a New Jersey corporation engaged in the manufacture, research, development, sale, and distribution of elevators and related products. Otis owns and operates a number of facilities, including a facility in Mahwah, New Jersey. *Id.* at 241. Local 989, United Automobile, Aerospace and Agricultural Implement Workers of America represents a unit of professional and technical employees in Otis' engineering division, which is headquartered in Mahwah, New Jersey. In December, 1977, there were approximately 274 employees in the bargaining unit. The parties entered into a collective bargaining agreement in April 1977 which was effective until March 31, 1980. *Id.* at 242 n.1.

[126]*Id.* at 236. In 1975, United Technologies Corporation acquired Otis. At the time of the takeover it was determined that Otis' engineering activity was very diffuse; the company's research and development activities were being performed in many locations throughout New Jersey, New York, Colorado and Canada and there was some overlapping of functions. United Technologies maintained a major research and development center with approximately 1,000 employees in East Hartford, Connecticut. *Id.* at 241. Following recommendations by a consulting firm and after its review of Otis' engineering operations, United's board of directors decided to centralize Otis' research and development operations with the parent corporation's facilities in and around the Hartford, Connecticut, area. Thus, in 1977, with construction of a new facility already under way in East Hartford, the company notified Local 989 of its decision to consolidate and restructure Otis' engineering functions. *Id.* at 242.

[127]*Id.* at 236. The union responded to Otis' unilateral relocation by filing a charge with the Board alleging that Otis violated § 8(a)(1) and (5) of the Act by refusing to bargain with the union over its decision to relocate work from Mahwah, New Jersey, to East Hartford, Connecticut, and the effects of that decision on unit employees. *Id.* at 241.

[128]*Id.* at 235.

improper for collective bargaining.[129] The Board rejected the employer's argument, however, reasoning that, (1) although it consolidated its research and development operations in one location, the employer continued to perform the relocated work, albeit at a different location; (2) such actions did not constitute a major corporate reorganization; and (3) while the employer spent in excess of three million dollars to construct a new facility, this investment did not signal any change in the direction of the employer's activities, or in the character of its enterprise.[130]

The circuit courts have not always agreed with the Board as to an employer's duty to bargain concerning a relocation, and, on occasion, have refused to enforce Board orders requiring employers to bargain about decisions to transfer unit work.[131] Thus, in *NLRB*

---

[129]*Id.* Otis argued that the transfer of employees and the construction of the new facility in Connecticut involved such a substantial shift in its assets and operations that bargaining about the decision to transfer the 17 unit employees would be a significant abridgment of its freedom to invest its capital and manage its business. *Id.*

[130]*Id.* The Board explained that bargaining with the union concerning the transfer of 17 unit employees would not significantly abridge Otis' prerogative to carry on its business. Moreover, while recognizing that Otis spent in excess of three million dollars to construct a new facility to house the relocated work, the Board noted that Otis continued to design and manufacture elevators, albeit with modernized facilities and with a more expeditious arrangement of its research and development personnel. Thus, the Board explained, Otis had not undergone a basic capital reorganization whereby it conveyed any portion of its assets or operations to another entity, terminated any of its activities or liquidated any of its holdings in achieving its objectives. *Id. Cf.* National Car Rental System, Inc., 252 N.L.R.B. 159 (1980) (Board held that employer did not unlawfully fail to bargain concerning its decision to sell most of its truck and lease accounts, close its existing Newark, New Jersey, facility and transfer all remaining accounts to another facility, reasoning that the employer's decision "involved a 'significant investment or withdrawal of capital' as to 'affect the scope and ultimate direction of the enterprise' and was essentially financial and managerial in nature") [relying on General Motors Corp., GMC Truck & Coach Div., 191 N.L.R.B. 951 (1971)], *enforced sub nom.* International Union, United Auto. Workers of Am. Local 864 v. NLRB, 470 F.2d 422 (D.C. Cir. 1972)), *enforced as modified,* 672 F.2d 1182 (3d Cir. 1982).

[131]*See e.g.,* NLRB v. International Harvester Co., 618 F.2d 85 (9th Cir. 1980) (company which was losing $10,000,000 per month on "fleet sales" of trucks under no duty to bargain over decision to reorganize its marketing structure and phase out fleet sales since it was highly unlikely that bargaining would have ameliorated the company's financial difficulties); NLRB v. Acme Indus. Prods., 439 F.2d 40 (6th Cir. 1971) (no obligation to bargain over decision to relocate standard production unit to another plant); NLRB v. Thompson Transp. Co., 406 F.2d 698, 703 (10th Cir. 1969) (no obligation to bargain over closing of a terminal where evidence indicated that

v. Transmarine Navigation Corp.,[132] the Ninth Circuit denied enforcement of a Board order requiring the employer to bargain with the union over its economically motivated decision to terminate its Los Angeles harbor operations and relocate to Long Beach, California.[133] The company was faced with the prospect of losing its main customer if it did not shut down its Los Angeles operations. The court concluded that requiring the employer to confer with the union would not have served any effective purpose.[134] Thus, the court held that "the Company's decision, based solely on greatly changed economic conditions, to terminate its business and reinvest its capital in a different enterprise in another location as a minority partner

---

employer had lost the "major part" of its business and relocation involved a major commitment of capital and a fundamental alteration of the corporate enterprise. Hence, the circuit court found that "[n]o amount of collective bargaining could erase the economic facts that gave rise to the Company's decision to close . . ."); NLRB v. Transmarine Navigation Corp., 380 F.2d 933 (9th Cir. 1967) (employer's decision, based solely on economic reasons, to terminate its business and reinvest in a different enterprise was not a mandatory subject of bargaining).

[132]152 N.L.R.B. 998 (1965), *enforcement denied and remanded for reconsideration on the merits*, 380 F.2d 933 (9th Cir. 1967), *on remand*, 170 N.L.R.B. 389 (1968).

[133]The employer operated as a freight agent, ship broker, steamship agent, and terminal operator at Los Angeles harbor. The company's guards were represented by the American Federation of Guards, Local No. 1. The employer had a collective bargaining agreement with the union which was executed in 1962, with an expiration date of June 30, 1965. The contract was in effect at the time of the events described herein. 380 F.2d at 934.

During the summer of 1963, the Japanese government ordered the consolidation of Japanese shipping companies. This order had a direct effect upon the company's principal customer, thus creating the need for Transmarine to maintain larger shipyard facilities. In September, 1963, the company executed a joint venture agreement with a stevedoring company. Pursuant to this agreement, the company was to terminate its operations in Los Angeles and relocate to Long Beach, California, as a minority partner. *Id.* After this agreement was executed, the company offered positions with the new company to most of its guards employed in the Los Angeles harbor. The guards declined the company's offer of employment, however, because at that time they were earning substantially higher wages than were offered at the new location. *Id.* at 935.

On October 24, 1963, the company announced in a bulletin sent to all employees that, effective November 1, 1963, all guards would be terminated. Thereafter, the company wrote to the union informing it that the company would soon cease business at its present location, and that the parties' collective bargaining agreement would no longer be in effect after relocation. The union filed charges with the Board alleging that the company had unlawfully refused to bargain over the decision to relocate its operations in violation of § 8(a)(1) and (5) of the Act. *Id.*

[134]*Id.* at 939.

280

was not a subject of mandatory collective bargaining within the meaning of section 8(a)(5)."[135]

Similarly, in *NLRB v. Acme Industrial Products, Inc.*,[136] the Sixth Circuit declared that an employer had no *absolute* duty to bargain with a union over the decision to relocate part of its manufacturing operations to another plant.[137] More recently, in *Royal Typewriter Co. v. NLRB*,[138] the Eighth Circuit rejected the Board's finding that

[135]380 F.2d at 939. The court relied on NLRB v. Rapid Bindery, Inc., 293 F.2d 170 (2d Cir. 1961). In that case, a bindery plant owner in Dunkirk, New York, became unable to adequately service its principal customers in Buffalo. Thus, the employer formed a new entity near Buffalo and transferred its operations from its old plant. *Id.* at 171. This relocation was dictated solely by economic considerations. The Board held that the employer violated § 8(a)(5) by failing to give notice to and bargain with the union. *Id.* at 172. In modifying the Board's order, the Second Circuit stated that the decision to relocate was not a mandatory subject of bargaining. *Id.* at 176. *See also* International Harvester Co., 227 N.L.R.B. 85 (1976) (where the court denied enforcement of a Board order requiring the employer to bargain over the restructuring of its fleet sales accounts), *enforced in part*, 618 F.2d 85 (9th Cir. 1980). *Cf.* NLRB v. Johnson, 368 F.2d 549, (9th Cir. 1966) (employer's plan to discontinue part of its operations and contract out floor-covering installation work mandatory subject of bargaining); Cooper Thermometer Co. v. NLRB, 376 F.2d 684 (2d Cir. 1967) (company's refusal to bargain with the union over partial termination of its operations and the employee's relocation to a new plant constituted a violation of § 8(a)(5)).

[136]439 F.2d 40 (6th Cir. 1971), *denying enforcement to* 180 N.L.R.B. 114 (1969). The employer maintained a plant in Madison Heights, Michigan, for a number of years. In September, 1968, the employer notified the union representing its employees that it was moving its operations to a new facility and that all employees would be offered the opportunity to transfer. The union requested negotiations. Thereafter several meetings were held between the parties. The employer refused to negotiate concerning the decision to relocate; however, it stood ready to bargain over effects of the relocation. The union filed § 8(a)(5) and (1) charges with the Board. *Id.* at 41.

[137]439 F.2d at 42–43. The court distinguished this case from its earlier decision in NLRB v. Weltronic Co., 419 F.2d 1120 (6th Cir. 1969), *cert. denied*, 398 U.S. 938 (1970). First, the court noted that its holding in *Weltronic* was limited to its facts. Second, the court noted that the employer in *Weltronic* moved a substantial portion of its unit work without any notice to the union and without bargaining over the effects of the transfer. In the instant case, the employer stood ready and willing to bargain over every aspect of the decision except the decision itself. 439 F.2d at 42–43. In 1979, the Sixth Circuit again imposed a duty to bargain over an economically motivated transfer of work and machinery to another site. *See* NLRB v. Production Molded Plastics, Inc., 604 F.2d 451, 452–53 (6th Cir. 1979). The court qualified its decision, however, by noting that the employer's decision did not involve "any major commitment of capital to a new enterprise nor any withdrawal from a previous line of company endeavor." *Id.* at 453.

[138]533 F.2d 1030 (8th Cir. 1976), *denying enforcement to* 209 N.L.R.B. 1006 (1974).

281

a company's decision to close one of its plants and transfer work to another plant was a mandatory subject of bargaining.[139] The court held that "absent union animus, a company has no legal duty to bargain with a union over the decision to partially shut down its operations because of economic reasons."[140]

2. After *First National Maintenance*. The Board's general rule requiring an employer to bargain over a decision to transfer bargaining unit work, as well as the circuit court decisions enforcing or denying Board orders on this issue, predate the Supreme Court's decision in *First National Maintenance Corp. v. NLRB*.[141] As previously discussed, the Court in *First National Maintenance* "intimate[d] no view as to other types of management decisions, such as plant relocations . . . which are to be considered on their particular facts."[142]

The Board and the courts have yet to apply *First National Maintenance* to an employer's decision to relocate or consolidate bargaining unit work.[143] However, an Administrative Law Judge (ALJ) recently applied the balancing test of *First National Maintenance*[144] to

[139]*Id.* at 1039. In March, 1969, Royal informed the union that it intended to shut down its plant and resume the production of portable electric typewriters elsewhere on a permanent basis. The union demanded that the company bargain over the decision to relocate its operations; the company refused but willingly engaged in effects bargaining. *Id.* at 1034. The union filed charges with the Board alleging violations of § (8)(a)(1) and (5) of the Act. The Board held that the employer violated § 8(a)(1) and (5) by failing to bargain with the union over its decision to close its plant and resume operations elsewhere. *Id.* at 1035.

[140]*Id.* at 1039. The court did not specifically address the question of whether an employer must bargain over the decision to relocate unit work; however, the fact that the employer in this case was closing its plant and relocating its operation renders the conclusion implicit in the court's decision.

[141]452 U.S. 666 (1981).

[142]*Id.* at 686 n.22.

[143]The Board's decision in Tocco Div. of Park-Ohio Indus., 257 N.L.R.B. 413, *enforced*, 112 L.R.R.M. 3089 (6th Cir. 1983), was issued on July 30, 1981, approximately one month after the Supreme Court's decision in *First Nat'l Maintenance*. The Board held that the employer violated § 8(a)(1) and (5) by refusing to bargain over the decision to relocate bargaining unit work. The Board did not rely on *First Nat'l Maintenance* for its holding. *Id.*

[144]The Supreme Court's balancing test provides that "bargaining over management decisions that have a substantial impact on the continued availability of employment should be required only if the benefit, for labor-management relations and the collective-bargaining process, outweighs the burden placed on the conduct of the business." 452 U.S. at 679.

determine that an employer unlawfully failed to bargain over the decision to relocate its operations during the term of its collective bargaining agreement where the motive for the relocation was to reduce labor rates.[145] Although recognizing that the Supreme Court in *First National Maintenance* intimated no view as to relocations,[146] the ALJ stated that "if the Court intended to apply a balancing test with respect to all cases of unit work relocation decisions, that test applied to the facts herein leads me to conclude that the [employer's] decision was a mandatory subject of bargaining."[147] The ALJ reasoned that since the employer's decision to relocate work was dependent upon its employees' willingness to agree to a lower wage rate, "[t]he managerial decision . . . was thus clearly amenable to the collective bargaining process."[148]

3. NLRB General Counsel and Division of Advice. The NLRB General Counsel has stated that, contrary to Board precedent, decisions to relocate will not automatically be viewed as a mandatory subject of bargaining. Rather, in accordance with the Supreme Court's balancing test in *First National Maintenance*, decisions to relocate (e.g., relocations, subcontracting, consolidations, etc.) will be scrutinized to determine whether they are "based on labor costs

[145]Heat Transfer Group, Gulf and Western Mfg. Co., No. JD-381-82 (Sept. 7, 1982) (no exception taken, unpublished decision). The employer did not file exceptions to the Administrative Law Judge's decision. Therefore, the Board automatically adopted the ALJ's decision and recommended order. *See* 29 C.F.R. § 102.48 (1982). The employer operated facilities in Illinois and Kentucky. In 1980, after it had entered into a renewal of its collective bargaining agreement covering the Illinois facility, the company began to experience a significant loss of business in its product line which was produced at that location. Slip op. at 4–5. It concluded that the loss was attributable to the company's high labor costs. To remedy its economic problem, the company decided on two alternatives: either gain concessions in its contractual wage rates from its Illinois employees, or relocate production to a facility where it would obtain lower wage rates. *Id.* at 5. Accordingly, the company approached the union representing its Illinois employees, and stated that it would be necessary for the union to lower the contractual wage rates to a par with its competitors, or the company would relocate the bargaining unit work. *Id.* at 8. When the union refused to grant concessions on wage rates, the company implemented the relocation. *Id.* at 11–12.

[146]*Heat Transfer*, slip op. at 18.

[147]*Id.* at 19. Accordingly, the ALJ ordered that the employer restore the equipment and fixtures used in the Illinois facility. *Id.* at 35.

[148]*Id.* at 19. A § 10(j) injunction *pendente lite* was also issued in the *Heat Transfer* case. *See* Zipp v. Bohn Heat Transfer Group, 110 L.R.R.M. 3013 (C.D. Ill. 1982).

or other factors that would be amenable to resolution through the collective bargaining process."[149]

Consonant with the General Counsel's application of the *First National Maintenance* balancing test, the NLRB's Division of Advice[150] concluded in *Stewart Sandwiches, Inc.*[151] that no further proceedings against an employer were warranted where the employer had closed a facility and transferred unit work to another location without first bargaining with the union.[152] There, the employer unilaterally decided to close its Detroit facility and consolidate remaining bargaining unit work at its Flint, Michigan, warehouse during the term of its contract with the union representing its employees.[153] The employer's decision was based solely on the fact that its overhead was too high to justify continued maintenance of a separate Detroit facility.[154] The employer informed the union that its Detroit contract would not be applied at Flint.[155]

Utilizing the *First National Maintenance* balancing test,[156] the Division reasoned that, while relocations of bargaining unit work are presumptively mandatory subjects of bargaining, "that presumption [in this case] is rebutted by evidence indicating that the Employer's determination to consolidate its operations . . . was based solely on economic considerations unrelated to labor costs or other factors which arguably would be amenable to the collective bargaining

[149]General Counsel's Memorandum, *supra* note 94, at 316.

[150]The Division of Advice is a division of the Office of the General Counsel. Its function is to render substantive legal advice in cases which involve novel or complex issues of national interest or which involve developing and changing areas of the law. The Division also processes requests for injunctive relief under § 10(j) of the Act, litigates injunction cases in Federal Appellate courts, and indexes and classifies Board and court decisions under the Act. *New Developments Summary of Operations,* N.L.R.B. Case Handling Manual (CCH) ¶ 30,340 (Feb. 23, 1983).

[151]112 L.R.R.M. (BNA) 1422 (NLRB Div. of Advice Sept. 15, 1982).

[152]*Id.* at 1423. *Cf.* Midwest Bus Lines, 9 N.L.R.B. Advice Memo. Rep. ¶ 19,045 (Jan. 22, 1982) (under *First Nat'l Maintenance* balancing test no duty to bargain over economically motivated decision to sell a distinct line of business). *But see* Polaris E-Z-Go, 9 N.L.R.B. Advice Memo. Rep. ¶ 19,006 (Oct. 30, 1981); United Wire & Supply Corp., 8 N.L.R.B. Advice Memo. Rep. ¶ 18,224 (Sept. 30, 1981); Toledo Foreign Trade Zone Operations, Inc., 8 N.L.R.B. Advice Memo. Rep. ¶ 18,207 (Aug. 28, 1981).

[153]112 L.R.R.M. at 1422.

[154]*Id.* at 1422.

[155]*Id.* at 1423.

[156]*Id.* (citing *First Nat'l Maintenance,* 452 U.S. 666 (1981)).

284

process."[157] The Division observed that "even if the Union had made labor cost concessions, such concessions would not have modified or reversed the Employer's closure decision."[158] Thus, it concluded that the employer was under no statutory obligation to bargain over the decision to consolidate its remaining Detroit operations into its Flint facility.[159]

In sum, the foregoing discussion illustrates that, despite over twenty years of Board and court precedent, the scope of an employer's duty to bargain concerning a decision to relocate bargaining unit work remains unsettled.[160]

B. Mid-Contract Restriction on Relocation

Prior to 1974, the focus of the Board's analysis with respect to a transfer of unit work was primarily limited to whether an employer

[157]*Id.* at 1424.

[158]*Id.*

[159]*Id.* The Division answered the union's allegations that the employer unlawfully modified the parties' contract by relocating its operations by stating that where "an employer's decision to transfer and consolidate unit work was not amenable to the collective bargaining process and thus was not a mandatory subject of bargaining under Section 8(d), it was considered unnecessary . . ." to reach the issue of whether the employer's relocation constituted a midterm modification. *Id.* at 1424 n.11. For further discussion see notes 232–34 *infra*.

[160]An employer violates § 8(a)(3) and (1) of the Act by engaging in conduct which is "inherently destructive" of important employee rights, even absent specific evidence of unlawful intent. *See* NLRB v. Great Dane Trailers, 388 U.S. 26, 33–34 (1967); NLRB v. Fleetwood Trailer Co., 389 U.S. 375, 380 (1967). Where, as part of a plan to escape the obligations of a collective bargaining agreement, an employer terminates and refuses to reinstate employees, such action clearly is "inherently destructive" of employee rights and thus violates § 8(a)(3). *See* NLRB v. Triumph Curing Center, 571 F.2d 462, 474 (9th Cir. 1978); Local 57, Int'l Ladies Garment Workers Union v. NLRB, 374 F.2d 295, 299 (D.C. Cir. 1967), *cert. denied*, 395 U.S. 980 (1967); NLRB v. Preston Feed Corp., 309 F.2d 346, 350 (4th Cir. 1962); NLRB v. Wallick, 198 F.2d 477, 484 (3d Cir. 1952); Coated Prods., 237 N.L.R.B. 159 (1978), *enforced*, 106 L.R.R.M. 2364 (3d Cir. 1980); Lloyd Wood Coal, 230 N.L.R.B. 234 (1977), *enforcement granted in part, denied in part*, 585 F.2d 752 (5th Cir. 1978). *See also* Am-Del Co. Inc., 225 N.L.R.B. 698 (1979) (employer converted employees to independent contractors to escape provisions of its contract with union); Big Bear Supermarkets No. 3, 239 N.L.R.B. 179 (1978) (employer franchised store to escape provisions of its contract with union), *enforced*, 640 F.2d 924 (9th Cir.), *cert. denied*, 449 U.S. 920 (1980); Rushton & Mercier Woodworking Co., 203 N.L.R.B. 123 (1973) (employer violated § 8(a)(1), (2), (3) and (5) by closing its facilities, laying off its union employees and resuming operations with another union under the name of its wholly owned subsidiary), *enforced by published opinion*, 86 L.R.R.M. 2151 (1st Cir. 1974); Rome Prods. Co., 77 N.L.R.B. 1217 (1948) (employer's sale of business to a sham corporation to avoid dealing with the union held to be an unfair labor practice).

had a duty to bargain over the decision to relocate.[161] In 1974, however, a new type of analysis was introduced:[162] Whether an employer may transfer bargaining unit work during the effective period of a collective bargaining agreement despite the fact that (1) such transfers are not prohibited by the contract, (2) the employer bargains in good faith with the union to impasse and (3) the employer is not motivated by union animus.[163] To the consternation of management, the Board, with limited approval by the circuit courts, has held that an employer may not effect such transfers under certain circumstances.[164]

In *University of Chicago*,[165] an employer operated a number of hospitals and clinics on its campus. All functions carried on in these buildings were placed under the administrative direction of the University's Biological Sciences Division (BSD).[166] The University employed approximately 10,500 persons, 900 of whom were represented by American Federation of State, County, and Municipal Employees' Union (AFSCME).[167] Of this number, approximately 200 were assigned to the BSD and were classified as custodians, responsible for cleaning patient and non-patient care areas in the hospital complex.[168] The University also had successive collective bargaining agreements with the Service Employees International Union (SEIU).[169] The SEIU represented approximately 300 of the

---

[161]*See* cases cited and discussed in notes 113–40 *supra* and accompanying text.

[162]*See* University of Chicago, 210 N.L.R.B. 190 (1974), *enforcement denied*, 514 F.2d 942 (7th Cir. 1975).

[163]514 F.2d at 949.

[164]*See* cases cited and discussed in notes 165–219 *infra* and accompanying text.

[165]210 N.L.R.B. 190 (1974).

[166]*Id.* at 191.

[167]*Id.* at 191–93.

[168]*Id.* at 193.

[169]*Id.* The principal function of the custodians who were represented by SEIU was to provide janitorial services in specifically designated areas of the hospital complex. Their primary responsibilities included the following: (1) wet-mopping classrooms, offices, laboratories and corridors, (2) picking up glass and other debris, (3) emptying wastepaper baskets and ashtrays, and (4) stripping and waxing floors. These employees did not wash walls, clean hospital bedrooms, operating rooms, or other areas devoted principally to the immediate treatment of clinical patients. *Id.*

University's employees, including 125 custodians, nineteen of whom were administratively placed under the auspices of the BSD.[170] In September 1970, the University and SEIU renewed their collective bargaining agreement for a two-year period.[171] In July 1971, the University advised SEIU that the hospital was experiencing difficulties stemming from the maintenance of its hospital complex by two bargaining units of janitorial employees.[172] The University informed the union that it wanted to raise the sanitation level in those portions of the hospital buildings then serviced by SEIU employees, and that the only feasible solution was to transfer all SEIU hospital custodial work to the jurisdiction of AFSCME.[173] SEIU objected to the proposed transfer, in part because it was to result in a pay cut for its members who were to be transferred and a net reduction in the overall bargaining unit.[174] The University nevertheless implemented the transfer.[175]

The Union responded by filing section 8(a)(1) and (5) charges.[176] The Board held that the University's unilateral removal of bargaining unit work from SEIU's jurisdiction in midterm of the parties' existing contract constituted an impermissible modification of the

[170]*Id.* Many of the areas of the complex to which AFSCME members were assigned were devoted to patient care, and therefore required a higher degree of cleanliness than did the complex's administrative offices, classrooms, and other areas which were cleaned by SEIU's members. For the most part, employees of the two unions utilized certain benchmarks, such as a doorway or an archway, to delineate the boundaries of their respective cleaning responsibilities. *Id.*

[171]*Id.* at 194.

[172]*Id.*

[173]*Id.*

[174]*Id.*

[175]*Id.* at 195. Of the 14 employees laid off, 12 accepted positions performing the transferred work under the jurisdiction of AFSCME. Of the 12 employees who accepted transfer, three received the same wages as before their transfer; the other nine employees suffered varying reductions in their hourly rates because they were assigned to labor grades whose wage rates were lower under AFSCME's agreement. Each of the 12 employees was required to join and pay dues to AFSCME since its contract contained a union security clause. *Id.*

[176]*Id.* at 191. The SEIU alleged that the University failed to bargain in good faith over the decision to transfer work to the jurisdiction of AFSCME, unlawfully modified the parties' collective bargaining agreement by implementing the transfer without the union's consent, and unlawfully rendered assistance and support to AFSCME by effecting the transfer. *Id.*

recognition clause of the contract, in violation of section 8(d).[177] The Board also held that "the payment of unit employees under different pay scales thus constitutes an impermissible modification of the wage provisions of the . . . [SEIU] contract in mid-term."[178]

The Seventh Circuit denied enforcement of the Board's decision and order.[179] The court held that the recognition clause in the parties' collective bargaining agreement could not be interpreted to provide that the University was prohibited from unilaterally effecting transfers within the employer's hospital complex, since (1) the contract did not specifically provide for such a prohibition[180] and (2) the parties' past practice indicated a history of unilateral tranfers.[181] The court explained that "unless transfers are specifically

[177]*Id.* at 199. The recognition clause of the collective bargaining agreement recognized SEIU as the exclusive bargaining agent for employees employed in specific job classifications. *Id.* at 193–94. The Board held that the recognition clause in the parties' collective bargaining agreement necessarily included the specific areas in the hospital complex in which the transferred SEIU employees had worked, and that, by effecting the transfer of work, the University repudiated both the recognition clause in the contract, as well as the terms and conditions of employment of SEIU members in violation of § 8(a)(1), (5) and § 8(d). *Id.* at 190, 199.

[178]*Id.* at 198. The Board had applied a similar analysis prior to its decision in *University of Chicago.* In Weltronic Co., 173 N.L.R.B. 235 (1968), *enforced,* 419 F.2d 1120 (6th Cir. 1969), the employer manufactured, sold and distributed resistance welding controls, plant central equipment and related products at its six plants located in Michigan and Ontario, Canada. In 1967, without prior notice to the union which represented its employees, the employer moved its wiring and assembly work during the term of its collective bargaining agreement from its Southfield, Michigan, facility to another plant located three miles away. 173 N.L.R.B. at 236. The Board adopted in relevant part the Trial Examiner's finding that the employer violated § 8(a)(1) and (5) by transferring unit work without first bargaining with the union over its decision, and by unilaterally changing terms and conditions of employment by paying employees at rates less than those provided for in its contract with the union. Unlike *University of Chicago,* however, the Board did not specifically rely on § 8(d) for its decison. *Id.* at 235, 237. It affirmed the Trial Examiner's recommendation and ordered the employer to bargain in good faith with the union over the decision to relocate. 173 N.L.R.B. 235, 238. The Sixth Circuit affirmed the Board's decision, 419 F.2d at 1120.

[179]University of Chicago v. NLRB, 514 F.2d at 942 (7th Cir. 1975).

[180]514 F.2d at 948. The Court rejected the Board's attempt to construe the enumeration of employee classifications in the recognition clause of the parties' agreement as a jurisdictional clause which restricted bargaining unit transfers. *Id.*

[181]*Id.* The Court emphasized that the University had a past practice of transferring custodial work from one union to the other; that there was never any definite line of demarcation as to the unions' division of cleaning responsibilities; and that no part of BSD was ever cleaned solely by the custodians of either union. *Id.*

prohibited by the bargaining agreement, an employer is free to transfer work out of the bargaining unit if, "(1) the employer complies with *Fibreboard Paper Products v. NLRB* . . . by bargaining in good faith to impasse; and (2) the employer is not motivated by anti-union animus. . . ."[182]

The Seventh Circuit observed that the University had fulfilled its bargaining obligation,[183] and that there was neither a contention nor any evidence that its transfer of work was motivated by union animus.[184] The court emphasized that "the sole reason for the decision to transfer the work was the necessity to raise the level of sanitation in the [hospital] complex."[185]

Three years later, in *Los Angeles Marine Hardware Co., a Division of Missions Marine Associates, Inc.*,[186] the Board adopted without comment an Administrative Law Judge's decision that an employer violated sections 8(a)(1), (3) and (5) when, without the union's consent, it laid off several of its employees and relocated bargaining unit work during the term of the parties' agreement.[187] The ruling was upheld despite evidence that the employer had bargained in good faith over the decison to remove the work, and was motivated solely by economic considerations.[188]

The employer was a party to a collective bargaining agreement

---

[182]514 F.2d at 949 (citing Textile Workers v. Darlington Mfg. Co., 380 U.S. 263 (1965)).

[183]*Id.* The Board conceded that the University had bargained in good faith with SEIU in advance of its decision to transfer the work. *Id.*

[184]*Id.*

[185]*Id.* Two years after the Court's decision in *University of Chicago*, the Board turned a deaf ear to the Seventh Circuit when it decided Boeing Co., 230 N.L.R.B. 696 (1977), *enforcement denied*, 581 F.2d 793 (9th Cir. 1978). In affirming without comment an Administrative Law Judge's rulings, findings and conclusions, the Board once again held that a clause in the parties' agreement recognizing the International Union of Operating Engineers, AFL-CIO, as bargaining agents for Boeing's welders, *id.* at 698, prohibited the employer from unilaterally reassigning bargaining unit work to the jurisdiction of another union during the term of a collective bargaining agreement. The employer's action in *Boeing* was held to be an unlawful modification of the agreement under § 8(d) and hence, a violation of § 8(a)(5) of the Act. 230 N.L.R.B. at 696, 704. The Ninth Circuit denied enforcement of the Board's order, relying on the Seventh Circuit's reasoning in *University of Chicago*. 581 F.2d at 793.

[186]235 N.L.R.B. 720 (1978).

[187]*Id.* at 720, 737–38.

[188]*Id.* at 732–33.

covering its recreational sales employees.[189] In 1975, faced with a substantial operating loss at that facility,[190] the company unsuccessfully sought to reduce the wages of its recreational sales employees during its negotiations for a renewal of its contract, and again in 1976 when the contract provided for a wage reopener.[191] After the union refused to grant wage concessions during the contract's wage reopener period,[192] the employer announced that it was relocating its recreational sales operations to two other plants in California.[193] Shortly thereafter, and without the union's consent, the employer terminated all of its twenty-three recreational sales employees and relocated its operation.[194]

The company did not apply the contract's terms to the newly hired recreational sales employess at the new facilities, and in fact, the new employees were paid less than the contractual rate.[195] The union filed charges with the Board alleging that the employer violated sections 8(d), 8(a)(1) and 8(a)(5) by unilaterally modifying its contract midterm.[196]

The Administrative Law Judge found that section 8(d) of the Act precluded the employer from making a midterm modification in the contract without the consent of the union, and that the parties' collective bargaining agreement applied to the other plants.[197] He

[189]*Id.* at 721.

[190]*Id.* at 722. In 1975 the employer determined that it was necessary to obtain economic relief from the union since a survey of its competitors disclosed that the employer's labor costs were $1.40 per hour higher than those of its highest paying competitor. By 1976, the employer determined that it would have an annual operating loss of $170,000, with additional cash flow problems. *Id.*

[191]*Id.* A wage reopener is a provision in a collective bargaining agreement which permits either party to reopen the contract during its term to renegotiate wages. H. Roberts, *supra* note 13, at 575.

During the 1975 negotiations leading to the execution of the agreement, and again in 1976 when the contract provided for a wage reopener, the employer attempted to obtain economic relief from the union in its recreational sales area. This effort proved unsuccessful on both occasions. 235 N.L.R.B. at 722.

[192]235 N.L.R.B. at 722.

[193]*Id.*

[194]*Id.* at 724–25.

[195]*Id.* at 732.

[196]*Id.* at 720, 738. The union also filed charges alleging that the employer's discharge of 23 unit employees, and the subsequent refusal to hire these individuals at the new locations, constituted a violation of § 8(a)(3). *Id.* at 731.

[197]*Id.* at 735–36.

explained that, "notwithstanding the persuasiveness and validity of the employer's economic straits, an employer is not free, without union consent, to make midterm modifications in wage rates . . ., nor to remove work from the bargaining unit . . ., nor to replace all unit employees."[198] The ALJ concluded: "[f]or to permit relocation alone to vary this result would mean that employers would be permitted to achieve by indirection that which . . . employers [are] denied the opportunity to achieve by direct means under Section 8(d) of the Act."[199] The Board adopted the ALJ's conclusions without comment, as well as his recommended order.[200] The Ninth Circuit enforced the Board's order,[201] observing that the employer's actions

[198]*Id.* The Administrative Law Judge reached these conclusions notwithstanding his findings that (1) the employer had been confronted with a legitimate adverse economic problem prior to and during its negotiations with the union, *id.* at 732–33, (2) the employer's decision to relocate "was an economic one and was not based upon unlawful considerations," *id.* at 733, (3) there was no basis for finding that the employer failed to satisfy its bargaining obligations owed to the union concerning the relocation and its effects on unit employees, *id.*, and (4) there was no basis for finding that the employer had made efforts to discourage employees from seeking employment at the employer's other plants, *id.*

[199]*Id.* at 735. The Board has recently sought and obtained injunctive relief under § 10(j) of the Act against employers who have threatened to relocate bargaining unit work. Thus, in Eisenberg v. Suburban Transit Corp., 112 L.R.R.M. 2708 (BNA) (D.N.J. 1983), the employer announced that it would relocate its bus service operations from one terminal to another, transfer bargaining employees, and make unilateral changes in terms and conditions of employment after the union refused to grant wage concessions during midterm negotiations. *Id.* at 2711. The union filed unfair labor practice charges with the Board alleging violations of § 8(a)(1), (3), (5) and § 8(d). *Id.* at 2708. The Board subsequently petitioned the New Jersey District Court for a temporary injunction to enjoin the employer from relocating its operations pending a final determination of the unfair labor practice charges before the Board. *Id.* The court granted the Board's petition and enjoined the employer from relocating its operations. *Id.* 2712. *See also* Kobell v. Thorson Tool Co., 112 L.R.R.M. (BNA) 2397 (M.D. Pa. 1982); Zipp v. Bohn Heat Transfer Group, 110 L.R.R.M. 3013 (D. Ill. 1982) (federal district courts of Pennsylvania and Illinois, respectively, granted Board petitions for temporary injunctive relief under § 10(j) of the Act, pending final determinations of the unfair labor practice charges by the Board).

[200]235 N.L.R.B. at 720.

[201]Los Angeles Marine Hardware Co. v. NLRB, 602 F.2d 1302 (9th Cir. 1979). *See* Brown Co., 243 N.L.R.B. 769, *enforcement denied and remanded for reconsideration on the merits*, 109 L.R.R.M. 2663 (9th Cir. 1981). In *Brown*, a Board majority found that the employer discontinued its cement hauling operations, laid off its drivers and transferred trucks to another division to evade its wage obligations under the collective bargaining agreement, in violation of § 8(a)(1) and (3). 243 N.L.R.B. at 772. The Board deemed it unnecessary to pass on the § 8(a)(5) allegation. *Id.* at 771. The

"amounted to a midterm repudiation of the [contract], in violation of Sections 8(d) and 8(a)(1) and (5)."[202]

The principles established by the foregoing cases were recently affirmed by the Board in *Milwaukee Spring Division, Illinois Coil Spring Co.*[203] There, a three-member panel held that an employer violated sections 8(a)(1), (3), (5) and 8(d) of the Act when it transferred assembly work in midcontract from its unionized plant to a non-union facility, after unsuccessful attempts to secure midterm wage concessions from the union.[204]

One of the employer's three divisions, Milwaukee Spring, was a party to a collective bargaining agreement covering its production employees.[205] The agreement was effective from April, 1980, through March, 1983.[206] In January, 1982, the employer asked the union to forego a contractual wage increase due on April 1 and grant other concessions.[207] This request was precipitated by the employer's loss of a major contract resulting in a $200,000 per month decline in revenues.[208]

During the employer's discussions with the union, it proposed relocating its assembly operations to another division.[209] During these discussions the employer informed the union that wage concessions were necessary to maintain the viability of the facility.[210]

---

§ 8(a)(3) violation was based on the *Los Angeles Marine* theory that the employer's actions were inherently destructive of employee interests. *Id.* at 771. See note 250 for further discussion of the Board's current application of the "inherently destructive" doctrine. The Ninth Circuit denied enforcement of the Board's decision and order and remanded the case to the Board for a determination of whether the employer was given the right under the terms of its collective bargaining agreement to transfer the work. 109 L.R.R.M. 2663 (9th Cir. 1982).

[202]602 F.2d at 1307. The court also agreed with the Board that the employer violated § 8(a)(3) of the Act by discharging 23 unit employees as a result of the relocation. *Id.* at 1307–08.

[203]265 N.L.R.B. No. 28, 111 L.R.R.M. 1486 (1982).

[204]111 L.R.R.M. at 1490.

[205]*Id.* at 1486–87. The Milwaukee Spring Division employees were represented by UAW, Local 547. The division employed approximately 99 bargaining unit employees; 35 of these employees worked in the company's assembly operations and 42 worked in molding operations. *Id.*

[206]*Id.* at 1487.

[207]*Id.*

[208]*Id.*

[209]*Id.*

[210]*Id.*

After notification of the union's vote against concessions,[211] the employer relocated its assembly operations.[212] The union filed charges alleging that the employer had unlawfully modified the parties' contract during its terms.[213]

Before the Board, the parties stipulated that the relocation of assembly operations was due solely to the comparatively higher labor costs under the agreement between the employer and the union.[214] It was further stipulated that the employer had fulfilled its duty to bargain with the union over the decision to relocate these assembly operations, and that the employer had been willing, and remained willing, to engage in bargaining with the union over the effects of its decision.[215]

The Board concluded that the employer's decision to transfer its assembly operations constituted a midterm modification within the meaning of section 8(d).[216] The Board held that the employer was not free to take such action without the consent of the union or without waiver of the union's statutory right to object to such action.[217] Since the union did not consent to the employer's relocation and the parties' agreement did not clearly and unequivocally waive the union's statutory right to object to such action,[218] the

[211]*Id.*

[212]*Id.*

[213]*Id.*

[214]*Id.*

[215]*Id.* For a discussion of an employer's duty to bargain concerning the effects of a relocation of bargaining unit work, as well as effects of other substantial alterations of its business enterprise, see note 51 *supra.*

[216]111 L.R.R.M. at 1490. The Board reached this decision even though the parties' collective bargaining agreement did not contain a restriction of the employer's right to transfer work. *Id.* at 1489. Chairman Van de Water stated that his finding of violations rested on the parties' stipulation that the employees' transfer of assembly operations was motivated by comparatively higher union wage rates and an inadequate return on investment. *Id.* at 1490 n.7. He also stated that the outcome of the Board's decision might have been different if the employer had faced bankruptcy or if the short-term viability of the corporation were in jeopardy. *Id.* at 1488 n.3.

[217]*Id.* at 1490. The Board also held that the resultant layoffs of bargaining unit employees as a consequence of the employer's decision to transfer constituted independent violations of § 8(a)(1) and (3). *Id.* The Board invoked the so-called *Los Angeles Marine* theory to find that the employer's unilateral relocation was inherently destructive of its employee's § 7 rights and thus a violation of § 8(a)(3). *Id.* at 1488.

[218]*Id.* at 1490.

Board ordered the employer to rescind its decision to transfer its assembly line operations and to restore the status quo ante.[219]

The Board's decision in *Milwaukee Spring* constitutes an unwarranted and unsupportable extension of section 8(d) which, if allowed to stand, should be limited to its facts. Distilled to its essence, the Board's holding should be applied only to those cases where an employer, presented with a union's refusal to accept midterm contract modifications, relocates bargaining unit work specifically to achieve the desired modification.[220] Where implementation of an employer's decision to relocate is not motivated by a desire to change mandatory subjects of bargaining contained in a collective bargaining agreement, its decision should not constitute a direct or

---

[219]*Id.* The Board also ordered the employer to recall and reinstate any employees laid off as a result of the decision to transfer its assembly operations and to make such employees whole for any loss of earnings they might have suffered, with back pay computed on a quarterly basis, with interest. *Id.*

The Board, on occasion, has ordered employers to recognize and bargain with the union representing its employees after relocating during a contract term. Thus, in Westwood Import Co., 251 N.L.R.B. 1213 (1980), *enforced,* 681 F.2d 664 (9th Cir. 1982) the employer bargained over the decision to relocate its plant during the term of its contract, and the effects of that decision on unit employees. Without reaching agreement, the employer closed and relocated its plant and refused to recognize the union as its employees' bargaining representative at the new location or to comply with the terms of its collective bargaining agreement. The union filed § 8(a)(5) charges with the Board, alleging that the employer had failed to bargain in good faith. 251 N.L.R.B. at 1213. The Board ordered the employer to recognize and bargain with the union at the new facility since there was a continuity of operations and a substantial percentage (40%) of the employees at the new plant were transferees from the former facility. *Id.* at 1214, 1216 n. 8. Interestingly, the union never alleged a midterm modification of the parties' contract in violation of § 8(d). *See also* Marine Optical, Inc., 255 N.L.R.B. 1241 (1981), *enforced,* 671 F.2d 11 (1st Cir. 1982); *cf.* Massachusetts Machine & Stamping, Inc., 231 N.L.R.B. 801 (1977) (employer lawfully withdrew recognition from union after relocating its plant at expiration of contract where only 11 of 22 employees transferred to new facility and the company moved to different state with an entirely different labor pool), *enforcement denied,* 578 F.2d 15 (1st Cir. 1978); Trell Restaurant, Inc. 9 N.L.R.B. Advice Memg. Rep. ¶ 19,100 (June 11, 1982).

[220]See note 244 *infra* for a further discussion of the Board's current extension of § 8(d) in the context of relocations. Pursuant to the Board's current application of § 8(d) principles, unlawful midterm modifications are not limited to contract terms which contain wages. Any contract term which expressly sets forth an agreed-upon term and condition of employment may not be modified for the duration of that agreement without the consent of both parties. *See* note 102 and 142 *supra* and accompanying text.

indirect violation of section 8(d).[221] Thus, the Board's decision should be read as a mere reaffirmance of the proposition that, under section 8(d), neither party to a contract may use its economic muscle to force midterm modifications of its agreement.[222] This conclusion was reached by the Board's Division of Advice in three recent memoranda.

In *Chino Mines Co.*,[223] an employer operated two geographically separated facilities, a mine and a concentrator.[224] It was a party to labor agreements with three unions, all of which represented maintenance employees at the concentrator.[225] As part of a modernization plan, the employer closed its concentrator, constructed a new facility, and created new classifications within one unit to perform all maintenance work at the new concentrator.[226] The remaining unions filed charges with the Board, alleging that the employer had unilaterally modified their contracts.[227]

---

[221]*See* Milwaukee Spring Div. Illinois Coil Spring Co., 265 N.L.R.B. No. 28, 111 L.R.R.M. 1486 (1982). Indeed, under the principles established by the Supreme Court in Allied Chem. Workers of Am., Local Union No. 1 v. Pittsburgh Plate Glass, Chem. Div., 404 U.S. 157 (1971), the Board's holding necessarily must be so limited. As discussed, *Pittsburgh Plate Glass* established the principle that § 8(d)'s protection against midterm modifications only extends to contract terms containing mandatory subjects of bargaining. *Id.* at 186–87. Relocations, unaccompanied by an employer's unsuccessful attempt to obtain mid-contract concessions, do not per se constitute unlawful modifications or terminations of a collective bargaining agreement. This conclusion is implicit in numerous Board decisions concerning relocations. Thus, in University of Chicago, 210 N.L.R.B. 190 (1974), *enforcement denied,* 514 F.2d 942 (7th Cir. 1975), the Board was compelled to proceed through a convoluted and strained conversion of the applicable labor agreement's recognition clause into a jurisdiction clause. Similarly, in *Milwaukee Spring,* 111 L.R.R.M. at 1486, if relocations per se constituted contract modifications, the entire analysis of unlawful indirect modification would have been unnecessary.

[222]*See* notes 165–219 *supra* and accompanying text. The Board also has held that a union commits an unfair labor practice when it engages in a strike to modify an existing bargaining agreement. *See* Brewery Delivery Employees Local Union 46, 236 N.L.R.B. 1160, 1173–74 (1978); Chauffeurs, Salesmen and Helpers Local 572, 223 N.L.R.B. 1003, 1008 (1976); New York Local No. 1190, Communication Workers of Am. 204 N.L.R.B. 782, 784–85 (1973); Telephone Workers Union of New Jersey, Local 827, 189 N.L.R.B. 726, 734 (1971).

[223]112 L.R.R.M. 1419 (BNA) (NLRB Div. of Advice Jan. 7, 1983).

[224]*Id.* at 1419.

[225]*Id.*

[226]112 L.R.R.M. at 1420.

[227]*Id.*

The Division of Advice found that the employer's decision to close its concentrator involved a significant investment of capital and was motivated by economic considerations unrelated to the labor costs of its union contracts.[228] Thus, the employer's decision did not constitute a mandatory subject of bargaining.[229] The Division also noted that, since the employer's decision was not a mandatory subject of bargaining, its implementation of that decision was not an unlawful midterm modification of the parties' contract in violation of section 8(d).[230] The Division reasoned that:

> the prohibition against mid-term modification contained in Section 8(d) is limited to unilateral changes involving mandatory subjects of bargaining. And, decisions which involve a significant investment or withdrawal of capital affecting the ultimate scope and direction of an enterprise generally are not deemed mandatory subjects of bargaining.[231]

Similarly, in *Stewart Sandwiches*,[232] the Division concluded that a refusal to bargain charge should be dismissed where the employer had relocated work from a union facility to a non-union facility during the term of a labor agreement.[233] The Division determined that the employer's decision was implemented for reasons unrelated to the terms of the labor agreement in effect at the union facility; it therefore refused to consider whether the employer's decision constituted a midterm modification.[234]

Finally, in *Greyhound Lines, Inc.*,[235] a union represented clerks at the employer's terminal in Chicago.[236] As part of a regional consolidation of accounting functions, the employer relocated the work of six accounting clerks from the Chicago facility to a facility in

---

[228]*Id.* at 1421. *See* National Car Rental Sys., Inc., 252 N.L.R.B. 159 (1980), *enforced as modified*, 672 F.2d 1182 (3d Cir. 1982); General Motors Corp., GMC Truck & Coach Div., 191 N.L.R.B. 951 (1971), *enforced sub nom.* International Union, United Auto. Workers of Am. Local 864, 470 F.2d 422 (D.C. Cir. 1972).

[229]112 L.R.R.M. at 1421.

[230]*Id.* at 1421–22.

[231]*Id.* at 1421.

[232]112 L.R.R.M. 1422 (NLRB Div. of Advice Sept. 15, 1982).

[233]*Id.*

[234]*Id.* at 1424 n.11 (*citing Pittsburgh Plate Glass*, 404 U.S. at 185–88).

[235]112 L.R.R.M. (BNA) 1437 (NLRB Div. of Advice March 2, 1983).

[236]*Id.*

Cleveland.[237] Although the Cleveland facility was organized, employees received $1.50 per hour less than their counterparts in Chicago.[238] The Regional Director sought advice whether it should issue a complaint alleging a violation of section 8(d) based upon the Board's decision in *Milwaukee Spring*.[239] The Division of Advice found that the employer's consolidation decision was purely "to improve convenience and speed in processing the work"[240] and not motivated by a desire to reduce contractual wage rates.[241] Consequently, the Division recommended dismissal of the section 8(d) allegations of the complaint.[242]

Although the Board attempted to portray its holding in *Milwaukee Spring* as a logical extension of prior decision,[243] in the opinion of the authors, the decision, as well as the precedent upon which it relied, constitutes an unwarranted and indeed unsupportable extension of section 8(d).[244] Moreover, it should be expected that

[237]*Id.*

[238]*Id.*

[239]*Id.* In *Greyhound Lines*, the Regional Director had previously issued a complaint alleging violations of § 8(a)(5) by the employer's failure to consult with the union prior to consolidating its operations. *Id.*

[240]*Id.*

[241]*Id.*

[242]*Id.* With regard to the wage differential between the Chicago and Cleveland facilities, the Division found:

Further, the mere fact that the Employer will save $1.50 per hour per employee in wages at the new location was not considered sufficient, in and of itself, to indicate labor cost was part of the Employer's motivation for the transfer. In this regard, it was noted that there is no other evidence that the Employer's asserted reason of consolidation is not actually the sole reason.

Id.

[243]111 L.R.R.M. at 1488–89.

[244]If limited to its facts, the Board's holding in *Milwaukee Spring* deems unlawful employer relocations based upon a desire to escape contractually established labor costs. However, this holding arguably lays the foundation upon which the Board may eventually prohibit employer relocations effected, in whole or in part, for other reasons. Thus, under the *Milwaukee Spring* rationale, a midterm relocation based even in part on an employer's desire to obtain relief from onerous *non-economic* contract terms (e.g., work rules, seniority provisions, etc.) may constitute an unlawful contract modification. 111 L.R.R.M at 1489; *see also Quarterly Report of NLRB General Counsel William A. Lubbers*, Daily Lab. Rep. (BNA) D-1 (Jan. 5, 1983) [hereinafter cited as *General Counsel's Quarterly Report*]; *Abbey Medical/Abbey Rents, Inc.*, 264 NLRB No. 129, 111 L.R.R.M. 1683, n.1 (1982); *Pet, Inc., Bakery Division*, 264 NLRB No. 166, 111 L.R.R.M. 1495 (1982). The possibility that *Milwaukee Spring* will be thus

extended underscores the critical need for re-examination of the decision.

It has long been established in this country that courts will not, and should not, rewrite contracts entered into between two or more parties which have been freely bargained for. NLRB v. Nash Finch Co., 211 F.2d 622, 626 (8th Cir. 1954) ("if there is one thing which more than another public policy requires it is that men of full age and competent understanding shall have the utmost liberty of contracting, and that their contracts, when entered into freely and voluntarily, shall be held sacred, and shall be enforced by courts of justice"). Moreover, it is clear that the Board is not authorized to control or set any terms of a collective bargaining agreement or otherwise sit in judgment upon the substantive terms of a collective bargaining agreement. H.K. Porter Co. v. NLRB, 397 U.S. 99 (1970); NLRB v. Insurance Agents, 361 U.S. 477 (1960); NLRB v. American Insurance Co., 343 U.S. 395 (1953). Indeed, the United States Constitution provides that: "No State shall . . . pass any . . . law impairing the obligation of contracts . . ." U.S. Const. art. 1, § 10, cl. 2. Although this provision does not by its terms extend to the federal government and its administrative bodies, it has been held to express a general public policy prohibiting the impairment of contracts by federal government action. See Hepburn v. Griswold, 75 U.S. 603 (1869); John McShain, Inc. v. District of Columbia, 205 F.2d 882 (D.C. Cir. 1953) (protection against impairment of contracts is provided by the Fifth Amendment); accord Rivera v. Patino, 524 F. Supp. 136 (N.D. Cal. 1981). The Milwaukee Spring decision is founded upon assumptions which represent an unwarranted circumvention of these longstanding principles of law.

Traditionally, collective bargaining has been viewed as a process by which organized labor secures rights from management which are, in turn, incorporated into the parties' contract. Pursuant to this process, if a union wishes to circumscribe an employer's right to relocate, or otherwise transfer work during the term of the parties' contract, it is incumbent upon the union to obtain through contractual negotiations language which prohibits or limits this right. Where a union is successful in this respect, the employer will ordinarily have gained from the union concessions in other areas in exchange for conceding the right to relocate. The Board ignored in Milwaukee Spring the principle that management retains certain inherent rights unless knowingly and affirmatively waived. Thus, unless contractually waived, management reserves the right to relocate work before, during or after the effective period of contract. The Board's approach turns traditional bargaining on its head by proceeding on the inaccurate premise that management has no inherent right to relocate work during the term of a labor agreement unless the employer has affirmatively obtained through negotiations the clear and unequivocal right to do so. See, e.g., Tocco Div. of Park-Ohio Indus., 257 N.L.R.B. 413 (1981). In effect, the Board has unilaterally written a clause into every collective bargaining agreement which prohibits midterm relocations. This intrusion into the arena of private sector collective bargaining appears to be part of the Board's longstanding attempt to inappropriately construe collective bargaining contracts as employment guarantees. See University of Chicago, 210 N.L.R.B. 190 (1974) (Board attempt to construe recognition clause in parties' contract as work jurisdiction clause); Boeing Co. 230 N.L.R.B. 696 (1977) (same). The Courts should continue to reject these attempts. See, e.g., University of Chicago v. NLRB, 514 F.2d 942, 948 (7th Cir. 1975) ("[a]s we read the cases, unless transfers are specifically prohibited by the bargaining agreement, an employer is free to transfer work out of the bargaining unit if: (1) the employer

the Board and the courts will soon face relocations[245] unattended

---

complies with *Fibreboard* . . . by bargaining in good faith to impasse; and (2) the employer is not motivated by anti-union animus . . ."').

The Board's approach also fails to recognize that by inferring a contractual prohibition on midterm employer actions which involve mandatory bargaining subjects, the employer loses the opportunity to consciously yield certain management rights to a union and to demand something in return for those rights which it has yielded. Thus, even contractual silence results in the acquisition of rights for the union; i.e., the union retains all it does not clearly and unmistakably yield.

Rather than engaging in convoluted, unwarranted and unsupportable contract analysis, the Board should defer such contractually based issues to arbitrators. The interpretation of labor contracts has historically been the province of arbitrators, subject, of course, to court review. *See* 29 U.S.C. § 185 (1976). Indeed, arbitrators have long been called upon by labor and management to decide issues concerning the permissibility of an employer's relocation of work in light of relevant contract language. *See* Spielberg Mfg. Co., 112 N.L.R.B. 1080 (1955); Linde Co., 40 Lab. Arb., 1073 (1963); Sivyer Steel Casting Co., 39 Lab. Arb. 449 (1962); ASA Brothers Co., Inc., 31 Lab. Arb. 426 (1958). Furthermore, court review of arbitration awards provides a workable system by which these awards may be kept consistent with established principles of law. Simply put, the Board should remove itself from the business of analyzing collective bargaining contracts, a business which it is not equipped to conduct.

Finally, the Board's action hinders the very collective bargaining system which it was long ago called upon to foster by discouraging bargaining and fostering deceit. Unions will have no incentive to negotiate solutions to employer economic problems; rather, they may simply refuse to negotiate during a contract term. If, in response, employers act unilaterally in the interest of marketplace survival, the Board may well continue to issue complaints and, perhaps, seek federal court injunctions under § 10(j) of the Act, 29 U.S.C. § 160(j) in order to enjoin employer from taking the desired actions. *See, e.g.,* Zipp v. Bohn Heat Transfer Group, 110 L.R.R.M. 3013 (D. Ill. 1982); Kobell v. Thorenson Tool Co., 112 L.R.R.M. (BNA) 2397 (M.D. Pa. 1982). As a future consequence, employers will be encouraged to construct "lawful" reasons upon which their relocation decisions are based in order to avoid unfavorable Board and court decisions. *See* Milwaukee Spring, 111 L.R.R.M. at 1486 n.4 (noting that employer admitted it had relocated to avoid onerous wage rates and implying that absent such a motivation, no violation would have been found). Moreover, employers may avoid midterm negotiation altogether for fear that the Board or a court may view their willingness to bargain as evidence that they were motivated by a desire to modify contract terms. *Id.*

[245]Cases involving unlawful relocations of bargaining unit work have quickly become of national interest. *See* notes 3 & 6 *supra*. Indeed the NLRB's General Counsel dedicated his first 1983 quarterly report to this topic. *General Counsel's Quarterly Report, supra* note 244, at D-1. In his report, the General Counsel examined several cases involving employer relocations which have recently come before the Board. These cases were decided upon a request for advice or on appeal from a regional director's dismissal of unfair labor practice charges. The report also covers

by employers' earlier attempts to obtain contract modifications, or later admissions that a decision to relocate was based upon a desire to modify existing contractual terms.[246] However, in light of the continuing support by the General Counsel,[247] the Division of Advice[248] and the courts,[249] for the Board's decision in *Milwaukee Spring,* the authors propose a rational approach which would limit the decision's impact.

VI. Proposed Three-Step Analysis

Under the Board's current approach to resolving issues arising from relocations of bargaining unit work, the reconciliation of section 8(d) of the Act with an employer's inherent right to manage its investment by determining the location of its business requires a three-step analysis. Initially, the employer's motivation for relocating must be determined. The outcome of this determination must then be considered in light of the Supreme Court's balancing test in *First National Maintenance* to determine whether the employer is under a duty to bargain with the union over the decision to relo-

---

relocation cases in which the Board authorized § 10(j) proceedings before federal district courts. Finally, the report contains a breakdown of all § 10(j) cases authorized by the Board for the first six months of calendar year 1982. *Id.*

[246]As a result of recent Board and court developments circumscribing an employer's right to relocate work during the term of a contract, employers who desire to repudiate or modify contract terms by relocating all or part of their operations may well be expected to present reasons other than onerous contract terms as a motivation for such action. This development would parallel those cases where employers have advanced legitimate business reasons for the discipline or discharge of employees for their union activities. *See* Wright Line, a Div. of Wright Line, Inc., 251 N.L.R.B. 1083 (1980), *enforced,* 662 F.2d 889 (1st Cir. 1981), where the Board stated that "[i]n modern day labor relations, an employer will rarely, if ever, baldly assert that it has disciplined an employee because it detests unions or will not tolerate employees engaging in union or other protected activities. Instead, it will generally advance what it asserts to be a legitimate business reason for its action." *Id.* at 1083–84. Indeed, the *General Counsel's Quarterly Report, supra* note 244, states that the Board will continue to face a proliferation of cases concerning relocations. *Id.* at D-1.

[247]*See General Counsel's Quarterly Report, supra* note 244.

[248]*See* Chino Mines, Co., Inc., 112 L.R.R.M. at 1419; Greyhound Lines, Inc., 112 L.R.R.M. (BNA) at 1437.

[249]*See* Hendrix v. Acme Markets, 113 L.R.R.M. 2036 (BNA) (D. Neb. 1983); Kobell v. Thorenson Tool Co., 112 L.R.R.M. 2397 (BNA) (M.D. Pa. 1982); Zipp v. Bohn Heat Transfer Group, 110 L.R.R.M. 3013 (D. Ill. 1982); Gottfried v. Echlin, 113 L.R.R.M. (BNA) 2349 (E.D. Mich. April 13, 1983).

cate.[250] Finally, where the employer has a duty to bargain over the decision, and there is a collective bargaining agreement in effect, the employer's motivation must be considered to determine whether a unilateral relocation would constitute an indirect midterm modification or repudiation of a term of that agreement.[251] Each of the above determinations are distinct yet inseparable steps in the analysis which must be conducted prior to a final determination of when and under what circumstances an employer may lawfully relocate bargaining unit work.

The critical inquiry in ascertaining the lawfulness of a relocation of bargaining unit work is the employer's motivation for such action.

---

[250]*See* Heat Transfer Group, Gulf and Western Mfg. Co., No. JD-381-82, slip op. at 19 (Sept. 7, 1982); Stewart Sandwiches, Inc., 112 L.R.R.M. (BNA) at 1424; General Counsel's Memorandum, *supra* note 94, at 316.

As one commentator has aptly noted, the Board has erroneously invoked its "inherently destructive" doctrine in the context of plant relocations. *See* Remarks on Plant Relocations By Attorney John S. Irving, Jr., Daily Lab. Rep (BNA), D-1 (May 9, 1983) [hereinafter cited as Remarks]. In three recent cases the Board held that employers' unilateral relocations were inherently destructive of employees' § 7 rights, and therefore no independent evidence of unlawful union animus was needed to establish violations of §§ 8(a)(1) and (3) of the Act. *See* Los Angeles Marine Hardware, 602 F.2d at 736; Brown Co., 243 N.L.R.B. at 771; *Milwaukee Spring*, 111 L.R.R.M. at 1488.

It is the opinion of the authors that the Board has mistakenly assumed that collective bargaining agreements are, in effect, job guarantees; that employees have an inherent right under § 7 of the Act not to have work relocated during the term of a labor agreement; thus, where an employer relocates without obtaining prior union consent, and the contract's management rights clause does not contain a waiver of the union's bargaining rights, such action is "inherently destructive" of the employees' § 7 rights.

The Board's current approach in this respect invokes the "inherently destructive" doctrine as a mere substitute for independent evidence of an employer's unlawful motive. In this way, the Board has circumvented the crucial yet controversial analysis of the inherent right of management to relocate its enterprise in the interest of business necessity, or even survival. Moreover, the present application of this doctrine allows the Board to arrive at the result which it appears to prefer without having to enunciate with any precision the source and nature of the § 7 rights which have allegedly been "inherently destroyed." Remarks, *supra*.

If the Board is going to continue to consider an employer's motivation in determining the lawfulness of a midterm relocation, the authors propose that it fairly conduct an extensive and detailed analysis of the facts underlying such motivation, rather than merely applying the sweeping "inherently destructive" doctrine as a substitute for careful evaluation of the evidence submitted in support of the unlawful motive allegations.

[251]*See Heat Transfer Group*, slip op. at 19.

With respect to the duty to bargain over a decision to relocate, the factors involved in an employer's decision may be determined by analyzing his motivation. If these factors are amenable to the collective bargaining process, the balancing test of *First National Maintenance* requires that the employer bargain over its decision to relocate.[252] With regard to unlawful midterm modifications, the employer's motivation reveals whether it is attempting to evade express contract terms covering mandatory subjects of bargaining.[253] Such evasion constitutes an unlawful midterm modification.[254]

Motivation is determined by viewing the employer's conduct as a whole.[255] In cases where an employer's decision involves a number of factors,[256] the authors propose an approach similar to that applied by the Board in employee discharge cases.[257] Relocations, as with discharges, are not per se unlawful under the Act.[258] Discharges,

[252]452 U.S. at 678–79.

[253]Los Angeles Marine Hardware Co., 602 F.2d at 1306–07; *Milwaukee Spring*, 265 N.L.R.B. No. 28, 111 L.R.R.M. at 1487–88; Boeing Co., 230 N.L.R.B. at 700–04.

[254]*See* cases cited in note 252 *supra*.

[255]In employee discharge cases where a union has alleged a § 8(a)(3) violation, the Board looks not only to direct evidence of union animus, *see, e.g.*, W.T. Grant Co., 210 N.L.R.B. 622 (1974) (anti-union comments prior to discharge), but also to such circumstantial evidence as: (1) delay in discharge after employer has knowledge of breach of work rules, National Grange Mut. Ins. Co., 207 N.L.R.B. 431 (1973); (2) a departure from established procedures for discharge, Richmond Refining Co., Inc., 212 N.L.R.B. 16 (1974); and (3) employer's subsequent change in position with respect to explaining the reason for discharge, Holiday Inn of Henryetta, 198 N.L.R.B. 410 (1972), *enforced*, 488 F.2d 498 (10th Cir. 1973). *See also Heat Transfer Group*, slip op. at 20 ("[h]owever, the Board may consider the totality of an employer's conduct 'to assess its motivation in determining whether it was really engaging in surface bargaining with no genuine interest of reaching agreement' ").

[256]An employer's decision to relocate bargaining unit work may be based in some cases on considerations completely unrelated to its employees' terms and conditions of employment, *see, e.g.*, Brooks-Scanlon, Inc., 246 N.L.R.B. 476 (1979) (insufficient supply of timber for sawmill operation); Raskin Packing Co., 246 N.L.R.B. 78 (1979) (bank suddenly cancelled employer's line of credit); or, in other cases, on considerations well within their scope. *See, e.g.*, Heat Transfer Group, Gulf and Western Mfg. Co., No. JD-381-82 (Sept. 7, 1982) (wages).

[257]*See* Bosanac, *Concession Bargaining, Work Transfers and Midcontract Modification: Los Angeles Marine Hardware Company*, 1983 Lab. L.J. 72, 78.

[258]Since Board and Court cases involving an employer's failure to bargain over a decision to relocate, as well as implementation of such a decision during the term of a collective bargaining agreement, most often arise within the context of unfair labor practice proceedings, § 10(c) of the N.L.R.A., 29 U.S.C. § 160(c) (1976), as well as § 7(c) of the Administrative Procedure Act, 5 U.S.C. § 556 (1976), requires the General Counsel to prove the employer's guilt by a preponderance of the evidence. *See* NLRB v. Wright Line, Div. of Wright Line, Inc., 662 F.2d 899 (1st Cir. 1981).

however, may not be made based upon union animus.[259] Similarly, relocations motivated by factors amenable to the collective bargaining process may not be made unilaterally.[260] Moreover, unilateral relocations motivated by a desire to modify terms of a contract covering mandatory subjects of bargaining are unlawful.[261]

In discharge cases where an employer's motivations are mixed, the Board in *Wright Line, Division of Wright Line, Inc.*[262] adopted a three-step approach. First, the General Counsel must make a prima facie showing that the decision to discharge was based upon union animus.[263] Once the General Counsel establishes his prima facie case, the burden of going forward shifts to the employer to show that it would have reached the same decision even in the absence of union animus.[264] The burden then shifts back to the General Counsel to demonstrate that the reasons proffered by the employer are pretextual, or that the discharge would not have occurred but for the employer's union animus.[265] This approach can be readily applied for determining an employer's motivation in relocation cases.

Under *First National Maintenance*, the nature and extent of an employer's bargaining obligation depends on whether the decision to relocate is amenable to collective bargaining. A decision is amenable to collective bargaining if the employer's intention is to change

[259]29 U.S.C. § 158(a)(3). *See* Edward G. Budd Mfg. Co. v. NLRB, 138 F.2d 86 (3d Cir. 1943).

[260]*See First Nat'l Maintenance*, 452 U.S. at 679.

[261]*Los Angeles Marine Hardware*, 602 F.2d at 1307; *Milwaukee Spring*, 265 N.L.R.B. No. 28, 111 L.R.R.M. at 1487; *Boeing Co.*, 230 N.L.R.B. at 700.

[262]662 F.2d 899 (1st Cir. 1981), *enforcing*, 251 N.L.R.B. 1083 (1980).

[263]662 F.2d at 904. The Board in its *Wright Line* decision held that once the General Counsel establishes his prima facie showing, the burden of proof shifts to the employer to show that it would have reached the same decision even in the absence of union animus. 251 N.L.R.B. at 1089. However, this approach has been rejected by several circuit courts. *See* NLRB v. Transportation Management Corp., 674 F.2d 130 (1st Cir. 1982), *cert. granted*, 51 U.S.L.W. 3378 (U.S. Nov. 15, 1982) (No. 82-168); NLRB v. Wright Line, Div. of Wright Line, Inc., 662 F.2d 899 (1st Cir. 1981). Throughout the authors' analysis, the burden of proof remains with the General Counsel to prove the employer's unfair labor practice by a preponderance of the evidence.

[264]662 F.2d at 904.

[265]251 N.L.R.B. at 1087.

the terms and conditions of employment of its bargaining unit employees.[266]

Where an employer has a duty to bargain over a decision to relocate, unilateral action on its part may constitute an unlawful midterm modification. Because section 8(d) prohibits any unilateral change in contractual terms, an employer may not unlawfully transfer its operations to effect a desired modification in contract terms. Thus, where an employer's sole motivation for relocating unit work is to reduce or otherwise modify specific contractual terms, section 8(d) prohibits such a transfer, absent union consent. Further, where the employer's reason for relocating work involves a combination of factors, application of the *Wright Line* approach will determine the propriety of its action.

VII. Conclusion

The conflicting and often confusing state of the law concerning an employer's duties under section 8(d) with respect to relocations of bargaining unit work may be resolved by focusing upon a critical issue—motive. It is an employer's motive for relocating which triggers rights and duties under the Act. Thus, if an employer is motivated by a desire to unilaterally change terms and conditions of employment, a relocation decision will probably be deemed a mandatory subject of bargaining. Conversely, if terms and conditions of employment do not form the controlling basis of a relocation

---

[266]452 U.S. at 677–78. The General Counsel arguably goes beyond the scope of the Supreme Court's balancing test by suggesting that a decision to relocate should be deemed amenable "[i]f the employer's decision is based on economic factors unrelated to labor costs (e.g., raise in rent), but union concessions in the area of labor costs could counterbalance these economic factors. . . ." General Counsel Memorandum, *supra* note 94, at 316 n.13. It is submitted that, where an employer's decision is based purely on economic factors unrelated to specific terms and conditions of employment, the employer is relieved from bargaining over the decision to relocate even though union concessions might counterbalance the factors underlying the employer's decision. The duty to bargain, and the penalties for an unlawful failure to do so, should not be contingent upon whether an after-the-fact review indicates a willingness by the union to offer concessions. Rather, in accordance with the *First National Maintenance* balancing test, the issue is whether the employer's reasons are per se amenable to the collective bargaining process. Where they are not, the employer's need to operate freely in deciding whether to relocate purely for economic reasons outweighs the incremental benefit that might be gained through the union's participation in making the decision itself. In such cases, the Supreme Court's decision in *First National Maintenance* dictates that the decision to relocate is not a subject over which Congress has mandated bargaining.

decision, an employer should be under no duty to bargain over that decision. Moreover, where a collective bargaining agreement is in effect, a unilateral relocation may constitute an unlawful midterm modification of the agreement only if that decision is motivated primarily by a desire to change one or more express terms contained in the agreement which cover mandatory subjects.

Most cases involving an employer's decision to relocate, however, do not present facts which clearly indicate the motivation behind the decision. In such cases, the foregoing three-step analysis should be applied under which the employer's motivation for relocating may be determined. A similar approach has been applied in unlawful employee discharge cases. It is submitted that such an approach would provide a logical and predictable basis upon which relocation cases may be decided in the future by the Board and the courts.

CONCLUSION

XV. Summary Remarks

Richard B. McKenzie

Opponents of plant-closing restrictions and other governmental efforts to alter the flow of human and physical capital face a perplexing problem: Readers often conclude, in spite of the detached quality of the analysis and the caveats to the contrary, that people who express the views presented here on plant-closing restrictions care little about the economic hardship experienced by workers and communities when their plants close down; that they fail to understand the economic realities of the recent high and unacceptable rate of unemployment in the country; that they carry only the torch of the business interests in this country. Such perceptions are deceiving. For this reason, several of the messages of the studies included in this volume can be usefully and succinctly restated.

Contrary to the good intentions of the sponsors of the National Employment Priorities Act of 1983, plant-closing restrictions will work to the detriment of the workers in this country. The general opinion of most writers in this volume is that such a bill should once again be set aside not because the noble objectives that gave birth to it are unimportant and uninspired, not because the country does not have economic troubles that warrant remedies, but because such a law will create more social mischief than it will remedy. For several very good reasons, the case *against* plant-closing restrictions is a case *for* workers and *for* the economic revitalization of this country.

• *First, the requirements for a one-year prenotification, severance pay, and community restitution embodied in the proposed legislation impose a disguised "tax" on U.S. firms for the employment of workers in this country.*

In order to meet the continued wage payments that are implied in keeping a failing business open for a year, firms must either buy insurance or set up a contingency fund that will allow for the continued payment of every worker employed for a year. Additional insurance must be bought or additional contingency funds

309

must be established by businesses to cover the severance pay and restitution claim of the community. Regardless of the financial mechanics of how the demands of the legislation are met, the cost of doing business in the United States is increased, just as it would be if Congress were to levy a special "head tax" on every employee a business hires.

Such a tax is not being imposed in other countries and is not applicable to equipment that can supplant workers in the plants. Obviously, the competitive position of the United States in the struggle for new industries will suffer. Proponents of this legislation should acknowledge that a growing concern among protectionists in this country is that the cost of production in a number of faltering basic industries is already higher here than elsewhere in the world. The potential closing costs implied in the legislation will be felt most keenly by these contracting industries, worsening their international competitive position and placing in further jeopardy the jobs of many American workers.

• *Second, restrictions on plant closings, such as the ones embodied in the proposed law, ultimately become restrictions on plant openings.*

Plant-closing restrictions will increase the cost of doing business in the United States and will thus deter the emergence of new firms, the movement of foreign firms into this country, and the expansion of established firms. Backers of the National Employment Priorities Act of 1983 may think restrictions on plant closings are a palliative for our current economic troubles and will save jobs. Restrictions may have such a favorable effect for the short term. However, in the long run they can only worsen our economic troubles.

Because new firms will not emerge and old ones will not expand because of closing restrictions, many workers will be unable to fill the jobs that would have been created by American industry. If such a bill is passed we can expect to find ourselves seeking a "new" national industrial policy to rectify the damage of the proposed law. And proponents should not forget that the impact of the proposed legislation in destroying jobs will probably be greater than that which may be implied by the restrictions incorporated in the current bill. The proposed restrictions, if passed, will likely be interpreted by investors and prospective employers as an indication that even more stringent restrictions, and more costs, will be imposed upon them in the future.

Proponents of the legislation may believe that through restrictions the country will acquire the proverbial "free lunch," since the restrictions are imposed on businesses and all costs are, presumably, incurred by businesses. However, the "lunch" will have a price tag on it. Because of the likely impact of such restrictions on economic development in the country, growth in wages and the taxes collected from wages and the property bought with wages will suffer. Furthermore, in order to maintain the country's relative competitive position in the struggle for jobs and a tax base, something in the way of explicit tax rates or other government regulatory actions will have to be given up. The old adage concerning the universal absence of free lunches will not be denied by the passage of an ordinance.

Proponents may think that the nation's serious economic troubles require drastic action by Congress, a good example of which is plant-closing restrictions. Our economic distress, however, can be construed as an argument against passing the plant-closing restrictions, because the communities experiencing the greatest hardship will tend to be the ones most adversely affected by the closing restrictions. Closing restrictions apply when firms fail. Communities experiencing a high rate of business failures will tend to be communities where, for whatever reason, the risk of failure is high and the closing costs implied in the restrictions will loom most ominously. Depressed communities will be the ones that capital will tend to avoid most.

Unfortunately, the political attraction of this kind of legislation lies precisely in the visibility of the jobs that are saved for a short period of time by restrictions on closings and the invisibility of the jobs that are destroyed by the implied restrictions on openings. Given current calls for a national industrial policy, it may take a great deal of foresight and calm reflection for our political leaders to see that, on balance and over the long run, more jobs will be destroyed by plant-closing restrictions than are saved. This is not a probusiness or antilabor public-policy posture. On the contrary, it is a policy position steeped in concern for workers and for the long-term economic development of this country.

● *Third, plant-closing laws will tend to have the unexpected consequence of closing some plants that could have remained open.*

When firms announce their intentions to close, their economic fates can be sealed. Workers will understandably accept other jobs; creditors can be expected to charge higher rates of interest and to deny credit; suppliers will be reluctant to provide the materials needed in production. At any moment, many firms in this country may be unsure of whether they can meet their current financial needs and last the next six months, the next year, or two years. When confronted with the prospects of having to provide a one-year notification—that is, pay wages and incur additional losses for a year after their closing announcement—a number of these firms can be expected to give notification of closure just to minimize their closing costs and, in the process, seal their failure. As a matter of probabilities implied in the concept of risk of failure, a number of these firms would be able to weather their financial crises. In the process of closing these plants, many jobs would be lost that could have been saved.

Further, many multiplant firms in financial difficulties that have to bear the additional cost of keeping one or more plants open to meet the requirements of this law may find that they must go bankrupt, closing in the process all their plants and putting many workers whose jobs would have otherwise been saved onto the unemployment rolls.

- *Fourth, the bill under consideration institutionalizes the Chrysler-style bailout.*

The backers of this legislation propose that federal funds be made available to support direct subsidies, loans, loan guarantees, and interest subsidies to business and that federal funds be made available to aid workers in buying their companies. This bill suggests to all modest- and large-size firms that when they get into financial trouble they can, like Chrysler, beat a path to the Treasury doors. Such a law will discourage firms, especially large, established ones that have the political muscle to attract the attention of the federal bureaucracy, from being attentive to their costs and revenues. To that extent, it will encourage business failures and will force many hard-working, lower-income taxpayers in this country to bail out many of their higher-paid colleagues in other industries. The justice of such a tax-subsidy arrangement must be called into question.

- *Fifth, firms differ in their ability to give notification. For some firms, a one-year notice may be appropriate; for many others, perhaps most, it will not be.*

Where differences exist, politically established closing standards will tend to reflect favorably the circumstances of the politically powerful. Such a standard will discriminate against those workers who would be willing and able to accept jobs in industries in which the politically established closing standard is not appropriate. I caution you against imposing laws that may help some people at the expense of others, especially the politically weak. Most who favor closing restrictions seem to imagine that their preferred closing restrictions will be the ones adopted by Congress. However, I remind the proponents that closing restrictions applicable to the automobile industry in Michigan and California may not be the preferred rules for the textile industry in South Carolina. Nevertheless, a federal law establishes a standard for all, giving rise in the process to a shift in the distribution of the country's capital stock.

- *Sixth and finally, private alternatives exist to publicly established closing restrictions.*

If workers truly value notification of a pending closing, then I admonish them to put their economic interests where their hearts are and negotiate the prenotification requirement. I encourage firms to establish legally binding closing policies suitable to their own circumstances, because to the extent such policies are desired by workers, they should be self-financing. Workers who acquire such a benefit as a part of their contract will have to give up something in the way of fringe benefits and/or wages. Admittedly, no one likes to give up anything for benefits received. Workers understandably want notification of a pending plant closing and severance pay at zero cost. However, I again remind you that publicly imposed closing restrictions will also come at a price. The difference between an ordinance and a contractual agreement is that the former is compulsory and applied to all, while the latter is voluntary and adjustable to individual circumstances.

In summary, imposition of plant-closing restrictions is an economic mistake that a country in the midst of economic distress can ill afford to make.

Statements in Support of the National Employment Priorities Act by U.S. Representative William D. Ford

National Employment Priorities Act of 1974*

Mr. Speaker, on March 18, I introduced the National Employment Priorities Act—NEPA. Since then I have been contacted by several of my colleagues who wish to join me in cosponsoring this legislation, so today I am reintroducing it with 19 additional cosponsors, bringing the total number of cosponsors to 42. The legislation has been referred to the Education and Labor Committee, and to the General Subcommittee on Labor which is chaired by my good friend and colleague, the distinguished gentleman from Pennsylvania (Mr. Dent). Similar legislation has been introduced in the other body by the senior Senator from Minnesota (Mr. Mondale) and cosponsored by Senators Hart, Schweiker, and Kennedy.

The National Employment Priorities Act is designed to provide assistance to workers, businesses, and communities that are adversely affected by the arbitrary and unnecessary closings or relocations of industrial plants and other business enterprises.

The legislation is based on the premise that such closings and transfers may cause irreparable harm—both economic and social— to workers, communities, and the Nation.

My own State of Michigan has been particularly hard hit by this "runaway plant" phenomenon. During the past two decades, hundreds, if not thousands, of plants have shut their doors and

*Reprinted from the *Congressional Record—House* (June 10, 1974), pp. 18559–61.

moved away from Michigan leaving behind hundreds of thousands of unemployed workers.

Using data provided to them by the Michigan Department of Commerce, the United Auto Workers estimates that over 3,000 plants have either closed down or moved out of Michigan since 1967, and that almost 200,000 workers—representing approximately 5 percent of Michigan's total work force—have been affected.

My own congressional district suffered the effects of the runaway plant in 1972 when the Garwood plant in Wayne moved and left 600 unemployed workers behind. Detroit experienced similar problems when plants operated by Federal Mogul, the Huck Co., and Detroit Macoid—just to name a few—closed their doors.

Mr. Speaker, the reason these firms are moving away is not economic necessity but economic greed. For instance, the Federal Mogul Co. in Detroit signed a contract in 1971 with the United Auto Workers and 6 months later announced it would be moving to Alabama. A spokesman for the company was quoted as saying they were moving "not because we are not making money in Detroit, but because we can make more money in Alabama."

Last year, the John Bean Co. in Lansing announced that it would be moving to Arkansas. The effect of this move would mean instant unemployment for 230 production workers and 87 salaried workers. The reason? Cheaper wages. By moving to Arkansas, it was estimated that the company could get away with paying their new workers poverty wages—from $1.75 to $2.25 an hour. This would mean that their new employees would be receiving average annual salaries of $3,640 to $4,680 per year.

Michigan is not the only state facing this problem. Many other states are suffering similarly. In Virginia, one-fifth of the town of Tazewell—population 5,000—lost their jobs when a company producing television components moved to Portugal. We have had reports of a tractor plant in Minnesota moving to Iowa leaving behind 2,000 workers, and the Maendler-Bauer paintbrush company moving from Minnesota to Louisiana. Still another example is the Mead Co., which last year moved from Alabama to Texas and left 1,300 to 1,400 jobless workers behind.

The Subcommittee on Agricultural Labor, which I chair, recently observed the catastrophic problems which the State of Hawaii is experiencing because of a runaway pineapple industry. Hawaii is now faced with the shutdown of almost its entire pineapple industry because the corporate giants, such as Dole and Del Monte, have

316

decided that it would be more profitable to grow and process pineapples elsewhere, such as Taiwan and the Philippines. The number of workers expected to lose their jobs because of corporate greed in the pineapple industry has been estimated to be as high as 15,000—and thousands more are expected to be affected by these moves indirectly.

Mr. Speaker, again, these are mere illustrations of the kinds of problems which can be found in nearly every state in the country. The National Employment Priorities Act is designed both to prevent these problems and to aid the victims when the problems cannot be solved.

Briefly, the bill would establish a National Employment Relocation Administration—NERA—to investigate and report on the economic justification for a plant closing or the transfer of an agricultural or business enterprise upon request of 10 percent of the employees or a collective bargaining representative. Based upon the recommendation of the NERA, the bill would authorize adjustment assistance to employees affected by relocations; assistance through grants and loans to communities that suffer substantial unemployment as the result of plant closings or relocations; or technical and financial assistance to business and agricultural concerns in order to prevent their closing or relocation. It would also authorize the denial of certain federal tax benefits to businesses which relocate contrary to the will of the NERA.

The legislation we are proposing is intended to be a starting point—a proposal for discussion and further consideration.

Those of us who are supporting it are not completely wedded to any specific approach, but we are committed to the goal of providing some form of assistance to workers and communities forced to suffer because of the arbitrary closings and transfers of business and agricultural enterprises.

Mr. Speaker, federal legislation affecting relocation of industry is not a new or revolutionary phenomenon. In fact, many of the major culprits—the multinational corporations—are well aware of the fact that several modern industrial countries already have laws which regulate plant relocation.

For instance, Sweden has a labor market board which must be informed when a company desires to move. Should the company be given permission to move, substantial payments must be made to any employee who is losing work as a result of the movement, and the company is required to move any employees who desire to do so to the new location and pay them a travel allowance. The employees who are left behind and are jobless as a result of the plant relocation are to be paid from 2 to 6 months' full pay. Furthermore, Sweden provides comprehensive training and retraining programs for employees left behind and, during the retraining period, the employee is paid enough to cover all expenses including care of his or her family and other obligations. I might also add that many American companies have located in Sweden and have accepted the application of these Swedish laws.

If a company wishes to move in England, it must receive a certificate from the Industrial Development Division of the British Government. Before issuing such a certificate, the division takes into consideration factors such as the rate of unemployment, housing facilities, school facilities, and other considerations. England also has a law which requires a company to pay substantial amounts to displaced employees who are left jobless as a result of any move. Once again, American companies operating in England have accepted the application of these laws. Similar laws exist in Germany and France also.

Mr. Speaker, the Congress has recently acted very responsibly in passing legislation to provide pension protection for workers who have been left behind as a result of companies moving or going out of business. Our next goal should be to provide job protection for workers and economic protection for communities.

We can do so by enacting legislation such as the National Employment Priorities Act.

National Employment Priorities Act of 1979*

Mr. Speaker, yesterday, together with 46 cosponsors, I introduced the National Employment Priorities Act of 1979. Similar legislation has been introduced in the other body by the senior Senator from New Jersey, Mr. Williams, and the senior Senator from Michigan, Mr. Riegle.

The legislation addresses a serious and increasingly pervasive problem in our society: The phenomenon of sudden plant closings, undertaken without warning to the affected workers and without adequate regard for the devastating social and economic costs a shutdown can have. The costs to a community of the closure of a large workplace—whether it be an automobile factory, a shipyard,

*Reprinted from the *Congressional Record—House* (August 2, 1979), pp. 7240–41.

or a department store—can be tremendous. And these costs are exacerbated when the closings occur without advance notice to the people who are affected by them.

Without warning, the tax base of local communities may be decimated, leaving schools and municipal services underfinanced and leading to layoffs of municipal employees; unemployment skyrockets before anyone can plan to bring in new industry and jobs; and small businesses that depended on the closed establishment as a customer are left without a market.

The experience of many of the cities in Ohio after their largest industries shut down and relocated elsewhere is well known. Schools closed, police and fire departments reduced their operations, and everybody suffered—school children, local industry, municipal employees—as well as the workers whose jobs were lost in the plant shutdown.

The costs to individual workers can be tragically high as well. Their families are left without health insurance; their pensions may be wiped out; older workers soon learn that it is impossible for them to find new employment; and the mental and physical health of the displaced workers declines at an alarming rate—just when the community is least able to afford and provide social services.

Studies have shown that the suicide rate among workers displaced by a permanent closing of their workplace is almost 30 times the national average. This sobering statistic should convince even the most skeptical observer that the problem of plant closings is a critical issue, separate and distinct from the issue of unemployment in general. Nearly one million manufacturing jobs have been lost from the Northeast and Midwest, alone, in the last decade, and the toll on workers, their families, and their communities has been staggering. It is well established that the affected workers suffer a far higher incidence of heart disease and hypertension, diabetes, peptic ulcers, gout, and joint swelling, than the general population. They also incur serious psychological problems, including extreme depression, insecurity, anxiety, and loss of self-esteem.

All of these consequences of plant closings are very real for the affected workers and their communities. It would be a tragedy for Congress not to recognize the costs to our nation, costs which the other advanced industrial nations have recognized and dealt with for years. Most European countries have had legislation for more than a decade which has successfully met the problems of economic dislocation without harm to their productivity and economic strength.

Many major American corporations have prospered in Europe, adapting easily to laws and regulations far more restrictive of business mobility and management prerogatives than the legislation I have introduced today. The profit margin of our automotive giants, for example, is greater in Europe than it is at home. It is time for us to learn from the experience of West Germany, France, and Sweden and to seek a comprehensive solution to this gnawing problem.

While the impact of plant closings is felt most heavily at the local level, and numerous states are considering legislation to regulate economic disinvestment, a real solution to the problem must be a national solution. The adverse consequences of plant closings occur on a massive scale nationwide and are actually encouraged by federal tax policies.

Accelerated depreciation of machinery and structures, the tax deduction of relocation expenses and operating losses as a plant is phased out, and the investment tax credit all provide major incentives for plant relocations and closures.

The argument is made that plant closings are only a problem for the North and that this legislation is "anti-Sunbelt." Any serious reflection will reveal that this argument is a red herring. The congressional delegation from Hawaii remembers the economic and social crisis they faced when the pineapple industry pulled up stakes and moved abroad to Taiwan and the Philippines in order to escape paying a decent wage to American workers.

Many of our friends in California and the Southwest know that the threat of industrial relocation in Mexico and Central America is real and growing—and that their constituents are already suffering from that threat.

I am sure that before long our friends throughout the South will realize that the problem of plant closings and relocations is a disease that, like cancer, respects no region of the country. Almost 60 percent of all textile mill closings during the period 1971–76, for both union and nonunion plants, occurred in the South at a cost of almost 50,000 jobs. And anyone with a sense of history will realize that the television industry barely stopped off in the South on its way to the Far East.

Finally, it is difficult to believe that anyone living in the last quarter of the 20th century and the 1st decade of our 3rd century as a nation can seriously argue that a social or economic ill affecting one region of our country does not affect us all.

Present policies and programs, such as unemployment insurance, which only take effect after the crisis and trauma have occurred, have proven totally inadequate to meet the challenge of disasters like the closing of the Campbell Works steel plant in Youngstown, Ohio, which left 5,000 workers unemployed with less than a week's notice.

In my own State of Michigan, the cities of Lyons and Hamtramck have been numbed by Chrysler Corporation's recent announcement that their major sources of employment will be shut down. In the case of Lyons, 700 jobs in a town of 800 will be wiped out in one stroke, most of them moving to Canada. There is no national or state law to prevent, minimize, or cure the destructive impact of this corporate decision on so many people who have made a steady, productive contribution to Chrysler and our national economy for years.

The legislation which I have introduced today, the National Employment Priorities Act of 1979, would provide a comprehensive program to prevent the disastrous consequences of sudden, large-scale plant closings. The act would meet the problem of economic dislocation in a number of ways.

First, the workers, their community, and the federal government would have between 6 months' and 2 years' advance notice of the plant closing—time to find ways to avert the shutdown; to attract new business if the shutdown were unavoidable; to apply for federal assistance in retraining the workers for other jobs, buying the plant and renovating or retooling it, or finding new ways to employ the displaced workers on projects of benefit to the community.

Second, the act would require the business concern to assume some responsibility for the welfare of the people who served it and the community that supported it. Any displaced worker would be entitled to transfer to a similar job with any establishment under the business concern's control. Workers who were not transferred would be entitled to severance payments from the business concern, supplementing any unemployment compensation or trade adjustment assistance which they received. The employees' pension and health benefits would be maintained for up to one year for young employees and longer for older employees. In addition, the business concern would be required to pay the local government 85 percent of any tax revenue loss caused by the decision to close or relocate a plant.

Third, the act would provide numerous forms of assistance to businesses and communities to create new employment opportunities.

321

Among the forms of assistance would be targeted federal procurement, loans, and grants for the purpose of buying or reconverting the closed establishment, technical assistance, and loans and grants for the development of local public works projects that would lead to permanent employment opportunities.

In short, the act directs federal aid and protection to prevent the crises and trauma of economic dislocation, rather than allowing a crisis to arise and then attempting a piecemeal patchup afterward.

In conclusion, Mr. Speaker, I would like to say that neither Senator Riegle nor I and the 46 cosponsors of this legislation, are wedded to its specific provisions. The bill reflects lessons learned and information gathered during years of hearings conducted by John Dent and his subcommittee, and important contributions by public-interest groups and labor organizations. We think it presents a reasoned and equitable approach to a serious and too-long neglected problem. In the months ahead we will closely examine the details of the bill, but we will ensure that the principles of the legislation—that the impact of private disinvestment decisions is a matter of national, public concern; that those decisions must factor in the economic and social costs to workers and their communities; that the workers should not bear the brunt of economic decisions that benefit investors and the whole country; that labor should not be as mobile as capital; and that the federal government must have a greater role in the nation's economic planning—are not compromised.

National Employment Priorities Act of 1983*

Mr. Speaker, today, joined by 32 cosponsors, I have introduced legislation which addresses one of the most serious problems facing the American economy—the dislocations caused by plant closings and permanent layoffs. Every State and region of the country is suffering from the effects of massive, sudden plant closings which wipe out hundreds or thousands of jobs in a single blow, leaving communities and workers unprepared for unemployment and unable to adjust. Not just the Northeast and Midwest, but the entire Nation is experiencing the wrenching dislocation which major shifts of capital and jobs can cause. In fact, according to the Bureau of National Affairs, more plant closings occurred in the Southeast than in any other region in 1982, and North Carolina was the State most

*Reprinted from the *Congressional Record—House* (May 2, 1983), pp. 2526–27.

heavily affected. Even California, for decades a dynamo of economic growth and prosperity, has lost hundreds of thousands of jobs in the past few years, most of them in the manufacturing sector, as businesses have closed or relocated facilities, often shifting their investment to overseas operations in order to exploit cheaper wages.

Nationwide, the number of jobs lost to plant closings in the last few years is staggering. A study conducted by the Brookings Institution and the Small Business Administration indicates that 4.8 million jobs were eliminated during the first 2 years of the current recession when businesses shut down facilities of all kinds—factories, mines, retail stores and offices. Most of those shutdowns were in very small facilities, but many involved hundreds or thousands of employees and severely disrupted the social and economic fabric of the communities where they occurred.

In the past, certain economists have argued that plant closings and relocations are good for the economy—are, in fact, an essential part of a dynamic and growing economy. These economists argued that any governmental action to restrict such closings would lead to inefficiency and would weaken our economy. They claimed that, ultimately, everyone benefited from unrestricted business mobility, since it meant cheaper goods, higher profits, and efficient production.

That argument was always wrong, but it had a certain plausibility when unemployment was low, our work force was growing, and our manufacturing sector was the world's unchallenged leader. Today, with 11.3 million Americans unemployed and millions more forced to work part time, a stagnant manufacturing sector, and growing import competition, the argument is no longer plausible. Today, when multinational corporations such as General Electric, North American Phillips and Warner Communications, Inc., close facilities and move to Singapore, Mexico or Taiwan, they leave behind workers and families with no prospect of finding equivalent work or, sometimes, any work. And the number of these dislocated workers is growing.

Governments at every level, business leaders and their organizations, and academics have all become aware—belatedly—of the problems that these shifts in investment have created. They are beginning to realize that the impoverishment of millions of formerly productive workers creates dangers for our economy and our democracy.

A recent meeting in Pittsburgh, entitled the National Conference on the Dislocated Worker, highlighted the need for more active governmental intervention to prevent or minimize the adverse effects of plant closings. Speaker after speaker pointed out the need for advance notice of shutdowns to permit local adjustment programs to go into effect and to allow workers an opportunity to begin searching for new employment before their termination. Nearly every speaker at this conference—which was sponsored by the National Alliance of Business, the National Association of Manufacturers, and the Chamber of Commerce—agreed that current Federal retraining efforts are inadequate and should be expanded. And, as the National Alliance of Business reports, the conference participants agreed that "dislocation can be prevented by early communication between management and labor, enabling them to examine options. It can also be eased through severance pay, extension of health benefits, early retirement, and outplacement services."

I agreed with these conclusions, but the fact of the matter is that only Federal regulation will cause the great majority of businesses to provide prenotification of plant shutdowns, to extend health benefits, or to provide adequate severance pay. Voluntarism has failed, and the result is sudden layoffs, such as the recent termination of 600 Atari employees, with less than 1 day's notice, even though Atari's management began planning their relocation to Taiwan nearly 1 year earlier.

For nearly a decade, the Trade Act of 1974 has encouraged employers to provide advance notice of overseas relocations and to help relocate their employees to other locations where employment opportunities exist. Section 2934 of title 19 of the United States Code provides that:

> Before moving productive facilities from the United States to a foreign country, every firm should—
> (1) provide notice of the move to its employees who are likely to be totally or partially separated as a result of the move at least 60 days before the date of such move, and
> (2) provide notice of the move to the Secretary of Labor and the Secretary of Commerce on the same day it notifies employees under paragraph (1).
> (b) It is the sense of the Congress that every such firm should—
>
> (1) apply for and use all adjustment assistance for which it is eligible under this subchapter,

324

(2) offer employment opportunities in the United States, if any exist, to its employees who are totally or partially separated workers as a result of the move, and

(3) assist in relocating employees to other locations in the United States where employment opportunities exist.

When I checked with the Labor Department and the Commerce Department recently, I was told that no firm had ever provided them with the notice called for by the law.

If businesses will not voluntarily give advance notice of a shutdown, how likely are they to provide adequate severance pay, share financial information with their employees, extend health benefits coverage, or provide early retirement or outplacement services? Experience shows that all of these actions which could ease the adjustment of workers and their communities are rarely undertaken, even by unionized companies.

The need for these forms of assistance is critical because plant closings and large scale layoffs differ from "normal unemployment." Plant closings are usually a crisis for the workers and communities they affect, and their consequences can be more devastating than the floods and other natural disasters for which the Federal Government provides emergency aid. Numerous congressional hearings, agency reports, and academic studies have documented these adverse effects, which include:

Severe Unemployment. Whereas the median duration of unemployment in the United States is 10 weeks, studies have found that 40 percent of workers laid off in major plant closings are unemployed for 40–60 weeks and a quarter are unemployed for more than 1 year. During a recession or where unemployment in an area is already high, the duration of unemployment can be even greater.

Health Effects. Victims of plant closings typically suffer from hypertension, abnormally high cholesterol and blood sugar levels, a higher incidence of ulcers, respiratory diseases, unduly high propensities to gout and diabetes, and hyperallergic reactions. The mental health effects can be even more critical: Depression, anxiety, substance abuse and aggressive feelings frequently translate into spouse abuse, child abuse, crime, or suicide.

Income Loss. Not only do workers lose their jobs in a plant closing, along with health benefits, pensions, and other fringe ben-

325

efits, but the new jobs they eventually get do not provide as much income or status. Careful long-term studies show that 6 years after a plant closing, workers in the automobile, steel, meat packing, and aerospace industries still earn an average 12.5 to 18.1 percent less than before the shutdown. Over a lifetime, this income loss can total $40,000 or more per worker.

Community Effects. When a major business closes, a wave of income loss and job loss usually sweeps through the community. Supplier firms lose contracts, retail stores lose customers, local governments and school systems lose tax revenues and lay off employees. A seemingly "private" decision eventually affects nearly everyone in town. The indirect job loss, or "employment multiplier," can be as high as two jobs for every direct job loss. The U.S. Department of Transportation has found that for every 100 automobile jobs lost directly, another 140 to 200 jobs would be destroyed in industries ranging from iron ore mining to advertising. And just when social services are most needed, payroll, property, and income tax revenue losses undermine the ability of local governments to respond.

The causes of plant shutdowns vary, from bankruptcy or a desire to abandon an unprofitable operation to a desire to thwart unionization, to relocate a profitable business to a more profitable location, or to "milk" a "cash cow" and exploit the tax advantages of paper losses. Nearly all of them, however, have several things in common. They occur with little or no warning to the affected workers and communities—and with no input from them in the decision; they put a burden on the taxpayers for public assistance and social services; and they leave behind families who have no health insurance or pension and no immediate prospect of finding alternative employment.

The National Employment Priorities Act is intended to prevent or minimize each of these problems. In summary, the legislation has four purposes:

First, to provide Federal financial assistance to businesses, communities or workers to prevent business failure and plant closings that can be avoided. Years of study have proven that many plant closings are economically unnecessary or avoidable and that access to sufficient loan capital will often be enough to prevent major dislocations. Firms ranging in size from the Chrysler Corp. down to a 50-employee sporting goods firm have been saved by Federal loans, loan guarantees, and technical assistance.

Second, to require that businesses provide enough advance notice of plant closings and major layoffs and sufficient financial information to allow local governments, employees, and small businesses to plan for and adjust to the loss of tax revenues, employment, and business which will occur. Firms would be required to give 6-months notice before permanently displacing 100 or fewer employees, and 1 year before displacing more than 100.

Third, to protect employees from dislocation and discourage unnecessary closings by requiring businesses to make severance payments, to continue health and welfare benefits and to provide transfer rights to other facilities to workers laid off in plant closings.

Fourth, to expand Federal assistance to dislocated workers and their communities. The bill makes retraining available to all dislocated workers and authorizes emergency assistance to local governments to fund social services, school systems, and employment projects when a major plant closing severely reduces local tax revenues and the employment base.

I also want to make it perfectly clear what the legislation will not do. It does not give any agency of government the power to prevent a plant closing or relocation. Rather, it only allows the Government to delay a shutdown for 6 months or 1 year, depending on the number of employees affected.

Nor will this bill restrict in any way the operations of small businesses. More than 90 percent of the Nation's businesses, those which do not employ 50 or more workers at a single facility, are excluded from coverage. If anything, these small companies will benefit, as will all citizens, from the advance notice they will receive of major shutdowns in their community that might affect their business.

Legislation similar to the National Employment Priorities Act has worked well for many years in Germany, Sweden, and other European countries. With unemployment in the United States climbing to levels unimaginable just 5 years ago and the number of dislocated workers growing every day, the time for us to act is here. Our Nation needs a just, rational, and effective mechanism to help our communities adjust to economic dislocation. I believe that the National Employment Priorities act provides such a mechanism.

INDEX

Nutter, G. Warren, 227

Ohio plant-closing law, proposed, 129, 130 tbl
Oil prices, 181
O'Keefe, Edward, 8, 253–305
Olson, Mancur, 200
"Organizational control" shifts, 35

Patrick, Hugh, 163
Phillips, Kevin, 193
Plant-closing laws (*see also* National Employment Priorities Act; National Labor Relations Act): advance notice of closing, 312–13; bailouts, 312; capital flight, 52–53; closing costs, 209–10, 309–10; competition, effect on, 214–15; corporate democratization, 11–12; economic liberty, restrictions on, 210–12; foreign investment, 217; job rights, 51; modifications in, 152; negative impacts of, 24–27; in Ohio, 129, 130 tbl; plant closures caused by, 311–12; plant openings, effect on, 68–69, 77, 212–14, 310–11; political concerns, 212, 311, 312–13; private alternatives, 313; proponents of, 3; provisions of, vii, 12–14, 128, 129–130 tbls, 131, 205–6, 321–22, 327; rationale for, 131; reinvestment plans, 4–5; severance-pay requirements, 143–51; social concerns, 206–7, 209; social *v.* private costs, 51–52; state-level, 4, 29–30, 50, 128; Sunbelt assisted by, 320; in Sweden, 7, 69–71, 76–77, 317–18; unwanted goods, promotion of, 214; work force reductions caused by, 147–51; worker purchase of plant, 217–18
Plant closures: communities, effect on, 319, 326; foreign relocation, 323, 324–25; Frostbelt, 6, 19–20, 58–59, 60 tbl, 62; income losses due to, 326; job losses due to, 17–18; local efforts to offset, 210, 218–19; management rights regarding, 233–34; plant profitability, 215–16; plant-closing laws, effect of, 311–12; reasons for, 20; severance-pay requirements, 143–46; size of business, 58–59, 60–61 tbls, 62; social responsibilities of businesses, 207–8; in Sunbelt, 58–59, 61 tbl, 62, 323; television coverage, 208, 213; timing of, 143–46; unemployment,

relation to, 6, 131–32, 139, 140–41 tbls, 207, 325; visibility of hardships, 212
Plant openings: plant-closing laws, effect of, 68–69, 77, 212–14, 310–11; in Sunbelt, 20–21
Plant relocation, 234–52, 257 n
Population migration, 15–16, 62, 63 tbl, 64, 120–22, 197–98
Premus, Robert, 6, 21, 119–26
Product cycle, 184
Productivity growth, decline in, 161–62
Profit motive, 214–15
Progressive Alliance, 17
Rees, John, 8, 23, 193–203
Regional development, factors influencing, 120–21
Regional economic structures, 26
Reich, Robert, 157
Reindustrialization policy. *See* Industrial policy.
Relocation. *See* Business migration; Manufacturing relocation; Plant relocation.
Restrictions on Business Mobility: A Study in Political Rhetoric and Economic Reality (McKenzie), 62
Restrictive legislation. *See* Plant-closing laws.
Riegle, Donald, 3, 214, 318, 322
Royal Typewriter Co. v. NLRB (1974), 281–82
Runaway plant phenomenon, 12–14

Santayana, George, 227
Schultze, Charles L., 7, 155–75
Schumpeter, Joseph A., 199, 200
Schweiker, Richard, 315
Schweke, William, *vii*
Service Employees International Union (SEIU), 286–88
Smith, Adam, 222, 225
South. *See* Sunbelt.
Southern Growth Policies Board, 194
Steel industry, 187
Stein, Herbert, 223, 228
Stern, Robert, 184
Stewart, Potter, 267 n, 269
Strong, John S., 6, 7, 19, 49–77
Sunbelt (*see also* Sunbelt/Frostbelt confrontation): employment change, 57 tbl, 58, 66, 67 tbl; job loss rate, 58, 59 tbl; plant-closing laws, effect of, 320; plant closures, 58–59, 61 tbl, 62, 323;

ABOUT THE EDITOR

Richard B. McKenzie is professor of economics at Clemson University and an adjunct scholar of the Cato Institute. He is the author of several books, including *Fugitive Industry: The Economics and Politics of Deindustrialization* (Pacific Institute, 1984) and *Bound to Be Free* (Hoover Institution, 1982), and the editor of *Constitutional Economics: Constraining the Economic Powers of Government* (Lexington Books, 1984). *The New World of Economics* (Richard D. Irwin, Inc., fourth edition, 1984), which he co-authored with Gordon Tullock, is widely used in colleges and universities.

Cato Institute

Founded in 1977, the Cato Institute is a public policy research foundation dedicated to broadening the parameters of policy debate to allow consideration of more options that are consistent with the traditional American principles of limited government, individual liberty, and peace. Toward that goal, the Institute strives to achieve a greater involvement of the intelligent, concerned lay public in questions of policy and the proper role of government.

The Institute is named for *Cato's Letters,* pamphlets that were widely read in the American Colonies in the early eighteenth century and played a major role in laying the philosophical foundation for the revolution that followed. Since that revolution, civil and economic liberties have been eroded as the number and complexity of social problems have grown. Today virtually no aspect of human life is free from the domination of a governing class of politico-economic interests. A pervasive intolerance for individual rights is shown by government's arbitrary intrusions into private economic transactions and its disregard for civil liberties.

To counter this trend the Cato Institute undertakes an extensive publications program dealing with the complete spectrum of policy issues. Books, monographs, and shorter studies are commissioned to examine the federal budget, social security, regulation, NATO, international trade, and a myriad of other issues. Major policy conferences are held throughout the year from which papers are published thrice yearly in the *Cato Journal.* The Institute maintains an informal joint publishing arrangement with the Johns Hopkins University Press.

In order to maintain an independent posture, the Cato Institute accepts no government funding. Contributions are received from foundations, corporations, and individuals, and other revenue is generated from the sale of publications. The Institute is a non-profit, tax-exempt, educational foundation under Section 501(c)3 of the Internal Revenue Code.

CATO INSTITUTE
224 Second St., S.E.
Washington, D.C. 20003